WOMEN IN AMERICAN HISTORY

Series Editors

Mari Jo Buhle
Nancy A. Hewitt
Anne Firor Scott
Stephanie Shaw

A list of books in the series appears at the end of this book.

Purifying America

Purifying America

Women, Cultural Reform, and
Pro-Censorship Activism, 1873-1933

ALISON M. PARKER

UNIVERSITY OF ILLINOIS PRESS
Urbana and Chicago

1 2 3 4 5 C P 5 4 3 2 1

This book is printed on acid-free paper.

Library of Congress Cataloging-in-Publication Data
Parker, Alison M. (Alison Marie)
Purifying America : women, cultural reform, and pro-censorship
activism, 1873–1933 / Alison M. Parker
p. cm. — (Women in American history)
Includes bibliographical references (p.   ) and index.
ISBN 0-252-02329-3 (cloth : acid-free paper). —
ISBN 0-252-06625-1 (pbk. : acid-free paper)
1. Women social reformers—United States—History. 2. Woman's Christian
Temperance Union—History. 3. Censorship—United States—History. 4. Popular
culture—Moral and ethical aspects—United States—History. 5. United States—
Moral conditions—History. I. Title. II. Series.
HQ1419.P27   1997
303.48'4'092273—dc21
96-45897
CIP

For Joanne J. Parker

Contents

Acknowledgments

Research for this project was greatly facilitated by fellowships from the Johns Hopkins University History Department, Frederick Jackson Turner travel funds, and Ford Foundation travel grants from the Women's Studies Program. Additional support was provided by a Dissertation Research Grant from the Schlesinger Library on the History of Women in America, Radcliffe College, 1991. The kind assistance of librarian Alfred Epstein at the Woman's Christian Temperance Union's Willard Memorial Library in Evanston, Illinois, made my trips there more productive and enjoyable.

This book began as a dissertation at Johns Hopkins University. My greatest debts go to Ronald G. Walters and Toby L. Ditz. Both read innumerable drafts of the entire manuscript, provided the perfect combination of expert advice and personal warmth, and offered moral and intellectual support. Equally important, they had faith in my project and pushed me ever harder to articulate my vision. My debt to them both is enormous, as is the extent of my gratitude and appreciation. I would also like to thank colleagues and friends who generously gave of their time to read and provide helpful and challenging comments on one or more chapters: Andrea Friedman, Cathy Jurca, Cathy Kerr, JoAnne Mancini, Dorothy Ross, and June Sochen. In addition, conference presentations of excerpts from chapters on film, art, and theater censorship elicited thoughtful criticism from commentators Nicki Beisel, Paul Boyer, Peter Buckley, Alice Echols, and Kathryn Oberdeck. Thanks are also due to my colleagues: first at Goucher College and now at the University of Texas at Arlington.

The University of Illinois Press has provided me with great support and wonderful editors, Karen Hewitt and Nancy A. Hewitt. Nancy Hewitt's careful comments on my manuscript and subsequent revisions were thoughtful, direct, and supportive. In addition, the critique provided by my second reader, Kathryn Kish Sklar, helped me to better articulate the goals and mission of my project.

I dedicate this book to my mother, Joanne Parker, an early pioneer in the field of women's studies. She has given me the gifts of her encouragement and guidance and has inspired me with a love of women's history. Her humane spirit and generous friendship have deeply touched and enriched my life. Finally, I thank Geoffrey Hale for his constant love and kindness.

Purifying America

Introduction

For most Americans in the late twentieth century, the word censorship raises fears of the repression of free speech and the invasion of personal privacy. From 1873 through the 1930s, however, censorship was popularly viewed
as a useful tool for social change. This book explores the advocacy of censorship as a popular reform and the social conditions whereby this movement was transformed and expanded into a debate about the regulation of
society's morals and the content of American culture. I focus primarily on
the Woman's Christian Temperance Union (WCTU), a women's moral reform organization that devoted considerable time and activism to fighting
for censorship legislation. The organization, with its large membership and
national prominence, can be taken to represent the views of a significant
segment of the American middle classes at this time. A discussion of the
American Library Association (ALA) serves to reinforce and substantiate my
claims about the extent of middle-class acceptance of and participation in
pro-censorship activities. As a professional organization, the ALA believed
in its right to decide which books would be accessible to the public. Librarians' support of their professional regulation of children's literature bolsters
the assertion that censorship in its various forms had widespread public
support. The female and male librarians who supported censorship did not
view it as simply a state-mandated duty, for they wanted to make it part of
their professional prerogative. By bridging social, cultural, and political history, this study demonstrates how both lay and professional organizations
worked to expand the legal definition of censorship to problems beyond the
reading or viewing of legally "obscene" images.

The history of legal censorship in the United States begins in the eighteenth century. The first censorship laws of the New Republic were the Alien and Sedition Acts of 1798. These Acts were aimed at controlling political expression and dissent.[1] Laws aimed at regulating culture came decades later, when "obscene" pictures and prints were first restricted from entry into the United States through provision in the 1842 Tariff Act. The government became more interested in regulation during the Civil War, when soldiers began trading and collecting French postcards of pictures of nude and semi-nude women. The postmaster general was subsequently (1865) given limited rights to confiscate "obscene" materials in the mail. The Comstock Act of 1873 went significantly further by making it illegal to sell or distribute through the mail a multitude of "obscene" images in literature and art, as well as information on birth control devices or abortions.[2]

As a history of censorship, this book focuses on the period from 1873 to 1933, loosely defined as the turn of the century (encompassing both the Gilded Age and the Progressive Era). During this time, censorship of cultural forms—via local and state laws as well as congressional legislation and Supreme Court rulings—was at its apogee in the United States. The Supreme Court upheld a definition of obscenity that created a standard for culture based on the lowest common denominator of acceptability: that which would not impair the moral development of children. Turn-of-the-century obscenity decisions transformed the potential for sexual arousal into the potential moral corruption of youths, thus expanding the legally actionable criteria of corruption and corruptibility. Throughout this era, the U.S. Supreme Court did not view arguments based on free speech and the First Amendment as sufficient challenges to obscenity laws and postal restrictions on literature or visual images, including movies. In fact, until 1957 the Supreme Court accepted with minimal modifications the British court's 1868 censorship decision in *Queen v. Hicklin*. Lord Cockburn's definition of obscenity based censorship rulings on "the tendency of the matter . . . to deprave and corrupt those whose minds are open to such immoral influences, and into whose hands such a publication might fall."[3]

From the 1870s through the mid-1930s, regulation of both printed materials and the new medium of motion pictures was at its most restrictive. Novels that are now regarded as classics were often legally kept from distribution in the United States, and many imported books were impounded and/or destroyed by U.S. Customs officials. The legal situation changed dramatically for literature when District Court Judge John M. Woolsey ruled in 1933 that Irish author James Joyce's *Ulysses* was not obscene. Woolsey concluded that the work should be judged as a whole and that prosecutors could not quote passages out of context as proof that a book was "obscene."

Later rulings allowed for further refinement of what could be considered legally "obscene," as the Supreme Court modified its definition to protect all writings that might be deemed to have some "social importance."[4] The Supreme Court heard its first case against motion pictures in 1915 and ruled that the movie industry was a profit motivated business, not an art form, and therefore was subject to regulation. This ruling allowed censorship by review boards before distribution of movies to the public by any state or locale that deemed it necessary or desirable. Beginning in 1934, motion pictures were subject to relatively rigorous self-regulation, through the Motion Picture Association of America and its production code, by a movie industry that was trying to avoid federal regulation.[5] This study ends in the mid-1930s because these more liberal approaches to literary and visual "speech" mark a significant shift in the history of censorship in the United States.

Historians have demonstrated that laws upholding or mandating censorship were most prevalent at the turn of the century, but they have not explored the question of whether these laws were actively supported by the general public. Large numbers of Americans, from wealthy urban businessmen and industrialists to middle-class women reformers and white-collar professionals, endorsed the legal definition of obscenity and the larger preoccupation with safeguarding youth that accompanied it. Indeed, their goal was to extend the protective boundary of the law to encompass a wider range of readers, language, and images. Historian Annette Kuhn identifies this willingness to regulate morality as a desire on the part of the government and concerned lay people to monitor culture and the public sphere, whereby immorality was defined as an "offense against the community."[6]

Most histories of censorship in the United States have not, however, focused on this broader movement, but rather on the efforts of shop-clerk Anthony Comstock and his supporters to pass a national bill outlawing the distribution of "obscenity" through the United States mails. Comstock was made an agent of the U.S. Post Office in order to help enforce the new anti-obscenity regulation; the resulting legislation is commonly referred to as the Comstock Act of 1873. Comstock's congressional lobbying was supported by elite industrialists and Protestant businessmen, many of whom were founders and trustees of the Young Men's Christian Association. His later enforcement efforts were underwritten by the same men, who organized and funded vice societies, or anti-obscenity organizations such as the New York Society for the Suppression of Vice and the New England Watch and Ward Society. The fact of this elite support has led historians to interpret the censorship campaigns of the 1870s through the 1930s as the actions of only a narrow segment of the American public.[7]

Other historical accounts dismiss the focus on the supposed attempts at cultural hegemony made by Comstock's industrialist supporters and argue that the most significant censorship activities were conducted by Comstock himself with a mere handful of his agents, while the rest of the country's citizens were uninterested, occasionally irritated, or amused.[8] A variant of this interpretation not only views Comstock as a lone crusader but also as an obsessed and maniacal one who was able to inflict much personal suffering and financial damage on free-love advocates, abortion providers, birth control advocates, and printers of "obscene" cheap literature.[9] In either case, because the vice societies were involved in a number of notorious arrests, lawsuits, and impoundments, historians have focused almost exclusively on censorship as the territory of Anthony Comstock and a few (elite) white males. For a generation, moreover, most historians have simply accepted as a given that "purity" campaigns were a misguided and deplorable residue of "Victorian prudery." This Whiggish view, which emphasizes progress and increasing tolerance, combines with democratic sentiment in favor of First Amendment rights to present a history wherein repression is overcome by the latter part of the twentieth century. This understandable sympathy with a free-speech position has kept historians of censorship from fully analyzing and understanding past reformers' goals and concerns.[10]

At the turn of the century, when censorship regulations went largely unchallenged by judges and lawmakers, organized opposition to the Comstock Act was minimal. During the nineteenth century, the most notable opponents to censorship were the free speech advocates Francis E. Abbot and Colonel Robert Ingersoll and their small group of active supporters in the National Liberal League of 1876 (called the National Defense Association from 1878 until its demise in the 1880s). They managed to gather almost 50,000 signatures on a petition asking Congress to overturn the Comstock Acts, but their campaign was ignored.[11] Given the choice between continued support of an anti-obscenity movement endorsed by organized Christians and business elites and a protest led by free thinkers and free-love advocates associated with atheism, federal legislators overwhelmingly chose the safer path. Most gave higher priority to the protection of youths from "obscene" literature than to unrestricted freedom of speech and the mail.

Censorship, in fact, gained middle-class approval among a significantly broad base of Americans, including women's groups, religious organizations, and some professional associations. Many welcomed a federal mandate against "obscenity" and campaigned for further restrictive legislation at the state and local levels. They aimed at stopping, for instance, the proliferation of cheap crime-story papers such as the *National Police Gazette*. Women's groups, including the National Congress of Mothers (later the Parent-Teacher Association), condemned the sale of "impure" literature. Later, the WCTU and then the General Federation of Women's Clubs supported state regulation of the movies. Canon William Chase and Reverend Wilbur Crafts led Christian men and women in a fight for censorship through their leadership of the Federal Motion Picture Council and the International Reform Bureau. Emerging professional organizations were less willing to associate themselves with pro-censorship legislation, yet groups like the American Library Association still hoped to regulate reading. They simply wanted to do so through professionals' expert guidance rather than through increased legal coercion.

* * *

The year that witnessed the passage of the Comstock law also marks the beginning of a women's reform organization that would play an important role in expanding middle-class censorship efforts and in promoting "pure" culture. In that year, 1873, an evangelical women's temperance movement gained momentum as middle-class women in small midwestern towns demonstrated and prayed in front of local saloons, asking the owners voluntarily to dump their alcohol and close their businesses. Some closed down immediately, but others resisted, only to find that some of these modest "crusaders" were willing to dump the alcohol themselves, thus defying the laws of property and propriety alike. These activities led to the creation in 1874 of the Woman's Christian Temperance Union (WCTU). The WCTU soon became the largest women's organization of the nineteenth century with over 200,000 members by 1892 and more than 344,000 by 1921.[12]

Many WCTU members were evangelical women who had not previously taken part in reform movements but who, under the slogan "Home Protection," became activists for political and social reform. They even worked for woman suffrage (the "Home Protection Ballot") as they sought control over social morality through governmental legislation that would protect their children.[13] The idealization of white middle-class women's domestic role in the antebellum Northeast has been fully delineated by historians such as Carroll Smith-Rosenberg, Mary Ryan, and Nancy Hewitt, who also demonstrate that bourgeois women almost immediately began to use the power of the domestic ideal to gain a place in public benevolence and reform movements. During the last quarter of the nineteenth century, women's transgressions of the increasingly fluid boundaries between private and public spheres accelerated.[14]

Under the leadership of Frances Willard (president from 1879 to 1898), the WCTU diversified, cultivating alliances with other groups such as the working-class Knights of Labor. The WCTU also structured its organization around some nineteen departments, each one devoted to achieving a specific social-reform goal, ranging from child-labor laws to international peace and from arbitration to social purity. WCTU members quickly realized that temperance could not be achieved by moral suasion alone and advocated the legal prohibition of alcohol. This campaign convinced many members that they could not effect change without securing voting rights for women. At its convention in 1880, the national WCTU (although not all of its local chapters or individual members) committed itself to obtaining woman suffrage as the most effective route to achieving its reform goals. Ballots, it was hoped, would provide more direct power than petitions and protests aimed at influencing male voters and legislators.[15]

The WCTU's interest in federal censorship laws was compatible with its support of governmental regulation in other areas, especially the legal prohibition of alcohol. The strength of the WCTU came from its grass-roots organizational structure and its active membership on a local level. Yet as an institution, it had committed itself to reform programs that required governmental intervention at the national as well as the state, municipal, and county level. WCTU support for federal censorship must be understood in the context of specific historical developments, such as increases in immigration to the United States and a series of economic slumps marked by violent and divisive labor strikes. These disturbing developments coincided with the increasing availability of modernist and avant-garde art forms from Europe, which challenged traditional ways of seeing, as well as with a burgeoning of American popular entertainment. Cultural changes and technological innovations were unsettling and diffuse but could be symbolized for reformers by a single concrete issue, such as young people's access to "immoral" literature. Children represented the future of the nation, both literally and symbolically, and "immoral" literature represented a danger that demanded a reassertion of parental authority. Most ominously, the proliferation of "impure" children's reading materials represented the potential breakdown of mothers' dominance within the home, warning them that they were losing control over their children's education and leisure time. For WCTU members who had dedicated themselves to reforming the domestic and public spheres through a national assault on alcoholism, the answer to such outrages lay in a public, political campaign for federal censorship laws that would ward off these negative influences.

The WCTU made its pro-censorship position concrete in 1883 by creating a Department for the Suppression of Impure Literature (later, the Department for the Promotion of Purity in Literature and Art and, even later, the Department of Motion Pictures). As a history of pro-censorship activism at the turn of the century, this study does not provide institutional histories of either the WCTU or the ALA. It should, however, add to our understanding of both organizations. Future historians of the WCTU, for instance, will have to take into account the continued strength of the Department of Purity in Literature and Art after Frances Willard's death in 1898. This study's close examination of a single, if central, department supplements Ruth Bordin's groundbreaking overview of the nineteenth-century WCTU, *Woman and Temperance*. Bordin introduced readers to those units involved in work for the prohibition of alcohol and for suffrage but was unable to discuss the many other WCTU departments.[16] This shaped Bordin's sense of the rise and decline of the WCTU's influence as a reform organization. She ends her account in 1900, just two years after Willard's death, but well before the WCTU's major campaigns for suffrage and Prohibition were completed, and before other campaigns, such as movie censorship, were even undertaken. In both the nineteenth and twentieth centuries, the WCTU pro-censorship department's agenda encompassed far more than a narrow pro-temperance or pro-Prohibition stance. Details of the pro-censorship department's work demonstrate that the WCTU's "Do Everything" policy was not, in fact, abandoned by 1900, as Bordin suggests.[17]

Over the fifty-year period from 1883 to 1933, the number and range of projects taken on by this one department is staggering. The initial mission of the WCTU's Department for the Suppression of Impure Literature was to try to protect children from crime-story papers. By targeting the *National Police Gazette,* a paper that illustrated and described "sensational" crimes, the department pointed to one of the new forms of standardized entertainment available at a cheap price in cities and small towns all over the country. Such mass entertainment, it argued, ignored variations in local norms and community standards. The department also fought against other forms of "immoral" literature, art, theater, advertisements, prizefights, living pictures (*tableaux vivants*), the ballet, kinetoscopes, gambling, and patent medicines all in the name of protecting the innocent child.[18] As this list of targeted forms of entertainment suggests, the middle-class WCTU worked extensively to censor both "high" and "low" cultural genres.

In the twentieth century, the department took aim at newer cultural forms or those that had gained increased attention or popularity, such as motion pictures, but also popular dances and the Sunday comic strips. The WCTU changed its focus over time as the popularity of crime-story papers waxed and then waned and as new cultural products, such as movies, eventually took their place. The Woman's Christian Temperance Union exemplifies the resistance of segments of the middle class vis-à-vis the "sacralization" of culture into "high art," for it simultaneously fought against nude sculptures, the ballet, and Theodore Dreiser's realism, as well as boxing, motion pictures, and dime-novel "sensationalism."[19] Its activities complicate a class-based

interpretation that characterizes the censorship movement as purely or simply elitist.[20]

The WCTU's critical approach to culture captures the breadth of its re-
formist impulses as well as the expansive view of its own powers as a reform organization. Its two-pronged plan for achieving or enforcing cultural
"purity" included fighting for legal censorship *and* creating what it deemed
to be appropriate entertainment. The WCTU, for example, produced an alternative canon of acceptable or "pure" children's literature in its own periodical, the *Young Crusader,* published from 1887 through the 1930s.[21] The
Crusader has not previously been examined by historians, but its "pure"
fiction offers the chance to analyze reformers' positive substitute for the "sensational" children's literature they opposed. It also allows us to explore middle-class aesthetic tastes and moral standards. My analysis of proper fiction
for youths will highlight what WCTU reformers believed the moral boundaries of American culture should be and thereby help us discover which
ideas, genres, and aesthetics particularly disturbed reformers and professionals. The didactic message sent by the cultural items produced and endorsed
by the WCTU was oppositional to a hegemonic commercial culture that
could exist outside of audience control. Yet the WCTU's "pure" literature and
art also contained a strong normative view that was informed by the larger
culture.

The enormously varied pro-censorship activity undertaken by the WCTU
demands a reconsideration of the organization's historical place in the censorship movement. The tendency of historians to focus on elite males has
obscured women's pro-censorship activism. Paul Boyer's seminal work on
the history of censorship, *Purity in Print: The Vice-Society Movement and Book
Censorship in America,* for example, viewed the WCTU's Department for the
Suppression of Impure Literature as simply an adjunct effort, supporting the
male vice societies without a long-term agenda of its own. Recent historians of sexuality have also dismissed the WCTU's Department of Purity in
Literature and Art as subordinate to Anthony Comstock's New York Society for the Suppression of Vice.[22] Moreover, even revisionist historian Barbara Epstein has underestimated the WCTU's extensive censorship work:
"The WCTU conducted campaigns against plays and books it found offensive, applauded the work of Anthony Comstock and his Society for the Suppression of Vice, and, in the late 1890s, took up a campaign for curfews for
young people."[23]

The Woman's Christian Temperance Union's complex social and political agenda invites contradictory, seemingly incompatible, historical interpretations. Historians of the Progressive Era on the whole considered the WCTU
to be a conservative and backward-looking organization.[24] In contrast, revi-

sionist historians Ruth Bordin and Barbara Epstein portray the WCTU as a proto-feminist (and in some cases, feminist) organization that mobilized middle-class women for political and public activism on the strength of a gendered political agenda. Both interpretations are partially correct.[25]

Repressive and conservative tendencies sometimes characterized the WCTU's political and social activism. In matters of sexuality, for example, WCTU members supported the Comstock Act that outlawed the advertising or sending of contraceptives or abortifacients through the United States mails, thus denying women (including themselves) the right to control their bodies and their sexuality. WCTU reformers responded to perceived threats to their children with demands for the legal suppression of varied cultural forms. This use of the mother-child relationship as a paradigm for the relationship between citizens and leaders placed citizens in the role of the child, thereby defusing the possibility of democratic change.

Yet the WCTU was also an important player in a range of Progressive programs, including those characterized by a strong centralized government run by expert caretakers. Many WCTU members turned to the government, expecting it to somehow help them protect their children against society's evils.[26] The WCTU's acceptance of an interventionist role for the federal government makes the organization a useful example of the pervasiveness of the Progressive Era's expansionist program for social change. Child labor laws, mandatory school attendance, and juvenile courts—all supported by WCTU members—marked an increase in the regulatory function of the state. WCTU members welcomed the ascendancy of experts and celebrated every legislative and regulatory advance as a victory for mothers and their children. Historian Molly Ladd-Taylor's assertion that "motherhood was a central organizing principle of Progressive era politics. . . . inextricably tied to state-building and public policy," accurately characterizes the agenda of the WCTU.[27] Thus, the WCTU translated its relatively conventional maternalist concern for youths into sympathy with the Progressive child-study and hygiene movements and with the field of psychology. Evangelical WCTU members were well within the progressive cohort and did not share the hostility to the intellectual and scientific realm of the post–World War I fundamentalists. Whereas some conservative women defined themselves in hostile relation to child-study experts, most union members tried to make innovative use of expert knowledge and apply it to their own concerns.[28] In fact, calls for governmental censorship were generally not considered to be repressive and reactionary; instead, they represented the public's growing acceptance of the influence of government in all aspects of American life in the Progressive Era.

The WCTU's focus on the moral safety of children was part of a larger turn-of-the-century trend in American society toward taking the child seriously as an object of scientific study, reform, and control.[29] The WCTU held Mothers' Meetings and tried to regulate "purity" in cultural forms. Its Kindergarten Department was instrumental in popularizing and setting up many local kindergartens. Kindergartens were established as places where children could play and learn, while they were simultaneously studied by their teachers and other educators.[30] The significance of the nineteenth-century ideology of domesticity, with its emphasis on the importance of mothering, was reinforced for the WCTU by the popularization of the category "adolescence" by professors such as G. Stanley Hall and by the social hygiene movement's focus on children's "purity" and cleanliness. The work of most American psychologists and sociologists in the Progressive Era confirmed the importance of early childhood and adolescence by insisting that both were distinct stages of development that demanded nurture and protection by mothers *and* experts. All served further to focus the public's attention on youth and to enlarge the notion of what could and should be censored.

The WCTU's appeal to the state to protect traditional values is ironic given government's reconstructive role. The union's members did not consider the possibility that their maternal role as moral caretakers of the family might be usurped by a male-dominated federal government with expanded regulatory powers. WCTU laywomen, for instance, favored federal censorship of motion pictures. They may have had too little fear that censorship regulations could invade personal privacy and replace maternal oversight with governmental control.[31] Instead, they were confident that they could achieve their goals more efficiently through the state. As a safeguard, they believed that they could control the terms of censorship by proposing specific wordings of laws, including mandates to appoint like-minded reformers and educators to movie censorship boards.

In the long run, however, a centralized government undercut the WCTU's emphasis on the moral efforts of women, either in voluntary organizations or in the home, as the source of social salvation. The WCTU's grassroots style of political action, which functioned so well through the use of petitions and voluntary actions at the state and local levels, was ultimately sacrificed by its call for federal regulation. When the government was able to control the terms of censorship or prohibition, for instance, neither remained primarily a women's issue. As judicial or movie-industry "experts" gained the power to decide who or what to prosecute, confront, or pressure into conformity, censorship lost its power as a grass-roots women's issue. Ladd-Taylor's work on the National Congress of Mothers further illustrates women's loss of power: "Although club members played a key role in the initial development of parent education and social welfare programs, the professionalization of those fields limited the role that women at the grass-roots could play in their administration."[32]

Later in the twentieth century, from the mid-1930s through the 1970s, judicial definitions of "obscenity" became more narrow, abstract, and arcane, as well as less restrictive and therefore less a matter of public debate. The recent push by anti-pornography feminists and new right conservatives for strengthened anti-pornography laws reflects a return to an earlier grass-roots activism but also suggests that some women are once again placing too much power and hope in national laws to regulate or enforce their social and cultural mores.

The WCTU's pro-censorship department responded to changes in popular and elite culture by redirecting its efforts toward whatever medium seemed to be the most dominant or influential at any given time. In order to reflect upon the course of these changes over time, chapters two, four, and five focus on WCTU campaigns against literature, then art, and finally movies. The chapter on literature is presented first because printed materials were the earliest targets of the department, which was initially named, after all, the "Department for the Suppression of Impure Literature." Early campaigns against crime-story papers reflect the dominance of the print media in 1883 when the WCTU's pro-censorship department was formed. Yet this chapter does not focus only on the 1880s, when campaigns against "sensational" literature were at their peak. Instead, it includes a discussion of the WCTU's support of a 1920s campaign against "impure" magazines, for instance, in order to demonstrate the department's ambitious determination to insist upon "purity" in all media, not just in whatever genre was currently occupying the greater part of its attention. The pro-censorship department's 1925 transformation into the Department of Motion Pictures reflects the WCTU's assessment that movies had eclipsed all other cultural forms as the most attractive, potent, and dangerous. Chapter five, on movie censorship, begins with an account of the WCTU's earliest activities against kinetoscopes and then nickelodeons in order to emphasize that WCTU members kept a close watch on all new cultural developments. It stresses, however, that the bulk of WCTU-organized campaigns took place in the 1920s and early 1930s, at a point when WCTU members and many other Americans agreed that movies were the dominant cultural force and so must be regulated. WCTU members addressed the whole range of available popular media from 1883 to 1933, even while determining that one, such as movies, had become more influential than the others.

The WCTU's censorship initiatives served some internal purposes for the organization. Campaigns against plays at local theaters, for instance, seem to have been attempts to assert the cultural tastes of local women who wanted to resist those plays that might have been acceptable in New York but contravened small-town standards of propriety. The WCTU's theater censorship campaigns supplied cultural confidence to women in small towns or rural areas who could act as cultural critics and censors. More importantly, WCTU censorship campaigns were intended to draw upon a wider vein of public discontent and fears over the effects on children of various cultural media. Although virtually all state unions participated at various points in pro-censorship campaigns, Illinois, New York, Pennsylvania, and Massachusetts had the most consistently active departments. This can be attributed to strong department leaders in those states, as well as to a high level of interest in the impact of culture in states that had large and vital cities such as Chicago, New York City, Philadelphia, and Boston, the sites of various experiments in high and popular culture. This suggests that censorship work was as important and active in thriving cities as in conservative small towns that were clinging to their traditional culture. Censorship campaigns were designed by the national WCTU to build the organization's dues-paying membership. Local unions usually responded positively to these national priorities, but others focused on more immediate concerns such as restricting the availability of crime-story papers in barber shops.

The passage of Prohibition, and then its failure as a tool for reforming American society, placed the WCTU in the unenviable position of having promised much (just as it and other women's groups had placed much faith in women's winning of suffrage to change America), but having gained little. Thus, the 1920s mark the point when the WCTU began to lose its credibility as a reform organization, as speakeasies and crime syndicates gained increased power and profit with the criminalization of alcohol. As an organization that was nationally identified as a temperance group, the WCTU had to find a new focus. In order to maintain a place for itself in United States politics and reform, it needed other clear, visible, and viable issues for its organization to address in the 1920s. Overall, it decided to focus attention on the enforcement of Prohibition, especially in the face of widespread disregard for the law. Other avenues were also explored, however, as a means to increase the WCTU's membership and give it greater viability into the 1930s.

WCTU campaigns for national movie censorship were conceived of in the 1920s and 1930s as one of those possible avenues for institutional development. The organization's national leaders recognized that there was widespread public concern over the content and potential harmfulness (especially to children) of motion pictures. They tried to capitalize on this in order to give the WCTU a purpose beyond temperance and Prohibition, while broadening the membership base of the WCTU. Membership had reached an impressively high level of 355,355 in 1931 but slowly declined during the 1930s.[33] The WCTU did have the strength of its huge membership to enable it to wage strong movie censorship campaigns, but it did not take center stage in these campaigns. A separate Catholic campaign that used the strategy of boycotting "impure" movies stole the limelight from all of the Protestant pro-censorship groups and had the most immediate impact on the development of a set of Motion Picture Codes by the movie industry in 1934.[34] As a "temperance union," the WCTU lost its national credibility and much of its influence when the Eighteenth Amendment was revoked in 1933. This is because, in spite of its efforts, the public linked the WCTU's success and influence in other areas of reform to the status of the Prohibition legislation that was overturned in 1933. Although the group still exists in the 1990s, the WCTU is merely a skeleton of the organization that had been so influential in American reform efforts from 1873 to 1933. Clearly, the WCTU's attempts to use campaigns for movie censorship to raise its membership numbers and to refocus its energies away from temperance and Prohibition met with only limited and temporary success.[35]

A discussion of the regulatory activities of the Woman's Christian Temperance Union and the American Library Association presents a whole spectrum of pro-censorship activism by women in various organizations. I intend to illuminate the range of possibilities that pro-censorship women took across the whole era from 1873 to 1933. Moreover, although men were also active in fights for censorship, this study argues that some important women's groups developed censorship agendas distinct from those of their male counterparts.

* * *

Using the Woman's Christian Temperance Union as the primary point of comparison, chapter three is devoted to examining the pro-censorship stance of a professional organization, the American Library Association (ALA). There are important commonalities between the positions of the ALA and the WCTU regarding censorship and regulation. The ALA's rhetoric against "immoral" literature is strikingly similar to that of the WCTU's, and ideologically places this professional group within the pro-censorship, pro-regulatory movement in the United States. Both librarians and WCTU members based much of their pro-regulatory arguments on the purportedly malleable nature of youth. Indeed, the child figured centrally in their debates over censorship and the regulation of cultural forms. Whether the end result was the WCTU's support of federal legislation or librarians' decisions to remove certain books from the shelves, regulation of children's literature by reform-oriented laywomen and by professionals was both accepted and prevalent.

Significant differences, however, existed between the approaches of the two groups to censorship. Indeed, as an organization of professionals, the American Library Association seems to represent the antithesis of a voluntary organization such as the Woman's Christian Temperance Union. Librarians were middle-class professionals, wage earners who had received some special training for their jobs. WCTU members were evangelical laywomen, most of them middle-class and married, without wage-earning jobs. Active participation in the WCTU constituted many of its members' most public and time-consuming role outside the home. The WCTU thought moral guardianship should be the burden of mothers but accepted assistance from the state. As a voluntary women's reform organization, it had two main options. Its members could either regulate their own children's reading (a fairly limited and necessarily fragmented goal), or they could attempt to pass state or national legislation, a strategy requiring the investment of a great deal of time and energy. In contrast, the American Library Association did not rely on legal censorship—its members were able to withhold or simply not purchase books they disliked.

The American Library Association was formed in 1876, three years after the passage of the Comstock Act. It immediately initiated a discussion about the necessity of careful censorship in its official organ, the *Library Journal*. Librarians believed that it was their duty to censor and regulate access to books in the public libraries. The ALA promoted librarians' authoritative role as arbiters of culture through a discourse about the positive nature and effects of censorship. As an organization, it did not advocate legal restrictions against literature beyond the scope of the Comstock laws, but it did accept the language and the standards of the courts that allowed for broader restrictions on "sensational" or "impure" literature that might harm a child's character or lead him or her to criminal acts. Attempts of newly emerging white collar professionals to increase their authority and respectability have been discussed by scholars of professionalization from C. Wright Mills to Olivier Zunz.[36] While some newly emerging professions used technical language to emphasize their unique role in society, the American Library Association used ideas about censorship.

Librarians advocated book regulation as a means for effecting the moral reform of American youths and asserted that reading good books in the safe space of children's reading rooms would keep youths well behaved and off the streets. By the 1930s, concerns about political censorship and restrictions on freedom of speech and thought caused many librarians to reject censorship of adult reading, even on moral grounds, as dangerous. There is, however, nothing to suggest that librarians altered their advocacy of regulation of children's literature.[37] Historians of the ALA have charted a decline in librarians' support of censorship by the early 1900s only by ignoring their continued advocacy of censorship of children's literature. Librarians' mission to spread culture stopped short when confronted with "sensational" children's literature.[38]

Women's entrance into emerging professions such as librarianship, moreover, necessitated a reconfiguration of the duties and responsibilities the career required. In the late nineteenth century, many women entered library work as children's librarians. This was made easy by the fact that male librarians had little interest in the practical, everyday aspect of work with children, preferring simply to debate about which children's books should be wholly excluded from libraries, or about the impact on boys of reading dime novels. As soon as public libraries began opening children's rooms in the 1890s, female library *assistants* (who were accorded lower pay and lower status) were transferred there amid paeans to the maternal, nurturing qualities present in every woman, including single career women. Children's librarians generally accepted this gendered definition of their professional role, perhaps attempting to increase their social acceptability or simply being more comfortable with conceptualizing their professional duties in gendered terms.

The mixed-gender composition of the American Library Association complicates the relationship between gender and professionalization in the organization; yet it also provoked debates among male and female librarians that help reveal the salience of gender in questions of censorship. As early as 1890, the majority of librarians were women, yet especially before 1910, the association's leadership was predominantly male and overwhelmingly favored the regulation of reading. Attempting to counter stereotypes of prudish female librarians imposing a censorship ethic on the ALA, historian Dee Garrison argues that the most vocal advocates for library censorship were men in leadership positions. In fact, both male and female librarians supported their professional right to censor.[39] Children's librarians, virtually all women, came closest to laywomen reformers by linking their duty to censor literature to their special obligation, as women, to protect children from "impure" reading. Children's librarians' emphasis on their qualities as women conflicted with their desire to be treated as equals with male librarians. Indeed, their own maternalist rhetoric may have undercut their ability to demand comparable wages, further marginalized them into lower-paid jobs in children's rooms, and denied them access to higher status, male-dominated jobs, such as library directors.

The role of female librarians as political actors and public advocates for legal censorship was limited by their commitment to act as members of an emerging profession. They were to regulate reading in libraries without publicity; they were not to claim a place in the public debate as women or mothers. Librarians shied away from governmental censorship laws, which interfered with their professional role as censors. For this reason, gendered role definitions had serious limitations politically as well as professionally; female librarians could not transfer their concern for children's reading into the political pro-censorship activism espoused by laywomen in groups like the Woman's Christian Temperance Union and still maintain their professional stance as "experts."

* * *

As a study of censorship this book provides readers with an historical perspective on current controversies over pornography, art funding, and "obscenity." With *Miller v. California*, which was decided by the Supreme Court in 1973, the only adult pornography subject to governmental regulation became that which "an average person" deemed was *wholly* without literary, artistic, political, social, or scientific value. This so-called LAPS test was weakened in 1987 when the court in *Pope v. Illinois* ruled that because community views varied, "reasonable person" should be substituted for "average person." Combinations of sex and violence soon began permeating not only low-budget pornographic films but mass-distributed movies, videos, and magazines, making violent portraits of adult sex readily available. By the 1990s, pornographic materials were a $10 billion operation in the United States alone.[40] At the turn of the century, by contrast, that which was "immoral" or "sensational," such as a hazy drawing of a seminude woman, could be defined as "obscene." Thus, a far broader range of literature and visual images, from erotic photographs to literary classics, was subject to legal censorship in the past compared to today.

Women's groups that advocated censorship of literature, art, and the movies from the 1870s through the 1930s offer historical precedents to contemporary women who are anti-pornography and pro-censorship. Yet these earlier calls for censorship focused on degrading or trivialized portrayals of women, crime scenes, partial female nudity, and romances between unmarried people—scenes that in general are no longer considered "obscene." Pro-censorship reformers in groups like the Woman's Christian Temperance Union often based their calls for censorship on an insistence that images of women in popular and high culture should focus on women's strength and moral character rather than on physical characteristics. The WCTU's Department for the Promotion of Purity in Literature and Art, for instance, condemned "suggestive" advertisements featuring seminude women as degrad-

ing to all women. Its arguments against depictions of women in advertisements featured both a "Victorian" rejection of sensuality *and* a feminist attack on the objectification of women.

Today there is an ideological and practical split between those feminists
who are anti-pornography and those who are anti-censorship.[41] Anti-pornography feminists are those who believe that many images in contemporary
pornography—especially those depicting violence against women and/or
nonconsensual sex—are harmful to the female actors themselves and, more
broadly, to all women. This belief in the danger of pornography is based on
the assumption that male viewers (in particular) watch and read pornography as if it were a manual or an instruction guide to behavior, including
relations between the sexes. Although the most extreme anti-pornography
activists assert that "pornography is the theory, rape is the practice," studies have not conclusively proven such a link. Some researchers have indicated that pornography diminishes male sensitivity to women's legal rights,
including the right to withhold consent to sex.[42] Feminists such as Catharine
MacKinnon and Andrea Dworkin oppose pornography both as "injurious
speech," because it seems to condone and encourage violence against wom-
en, and as a violation of women's civil rights. They successfully proposed,
in the 1980s, local censorship ordinances in the cities of Minneapolis, Bell-
ingham (Washington state), and Indianapolis, which were subsequently
ruled unconstitutional on First Amendment grounds.[43]

Anti-censorship feminists today focus more attention on the issue of free
speech. They are also often bothered by images of violence against women
but argue that it should nevertheless be a protected form of speech. Rejecting the notion that people respond to pornographic movies or books by copying the actions of characters within them, they argue that pornography may
in fact serve as a safety valve that deters real violence against women by
acting as a form of fantasy and "safe sex" for women and men. They suggest that pornography's most objectionable images could be counteracted
if feminist women and men produced their own pornography that challenged patriarchal and heterosexual notions about women's place in society. Anti-censorship feminists also doubt the efficacy of censorship and fear
its tendency to be used against political minorities such as homosexuals.
They also point out that violence against women was a problem before pornography was as widely available or as graphic as it has been since the 1960s
and conclude that banning pornography would probably not stop the physical abuse of women.[44]

The Woman's Christian Temperance Union's support of censorship parallels the contemporary willingness of grass roots groups as diverse as Christian right-wing conservatives and anti-pornography feminists to demand

governmental intervention against the production of "obscenity." The uneasy cooperation of activists on the right and the left is based on a shared belief in the dangers of pornography. Yet the anti-pornography feminists are concerned with stopping violence against women, whereas the religious right is interested in maintaining traditional sex roles. At the turn of the century and today, censorship advocates have found their most common ideological ground on the subject of the vulnerability of youths. Reformers, judges, and legislators of the Progressive Era focused on the susceptibility of youths when deciding what to censor and how to regulate access to books, newspapers, and movies. WCTU laywomen's rhetoric defined censorship campaigns as programs to "mother the movies" and led to high levels of grass roots activism among the very women who advocated traditional values for themselves and their families.[45] New right and feminist anti-pornography activists also use a rhetoric of child protection as a means to gain support for censorship. Much of the American public, for example, currently supports laws restricting the access of youths to pornographic films and supports harsh actions against those who create child pornography. Like earlier reformers, the new right argues that censorship is necessary to protect children and conservative "family values." The new right condemns premarital sex and believes that pornography destroys the nuclear family unit and leads women to engage in freer sexual behavior and/or to reject the role of wife and mother.

There are also important differences between the contemporary pro-censorship movement and its historical predecessor. Again, at the turn of the century, that which was merely "immoral," not "pornographic," was considered to be subject to censorship. Pornography is now more violent, graphic, and accessible. The WCTU, moreover, combined a program for the repression of "impure" and the production of "pure" culture without problems or tensions. Today's anti-pornography feminists are uncomfortable with their alliance with the new right, as well as with the fact that their position seems to condone censorship. The paradoxical nature of a women's pro-censorship stance is demonstrated by its continued viability—and by the divisiveness it incurs—with women on both the right and the left of the political spectrum. Turn-of-the-century pro-censorship arguments have been both resurrected and transformed in the current debates over pornography and the larger problem of the commercial exploitation of female sexuality.

* * *

Culture is a likely object of censorship, for it is the transfer point of societal values. As popular cultural forms multiplied at the turn of the century, they became the contested terrain of activists in voluntary and professional groups as different as the Woman's Christian Temperance Union and the American Library Association. This study modifies cultural historian Lawrence Levine's argument that, by 1900, debates about aesthetics and "high art" had aligned the upper and middle classes against a "low" or popular culture.[46] By exploring the complex aesthetic and moral pro-censorship perspective of the solidly middle-class WCTU, the place of the middle classes in this transformation is problematized. My discussion of the WCTU and the ALA contributes a significant chapter to women's history at the turn of the century by demonstrating women's complex and deep involvement in the politics of censorship, state regulation, and the production of "pure" culture. An examination of the WCTU and the ALA highlights the tensions between laywomen's advocacy of legal censorship and professionals' emphasis on more localized forms of control and between images of mothers as part of the solution and as part of the problem in assuring the purity of children's reading materials.

When the WCTU created the Department for the Suppression of Impure Literature in 1883, few Americans questioned those contemporary legal obscenity decisions that based restriction of public access to things "immoral" on a concern for children. The WCTU held in common with many progressives and conservatives alike the belief, as Annette Kuhn defines it, that "morality was a matter of public concern, and could and should be subject to regulation."[47] The notion that the law must protect the "most vulnerable" in the community (usually children) was the rationale of obscenity laws and court decisions on censorship. Although by the Progressive Era and the 1920s, "the community" was being fragmented—so much so that social scientists were focused on trying to *save* it—the WCTU and other reform organizations supported court decisions upholding a "community standard" of decency. Overall, a focus on the morality of youths was central to the public's support of all censorship campaigns. The goal of the protection of youths linked librarians and teachers to women's reform groups and helped reformers weave together their concerns about culture, education, immigration, morality, the family, and class divisions.

CHAPTER 1

Women's Activism and Alliances

WCTU Crusades and the Quest for Political Power

The Woman's Christian Temperance Union had a deep interest in censorship and the regulation of social morality that went far beyond what most historians have previously assumed.[1] This interest was not purely rhetorical; rather, for fifty years, the WCTU's Department of Purity in Literature and Art, together with other pro-censorship reformers, left a legacy of legislative restrictions on "impure" cultural forms at the local, state, and federal levels. Key to the department's calls for censorship was its model of child development, one that equated consumption of any given cultural form with mimetic action; children were vulnerable, suggestible, and could potentially act out any criminal or immoral act they read about in a book or viewed in a movie.[2] Literature, art, and movies, therefore, had to be judged on moral, not aesthetic, grounds and circulated or repressed accordingly. The first half of this chapter explores the WCTU's ideas about "impure" culture; the second establishes that the WCTU's pro-regulatory work was not unusual and points to the acceptability of censorship among other middle-class and even some working-class Americans. The WCTU's support of censorship parallels the pro-censorship positions of a wide variety of organizations: religious groups and Christian ministers, professional associations (including the National Education Association), and women's reform groups and clubs, such as the National Association of Colored Women and the National Congress of Mothers (later the P.T.A.).

The WCTU's determination to fight for censorship laws can only be understood in conjunction with an analysis of its estimation of the power of cultural forms. New York state's superintendent of the Department of Purity in Literature and Art, Harriet Pritchard, dramatically declared that even the mere *"sight* of an evilly suggestive picture on the wall, easel, [or] book . . . often draws a young woman or man over the brink of destruction."[3] Thus no person, and particularly no youth, could look at anything "impure" without putting his or her own good morals into serious danger. Pritchard employed a model of personality development that focused on the interaction of the individual with society. She believed that if the hero or heroine of a book or movie was divorced yet still characterized as a respectable and desirable suitor of "innocent parties," for instance, that real people would follow suit and view divorce and remarriage as reasonable social options. Discussing youths' propensity to imitate movies, WCTU activists echoed the language of influential sociologists, psychologists, and criminologists, such as William James and Gabriel Tarde. Examining the development of modern American social thought, Ruth Leys argues that "the imitation-suggestion theory . . . introduced a new approach to crime and delinquency by proposing that these were the product not of biological degeneration but of the appropriation or incorporation of deviant forms of behavior."[4] Imitation-suggestion theory was translated, even if indirectly, by WCTU leaders to mean that "suggestive" novels and movies resulted in an actual increase in divorces as evidenced "in the news of court trials and in the press."[5] The department's leaders insisted that visual images and the written word could fundamentally alter a person's character for the worse: "Art and literature are like two levers which lift the world, when rightly applied, to a higher level, even to the highest pinnacle of thought, and consequently to the plane of best living, but if used to portray the lower instincts or reckless actions, tend to bring the human soul to a debauched and demoralized state."[6] Acting on this understanding of art and literature, the organization defined and created an alternative cultural hierarchy based on morality rather than aesthetics or class.

The Woman's Christian Temperance Union used the word "immoral" to describe art or literature it disapproved of and to suggest that censorship laws needed to be expanded to include more than that which was already legally "obscene." Pinning down the WCTU's definition of "immoral" literature or art is difficult. Yet the word's lack of specificity served pro-censorship activists' needs well. To illustrate the inclusiveness of their concerns, I have compiled a list of words used seemingly interchangeably by members of the WCTU to mean "immoral":

> "suggestive," "questionable," "doubtful," "objectionable," "obscene," "impure," "improper," "lewd," "lascivious," "disgusting," "indecent," "bad," "trashy," "a contagion," "unclean," "filthy," "dirty," "poisonous," "coarse,"

"life-destroying," "vicious," "vile," "sensual," "ignoble," "low," "debasing," "demoralizing," "forbidden," "pernicious," "evil," "sensational," "unsafe," "revolting," "spurious," "insidious," "salacious," "harmful," "immodest," "sensuous," "unchaste," "unseemly."[7]

These adjectives are obviously not in fact interchangeable. That which is "doubtful" or "immodest" is not necessarily "obscene" from a legal standpoint. WCTU members generally used the words "obscene" and "lewd" when referring to the types of literature and picture postcards that clearly fell under the existing legal sanctions as "obscenity." They talked more frequently about "immoral" and "impure" culture because their target was broader. There is a purposeful amorphousness in the WCTU's conception of the sources of corruption: Some words are descriptive, such as "sensational," while others are effects, such as "poisonous," but all reveal a causal model whereby cultural forms can directly affect an individual's health, character, and actions. All the words listed above revolve around each other to create a multifaceted definition of "immorality."

These subtle variations demonstrate how the WCTU mobilized language developed by professionals to justify campaigns for the greater regulation of cultural forms. The social hygiene movement, for instance, provided moral reformers with a quasi-scientific language and professionally accepted metaphors of disease to describe the dangers of "immorality." Led by teachers and professors, it focused public attention on diet, cleanliness, and sex education, positing youths as the recipients and primary beneficiaries of social hygiene education.[8] The social hygiene movement publicized the dangers of dirt and trash to both morality and health. The American Medical Association tried to assure the public that its members could rid society of these contagions and poisons. The WCTU gladly quoted Dr. David Starr Jordan's speech at the 1912 National Education Association convention, for he linked the social hygiene rhetoric to temperance. Jordan argued that it was in the interest of sanitation (as well as morals) to stop the "liquor traffic" and connected saloons and intemperance to the "white slave traffic" and contagious diseases.[9]

WCTU laywomen themselves drew upon a medical vocabulary, speaking of "poisonous droughts" of "immoral" literature. They suggested that mothers and nurturing women should be accepted as the true professionals who could administer literature in "corrective, antiseptic doses."[10] Metaphors of disease appear in almost every discussion of "impure" literature; indeed, moral reformers exploited medical knowledge about germ theory and the spread of disease to impress upon their audiences the dangers of impurity in literature: "Every home should be quarantined against this stream of vice and corruption. Exclude it from the house as you would the germs of a deadly pestilence."[11] Anti-obscenity crusader Anthony Comstock hyperbolically exclaimed in the WCTU's official organ, the *Union Signal*, that if one "combine[s] intemperance with evil reading, it is an influence more to be dreaded than the microbes of smallpox, scarlet fever or Asiatic cholera."[12] Not only the mind and subsequent behavior, but the physical body, too, would be damaged by "impure" reading; reformers sometimes claimed that youths who read sensational stories were sure to become "*addicted* to the solitary vice [masturbation]."[13] The WCTU asserted that mothers with Christian homes wanted their children's "bodies free from the effects of dissipation in reading sensational and vicious books."[14] The WCTU yoked the languages of social hygiene and disease to its own concerns about morality in order to address long-standing social problems.

Since impurities shown in popular culture were "contagious," it logically followed that crime stories and, later, movies could lead youths to the violent extremes of murder and accidental suicide. The WCTU reported to its members any evidence it could discover of such connections between reading and criminal behavior:

> The following is a clipping we received from a paper that shows the effect of such pictures upon a child's mind: "John Barry, 12, . . . showed his dog Bessie the tricks he saw cowboys and bandits do in a motion picture show his mother took him to last night. Playing bandit, he took the leash off the dog, tied one end around his neck and the other to the gas chandelier. He then stood on a packing box. The box accidentally tipped and Johnnie's neck was broken. . . . Dr. Homerick pronounced the boy dead."[15]

Seemingly innocent imitations of the movies, it warned, could result in a child's death. In other cases, the department made its own correlations between "impure" literature and violence: "On August 26, at Belmar, New Jersey, two boys were arrested and charged with burning to death at the stake two younger boys, one of whom was a younger brother of one of the culprits. No doubt they were imitating what they had read or heard told, of Indian massacres. Such reading should not be allowed where the young may have access to it."[16] Concern for control over the leisure time of youths was sometimes translated by local unions into a mandate to petition for curfew laws, a (compelling) way to keep children at home.[17] Moreover, the probability that children might mimic the harmful actions of characters from literature or the screen denied the possibility of innocent, if sensational, fantasies. By defining fictional "immorality" or fantasy as leading to harmful acts, WCTU reformers necessitated the legal suppression of suspect cultural forms.[18]

The WCTU favored and publicly voiced support for governmental censorship, unlike those middle-class groups that merely favored regulating books within the boundaries of their profession. Emilie Martin, the influential WCTU leader and national superintendent for the Department of Purity in Literature and Art, gave a description of the department's campaign against Hal Caine's book *The Woman Thou Gavest Me.* Martin reported that "a thunder of censor has been uttered against the book."[19] Here, censorship was not an embarrassing activity to be done surreptitiously but was as loud and as commanding as thunder. Superintendent Martin further described successful pro-censorship work in the following terms: "The Sunday comic supplement has caused *an arrest of thought,* and many [comic strips] are modified."[20] To Martin an "arrest of thought" implied a cessation of "wrong" thinking, corresponding to a massive change in public opinion initiated, she hoped, by WCTU campaigns. Martin argued that literature and art were living expressions of thought and that "the aim of this department is to set people thinking right."[21] In this instance, the WCTU viewed itself as an activist minority, but one that would ultimately prevail with the majority of Americans and end complacency by pointing out the negative effects of "impure" popular culture. The WCTU's pro-censorship department supported regulation as a means for creating an ideal American society based on a vision of future democratic harmony. In effect, the WCTU believed that it represented what in recent years has been called the "moral majority."

The WCTU had a much broader program than simple censorship. In seeking control over cultural production, it pursued an active strategy of promoting and creating its own "pure" literature, as well as a reactive one of banning the "impure" variety. Not content to wait for professional writers to create "clean" literature, the WCTU wrote and published its own magazines for children and young people beginning in 1883, the same year that its pro-censorship department was created.[22] The organization expanded the need for a women's pro-censorship movement through a subtle redefinition of the task at hand. Its job was not to supervise literature but rather to make children's lives wholesome. Claiming that "this department works largely for the children," WCTU activists believed they had the broadest possible mandate because "if we would help our child's life, we must help the lives of all other children, for they make up the world in which our child must live."[23] The department also encouraged cross-class networking based on the solidarity of women as potential mothers: "Our work lies in getting young mothers together . . . helping them to realize how much is given to them in the training of the young lives entrusted to them."[24] WCTU superintendents advised sending "clean, interesting reading matter to the mills and factories for the girls and men to read and take home."[25] The WCTU willingly used the government's legal and penal systems to help it fight the "impure" more effectively, yet censorship was conceived of primarily as a means to increase women's control over children's developing characters. Although national censorship might increase the power of the government and its experts, thereby threatening women's regulatory authority, this possibility was not raised by WCTU members.[26]

The censorship activities of the Department of Purity in Literature and Art were regularly presented in a language that stressed women's responsibilities to children and domesticity: "This Department of Purity in Literature and Art means much, because it touches directly the home, and the life connected with it. Our American home is the heart of our great country, and we must see to it, by our influence, that it is kept clean."[27] The WCTU justified its work of censorship and supervision of American culture by insisting that all women, as official caretakers of the American home, needed to be in the front lines fighting against immorality. When demanding legislative changes, WCTU members carefully constructed their petitions to emphasize their role as mothers concerned for their children. One letter concluded with a modest portrayal of the role of women and their alliance with the government: "We confidently appeal to our Chief Executive, and the heads of the legal and postal departments of this government, to aid us as women to protect the innocent and helpless—the children—from an enemy that we seem powerless to stay in any other way. We pray you to grant our petition."[28] This rhetoric was calculated to appeal to the paternalist notions of the president and legislators, asking them "to aid us" against the "enemy." WCTU members identified themselves as "powerless" yet asserted "confidently" their belief that their petition would move the president of the United States to initiate change and to more vigorously enforce extant censorship laws.

Thus, the department justified its activities by an extended discussion of the need for WCTU women to protect the nation's children. Any discussion of censorship and regulation eventually led back to youths:

> We stand for over twenty-two millions of youth under twenty-one years of age. Fully one-third of the population of the United States. We want to reach the mothers of this land and warn them of the perils and dangers that surround their children upon the very threshold of their lives. We seek to create public sentiment for the right training, culture and development of children. Throw out a sheet anchor of safety to parents and others and thus secure the moral purity of the rising generation. *There is no organization or society in this world that can do this work as well as our own.*[29]

As mothers protecting children, WCTU members claimed sweeping powers for themselves and their organization. The department argued that its pro-censorship fight was also relevant to the organization's temperance goals: "Thousands of youth are defiled and unclean before they ever touch liquor, through reading impure literature and the debasing influence of bad pictures."[30] The WCTU's advocacy of woman suffrage in the late nineteenth century was not generally discussed as a means for asserting women's individual rights but was instead celebrated as the "Home Protection Ballot" in order to gain support for suffrage from moderate reform-oriented women and their families. Similarly, the Department of Purity in Literature and Art ensured the wide acceptance of its censorship goals by focusing on the dire effects of "immoral" literature and art upon youths rather than on controlling adults.

* * *

The alleged transformation in the WCTU's agenda, after President Frances Willard's death in 1898, from a "Do Everything" policy—encouraging a program of action on a wide range of social concerns—into a putatively single-issue lobbying group for the national prohibition of alcohol, was never as abrupt or complete as most historians have asserted. Ruth Bordin, for instance, has mistakenly asserted that "for whatever reason, the WCTU's program emphasis changed after Willard's death. The union shifted to a single-issue approach, an emphasis on temperance."[31] In reality, throughout the first three decades of the twentieth century, the WCTU fought hard for many issues other than prohibition. During a much shorter period, from 1915 to 1919, many local unions did seem to undergo a temporary contraction of activities in their numerous departments, for at that time the constitutional prohibition of alcohol and the passage of a woman suffrage amendment were imminent realities. Not surprisingly, WCTU women were inspired to put the majority of their time and energy into these winning campaigns.[32] In the 1920s, after the passage of the Eighteenth and Nineteenth Amendments, there was a resurgence of the activities of other departments that went significantly beyond the WCTU's obvious interest in the rigorous enforcement of Prohibition. Surviving national WCTU records indicate that through the 1930s, all states had active and diverse departments.[33] The pro-censorship department is a good example of the continuation of the WCTU's "Do Everything" policy. This department was reorganized into the Department of Motion Pictures as late as 1925, which suggests that well after Willard's death, broad reform goals were actively being pursued. Rather than abandon a pro-censorship program whose early focus on crime-story papers had become obsolete, the WCTU committed itself to continuing its pro-censorship work with a stronger focus on the then most popular cultural form—movies. While the Department of Motion Pictures certainly embraced temperance and was concerned with the portrayal and use of alcohol in the movies, it focused much attention upon more general concerns for "purity." Social morality was the department's motive for political activism in favor of movie censorship.

The organization's twentieth-century agenda, therefore, was not simply or narrowly connected to the Prohibition cause.

The vitality and variety of the WCTU's departments and reform goals through the first three decades of the twentieth century (exemplified by the creation of the Department of Motion Pictures) demonstrates the organization's continued commitment to a comprehensive reform of American society. From 1900 to 1933, many local branches of the WCTU had departments such as Child Welfare, Mother's Meetings, Juvenile Court, Americanization (also called Christian Citizenship), Motion Pictures, Scientific Temperance Instruction, Radio, Peace and Arbitration, Evangelistic (including the Bible in Public Schools), Fairs and Exhibits, Child Health and Protection, and Purity in Literature and Art. The organization's interest in the broad reforms for social morality persisted through 1933. Only the end of Prohibition signaled the WCTU's demise as an effective national reform organization.

The WCTU's flexibility in meeting the varied and changing interests of its members is demonstrated by its official structure. Members could act at the state and local levels to set up whichever branches of the nationally created WCTU departments interested them the most. Loosely controlled by the national WCTU, the state unions maintained local autonomy. It was this ability of local chapters to choose their agenda from a wide selection of social reform issues, including pro-censorship activism, that helped the WCTU to thrive for over fifty years.[34] Emilie Martin emphasized that much pro-censorship work was done at the individual initiative of local leaders: "There has been heroic work done by many of the Superintendents." She implied that the initiative of local and state leaders was critical to the department's success.[35] State WCTU annual reports demonstrate, moreover, that state unions often continued activities in certain departments even after they had been formally disbanded at the national level. When the national WCTU decided to eliminate the Department of Purity in Literature and Art in 1925, for instance, in order to replace it with a Department of Motion Pictures, some state unions kept the former department. They simply added a Department of Motion Pictures without eliminating the other.[36] The absence of a Department of Purity in Literature and Art in some state annual reports does not automatically signal an end to its members' interest in censorship and regulation. The departmental names agreed upon at the national conventions often had local variations; in northern California, for instance, the pro-censorship department was called the "Department of Social Morality."[37] The Pennsylvania WCTU reported that in one local union, "Mrs. A. T. Bell continues to work on this line [censorship] through several departments."[38] In one New York town, "this department is combined with that of Moral Education."[39] Attempts to identify the range of the department's pro-censorship activities are thus somewhat complicated by state and local independence.

The WCTU continued to be a viable reform organization well beyond 1900, although no subsequent national WCTU president after Frances Willard had a comparable level of charisma, national attention and recognition, or power. This certainly had a negative effect on the strength of the WCTU as a national organization, but it overcame this disadvantage through its vast grass-roots network of local unions. WCTU membership increased, for instance, in the first decades of the twentieth century before peaking at 355,355 in 1931.[40] This strength, along with its well-organized system of departments, enabled the organization to perform at a high level of planning and activism even without its most dynamic president. Its continued strength can also be attributed to the leadership capabilities of the national superintendents, as well as to state and local leaders who built up loyal and devoted memberships that were determined to push forward their agendas.

The scattered but suggestive evidence indicates the variety and unpredictability of the type of work the unions pursued, especially in comparison to national statements and goals. Unfortunately, state annual reports at the national WCTU library are not complete; in particular, many of the states' reports written before 1930 did not survive. For this reason, it is difficult to trace the history of these departments at the state level as thoroughly as one might wish. Sources for local activism used here include annual reports issued by state unions (these are on file at the national WCTU headquarters), the *Union Signal*, the *Young Crusader*, and the *National Minutes*. State independence is exemplified by Jessie Leonard, the superintendent of motion pictures for Massachusetts. Leonard offered a different agenda from that of the national pro-censorship department. She did not actively support federal censorship of movies. Instead, she argued that women "must mother the movies" by attending the shows and then responding as helpful critics with letters to the movie producers. In 1928, when the national department was gearing up for a huge campaign for federal censorship, Leonard looked at the movies and concluded that "*progress* . . . is all she [Leonard] can report at this time." Leonard argued that the movie industry was already cooperating with reformers and even had "an active code of ethics." Instead of criticizing the industry, Leonard reported that "she has kept in touch with the makers of movies and praised every forward step taken." Leonard's agenda for Massachusetts was quite different from that of the national WCTU, but she was unapologetic about modifying it.[41] This example suggests that extensive use of local archives could produce some fascinating institutional histories of the WCTU with more specifically local perspectives.[42]

Brief sketches of three WCTU leaders help to demonstrate the range of political activities and types of activism undertaken by state and local unions. Detailed information is difficult to obtain on individual women in the WCTU, even about those women who led national departments. WCTU leaders at the state as well as the national level seem to have been more politically active than most other middle-class women at the turn of the century. Illinois state had an effective superintendent of the Department for the Suppression of Impure Literature, Mrs. Ada Kepley. She worked in an important state union, for Illinois was the home of the WCTU's national headquarters, located in the Chicago suburb of Evanston. As the state's leader of WCTU censorship campaigns during the nineteenth century, Kepley supported the national organization's principal strategy of attempting, by petition drives and political lobbying, to pass stricter censorship laws at the federal and state levels. Simultaneously, she encouraged campaigns to pass or better enforce local censorship laws.[43] Kepley noted in 1887 that the city council of Delavan, Illinois, for instance, had "passed an ordinance which fully reaches all evil literature." She explained to local superintendents that "our State law gives all municipalities the power to legislate evil literature. Therefore imitate Delavan, and labor for ordinances in your towns that will reach evil publications of all sorts."[44] Local censorship measures were viewed by both Kepley and the national WCTU as good temporary measures that would help enforce community standards while the fight continued for the more comprehensive solution of federal censorship.

Kepley brought important professional skills to the organization's fights for censorship regulations, for she had a B.L. from the Union College of Law in Chicago and a Ph.D. from Austin College. She became a practicing member of the bar in 1870.[45] Frances Willard included Kepley in a book she edited of biographies of important nineteenth-century women, noting that Kepley later became a city marshall and an ordained Unitarian minister (1892). To explain her connection to the Unitarian faith, Willard wrote that "Mrs Kepley's ancestors were Episcopalians, Catholics and Methodists in religion, from which combination she is, by a natural process, a Unitarian in belief."[46] Using her familiarity with the legal system, lawyer Kepley worked with agents of the Western Society for the Suppression of Vice and her Illinois state legislators as they designed a bill for the "suppression of evil literature." This bill did not pass, yet it demonstrates that Kepley worked with ease in the male-dominated structures of law and politics.[47] Willard's biographical sketch also highlighted Kepley's work as a newspaper correspondent and as "editor of the *Friend of Home,* a flourishing monthly." Her editorial work was important to the pro-censorship cause, because "in its pages she expounds the law, demands its enforcement, declares for new laws and suggests ways to secure them." Willard also made sure to note appreciatively that "she and her husband [also a lawyer] erected and support 'The Temple,' in Effingham [Illinois], a beautiful building, which is headquarters for the Woman's Christian Temperance Union, prohibition, and general reform work."[48] Kepley provided both leadership and institutional support for the Illinois WCTU.

Aiming to awaken women to their exploitation and to thereby eliminate the hated "average of feminine placidity," Frances Willard used her annual presidential address of 1889 to celebrate Ada Kepley as a laudable role model. In addition to her above activities, Kepley led a fight in the late 1880s to remove from Illinois both burlesque "exhibitions ('for men only')" and the billboards that advertised them. Ironically, Willard praised the state superintendent not for her skills as a lawyer, but instead for her willingness to break the law in pursuit of a higher moral standard. Angered at the continued presence of "indecent" billboards, Kepley purposefully tore an "indecent" poster off the wall—aided by other WCTU members, who stood beside her and "poured out fervent prayer[s] to God." She was immediately arrested. Willard commended her courageous and decisive act, as well as the judge's decision to acquit her, and claimed that Kepley's actions succeeded in securing a "helpful new law."[49] Like the early female temperance crusaders of 1873 who destroyed private property (barrels of alcohol) in the interest of forcing political and social change, Willard and local WCTU members endorsed Kepley's action as civil disobedience and not vigilante justice because they believed that Kepley was following God's higher moral laws. Here was an instance when the WCTU could not trust the moral authority of the government of "the people" and so vested that authority in God. Kepley's pro-censorship work was also praised by Lucy Holmes, the first national superintendent of the Department for the Suppression of Impure Literature. In her annual report, Holmes said that "Mrs. Ada Kepley, of Effingham, has been so successful in her work that I commend her methods to all workers in this department." Holmes explained that Kepley's "first work was to send out to the local societies a circular, setting forth her plans for the year, and directing the local Unions how to carry them out. Eighty societies report efforts made."[50] One state's leader could provide an example for all the others.

Mrs. Margaret Dye Ellis, national superintendent of legislation in Washington, D.C., served as the organization's chief political lobbyist in the nation's capital. Ellis was also the principal correspondent to WCTU journals on the status of legislation in the House and Senate for about seventeen years, from the mid-1890s through at least 1914.[51] Explaining the reason for her WCTU work, Ellis stated that WCTU members' earlier belief in the power of prayers to close the saloons had given way to an understanding about the

need to change the laws: "We found that there must be law back of sentiment and sentiment back of law. We found that women must study law."[52]
Ellis's political and legal reform interests also led her to join other organizations, including the National Consumers' League, the Woman's Suffrage
League, and the Woman's Welfare Department of the Civic League.[53] Ellis's
Union Signal reports create an impressive record of the extent of her own
political lobbying work. In the space of one week in 1904, for instance, she
reports having gone to "the Senate Post Office Committee to again urge action" on a bill forbidding mail carriers from delivering liquor. She then con-
ferred with "clerks and secretaries" until she managed to talk to a senator
who agreed to add this proposal (successfully) to the current postal bill. Next,
Ellis consulted with Minister Wu and Secretary Gage to make sure that all
Chinese women brought to America to participate in the St. Louis World's
Exhibition would be protected against sexual slavery and kidnapping—a
likely and "dire calamity" that Ellis asserted had occurred at the previous
world's fair. Ellis was promised that a five-hundred-dollar bond would be
given for every woman who came to the United States and that a governmental inspector would check on them each day to make sure they were not
missing.[54] In each of the above instances, Ellis unhesitatingly negotiated with
representatives of foreign states and United States Senate committees, representing the WCTU's position on disparate causes and pieces of legislation.
Ellis also helped the WCTU's pro-censorship activists keep informed about
the status of various proposed federal censorship laws.

Mrs. Emilie D. Martin, of New York City, was the world's and national
superintendent of the Department for the Promotion of Purity in Literature
and Art for twenty years, from 1891 until 1911. Like Kepley and Ellis, Martin embraced her role as a political activist. Apart from the scant personal
information we can glean from her monthly departmental reports, Martin's
1911 obituary in the *Union Signal* tells us that Martin was present at the
founding meeting of the WCTU in 1874. As early as 1880, eleven years before Martin officially took over leadership of the pro-censorship department,
"she became the associate of Frances E. Willard for the promotion of purity
in literature and art." In addition to her work promoting and securing censorship laws, she was "one of the early members of the Foreign Missionary
Society of the Presbyterian church, and served on the executive committee
of the Home Missionary Board." Martin had gained some speaking and leadership experience before she joined the WCTU, for "she was one of the speakers at the International Council of Women in London, in 1869." She was also
a "member of the Synodical Committee of the Synod of New York, Vice-Pres-
ident of the Women's Press Association of New York, and a member of the
New York City Woman's Press Club."[55] Throughout her WCTU career, Mar-

tin used her connections to the press to push for the WCTU's reform agendas. She frequently spoke in favor of censorship at the annual conventions of professional groups such as the National Editorial Association. Martin also supported "pure" literature in speeches at the conventions of other women's groups such as the National Congress of Mothers. Like the Kepleys, Martin and her husband used their wealth to support the national activities of her department.

As head of the Department of Purity in Literature and Art, Martin wrote personal letters and sent large collections of petitions to several consecutive presidents of the United States, usually demanding legal regulations that would ensure purity in newspaper stories or in art. Immediately upon becoming national superintendent of the department, Martin initiated a large petition and letter-writing campaign directed to the managers of the upcoming World's Columbian Exposition of 1893 in Chicago. These letters demanded that the art exhibited at the world's fair be "pure"—meaning without representations of female nudity.[56]

Martin's strong leadership of the pro-censorship department ensured an active New York state union, with an especially well-organized and active branch in New York City, where examples of "impurities" were so pervasive in both popular and avant-garde art. Martin herself commented in one report that "New York City is the storm center, and whatever is produced and made attractive here is copied in the cities and towns all over our country." She thus insisted that New York censorship laws needed to be particularly tough.[57] To be certain that the WCTU was right in the "storm center," Martin established the department's national offices in the Times Building in Manhattan. This is the same building that held the offices for Anthony Comstock and his New York Society for the Suppression of Vice. The strength of the national department and of the New York union did not suffer terribly after Martin's death in 1911, for Harriet Pritchard, New York state's pro-censorship leader, was Martin's protégée and colleague. Pritchard took over the leadership of the national department and kept its headquarters in Manhattan. Leaders like Kepley, Ellis, Martin, and Pritchard proved that they could adapt to a male-dominated political game, but they also changed the game itself by bringing into politics issues of "home life" and by raising concerns conventionally identified as those of women and/or mothers.

The WCTU insisted on the ability of average, individual women, not just WCTU state and national leaders, to initiate change. This belief is exemplified in many incidents of individual action recounted in the organization's records and journals. The local activities of the Department of Purity in Literature and Art highlight the significance of historian Ruth Bordin's observation that "the most important long-range result of the WCTU's politici-

zation was that a large group of women who previously had little experience in the political arena learned the practice of politics."[58] Women who
could not vote practiced politics through the WCTU.[59] Examples of individual protest range from a woman who "told her grocer she would not trade
with him as long as he showed an objectionable billboard. It disappeared,"
to a Michigan union that successfully intervened to have "an objectionable
picture removed from a drug store window."[60] Local members went to the
police commissioners to protest advertisements and often convinced them
to cooperate. They also wrote letters to groups like "the Bill Posters Union
urging them not to lay themselves liable to prosecution."[61] Local campaign-
ing included door-to-door efforts by individual activists: "she made nearly
100 calls at that time to the most important influential homes on every street
in the village, requesting that the cards be put in the front windows, and interviewed many people regarding their temperance vote at election."[62]
WCTU members seem to have played the political game differently than men
by relying on a more diffuse, less hierarchical system of organization that
emphasized the importance of local grass-roots politics.

Clearly hoping to inspire others, Illinois Superintendent Kepley wrote:
"One of our women reports a picture of evil tendencies in a hotel, which she
turned with its face to the wall and across the back she wrote a protest in
the name of the W.C.T.U. with the result that the picture was removed."[63]
Private property could be defaced with good conscience in the name of "purity" in art. The Washington, D.C., department superintendent, Mrs. E. A.
Chambers, boldly stated: "I have the honor to report that through the influence and labors of the W.C.T.U. our city is free from all display of obscene
pictures, which were formerly used by tobacconists and bill-posters as advertising mediums. These men begin to fear the *power* of this organization,
and no longer make any attempt to attract the eye of the public through the
nude form of woman."[64] The power of women's activism was, she claimed,
visible throughout the city's public places just as "obscene" advertisements
had been before. Most suggestive about the WCTU's censorship work is how
women's moral and ideological concerns were translated into political and
social action.

Articles in the WCTU's *Union Signal* detailed the breadth of legal and
political regulatory options available to local unions, including petition
drives, citizens' seizure actions, frequent editorial contributions to the local
and national press, Mother's Meetings, and more. A version of the English
Seizure Clause Law enacted in the United States, for instance, was quoted
in the *National Minutes* of 1892 to alert members that it gave "our WCTU
women . . . power to seize anything improper in character" and turn it over
to the District Attorney, who "may have the offensive matter destroyed."[65]

Pro-censorship work typically began for local unions with a review of the federal, state, or local laws "relating to profanity and obscenity." If an appropriate law was already on the books, copies of it would be prominently posted in public places and "widely distributed" to stores and merchants.[66] Next, "a committee was sent to visit stores" to see if any "impure" articles or advertisements were being sold or displayed.[67] Some local WCTU's created committees for "securing evidence preparatory to taking action against a person for exhibiting impure pictures in a public place."[68] This last step involved attempting to enforce the already extant law; members were exhorted to, "inform your public officials of conditions. If they do not act, notify other citizens and organizations of conditions."[69]

State and local WCTU leaders periodically assessed their pro-regulatory successes and failures. Many pragmatically concluded that it was easier to secure local laws: "Municipal law is more easily secured than state [or federal], and can be better enforced. But few town boards will refuse the petition of its best citizens for the passage of a law prohibiting the sale of impure books and pictures."[70] Historian Paula Baker presents a picture of women in this era as relatively uninvolved in local politics. Instead, she argues that they engaged in national work for those issues, including temperance, that could avoid placing them in direct conflict with the local power structure and/or the important men in their personal lives.[71] WCTU members' activities do not support this characterization, however, for they openly participated in local politics—including pro-censorship work—not as secondary figures, but as prominent community members and active enforcers and supporters of all levels of legal intervention into reform and regulations. Asserting their authority and ability to instigate change in the legislative and public spheres, WCTU members believed that they had the right as citizens to enter the offices of any local politician or law-enforcement official and receive respect and prompt attention to their concerns. They did not hesitate to hold the government responsible for the higher standards and regulations they advocated.

* * *

The Woman's Christian Temperance Union was not alone in its pro-censorship activism; it occasionally collaborated with and often worked on programs that paralleled those of other middle-class organizations and women's groups that promoted censorship. The remainder of this chapter focuses on some of those instances when the WCTU cooperated with or complemented the efforts of a variety of other groups that supported censorship goals. From the 1880s through the 1930s, the New York Society for the Suppression of Vice, the Young Men's Christian Association, the Christian Endeavor, the

Protestant Church, the Catholic Church, the League of American Mothers, the National Congress of Mothers, the American Literary Railway Union, the Society for the Prevention of Cruelty to Children, the General Federation of Women's Clubs, the Watch and Ward Society, the National Association of Colored Women, and the International Reform Bureau all supported pro-censorship positions and laws. Each also cooperated at times with the WCTU in some aspects of pro-censorship work. The WCTU as an organization had ties to the woman suffrage movement, strengthened by the mutual respect and friendship between Frances Willard and Susan B. Anthony. Yet WCTU ties with liberal feminist organizations are not as visible in this account, for the work of its Department for the Promotion of Purity in Literature and Art was more compatible with that of moral reform and religious organizations. WCTU activists were often members of other organizations, such as religious associations or churches and women's clubs. Those who had memberships in other organizations spread the department's message by speaking publicly at their other club meetings against "impure" literature and on the need to support censorship legislation.[72] Taken as a whole, the agreement of these groups on the need for censorship and regulation reinforces my claim for censorship's broad-based appeal in the Gilded Age and the Progressive Era.

Censorship was not the primary focus of many of these groups, including the WCTU; for others, such as Anthony Comstock's New York Society for the Suppression of Vice, it was their sole reason for being. Yet what differed was the amount of time each group spent at pro-censorship work, not the degree of agreement over the need for censorship. Together, these organizations and their members created public support for censorship and advocated the regulation of culture for reasons of morality. We will see that pro-censorship activism among these different groups reached its peak of cooperation and cohesion in campaigns for movie censorship in the late 1920s and early 1930s.

The WCTU's Department of Purity in Literature and Art worked with male vice societies and other religious organizations that were organized solely to fight for censorship and regulation. The department itself rarely interpreted either purity or morality as religious constructs. Its notions of what should be censored were seldom directly tied to Christian notions of sin. Although many WCTU members were Methodists or belonged to other Christian denominations, the *Union Signal* did not explicitly stress or privilege a specific religious orientation. This is because the organization was devoted, at least theoretically, to reaching all Americans through its literature. Yet the WCTU did print articles by Christian leaders in the *Union Signal*. It also reprinted articles from the Christian press that presented the censorship battle as a fight against the rise of a secular American culture.

WCTU members cited articles from the Christian press to bolster their pro-censorship position. Arguing for the necessity of strict movie censorship legislation, for example, a member quoted arguments presented in the respectable, nondenominational *Christian Century:* "Ten years ago, says Prof. Fred Eastman in *Christian Century*—high screen officials promised—'Put the motion picture industry on its word one year—we will show you how to clean up the business.' Well, nine years have passed but the scenes they promised to eliminate have increased rather than diminished. . . . The industry has basely repudiated its promises."[73] *Union Signal* editors published articles by ministers who described the censorship battle as religiously motivated. Reverend B. W. Williams, for instance, claimed that a Christian crusade against "vicious literature" was necessary since "boys and girls are often rendered mentally dyspeptic by reading the high-wrought fiction and demoralizing trash that is constantly being issued by the *secular* press."[74] The WCTU also praised the Young Men's Christian Association (YMCA) and presented censorship as part of the YMCA's noble fight to keep young men respectable and sober: "Many of the magazines are becoming so salacious in their pictures that several YMCA secretaries . . . have to expurgate (better expel) them before putting them on the files."[75] The *Union Signal* recorded and supported the pro-censorship activities of YMCAs and YWCAs. The YMCA, it noted, had fought against nudity in fine art by protesting against a mixed sex reception to be held at the Boston Museum of Fine Arts, because "nude art never helped a soul to belief in the Lord Jesus."[76] Demanding "pure" representations of women, local YMCAs passed resolutions demanding the removal of "indecent theatrical show bills" from public display.[77] The Young Women's Christian Associations (YWCA) were also involved in the fight against immorality. They set up their own libraries for young working women. YWCAs created Library Committees to read and approve all books before they were placed on the shelves of their private libraries. YWCAs thus implicitly denigrated book selections in the competing public libraries, while they engaged in the careful regulation of reading.[78]

From its inception, the WCTU's Department of Purity in Literature and Art made pro-censorship appeals to Christian ministers. Its "plan of work" asked local members to provide their town ministers with enough literature to enable them to write sermons urging their parishioners to fight against "immoral" literature. Yearly departmental reports indicate success in this goal. More dramatically, in the host city of each annual national convention, WCTU women spoke from the pulpits of all or most of the host city's Protestant churches. The department perceived its relationship with ministers to be harmonious and mutually supportive: "Ministers are expressing thanks that women have the courage of their convictions."[79]

The WCTU worked with those individual ministers most dedicated to taking an activist role in regulation and reform. The Reverend Josiah Leeds, a wealthy Philadelphian minister of the Society of Friends, contributed articles to the *Union Signal* on the evils of "immoral" plays and magazine advertisements. Leeds advocated that WCTU members withdraw their patronage from barber shops that subscribed to the *Police Gazette* or displayed "indecent pictures on the wall." He also advised them to discontinue magazine and paper subscriptions and to include an explanatory letter if more than one incident of "impurity" occurred.[80] Reverend Leeds was further connected to the WCTU through his wife, Deborah Leeds, who headed the Department for the Suppression of Impure Literature from 1888 to 1889. Deborah Leeds joined with her husband in encouraging local WCTU members to request that "blood and thunder" papers be removed from barber shops, noting that individual customer complaints were often effective.[81]

From the 1880s through the early 1930s, the Reverend Wilbur Crafts, superintendent of the International Reform Bureau, actively courted the WCTU's assistance. Based in Washington, D.C., the bureau lobbied for and monitored the status of reform bills before Congress. At the turn of the century, Crafts's organization worked with the WCTU, the Anti-Saloon League, and the National Temperance League to fight for dry laws and for Sunday "blue" laws.[82] Crafts periodically contributed articles to the *Union Signal* detailing the status of national legislation against "immoral" literature and then detailing the status of particular movie censorship battles, encouraging WCTU members to support various reform laws through letter writing and petition campaigns. An 1899 article by Crafts, "Reform Gains and Losses," discussed a peace arbitration campaign, efforts to suppress prizefighting, restrictive divorce laws, anti-gambling laws, and municipal censorship of theatrical productions.[83] The International Reform Bureau's wide scope of interest paralleled, with variations, that of the WCTU's.

In the 1910s and 1920s, Reverend Crafts, as general secretary of the Federal Motion Picture Council, became one of the most visible proponents of federal movie censorship, along with Canon William Chase of Brooklyn's Christ Church.[84] When representatives of the nascent movie industry met with pro-censorship forces in 1914 (in an unsuccessful attempt to convince reformers to abandon their demands and agree to industry self-regulation), Crafts was leader of the pro-censorship delegation, representing his International Reform Bureau. Crafts was joined in the meeting by leaders from three major New York reform organizations: the City Federation of Women's Clubs, the Society for the Prevention of Crime, and the Woman's Christian Temperance Union, represented by New York state president Ella Boole.[85] As late as 1931, Nebraska WCTU Director Dr. Jennie Laird wrote of the continued close ties between Crafts's organization and the WCTU: "The International Reform Federation of Washington, D.C., are among our most faithful allies. Copies of their publication 'Twentieth Century Magazine,' were sent with letters and resolutions and motion picture bill literature to 38 P.T.A. presidents in Omaha, 50 letters to Nebraska WCTU directors and 100 letters and literature to county WCTU presidents and workers."[86]

On the subject of censorship, the Woman's Christian Temperance Union has been linked most consistently by historians to the New York Society for the Suppression of Vice and to Anthony Comstock. This relationship is more complicated than many have suggested.[87] Comstock and his society, most importantly, did not direct the pro-censorship agenda of the WCTU. My demonstration of widespread support for censorship at the turn of the century challenges the now-dominant interpretation that places the efforts of women's groups like the WCTU under the umbrella of elite men's desire to promote "high" culture and regulate and control "low" culture. Instead, the WCTU worked from a distinct set of assumptions about culture. It differentiated between "pure" and "impure" within both "high" and "low" genres. The primary goal of the vice societies—reporting "obscene" materials to legal authorities for search and seizure—was not the primary goal or project of the Department of Purity in Literature and Art. The WCTU did not focus solely on enforcing repressive legal measures but also sponsored and produced "pure" literature, art, and movies. The WCTU, moreover, focused less on the problem of the masturbating boy—a favorite topic for Comstock— and more on creating support for censorship based on a program of maternal activism. The WCTU program became a form of women-centered activism when its members targeted ads featuring sexualized images of women as degrading. WCTU members, however, agreed with Comstock's central thesis: "Without morals no public order."[88] The organization wholeheartedly concurred with Comstock on some of his basic ideas regarding the dangers of immorality. In particular, the WCTU shared his belief that "evil thoughts are an introduction to every debasing practice." This assertion put immoral literature in the forefront as the "great crime breeder," thereby ensuring the necessity of pro-censorship campaigns.[89]

As the leader of the Society for the Suppression of Vice, Comstock was, on occasion, a featured guest speaker at state, national, and world WCTU conventions, where he warned of the evils of dime novels, "sensational" literature, and the daily papers. In this capacity, he urged WCTU members to focus on their roles as mothers and guardians to control the reading of youths. When speaking at WCTU conventions, Comstock could be both condescending and self-aggrandizing. Unlike the Reverend Wilbur Crafts, Comstock was often unwilling to acknowledge that his organization needed women to work actively against the "impure." He stressed instead his desire for the mere "moral support" of WCTU women.[90] Comstock stated, for instance, that all the society wanted was that the women's "prayers may stand by us, so that through the efforts of these societies [not the WCTU itself] we may secure legislation."[91] In fact, in his capacity as post office inspector, Comstock and his Society for the Suppression of Vice relied upon a broad network of reformers, including WCTU members, to lobby for stricter censorship laws and to enforce extant laws by informing the society of any potentially obscene and therefore legally repressible materials.[92] Members of the WCTU and other organizations reported on local book dealers and newsstand owners who sold crime papers or dime novels and secured evidence against these sellers by recording the purchases of "impure" literature.[93]

Comstock's practical influence on the WCTU's agenda was generally limited to a number of subsidiary regulatory issues that were periodically mentioned in its departmental reports of state and local work. Specifically, sporadic work against lotteries and false advertising was probably encouraged by Comstock's campaigns against gambling at slot machines or through the lottery.[94] This is an instance where local concerns and individual initiative were more important instigators of action than the department's national agenda. WCTU Superintendent Ada Kepley described her own work against the lottery as personally motivated, for instance, rather than as part of a systematic WCTU pro-censorship program:

> Last winter I stopped the distribution of advertisements of the Louisiana Lottery. I accidentally came upon a copy which was in the shape of a book of stories called *Family Fiction*. Several thousands of copies had been sent to our town, and three parties were out distributing them. The inside cover was a big advertisement of the lottery. I hunted till I found the men, and forbade any further distribution but had to threaten the distributors that the matter should be brought before the State's attorney if they did not cease.[95]

Actions against "questionable" advertisements for lotteries and gambling in the papers were inspired by a desire to protect the average person against the unscrupulous who advertised false get-rich-quick schemes. When Kepley, for instance, found that "certain parties . . . are sending out advertisements of counterfeit money, to catch the unwary and relieve them of their means," she then sent the ads to Comstock "and he stop[ped] the mail matter."[96] On these issues, WCTU members supported Comstock's Society for the Suppression of Vice but did not lead the crusade.[97]

Work against "questionable" advertisements further suggests that the WCTU had a different emphasis from the Society for the Suppression of Vice, with the exception of the activities of some local unions. Comstock focused on ads that catered (however ineffectively) to the needs of those men and women engaging in sexual intercourse, discreetly offering everything from cures for venereal diseases to birth control devices and abortifacients.[98] Comstock put the majority of his society's effort into prosecuting free-love advocates, abortion providers, and those who advertised birth control devices or wrote sex education manuals.[99] Some state unions occasionally lent their support to the anti-abortion campaigns of male vice societies.[100] Like most other women's groups, the WCTU's sympathy for the "fallen woman" did not extend to her need for an abortion. Its department, however, rarely alluded to this type of advertisement.[101] It was more concerned with the fact that many advertised patent medicines consisted primarily of alcohol.[102] In 1908, for instance, the department sent out appeals to "all the leading journals" to refuse liquor and patent medicine ads and reported winning the cooperation of sixty magazines.[103] Middle-class women concerned with "impure" (more than "obscene") materials differed from the male vice societies in their approaches to resolving the problem. The WCTU promoted local, state, and federal censorship laws while producing, at the same time, alternative "pure" forms of popular culture.

When trying to build a pro-censorship consensus with other more secular groups, WCTU members downplayed their religiosity and instead based their appeals upon the assumption that all women held in common a concern for the welfare of youths. The WCTU sought a plan of work that would be successful and compatible with other women's professional and reform priorities. Department leaders considered teachers, for example, to be logical allies of mothers in the moral education of children. Teachers were potential allies because they were predominantly women who worked closely with children as educators and nurturing caretakers. Union leaders advised mothers to provide teachers with lists of "choice books" for children and to appeal to teachers to help them regulate their children's reading.[104] The WCTU also reported any instances when teachers actively sought cooperation from mothers, as when a "faithful teacher suspected from the conduct of some of his older boys that they had a bad book in their possession. . . . He then informed every mother of his suspicions. These mothers at once held a meeting and arranged to hunt for facts. Inside of three weeks ten bad books were burned by them."[105] Less anecdotally, the department was satisfied to report in 1910 that the National Education Association had established a department of school patrons that gave women's organizations, including the WCTU, a formal opportunity for regulatory involvement in the public schools. School patrons worked in their communities for pro-school legislation, entered the school libraries to examine and remove any "objectionable" literature, and advocated the teaching of the Bible as literature in public schools.[106]

WCTU members' cooperation with teachers over censorship issues was not guaranteed, however, for the relationship between the two groups was fraught with conflict in other areas. WCTU members were perceived by teachers as interfering with their professional prerogative when they tried to direct and control the curriculum. Specifically, the national WCTU had successfully passed legislation by 1903 in every state mandating the teaching of "Scientific Temperance," or anti-alcohol health lessons, in all public schools. The organization faced challenges from teachers as it tried to ensure that they all complied with the new legislation.[107] This battle suggests that the WCTU work against "impure" literature in public school libraries may not have been uniformly welcomed by teachers who worried that their professional authority was being challenged by WCTU laywomen.

The National Congress of Mothers (later the Parent-Teacher Association) offers an instructive point of comparison to the pro-censorship work of the WCTU.[108] The National Congress of Mothers, formed in 1897, was the "aggregate of the thousands of Child Study Circles throughout the country" for mothers and teachers.[109] Initially, there was some rivalry between the WCTU and the congress for, in a weak moment, the editors of the *Union Signal* complained: "The National Congress of Mothers took up the teaching and lines of work taught and wrought by the W.C.T.U. for years. The very year of its first meeting [1897] there were in the state of Illinois alone 2,000 mother's meetings held under the auspices of the W.C.T.U. . . . including fathers as well as mothers in its thought, and every phase of child life, and yet the Congress reported its lines of work as though originated then for the first time."[110] In spite of its desire to assert the WCTU's precedence in the field, most *Union Signal* articles about the National Congress of Mothers enthusiastically welcomed its efforts. The congress's convention programs, for instance, were praised for clarifying the links between mothers, children, and teachers, on the one hand, and regulation and reform, on the other. At one convention of the congress, a minister gave a speech on "The Duty of the *State* in Training Children," while a woman who was "a member of the Philadelphia Board of Education read an essay on '*Parental* Duty in Education.' " The WCTU endorsed both parental and state duties toward youths and praised the various speakers for their concern with "the education of the child, from prenatal condition to adolescence." It believed that such an emphasis almost invariably led to a pro-regulatory stance, based on the need to protect the developing child.[111]

WCTU members were directly involved in encouraging the National Congress of Mothers to create and pass resolutions against "impure" crime-story papers; they did this by holding memberships in both groups. A number of WCTU members were delegates to the annual congress conventions, where they participated as representatives of their local branches of the WCTU.[112] At the congress's second annual convention, in 1898, two WCTU leaders, Emilie Martin and Dr. Mary Wood-Allen, the world's superintendent of purity, were featured speakers on saloons and purity.[113] Martin, in her capacities as a convention speaker, a congress delegate, and the leader of the WCTU's pro-censorship department, convinced the congress to adopt a resolution against "impure" papers and "indecent" pictures and advertisements: "Resolved, That we will endeavor to exclude from our homes those papers which do not educate or inspire to noble thought and deed, and that our influence will be used to cultivate the public taste so that it will exact from the Press and artists that which educates and refines."[114] The resolution did not discuss federal censorship and instead encouraged mothers to act as censors for their own children, while trying to elevate "public taste." The two groups were also in agreement in their condemnation of divorce and remarriage.[115] The congress observed that "marriage presupposes monogamy [and chastity outside of marriage]. . . . The obedience to this law establishes a well ordered social condition—disobedience makes social anarchy."[116] *Union Signal* editors voiced similar concerns when they asked parents to stop buying magazines that treated divorce lightly and thus gave "to young readers an entirely false idea of the seriousness of the marriage relation."[117]

The Woman's Christian Temperance Union and the National Congress of Mothers both worried about the negative influence of "vicious" literature and movies. The differences between the two organizations are, however, as striking as the similarities. In particular, the congress was more ambivalent about the propriety of women's calls for state intervention in issues of morality and was often concerned with the type of impression it would create if its members demanded action from the government. Historian Molly Ladd-Taylor's study of the National Congress of Mothers argues that the "Red Scare of the early 1920s brought the long-standing political differences within the PTA to the surface," as some of its leaders were accused of being communists and were forced to resign. In response, congress leaders focused on "less controversial aims," while some insisted that "the average homemaker is not and never should become a public woman."[118]

The WCTU founded its Department for the Suppression of Impure Literature in 1883 in order to fight for stricter legislation, immediately confronting the public and the government with its condemnations of various crime papers. In contrast, in 1926, the congress's Committee on Standards in Literature was mostly content to publish "list[s] of good magazines" and books. The committee chair, Mrs. Curtis Bynum, was concerned with the need to be discrete. Explaining that "the sale of undesirable magazines and books is invariably increased by *public* black-listing and abusive criticism," Bynum argued against "arousing antagonism." Bynum was clearly worried that censorship itself might promote a discourse she wished to suppress. (Drawing on the work of Michel Foucault, theorist Judith Butler's arguments suggest that perhaps Bynum was right. Butler proposes that the paradox of censorship and regulation is that these very acts of prohibition "end up inadvertently but inevitably producing and authorizing in their own discursive actions precisely the scenes of sexual violence and aggression that they seek to censor."[119]) Significantly, Bynum derided those "men and women of the ultra-reforming type," such as women in the WCTU, who were willing to take a public stand. She argued that producers of "objectionable" literature "know their psychology" and readily used reformers' criticisms to increase sales.[120]

The real concern, however, seemed to be the congress's desire to shun an overtly political role. Ladd-Taylor argues that in the 1920s, congress "members were sharply divided over the questions of women's involvement in politics and the state's responsibility for social welfare."[121] The National Congress of Mothers' 1926 plan of work, for instance, concluded: "The local and state chairmen are advised against making arrests, bringing bills into the state legislatures, or committing any act which might involve the state president or National Board in *embarrassing* law-suits."[122] The congress's restrictions read like a list of WCTU-mandated actions against "impure" culture during any given year in the same decade. The congress's reluctance to fight its regulatory battles openly in the legislative and political arenas serves to highlight the unabashedly aggressive political tactics of the WCTU. Union members seem like daring activists when compared to this middle-class women's group that was more concerned with the possibility of social or political "embarrassment" and their image as unruly women. The need to issue such orders, however, suggests that some rank and file congress members were more zealous than the leaders of the national organization. Indeed, Ladd-Taylor concludes that "most PTA *members* seem to have welcomed the Progressive Era politicization of motherhood, but the organization's growing involvement in civic and legislative work did not go unquestioned."[123]

By the late 1920s, the congress's Committee on Motion Pictures began to take a less reticent, pro-activist stance, even as its Committee on Standards in Literature issued conservative reports reflecting its fears that political activism would harm women's social standing (based on an idealization of women's role in the domestic sphere). Although as early as 1917, "the Denver PTA presented a petition with ten thousand signatures to the Film Exchange Board and won a permanent committee to judge the suitability of films," the first years of the 1920s signaled a retreat.[124] A National Congress of Mothers' report blandly recommended that the organization "furnish lists of the best films." A resolution at the annual convention of 1923 charged that teachers' efforts to "foster a love of the classics among our boys and girls" were being harmed by the movie industry's "impure" film versions of classic novels. These films, they complained, were subject to plot changes that were made solely to increase profits. The congress did not try to demand legal regulation but asked film producers "to adhere strictly to the theme of these stories [classic novels], so sacred to us."[125]

From 1926 to 1932, the movie censorship goals and methods of the Woman's Christian Temperance Union and the National Congress of Parents and Teachers (former National Congress of Mothers) became almost indistinguishable, as a Protestant-led movie censorship movement united and reached its peak of influence. By that point, many groups, such as the Methodists, the Religious Education Association, and the General Federation of Women's Clubs, all firmly believed that films were "encouraging disrespect for the law" and dedicated themselves to ridding movies of seductive portrayals of "lawlessness."[126] The National Congress of Parents and Teachers created a committee on motion pictures that worked with the WCTU's Department on Motion Pictures as "a matter of public welfare."[127] At its 1927 convention, the congress denounced "salacious magazines and . . . the showing of cheap motion pictures" and passed a resolution in favor of "a return to the home as a center of recreational life."[128] More importantly, the congress's legislative committee participated directly in a campaign for national censorship by asking parents to support the Brookhart Senate Bill in 1928. This bill aimed to stop the system of block booking that forced exhibitors to rent ten to twelve movies at a time, without any veto power over "objectionable" films. The committee wrote, "as parents you realized as far back as 1925 that the block booking system was responsible for many unwholesome pictures. . . . This is your opportunity. Write to your Senators. Make every effort to have this bill passed."[129]

By 1930, as its misgivings about movies multiplied and producers seemed unmoved, the congress began to echo calls for national censorship that the WCTU had been making for many years. The chair of the Committee on Motion Pictures, for instance, expressed concern that exhibitors were "continually show[ing] films dealing with sex, crime, coarse ridicule of family life, defiance of law."[130] This was particularly problematic because, like the WCTU, the congress believed that "a child's idea of what real people are like, if taken from the movies, is too often not that which 'founds and keeps a nation well.'"[131] Such discussions of the harmfulness of movies led the congress to a direct involvement with political lobbying for censorship legislation. Protestant efforts at censorship converged with and culminated in a 1934 movie boycott campaign led by Catholics in the Legion of Decency, a campaign that included a wider spectrum of Christians and immigrants in a pro-regulatory coalition.[132]

* * *

Although this study focuses on demonstrating white middle-class support for censorship, there is evidence that some segments of the working classes and some African-Americans also supported fights against "immoral" culture. Labor historians Roy Rosenzweig and Kathy Peiss argue persuasively that, overall, working-class and immigrant groups did not support censorship campaigns. The younger generation, in particular, welcomed new forms of leisure activities and the creation of a "heterosocial" public space.[133] Evidence from their own work suggests, however, that the working classes did not have one monolithic position on popular culture and "immorality." Some members of the working class, especially first generation immigrants, were concerned with the impact of American commercial culture on their children's ethnic heritage, values, and religious beliefs. Kathy Peiss points out, for example, that unmarried Italian girls and women "found their social participation curtailed by conservative cultural traditions regulating women's familial roles and affirming patriarchal authority."[134] Similarly, Leslie Woodcock Tentler observes that "many parents, especially those of the immigrant generation, could not . . . tolerate the allegiance of daughters to the alien norms of urban mass culture."[135] Immigrant parents regulated their children's morality by trying to restrict their access to popular culture.

Segments of the working class that supported temperance campaigns sometimes advocated censorship and purity campaigns as well. Earlier, in the 1830s, those journeymen who supported temperance and attended church regularly moved up into positions as master craftsmen more frequently than other journeymen. With the evangelical revival of Charles Finney, upward social and economic mobility was tied to abstinence from alcohol and to church-going.[136] In his study of working-class life in Worcester, Massachusetts, Roy Rosenzweig found that some upwardly mobile "ethnic constituencies" gave "zealous censorship" their "wholehearted support." The Catholic Messenger, a leading journal for Irish Americans, for instance, "denounced moving pictures as 'the Devil's Lieutenants,'" supported police raids on movies, and even advocated that the police close down the city's movie theaters in 1910.[137] Interestingly, Rosenzweig argues that the Catholic Messenger "spoke more for the emerging middle-class and second-generation Irish American than it did for the laborer or the recent immigrant." Rosenzweig suggests that it was their desire for middle-class status that led these Irish Americans to support censorship, yet he also points out that from 1885 to 1910, James H. Mellen, a leading "champion of the Worcester worker" and editor of a journal with openly working-class sympathies, had written with "moralistic strictures" first against "showbills . . . of shameless women" and later against motion pictures.[138] This is consistent with the Knights of Labor's endorsement of WCTU resolutions against "shameless" showbills in the 1880s.[139] During the same period, Knights of Labor cigar makers were praised by the WCTU's department superintendent, Deborah Leeds, for having "adopted a resolution 'condemning the placing of pictures of nude women on cigar boxes'—these humble workmen having at least the courage and the grace to do what their employers have not, or will not."[140] Significantly, James Mellen, the champion of the workers, called for a state investigation into movies and hoped that they would become "a great educational and instructive institution." This goal is similar to that of the WCTU's pro-censorship department. Worcester's ethnic community surrounding the Swedish evangelical churches took an even stronger stand against movies by forbidding members of their congregations to attend.[141] Both Tentler and Rosenzweig note that some immigrants even resisted public education, a sentiment symptomatic of parents' desires to restrict the process of Americanization that often involved a rejection of religious or traditional ethnic values by their children. Rosenzweig quotes a "Slovak commentator [who] explained that with 'a public school education' children are lost completely to the Slovaks. Their idea of life is a breezy and snappy novel, a blood curdling *movie* and lots of money.' "[142] Collectively, these incidents suggest that some members of the working classes had their own pro-censorship agenda.

Middle-class African-American women also supported censorship and fought against "immorality." Historian Dorothy Salem suggests that black women's interest in protecting the morals of youths was in part a positive assertion of their own high moral values in response to repeated racist public attacks that charged African-American women with immorality. Black women's clubs and meetings, such as the First National Conference of Colored Women of America in 1895, therefore included calls for "religious and moral reform" in their political and social agenda.[143] Significantly, the National Association of Colored Women (NACW) saw its work, which included condemnations of lynchings and segregated streetcars, as being in harmony with that of the pro-censorship WCTU. The NACW resolved in 1904 to endorse "temperance, educational mothers' meetings, and the elimination of immoral literature."[144] Condemnations of immoral literature were part of middle-class black women's assertions of their moral purity. Salem also argues that there were important links between the National Association of

Colored Women and the "colored" and integrated branches of the Woman's Christian Temperance Union. Both organizations supported moral, educational, and temperance reform projects: "The NACW resolved to work vigorously for suffrage, to develop closer ties to the WCTU, and to create a better environment for children."[145] Unfortunately, the nature of the WCTU's "colored" branches' participation in pro-censorship work is not recorded in the department's national records, nor are the WCTU's "colored" branches' possible connections to the NACW.

The prominent organization, the National Association for the Advancement of Colored People (NAACP), accepted censorship as a viable means to address the problem of how to protest against and stop the showing of specific racist films. D. W. Griffith's "Birth of a Nation" of 1915, for example, was attacked because it celebrated the Ku Klux Klan and presented a distorted history of the Civil War and Reconstruction as a time of lawlessness among blacks. The film generated protests by African-Americans and some liberal white supporters. In her history of the NAACP, Minnie Finch explains that "the Association protested this gross distortion of facts and felt that the showing of the film would foster racial hatred and mob violence. Protest meetings and picket lines were organized in cities where the film was shown. This massive campaign did not restrict the film's distribution, but in some cities the worst of its anti-Negro scenes were cut and in several other cities the entire film was banned."[146] The NAACP became part of a pro-censorship movement through its calls for the suppression of this racist film. As late as 1954, Joanne Meyerowitz has documented that in "the African-American magazines, some readers, women and men both, objected to the photos of semiclad women."[147] Readers thought that these titillating images would only contribute to racist fantasies of black women as highly sexed. Clearly, segments of the African-American and working-class communities supported governmental censorship and direct parental control over their children's access to popular urban culture. They attempted to insist that cultural products reflect or maintain their moral and religious standards. Their support of "pure" culture and of censorship links them to the pro-censorship efforts of middle-class Americans and reinforces my contention that censorship and moral considerations received widespread public support at the turn of the century.

This brief outline of the censorship activities of other organizations demonstrates that the regulation of "impure" cultural forms was supported by many Americans. Broad-based support for censorship must also include the pro-regulatory position of the American Library Association, the members of which were aspiring professionals. This part of the middle class claimed the right to censor children's fiction based on its professional identity as "guardians of morality," not on campaigns for legal censorship. The following chapters demonstrate the determination of women to assert their moral authority in the political, professional, and public realms. They also provide the first detailed examination of the workings of a single department of the WCTU. The concerns of the WCTU's Department for the Promotion of Purity in Literature and Art changed and expanded from the 1880s through the 1930s, moving generally from literature to art and then to movies. Much was at stake for pro-censorship reformers. Literature and other art forms influenced the moral character and behavior of both native-born and immigrant youths, who together represented the future potential or downfall of the United States. WCTU members were explicit about what they desired, openly calling it "power"; their goal was ultimately to ensure that any "demand" of the "white-ribboned army" would be readily complied with.[148] Union members desired this power precisely because they saw that real power was located at the sites of cultural production. For this reason, they tried to produce, distribute, and advertise their own "pure" movies, as well as their own children's literature. The WCTU grasped that commercial popular culture was based on mass reproduction and so utilized as many popular tastes and styles as possible while highlighting its own "pure" moral message. These aspects of the organization's work show its awareness that producing culture was as important as censoring it.

CHAPTER 2

The Suppression of Impure Literature

Impressionable Children, Protective Mothers

The Woman's Christian Temperance Union's pro-censorship activity was officially initiated by President Frances Willard at the National Convention of 1883. Pointing to the availability of "impure" novels and fictional stories, Willard alerted women to the need for, and reasonableness of, regulating reading through national censorship laws. Willard conceived of the WCTU's work against "immorality" in culture as a subdivision of the Department of Social Purity. This linkage of censorship and social purity illustrates the fact that WCTU leaders and members believed strongly in the connection between words or images and subsequent action.

The pro-censorship agenda of the WCTU's new Department for the Suppression of Impure Literature was broad enough to eventually expand to include many cultural forms or media. It was first organized, however, around a concern with the power of the written word. After the Civil War, the cost of reading materials had decreased while the amount and variety increased; this proliferation was symbolized in the 1870s and 1880s by children's easy access to crime-story papers like the *National Police Gazette* at book stalls and railroad stands. WCTU activists regularly pointed to disturbing increases in the production of literature—"in one year's time from seven to eight million volumes of fiction are issued in the United States, together with uncounted millions of serials and short stories"—as a reason to support regulation.[1] Indeed, the proliferation of printing, the burgeoning of visual arts, and the growing acceptability of risqué female sexuality all reflected a growing diversity in the popular culture of the late nineteenth century.[2] To then help mothers solve the problem of increasing availability and variation in children's leisure reading, the WCTU's journal advocated the censorship of "impure" literature. Articles focusing specifically on literature appeared in the *Union Signal* from 1883 through the 1920s, although censorship of the printed word became less of a priority as the twentieth century progressed.[3] During the time that the WCTU flourished, a focus on "impure" literature alone became less tenable. Even printed magazines were fast becoming more visual; the *Police Gazette* was extensively illustrated, for instance, making a strict dichotomy between written and visual materials increasingly irrelevant. The WCTU recognized this reality and changed its emphasis accordingly. For the sake of clarity, this chapter focuses on the WCTU's actions against all forms of literature, while subsequent chapters discuss, in rough chronological order, the department's metamorphosis into the Department of Purity in Literature and Art by 1889, and then into the Department of Motion Pictures in 1925.

The Woman's Christian Temperance Union's pro-censorship stance was complicated by its notions of how people respond to what they read. Occasionally, WCTU activists echoed a part of what today's theorists of the Birmingham school, such as John Fiske, believe. Fiske views popular culture as a realm of contestation. While the WCTU argued that a "moral," activist-oriented middle class should have the right to determine the proper meaning of any given text, it believed, more importantly, that WCTU members could influence popular culture by offering the public "pure" literature of their own creation, such as the WCTU's *Young Crusader* magazine for children. A departmental spokeswoman argued that "we will control public opinion in about the same measure that we *control the production* of the people's chosen literature."[4] The notion that producers of culture determine the meaning of texts increased the need for censorship at the preproduction level: "He who would influence public opinion must control the production of the songs or ballards [*sic*] or whatever form of literature appeals to the emotional side. . . . [People] give the novel the same transient [i.e., careless] attention . . . and are alike at the mercy of the man who entertains them."[5] WCTU women believed that they could resist and critique "impure" meanings in texts, offer the public alternative "pure" texts, and thereby adapt any cultural form to their own uses.

Theorists of the Birmingham school further argue that the concept of contestation implies that meanings are not fixed but are determined by the individual reader.[6] With this assertion WCTU members could not have unconditionally agreed, for they also believed that texts had fixed meanings that could directly influence behavior. Some people (especially youths) might imitate the actions of "immoral" characters in a book or on screen. In this scenario, they feared that meaning could not be reinterpreted or contained and that censorship was therefore the only answer. Basing its activities on this fear, the WCTU's Department for the Suppression of Impure Literature embraced censorship, concluding that "fiction is too powerful a weapon to be left in careless hands."[7]

The WCTU's public fight for literary censorship emphasized the need for its members to work as mothers or nurturing women for the morals of all youths, including immigrant and working-class children. Mary Allen West, Round the World Missionary for the World's WCTU and editor of the *Union Signal*, published a book for mothers entitled *Childhood, Its Care and Culture* (1892). West's chapter on "Conversation and Reading" explained that the WCTU's pro-censorship department focused on regulating "immoral" or borderline, rather than "obscene," literature precisely because of its greater accessibility to children. West succinctly categorized "impure" versus "obscene" literature: "Bad literature comes under three heads: obscene, stories of crime and criminals, and trashy. . . . Obscene literature, which can be reached by the law, is really not so dangerous as the other two classes, for they abound everywhere."[8] According to West, boys would read crime papers and trashy fiction, emulate the actions of the characters, and actually run away, rob stores, use guns, and exhibit disrespect toward women. To bolster these contentions, the department's leaders cited expert witnesses, such as judges from the newly created juvenile courts. These experts testified that all boys and girls who came before the bench had been influenced into a life of crime by reading seemingly harmless (but really "demoralizing") crime papers and dime novels, not by reading literature that was legally "obscene." Claiming to be allied with Progressive Era "experts" such as juvenile court judges, laywomen reformers popularized and disseminated professional ideas about child psychology and pedagogy—but for the perhaps unanticipated purpose of encouraging pro-censorship activism.[9]

More than the "obscene," *Union Signal* editor Mary West objected to "trashy reading" because "it engenders a dreamy sentimentalism which makes real work distasteful, thus leading to discontent with one's surroundings."[10] West's comment regarding "dreamy sentimentalism" reflects the long-standing nineteenth-century attack on sentimental fiction, especially that written by women writers, and suggests that she was thinking in part of middle-class female novel readers.[11] Yet her comment regarding "real work" implies that her focus was wage-earning young men and women. On the one hand, hers was a realistic view of what upward mobility and assimilation entailed; instead of "dreamy sentimentalism," the meaning of life and of morality was in living, in coming to grips with the real world. On the other hand, her statement revealed the WCTU's interest in maintaining the social order, implying that the working classes should be satisfied with their labor, rather than dreaming of leisure or upward mobility. The WCTU's concern with public order and the responsibilities of citizens was sometimes tied to a defense of the status quo, against those seeking too much social mobility. The WCTU implied that "low" readings were most popular in the slums, fed by working-class audience demands for the exotic and "sensational." Accordingly, a prize-winning child's essay, reprinted in the *Union Signal* in 1900, closed with the author's approval of Frances Hodgson Burnett's story *Little Lord Fauntleroy*, because the character's life showed "that it is brave to be content and happy in the sphere in which one is placed by an All Wise Providence."[12] Historian Anne MacLeod notes that in comparison to Horatio Alger's *Ragged Dick*, "Burnett's story is also very much concerned with class but not at all with class mobility. . . . Just as Alger's promise of democratic opportunity encouraged the ambitious have-nots of American society, so Burnett's suggestion of inborn superiority warmed those who had arrived."[13] The WCTU judges had a similar interpretation of Burnett's story.

Fearing that otherwise sheltered middle-class boys might use "sensational" stories as textbooks on how to commit crimes, or as tour books for the unknown, poorer areas of the city, WCTU authors warned in 1886 that "the whole vile life of the slums of great cities reeks and steams in the pages of these books; vile women, vile men, the knife, the pistol, and the whole paraphernalia of vice is opened to the impressionable gaze of youth."[14] By stating that juvenile delinquents often came from "good families" and were "American boys . . . and not of foreign birth as is generally supposed," the WCTU emphasized the dangerous "polluting" influence of popular culture to the middle classes.[15] Nevertheless, fear of immigrant ghettos motivated much of the WCTU's early work against "sensational" literature. Middle-class parents in urban as well as rural areas hoped to contain the negative influence of America's cities (populated by immigrants and their foreign cultures) by regulating children's access to reading materials.

In the context of later national controversies over immigration admission policies, the WCTU was more interested in assimilation than exclusion.[16] The department hoped to direct and control the literature available to immigrant children and to modify their behavior by introducing them to uplifting literature. National WCTU Director of Child Welfare Elizabeth A. Perkins's 1921 article, "Children and Books," expressed an interest in influencing children: "Obviously the education to fit the coming citizens of the republic for the proper performance of their duties as citizens must begin with the child in the home."[17] Thinking at least in part of a program of Americanization, Perkins underlined the responsibility of parents, librarians, and teachers to direct all children's reading. Concerned with regulating the production and

distribution of "impure" culture, the department tried to convince members of the middle classes and the elites—including purveyors of literature—to censor their own products. The department also held "Mothers' Meetings" to encourage mothers and teachers to reinforce any extant legal sanctions on "immorality" by personally selecting the reading materials that entered homes and schools.[18]

* * *

Frances Willard consistently presented her own and her organization's resistance to "impure" literature as a feminist affirmation of self. An 1884 essay began with a childhood memory: "Much as I disliked the restriction then, I am now sincerely grateful that my Puritan father not only commanded me not to read novels, but successfully prohibited the temptation from coming in his children's way." Willard then recounted her subsequent horror upon first reading novels like *Jane Eyre* at age fifteen:

> But the glamour of those highly seasoned pages was unhealthful and made "human nature's daily food," the common pastoral life we led, and nature's soothing beauty seem so tame and tasteless that the revulsion was my life's first sorrow. How evanescent and unreal was the pleasure of such reading; a sort of spiritual hasheesh eating with hard and painful waking. . . . In all the years since then I have believed that novel writing, save for some high, heroic moral aim, while the most diversified, is the most unproductive of all industries![19]

Here, Willard characterized novel reading as destructive and addictive like a drug precisely because it created an unproductive dissatisfaction with ordinary experience without offering activist or progressive alternatives to life's problems.

Deriding the popular novel as a fictional panacea used to ward off real power by women in "the great world," Willard asked youths and women to refrain from most novel reading:

> I would have each generous youth and maiden say to every story-spinner, except the few great names that can be counted on the fingers of one hand: "I really can not patronize your wares, and will not furnish you my head for a football, or my fancy for a sieve. By writing these books you get money and a fleeting, unsubstantial fame, but by reading them I should turn my possibility of success in life to the certainty of failure. *Myself plus time* is the capital stock with which the good Heavenly Father has pitted me against the world to see if I can gain some foothold."[20]

Willard stressed the necessity for women's activism and employed a capitalist metaphor more common to time-management proponents and industrialists who believed that a careful use of time and self-control could bring success to striving young entrepreneurs. Willard also implored her readers to declare: "I am a wrestler for the laurel in life's Olympian games. I can make history, why should I maunder [*sic*] in a hammock and read the endless repetitions of romance?"[21] Willard used sports analogies and equated competition with success. She appropriated a conventionally "masculine" language in order to forecast a female victory. Willard's opposition to romance and fantasy was an outgrowth of two philosophical views: a repudiation of a well-entrenched image of feminine passivity and an assertion of an experimental activist ethic, much like the one found in Jane Addams's progressivism. By positioning women as makers of history rather than passive recipients of "unhealthful" novels, Willard presented censorship as an act of political and personal empowerment. Willard wanted women to be the principal actors and writers, not simply the audience.

Department leaders also stressed that girls who read romantic novels were wasting "precious time" that could be spent on education or on activism in favor of rights for their sex. Not coincidentally, many of those novels condemned as "impure" in the pages of the *Union Signal* were those that appealed to an audience of adolescents and young adults.[22] One 1890 article by a "Friend of Girls" asked, "think you that Frances Willard would stand where she does today had she frittered away her precious years of youth and study" reading novels? Explaining that "this is an age of progress and advancement for our sex," the writer declared:

> We have it in our power to make our lives good, useful, noble ones, or the very reverse. One of the principal arguments adduced against extending the suffrage to woman, is her ignorance of the laws and constitution of her country. . . . You girls can begin reading now the class of literature which will teach you all about such things, and by and by, when you are grown to woman's estate, you will be able to cast your vote rightly, intelligently, and understandingly.[23]

On the one hand, the author's logic faulted girls, who had little incentive to read anything else, for reading those materials that unfitted them for political participation that they did not have and did not necessarily expect. On the other hand, the author's logic uplifted girls by encouraging them to read materials on the laws and political system of the United States so that they might strive for women's political advancement and the right to vote.

Other WCTU authors condemned popular novels for more conventional reasons. Romantic love stories that included the subject of adultery were objected to because they ostensibly gave young women unrealistic views of courtship and marriage: "Immorality is presented as the mere outburst of passionate love, whose worse results may later be lived down."[24] Such views, they argued, could lead women to lose their "virtue" before marriage or to want a divorce if unhappily married. As "immature people," adolescent girls would see only the attractive false "glamour" of the fashionable novel, be unhappy with their own more mundane lives, and even "unconsciously strive to imitate" the "immoral" lives of the characters they read about.[25]

The WCTU's concern for the morality of youths was complemented and modified by a desire to protect the respected role and status of women. The department warned women, as mothers and moral educators, that " 'the hand that rocks the cradle,' will not 'rule the world,' to any good purpose if its mate, meanwhile, turns the pages of the last fashionable novel."[26] WCTU activists insisted that regulating the content of women's fiction reading was as important as monitoring their children's reading.[27] They therefore tied the advocacy of censorship and the regulation of reading to increasing women's political power and social responsibility.

* * *

The Department for the Suppression of Impure Literature outlined its first "plan of work" in 1883. It took as its initial task the securing of state legislation against the daily illustrated "blood and thunder" papers that detailed stories of crimes, such as the *National Police Gazette* and the *Illustrated Police News*. The *Police Gazette* was first published in 1845 but was not successful until it was purchased and revamped by Richard K. Fox in 1876. The *Gazette* had been flourishing for almost a decade when the WCTU decided to try to ban it; a perusal of its pages makes this decision easily comprehensible in light of its reform goals.[28] Gene Smith, a scholar of the *Police Gazette*, claims that the paper "almost alone, made boxing big business" and that its publisher, Richard Fox, "campaigned to make boxing not only popular but legal."[29] The WCTU had very different ideas about boxing and saw the sport as a contributor to greater levels of societal violence. It consistently supported laws forbidding prizefights and, later, films of those events.[30] The *Police Gazette* also published numerous stories about violent crimes that recounted all the details and then lingered over the punishments of the "criminals." Notably, the *Police Gazette* seemed to take its greatest pleasure in describing brutal punishments meted out by white vigilantes to black men. The October 1878 issue, for example, featured a full-page woodcut illustration of the murders of six African-American men in Indiana for an alleged "brutal assault on the [white] women." The illustration depicts six scenes, beginning with a black man grasping a white woman, followed by acts of white "revenge," including the shooting of one man, the lynching of four others, and the mortal stabbing of a sixth. These acts are vividly portrayed and celebrated in the *Gazette*. Although the WCTU was chided by some black women reformers for not having a sufficiently vocal anti-lynching position, it did have "colored" members and could not condone a paper that encouraged brutal, racially motivated attacks.[31]

Even more important was the fact that every image of white women in the *Police Gazette* earned the wrath of WCTU members. One issue, for instance, mocked women who tried to vote in municipal elections, an action that was supported by most WCTU members. Another reported sensationalistically on the presence of white women in Chinese opium dens in New York City. The accompanying illustration shows young girls sprawled about in compromising poses. In the center, a Chinese man with a long braid has his arms around a white girl who is too drugged to notice or protest. Sexual predation and the use of opium imply that these girls are "white slaves" who have been (or will be) forced into prostitution (see figure 1).[32] This was the type of reporting that WCTU activists resented as demeaning to the "purity" of women. Most issues also included a page or two of illustrations of the "plump and pleasing" burlesque performers whose legs were covered only by tights (see figure 2). The cover of an 1895 issue pictured a woman in tights and proclaimed "Chorus Girls are Anxious to Display their Figures."[33] In 1894, the WCTU's department had organized a fight against *tableaux vivants*, or living pictures, precisely because performers' similarly suggestive attire mocked and challenged women's innate purity. Other articles told of a "vivacious widow" who had "too many male callers" or of "Girls Who Can Fight."[34] WCTU members insisted on the purity of women and rejected these sexualized and titillating images of their sex.

The *Police Gazette* regularly ran a column entitled "Religious Notes," moreover, that called attention to crimes and foibles of clergy members and their female-dominated church congregations. One issue told of a reverend in Illinois—a "sanctimonious villain"—who was allegedly arrested for trying to rape a young woman who sang in the church choir.[35] This was an attempt to discredit those ministers and members of their congregations who often spoke out against the *Gazette*. An 1888 article highlighted "The Sad Effects of the Work of the Salvation Army" by claiming that "Flora M. Ellis, a middle-aged woman of Boston," had become "crazed by religion" and had subsequently taken to wandering the streets, shouting and praying.[36] Parodies of religious women and their pastors were probably appreciated by *Gazette* readers as part of an irreverent anti-censorship gesture on the part of the crime-paper's editors. Its images of women and of religion were unacceptable to WCTU members, who believed that the portrayals were patently false and unfairly maligned woman's nature and the sanctity of religion. The *Police Gazette* was, overall, a natural first target of the WCTU's Department for the Suppression of Impure Literature. The department argued that detailed reports of crime would turn young readers into juvenile

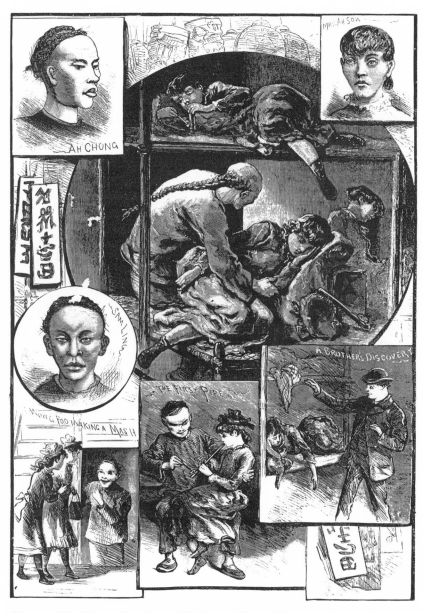

Figure 1. "The Mongolian Curse. Blighting effects of the introduction of a debasing celestial habit among the young girls of New York—scenes in and around the Chinese opium joints in Mott Street." (*Police Gazette*, Apr. 28, 1883)

Figure 2. Pictured counterclockwise: Estelle Clayton ("a much discussed and quite expensive professional beauty who occasionally tries her hand at acting"); Josie Sadler Gregory ("a charming burlesque and farce-comedy artist of some reputation and with many friends and admirers"); Delia Stacey ("a plump and pleasing warbler and dancer in the 'Straight Tip' Company, now at the New Park Theatre, New York"). (*Police Gazette*, May 16 and 23, 1891)

delinquents; that sports, especially boxing and prizefighting, led to brutality and racial hostilities; and that the sexual objectification of women lessened
their power as models of purity for men and children, both at home and in
the public sphere. Department leaders justified censorship by explaining that
"these publications are wholly unfit to be placed within the reach of boys,
young men or indeed men of any age. They are demoralizing and degrading to any reader of any age or sex."[37]

The 1880s and early 1890s were the height of the pro-censorship department's activities against these "impure" crime-story papers. To coincide with
this campaign and to encourage its members to take part, *Union Signal* articles highlighted the ways that crime-story papers negatively influenced
youths. The department's first national superintendent, Lucy Holmes, of
New Hampshire, wrote her initial annual report in 1884. Illinois and New
Hampshire were two states to experience early WCTU-organized censorship
campaigns. Holmes described Ada Kepley's Illinois work for the new department. Kepley began "by first soliciting and then causing the publication of
the Attorney General's decision, viz: that the law in regard to obscene publications applies to newspapers." Holmes explained that "in consequence of
these efforts, seconded by the Society for the Suppression of Vice, and sus-
tained by some of the leading Western newspapers, these vile periodicals
have quite generally disappeared from the stands of newsdealers in Illinois."
She then reported that "through Mr. Anthony Comstock, I learn that there
are laws covering the sale or exhibition of illustrated criminal papers, such
as the *Police News, Police Gazette,* and New York *Illustrated Times* in the States
of Ohio, Illinois, Georgia, Missouri and Virginia, while nearly all have laws
against what are known as obscene publications." Having tried to establish
the status of censorship laws both nationally and at the state level, Holmes
recommended that the "State Superintendents make efforts to secure laws
similar to those passed in Illinois and a few other States, making it a crime
to sell or exhibit obscene publications, including the newspapers above
mentioned."[38]

By 1885, New Hampshire's state union was praised at the WCTU's national convention for having circulated a petition "against the sale of pernicious literature." The corresponding secretary reported that the "petition received the courteous favor of the committee to whom it was referred, also
the favorable vote of the legislature and the bill has become a law."[39] National
Superintendent Holmes described her home state's work in the following
manner: "Mrs. Fellows, of Centre Sandwich, has accomplished a great work
during the past two years; first arousing public sentiment by sending out
special circulars addressed to pastors, teachers, and editors, and then presenting to the Legislature a petition to which 1,300 signatures were attached,

asking for the passage of the bill which in the following June became a law."
The department's state superintendent did the majority of the work in New
Hampshire, while Holmes coordinated nationwide pro-censorship efforts.
Strong individual leadership clearly made the difference in statewide campaigns. After influencing public opinion and getting the law passed, state
Superintendent Fellows still had much work to do, for as Holmes explained:
"During the past year she has faithfully guarded its enforcement—has sent
printed copies to be placed in each post-office, and asked that any violation
of this statute be promptly reported to her. The result has been a wholesome
fear of righteous law, and a perceptible lessening of the circulation of pernicious literature."[40]

These legal victories did not go unnoticed by other state unions. In fact,
they encouraged other state superintendents to mobilize their members to
win similar legislative successes. Holmes reported in 1886, for instance, that
Mrs. Bittenbender of Lincoln, Nebraska, "is now preparing a bill relative to
the Suppression of Impure Literature, to present to the State Legislature at
its next session."[41] The WCTU helped restrict criminal-story papers in several other states within two years of its initial campaigns.[42]

The department's early pro-censorship efforts were noticed and praised
by the New York Society for the Suppression of Vice in its 1887–88 annual
report: "They are doing much good, by their own sweet and pure publications, and by their heroic assaults against the criminal and indecent illustrated papers, cigarette pictures, etc." Here, the society identified the WCTU's
"pure publications" as a complement to its pro-censorship work. The report
went on to explain that WCTU members "have secured State laws in States
where no law existed. In some instances they have secured the passage of
City and Town ordinances suppressing these evils, and then they have seen
to it that these ordinances were enforced." The society enthusiastically concluded that "under the leadership of one of the noblest women of this or any
other land, Miss Frances E. Willard, their President, these noble Christian
women are a power of good, and a terror to many a miscreant who seeks to
fatten upon the weakness or vices of mankind." On her personal copy of the
society's report, Frances Willard wrote "Amen and Amen" in the margin near
the laudatory sentence.[43]

Compliance with state censorship laws was incomplete, however, so local
WCTU involvement in law enforcement was necessary to maintain effective
censorship. In Illinois, the department reported that "clubs of *Police Gazettes*
have been discovered by the vigilant women and efforts made to break them
up."[44] In Iowa, after a law was passed against the crime-story papers, the
local union at Muscatine established a committee that "visited ten shops,
were very kindly received, found the *Police News* in two or three, spoke to

them of the new laws against their being sold, or given to individuals to read."[45] Iowa WCTU members created a system of enforcement based on monitoring the local shops to see that the law was being complied with and that no issues were being sold.

State-by-state efforts did not wholly satisfy either the department's national or state superintendents, who stressed the need for federal legislation and supported adding "impure" papers to the extant federal obscenity (Comstock) laws. Even in Illinois, where state and local ordinances against the *Police Gazette* existed, state Superintendent Ada Kepley argued in 1887 that the problem needed a national solution: "The *Police Gazette*, [is] one of the most obnoxious of bad publications. . . . We are powerless to fully check it until we have a [federal] law against it. Therefore I ask you to circulate a petition I shall send you later, addressed to your Congressman, asking him to work individually and in conjunction with others to get a law passed to stop the passage of the *Police Gazette* and similar publications through our United States mails."[46] WCTU members reasoned that the extent of the problem and the easy accessibility of reading materials demanded measures beyond maternal direction of children's reading—dramatic measures such as federal censorship.

The WCTU's Department for the Suppression of Impure Literature underwent some growing pains between 1887 and 1891. It gained and lost three new national superintendents, and even its name changed. Naomi Tomlinson of Indiana was national superintendent for only one year, 1887, before Deborah C. Leeds of Philadelphia, Pennsylvania, took over from 1888 to 1889. Both women, during their tenures as national superintendent, focused on local enforcement of bans on the sale of "the unsavory *Police Gazette*, and *Police News*."[47]

When Mrs. Samuel Clements of Philadelphia, Pennsylvania, became national superintendent in 1889, she moved immediately to make some symbolic changes. Most important, she "at first asked permission at National Headquarters to change the name of the Department, that it might suggest what we seek rather than what we would avoid." Clements explained that she wanted "a positive, rather than a negative; and, having received the sanction sought, the name became the Department of Purity in Literature and Art." In spite of the lack of clear national leadership from 1887 through 1889, Clements found that work had taken place in several state unions, with New Hampshire, Indiana, Iowa, and Pennsylvania taking the lead. Three out of these four states were the home states of the department's national superintendents, suggesting that their leadership was critical for the success of regulatory efforts. In addition, Clements reported that "from the State Superintendent of Maine, I have cheering words. She writes: 'We have doubled our number of [local] superintendents; stopped the sale of the *Police Gazette* and like papers; . . . posted State laws, in regard to impure literature, in conspicuous places; held mothers' meetings for the discussion of this subject.' "[48]

The national department finally regained and built upon the work it had begun to achieve under Lucy Holmes when Emilie D. Martin was appointed the world's and national superintendent in 1890. Martin brought great commitment and stability to the department, for she remained in the position for twenty-one years, until her death in 1911. Within a year of taking over, Martin could claim "this department is now thoroughly organized." Martin strategized about how to increase the effectiveness of her department's work against "impurities." Her first major campaign shifted the focus from literature to the nudity in art that she expected to see on exhibition at the Chicago World's Fair of 1893. Yet Martin did not abandon the department's work against literature. She discovered that by "an act of Congress in 1873, a Seizure Clause was enacted, applying to the Territories, the District of Columbia and over all provinces over which Congress has exclusive jurisdiction. Therefore our W.C.T.U. women in these sections have power to seize anything improper in character through the civil authorities." Martin explained that she, as the "National Superintendent has worked [in New York] for the enforcement of the model [censorship] law with Seizure Clause." Other unions, including Pennsylvania, adopted the same strategy: "State law defective. The women will work for Model Law and Seizure Clause at the next legislature."[49]

Whereas the regulatory focus of the 1880s campaigns against "impure" literature had been on crime-story papers, the 1890s marked the beginning of the WCTU's campaign against "sensationalism" in the daily newspapers.[50] The *Police Gazette* went into decline by 1900, probably not because of WCTU activism since regulation was inconsistent, but mainly because of competition from Hearst dailies.[51] The WCTU's shift of focus can be attributed to the influence of the new national superintendent, Emilie Martin, who was more interested in the impact of the mainstream press. Legitimate daily newspapers were accessible to children in almost every home, she argued, and so more immediately frightening to most parents than crime-story papers. Condemning daily newspapers for favoring brutal crime stories over other national and international news reports, WCTU members charged that even factual newspaper reports made crime seem so exciting that young boys, and possibly girls, could be seduced into a life of crime: "The idea, though at first horrifying, takes such a strong hold of the mind that it finally leads to the committal of a similar act."[52] This explanation—that once mentioned, a repellent thing or action must eventually become desirable—was repeated frequently over the years by WCTU activists to describe how even those children (or adults) with the strongest characters could succumb to immorality without the helpful intervention of careful censorship. WCTU activists firmly believed in the power of words and images to suggest a new course of behavior to the innocent viewer. The department further charged that newspapers focused too much attention on divorce and adultery cases, thereby undermining the moral structure of society for the following generation. Martin recommended that mothers clip out all the stories of crimes and immorality before letting children read the daily newspapers.[53]

Since the strategy of clipping out worrisome articles on a daily basis was tiresome and less than foolproof, the WCTU attempted to gain the consent and cooperation of the newspaper editors and publishers themselves. The department, with Emilie Martin leading the way, threatened to organize the public to take the role of censor into its own hands. To avoid this, newspaper editors were advised to recognize their role as powerful cultural influences, report on more philanthropic deeds, and voluntarily improve the moral tenor of their stories by excluding details of crimes. The department argued that because weekly and daily papers had the largest readership of any form of literature, newspaper editors should understand, accept, and be held responsible for the "purity" of their reporting.

Superintendent Martin may have utilized her influence as vice president of the Women's Press Association of New York when she extracted pledges from the media's professional organizations such as the National Editorial Association, which promised to report criminal stories with greater discretion. The wording of the association's 1894 resolution is interesting because it singled out women's organizations and their impact on public opinion as the motivating force behind its pledge to uphold "good" morals: "Resolved, That the National Editorial Association is heartily in accord with every effort in the direction of elevating the moral standard of the press. We appreciate the interest that is being taken by the various woman's organizations in educating public sentiment in this direction, and will lend our united aid and influence in furthering the object."[54] The fact that the WCTU was able to secure even the nominal cooperation of editors is one indication that middle-class businessmen legitimated WCTU activities by their seeming acquiescence to the women's concerns. In 1895, local WCTU workers in New York City and Brooklyn alone collected 60,000 signatures favoring a "pure press."[55]

Before her death in 1898, WCTU President Frances Willard made a final push for "purity," lobbying for the wide circulation of her "Plea of the Women to the Press." This petition was to be signed by important and respected women leaders and then sent to the newspaper publishers, confronting them with the charge that "inaccuracy of statement, sensationalism and undue space given to recitals of crime and descriptions of brutal exhibitions make the newspaper a conglomerate of influence that we grieve to have come into the homes where our children and youth are being bred for beneficent lives." In light of their de facto role as moral educators of the nation, Willard asserted that members of the press should instead "tell the story of today so as to make the world more brotherly tomorrow."[56] Superintendent Martin and the state superintendents widely circulated this petition after Willard's death.

* * *

Into the twentieth century, the WCTU's regulatory agenda for literature focused on censorship of crime-story papers, daily newspapers, "yellow" or "sensational" novels featuring crimes or romance, and some "modernist" literature, as well as on particular books that challenged its temperance goals or its morality. Frustrated over what it perceived to be the slow progress of some mothers in directing their children's reading, a 1905 *Union Signal* editorial entitled "Help the Children to Read" remonstrated with those women who were not increasing their power and influence as reformers, mothers, or professionals: "The boy only needed skillful baiting [to get him to read good books] . . . mothers who spend their lives in the kitchen and keep their brains in the bread-box need not expect to have children who 'will read.' "[57] According to the WCTU, a good mother was an activist who was involved in social housekeeping on a local and national level. Members' speeches at conventions aimed to convince mothers of the need for maintaining strict vigilance over their children's reading.

Mother's Meetings from the 1880s through the early decades of the 1900s periodically featured sessions on "Purity in Literature and Art." An anecdote dramatizing the negative consequences of a mother's complacency usually opened these meetings: "A mother's boy . . . seemed changed for the worse, used slang, threatened to leave home, etc. . . . After some urging she decided to open his private boxes. The contents were half a hundred stories of the worst class, three pistols, a sand bag, and a masquerade suit. This is perhaps an extreme case, but three-fourths of all the girls and boys who are criminal, in one state, say they read nothing but papers of this class."[58] The meetings also featured lectures devoted to regulating children's reading, followed by discussion sessions on topics such as "How shall we guard our school and homes from impure literature?"[59] Department leaders advised mothers to create reading groups for youths so that they could share book expenses and cultivate a taste for "better" reading. Exciting episodes from Roman history, for example, were read aloud at Anti-Dime Novel Society meetings for younger boys.[60] In other book clubs, boys and girls shared and circulated "books of travel, popular scientific works, and short biographies," and "some good stories," all selected with the aid of an adult.[61]

During 1905 to 1906, Mrs. Jean McArthur Hyde, a national lecturer for the department, took up Willard's earlier challenge to evaluate the effects of reading popular novels. In a series of articles for the *Union Signal* with titles such as "Immoral Tendency in Modern Fiction," "A Book Conscience," and "Books as Moral Educators," Hyde argued that novels for both adolescents and adults needed more rigorous regulation and suppression.[62] Hyde's campaign provides insight into the WCTU's critique of "popular novels," "fashionable novels," and even some historical fiction. The now little-known book by James Lane Allen, *The Mettle of the Pasture*, and an unspecified Henry James novel, for instance, were both cited as examples of the "perversion of God's moral laws" because their upper-middle-class characters openly and unrepentingly lie and drink. The WCTU objected to other popular novels wherein "insults" were "heaped" on the Christian faith. Hyde encouraged Americans to have a "book conscience" and challenged WCTU members to fight against the increasing secularization of society by asking, "can a 'Christian' union afford to ignore an influence which acts steadily to overthrow religious beliefs from the minds of the people?"[63]

Documenting as many offensive passages and ideas as possible, Hyde encouraged her readers to protest the popularity and easy acceptance of such literature but took care not to print the worst books' titles or the names of their authors. In an extensive discussion of a "blasphemous" novel, whose subject was a man's "emancipation" from religion, the novel itself remained unnamed. This precaution was aimed at discouraging youths and other weak readers of the *Union Signal* from trying to acquire "impure" books precisely because of their forbidden and therefore potentially titillating quality.[64] Perhaps, too, Hyde's unwillingness to name the offending books symbolizes the degree to which censorship was not really about condemning specific texts, but about values—an assertion of what *ought* to be written, as well as an attack on what *was* written.

Hyde argued that historical novels, especially those depicting battles and bloodshed, tended to encourage war and other violent irrational acts, including the assassination of President McKinley! Favoring international cooperation in the 1890s, the WCTU opposed teaching about wars and war "heroes" such as Napoleon in school textbooks. Likewise, *Union Signal* editors disapproved of literary accounts of war that romanticized it and gave youths "the thirst for blood."[65] Although historical novels were studiously discussed by other women's reading clubs and social groups that were interested in self-education, the WCTU rejected literary accounts of wars.

As critiqued by Hyde, the popular novel cultivated the use of alcohol and cigarettes, produced "a race of criminals," encouraged divorce, caused "truth to be undervalued," robbed "the people of higher ideals," and last, but not least, was *"breaking down barriers,* destroying respect for creeds and ceremonials, and endangering the home and our national institutions."[66] Hyde's xenophobic invocation of sacred "national institutions" points to another type of fiction that was considered threatening—the "realistic" foreign novel. In an article entitled "The Domination of the 'French Novel,' and the Struggle against it," Philadelphia activist Reverend Josiah Leeds rejected the realistic novel as "the embodiment of nastiness" and urged that all such fiction be excluded from public libraries.[67] "Tainted" French literature was rarely acceptable to the WCTU, nor were the writings of European aristocrats who legitimized the double standard of sexual behavior: "A demoralizing book by Princess Charlotte of Saxe-Meiningen . . . follows the old line of argument in favor of legalizing sin—because men will be bad."[68] According to the WCTU, Princess Charlotte represented the literally "demoralizing" ideas of the woman's movement on the European continent that favored the regulation of prostitution. The WCTU's preferred position, common to most English and American women's rights activists, stressed purity and repression over legalization.[69]

Union Signal editorials pointed hopefully to religious and reform influences in some contemporary literature as signs that American novelists would be able to create "Truth, intangible, ideal."[70] Some *Union Signal* articles argued that the "saturation" of novels with representations of alcohol as a form of jovial socializing constituted an "indirect plea for alcoholic beverages."[71] Still others praised authors such as Leo Tolstoy, Thomas Hardy, and Emile Zola who wrote with "antagonism to drink" in their stories of miserable and ruined alcoholics. Zola's *L'Assommoir* or *Drink,* for instance, was praised for "the most awful descriptions of delirium tremens."[72] Clearly, WCTU readings produced different results depending on the issue at hand. When temperance was in the foreground, a positive evaluation of literary realism or naturalism was forthcoming, while in other contexts, such as critiques of Hardy's tale of seduction and betrayal, *Tess of the d'Urbervilles,* or Zola's *Nana,* the author's realism was likely to be condemned. The department, therefore, was pleased to report that "libraries have acceded to our requests to take out certain realistic works."[73] "Realism" was the WCTU's preferred mode, but not its central concern; members often assumed that texts had fixed meanings, so a realistic literary account could be good if it inspired "pure" behavior, and bad if it portrayed positively what "civilization" ought to transcend.

Hoping to establish an authentic, "pure" American literature, the WCTU developed a complicated cultural hierarchy in which "high" culture was as suspect as "low." These attempts suggest that a "middlebrow" culture emerged prior to the 1920s.[74] Reflecting a nativist nostalgia for the rugged American "woods and prairie," an article entitled "Tainted Literature" asked that reformers "sweep from our libraries" books that are not " 'genuine American' " and exclaimed, "we are surfeited with bankrupt earls and marquises."[75] European aristocratic writers did not abound, of course, yet they aptly symbolized the anti-democratic "high" culture emanating from Europe to the United States. The novel *Good Americans,* for instance, was praised by a *Union Signal* book reviewer for setting "forth the Anglo-American traits of character."[76] WCTU censorship efforts can be linked to a middle-class rejection of European "high" culture and to the creation of a native middlebrow culture in the twentieth century.

WCTU President Lillian Stevens's 1907 Address to the national convention supported Hyde's recent series of articles and lectures and developed an argument against six features of modern fiction. Asking local members to be methodical censors by reviewing books in public libraries and creating lists or reviews of "good" books, she outlined more systematically the kinds of "immorality" in fiction that the WCTU must fight:

> Condemning First, Books in which temperance and religious work are ridiculed and made light of. . . . Second, Books in which the hero, [or] heroine . . . is pictured as an habitual user of liquors and cigarettes without condemnation of such habits. Third, Books in which modern American life, in social, business, or domestic circles is represented as normally intemperate, impure, or immoral. Fourth, Books in which . . . a distinction is made between the two sexes as to the obligation of virtuous and moral actions. Fifth, Books in which clever evasion of the law is made to appear heroic. . . . Sixth, Books in which alcohol is treated as a benefit to mankind, and is administered to the saving of persons in physical distress or danger.[77]

President Sevens worried that cultural norms valuing religion, purity, and generally temperate behavior were disappearing from most early twentieth-century modern novels. Half of her categories dealt solely with alcohol or cigarettes; the others identified literary representations of a changed, "modern American life," as potentially marginalizing and threatening to the belief system of the middle classes.[78] Significantly, the Victorian double-standard of sexual morality was wholeheartedly rejected in favor of a single, stricter moral standard for both sexes—not the development of freer sexual expression for both women and men that eventually took precedence in American culture. The department's national superintendent, Emilie Martin, publicized Stevens's speech and pushed for more uniformity among the local unions. She urged they employ Stevens's six categories as the basis for book evaluation when acting as censors.

* * *

In spite of the fact that the WCTU clearly rejected many books as "immoral," and although Frances Willard declared that she could count all good novel writers on one hand, the department was more open-minded than this information might suggest.[79] In fact, the WCTU sanctioned a large amount of fiction for both adults and children. Mother's Meetings trained mothers themselves to read "good" books and magazines. A recommended WCTU reading list from 1900 for mothers included historical fiction, biographies, natural science, and poetry, as well as a generous selection of American and British novels by writers such as Louisa May Alcott, Charles Dickens, Nathaniel Hawthorne, and Sir Walter Scott.[80] Some articles on books for young boys and girls were gender specific, such as "Keeping the Boys at Home in the Evening" and "Books and Book-Lovers: A Talk to Girls." The boys' and girls' lists of suggested readings overlapped with authors such as Dickens and Shakespeare ("Hudson's expunged edition should be used") but diverged at *Westward Ho!* by Charles Kingsley, for boys, and *The Old Fashioned Girl*, by Louisa May Alcott, or *Girlhood of Shakespeare's Heroines*, by Mary Clarke, for girls.[81] WCTU members' acceptance of Hawthorne, Dickens, and Shakespeare for youths, even in abridged editions, shows a flexibility that is not usually associated with those who advocated censorship. An 1885 "Book Notices" column in the *Union Signal* provided mothers with a list of appropriate books for the youngest children, who needed to have books read aloud to them. Editorial comments accompanied each listing, such as "its lessons are pure and elevating, and we can recommend it as a safe book."[82] A perusal of these columns reveals that "safe" books emphasized "homely subjects" that could "instill lessons" in a story-book format.

Recommended WCTU book lists suggest that we need to revise our understanding of the censorship movement's ability to appreciate fiction even while advocating its regulation. This is particularly apparent if we look at WCTU book lists for teenagers and young adults from the 1920s. The WCTU's Young People's Branch (whose members ranged from high school aged through their mid-twenties) instituted "Bring a Book" evenings. In part, this was an effort to combat the influence of the "flapper" youth culture that was overtaking college campuses. In these meetings, students read and reported on biographies of celebrated WCTU missionaries who worked in foreign countries or on books providing arguments in favor of Prohibition. Many of the books were chosen because they might inspire young people, especially women, to pursue careers in WCTU missionary or reform work.[83] Each young people's branch had a "Leader for Reading and Reference," whose job it was to provide members with suggestions for good books in a variety of categories. WCTU youth leaders made their choices based on book lists, including those from "respectable" publishing houses, that were periodically printed in the *Union Signal*.[84] A 1923 book list included the following nonfiction reading suggestions: *The Making of an American*, by Jacob Riis (in the category "Americanization"); *The Christian Crusade for a Warless World*, by Dr. Sidney Gulick ("Internationalism"); *Travels in Alaska*, by John Muir ("Science and Travels"); *The Long Road of a Woman's Memory*, by Jane Addams ("History and Civics"); *Alcohol & the Human Body*, by Sir Victor Horsley & Mary D. Sturge ("The Liquor Problem"). In the fiction category, the *Signal* suggested titles by over thirty authors, including *David Copperfield*, by Charles Dickens; *The Strange Case of Dr. Jekyll and Mr. Hyde*, by Robert L. Stevenson; *Mill on the Floss* and *Adam Bede*, by George Eliot; and *Call of the Wild*, by Jack London.[85] Nonfiction books on natural science, history, and travel were always strongly emphasized and favored over fiction in discussions of proper reading materials. Yet these lists suggest that WCTU members should not be caricatured as anti-intellectuals. These sample recommended reading lists from 1885 and 1923 were not narrow nor did they avoid aesthetic or moral complexity, as the inclusion of Muir, Addams, Dickens, and Eliot indicates.

While the department as a whole clearly maintained an interest in recommended book lists, some state unions seem to have abdicated some of their responsibility for choosing which books or magazines were to be targeted for censorship as the WCTU became more involved in working for the federal censorship of motion pictures in the mid- to late 1920s. Campaigns against magazines in the 1920s, discussed by Paul Boyer in *Purity in Print*, for instance, did not include the WCTU. The *Union Signal* simply praised the efforts of other activists. One editorial commended thirty-two women's organizations in Huntington, West Virginia, that had successfully joined together to demand that news dealers refuse to carry "obscene magazines." In response to their protests, some advertising agencies had declined to print ads in magazines that published "notoriously offensive stories" until "the writers of these stories were dropped from the list of contributors."[86] During the 1920s, rather than monitor and create lists of "immoral" literature themselves, some states, such as Massachusetts, simply relied upon lists supplied by the New England Watch and Ward Society to aid it in deciding what books should be suppressed. The 1924 Watch and Ward's list of "bad" books included: "Non-Fiction: 'Jurgen, the Satyrican of Petronius Arbitu'; 'A Young Girl's Diary.' Fiction: 'Flaming Youth,' 'Black Oxen,' 'Janet March,' 'Skeeters Kirby,' 'Eric Dorn,' 'Many Marriages,' 'Women in Love,' 'Anne Severing and the Fieldings,' 'Cassanova's Homecoming.' "[87] These novels were clearly written for adults and have little to do with the WCTU's typical concern for "questionable" children's books, crime-story papers, or romance novels that appealed to adolescents. The fact that many of these books, by writers such as D. H. Lawrence, were illegal in the United States during this era highlights the differences in the Watch and Ward's agenda against legally "obscene" literature, compared to the more common WCTU agenda against "immorality" in literature. The department's acceptance of Watch and Ward categories reveals a diminishing interest in censorship of literature by the 1920s and an increased interest in regulating the "purity" of art and movies.

* * *

The commitment of WCTU members to improving children's and young adults' reading led these laywomen to interfere in a domain of professionals—the public library. Librarians organized themselves into the American Library Association in order to improve their professional status. They often asserted that they should be the sole authorities who would help to choose and guide the reading of children. Superintendent Emilie Martin ignored librarians' moves to protect their professional turf and instead encouraged local unions to designate members who would monitor library book selections and, if possible, work with their public librarians. Martin suggested that each local union form "a standing committee of two or more . . . to confer with the library committee [usually composed of laywomen volunteers] and secure if possible a rigid inspection of all books before placing them in circulation."[88] WCTU members joined these library committees whenever they could.

Workers in the Department of Purity in Literature and Art envisioned themselves as at odds with the "worst element" of publishing and advertising interests, while generally in alliance with most public librarians and teachers. Therefore, the tone of its campaigns for pure books in libraries was not hostile, although it was perhaps patronizing. If libraries had "immoral" papers and books in their libraries, WCTU members were sure that it was simply because librarians were unaware of the dangers contained within. The department assumed (often correctly) that boards of trustees and librarians would act quickly and forcefully to remove or restrict many of those books that they belatedly discovered to be "impure." The WCTU's characterization of public librarians was thus guardedly optimistic—librarians could be careless and accept a wide variety of "bad" books and magazines, but they were not purposefully sanctioning "immorality."

Department members were encouraged to inspect the shelves of school libraries, public libraries, smaller circulating libraries, and Sunday school libraries. They would then write letters to the librarians and boards of trustees if they found any "immoral" novels.[89] Librarians' possibly inadvertent carelessness ensured that WCTU campaigns had to be waged to clean public library shelves. Many state unions formed "vigilance committees" to look for "uncleanness."[90] In states across the nation, from California to Maine, WCTU members organized themselves to review all the books "before [they were] placed on shelves in public libraries."[91] Department members spoke personally to librarians and wrote letters to them and to their boards of trustees. The department advised members to "get permission to go over the books, point out the objectionable ones, and if possible have them destroyed, or at least taken out of circulation."[92] This probably brought WCTU activists into conflict with librarians who were determined to assert their own authority within their professional realm. Librarians, however, were often willing to remove many books that were objected to by community members. In one year in Kansas, for example, under WCTU-led community pressure, ninety-seven "bad books and pictures [were] destroyed." Expelling and destroying books such as those by Oscar Wilde came under the rubric of library improvement.[93] This may have been motivated in part from a desire to avoid conflict, but also because librarians themselves were concerned with the morals of children. WCTU members successfully removed books "teaching the Mormon doctrine" of polygamy, for instance, to which they were adamantly opposed. They also made certain that only "pure and safe books" were allowed into the Sunday schools, a task made easier by the fact that many union members were themselves Sunday school and elementary school teachers.[94] Taking a more legalistic approach, state unions notified owners of private circulating libraries "that they would come under the indictment of the law" if they did not "clean" up their collections.[95]

To address their concerns about "impure" books that remained in both public and for-profit circulating libraries, local and state WCTU's created their own free reading-rooms, circulating loan-libraries, and purity libraries from 1880 through the 1920s. WCTU libraries were dedicated to offering "true and wholesome books" to anyone interested.[96] "Purity libraries," for instance, were set up by local unions as supplements to the public libraries. They offered books and pamphlets against the legal regulation of prostitution and in favor of social purity and modest sex education. The *Union Signal* advised members to stock their circulating loan-libraries with "books by our [WCTU] workers, including this one, *A Paradise Girl*, by Mrs. S[usanna] M.D. Fry."[97] Union members created circulating libraries for rural areas as well as cities. WCTU libraries and temperance reading rooms were not devoted solely to temperance literature but, rather, included approved fiction, history, biographies, and natural science.[98] Members were asked to add to the book collections of WCTU libraries but were warned, "do not put *one* of the donated books into your library until it has been examined and passed upon by each one of a committee of three."[99] Loyal Temperance Legions, WCTU auxiliary groups for young boys and girls, committed themselves at state conventions to donating at least one book per local legion in order to create state WCTU lending libraries, as a measure "to save the boys."[100]

The WCTU's argument that the "stability of the state" depended upon "censorship over books [in libraries] as well as other agencies" put it at odds with librarians. This is especially true when the WCTU called for public control of and censorship over books in public libraries. It claimed that public libraries had become sites of "unguarded access" to modern fiction that could corrupt youths even more than "a saloon or gambling den."[101] This negative characterization of public libraries was certainly rejected by members of the American Library Association. In 1915, New York Superintendent Harriet Pritchard declared that "one of the most deplorable conditions today is the easy access that our youthful readers have to the trash and degrading stories that are offered to them, free of charge, in our public libraries." Aware, however, of the value of free libraries, Pritchard took care to praise the positive educative function of public access to books: "But these libraries also furnish excellent brain food free to many struggling people who are aspiring to a more liberal education. If our women would only encourage the circulation of the best, they would inspire for books that they know to be edifying and interesting at the same time."[102] By the following year, she reported with satisfaction that "protests have been made against obscene and objectionable books in public libraries and in school libraries. Good clean books have replaced objectionable ones in many places. A professor in a Cattaraugus County High School burned the books objected to and also obscene post cards."[103] The WCTU condoned book burning by zealous teachers and librarians.

Laywomen's library committees, as well as the presence of vigilant librarians, can take some of the credit for the careful regulation of children's reading materials by the 1920s. Massachusetts Department Superintendent Lillian Stone reported: "I find there is a great advance in the children's department of our libraries. Competent young women are in charge, who know what books to recommend to the children. This is a great help in the line of education, along the right lines."[104] Stone noted another possible reason why "many books have been suppressed." She explained that "as a rule the reports from the public libraries show that the books placed there have been carefully examined by a responsible committee. The circulating libraries, however, need our careful attention."[105] Volunteer laywomen seemed to be making an impact, yet there was always more work to be done.

The *Union Signal* periodically published lists of pro-alcohol and anti-Prohibition books that had been "placed there [in libraries] by the liquor interests." These lists, called "black lists," were meant to provide WCTU members with specific titles to search for in libraries. Members would then try to have those books removed. The *Union Signal* also published lists of acceptable books that "give the truth on the liquor question." WCTU-sanctioned books were donated by local members and unions to their public libraries.[106] An article entitled "A Good Letter to Pass on to Your Librarian" asked public librarians to purchase a subscription or accept a donation of the WCTU's *Union Signal*, wherein people could find "pure" articles about a range of social, cultural, and political issues. The sample letter then asked librarians to exclude pro-alcohol or anti-Prohibition books published by the U.S. Brewers' Association.[107] It appears that libraries may have accepted donations of the *Union Signal* and other WCTU-sanctioned publications, for the WCTU did not protest or condemn librarians for rejecting these materials.

The relationship between WCTU members and public librarians was complex. Librarians were indeed concerned about "purity" in literature, yet they did not uniformly or unconditionally welcome WCTU input into their professional domain of book acquisitions and restriction decisions. There is no evidence of much, if any, overlap of membership in the American Library Association and the Woman's Christian Temperance Union. There was, however, a great deal of interaction between members of the two groups. WCTU members believed that they had a right to influence the decisions of their local librarians. Cooperation is evidenced by the fact that most libraries had volunteer library committees that participated in their acquisitions decisions. In keeping with the Woman's Christian Temperance Union's work against literature, the American Library Association censored books according to a primary evaluative criterion that focused on the "sensational," including descriptions of crime, violence, or rapid upward mobility, rather than on nudity or sexuality. The ALA, like the WCTU, had an amorphous conception of "immorality" that sometimes allowed it to censor and regulate a broad array of literature that was not officially "obscene." The complicated role of the American Library Association in book censorship and regulation is explored in the following chapter.

CHAPTER 3

Guardians of Public Morals

Professional Identity and the American Library Association

An analysis of the American Library Association provides a point of comparison to the WCTU that can help us better understand the range of styles and methods used by those who favored censorship. It can also clarify the relationship between gender and professionalization in questions of social action, as well as establish the breadth of support for censorship. Librarians began the difficult process of professional self-definition in 1876 when they formed the American Library Association (ALA); from that point through the first decades of the twentieth century, they struggled to increase their prestige and status. By identifying their role as similar, variously, to that of the doctor, teacher, and social worker, librarians sought to ally themselves with the emerging "helping" professions of hygiene, social work, education, and psychology that gained such prominence during the Progressive Era (defined broadly as the 1870s to the 1920s). These "helping" professions positioned themselves as possessing special knowledge regarding proper child-raising techniques that parents supposedly lacked, thereby signaling the re-casting of parents as amateurs or clients who needed "expert" guidance. The focus of this struggle was a debate about the moral education of children. Which profession, in particular, would determine the pedagogy appropriate to the child's moral upbringing—or would that determination be made solely by the child's mother and father?[1] Although the American Library Association put its faith in social science to manage problems related to children's reading, social class issues, and urban life, it exhibited tremendous touchiness about professional turf and boundaries precisely because it faced stiff competition from other potential sources of authority laying claim to the same rhetoric.

Librarians censored only at the site of consumption, rather than at the point of production. They did not write their own children's books, nor did their organization publish its own magazine for youths. On that score, they had a less bold agenda than reform groups like the WCTU that wrote their own children's fiction, for they could only cull through books written by others. Moreover, they paid a price for professionalization; one of its characteristics is specialization, and librarianship represented a form of it. Librarians' professional efforts at censorship were difficult because their institutions were only one of many sources of reading materials; they competed with books displayed in shop windows, as well as with circulating libraries. Their problems were how to use the library to restrict access in the face of competing sites for reading and how to set general moral and aesthetic standards for society to follow.

Librarians' self-identification of their role as "guardians of public morals" allowed them to regulate books based on the criterion of moral acceptability. Their debates about censorship reveal conflicts over how to achieve both professionalization and the moral education of children. Although the first library schools were established at Columbia College and the University of the State of New York in the 1880s, librarians were unable to claim and restrict access to special knowledge that would give them the level of prestige they desired.[2] The Dewey decimal system for card filing was a distinctive language developed by librarians for themselves and their clients, but it seemed to be too accessible—unlike the more mystifying professional language of psychologists or doctors. The public persistently viewed librarians as caretakers of books, not as educators or guardians of children. Librarians' conflicted and uncertain professional status was complicated by the increasing number of women entering the occupation at the turn of the century, keeping wages low or even driving them lower, since women's wage work was (and still is) automatically devalued.[3] Moreover, as tax-funded institutions, public libraries could not pay salaries comparable to most other professions.

The American Library Association had different ideas about how and why it should censor books for children versus those for adults. Dee Garrison's lucid study *Apostles of Culture* presents a thorough discussion of the ALA's top-level debates about censorship of books for adults but underemphasizes the pervasiveness and significance of library censorship of children's literature.[4] Garrison separates her discussion of the censorship of children's literature from the section called "Moral Passage: The Fiction Problem," where she explores librarians' ideas regarding "immoral" adult fiction and their resistance to a cultural shift in attitudes regarding popular fiction. Instead, she discusses the regulation of children's reading in a chapter called "Maid Militant: The Progressive Years and World War I" and sees it as a natural outgrowth of Progressives' interest in regulation as a reform tool, the popularity of child study, and the concerned "maternalism" of female librarians. These are all certainly relevant aspects of the supervision of children's fiction, but they serve to deflect attention away from the phenomenon as proof of librarians' continued interest in censorship and restriction of reading. They also hide some of the motivations for regulation, such as the imposition of cultural and moral standards on children. Moreover, while Garrison's consideration of censored adult's fiction highlights a different set of concerns about the "New Woman" and changing standards of sexuality, a consideration of censored children's fiction highlights concerns about the diffusion of knowledge, control over cultural production, morality, and women's place in professional organizations.[5]

Librarians revealed in an 1893 survey that the purchase of *any* work of fiction—regardless of its "purity"—caused discomfort among the majority of them, who worried that they were betraying their mission as educators and moral guardians.[6] In reality, librarians purchased fiction; the practical debates concerned where exactly the cut-off point should be in both adults' and children's fiction. Librarians agreed that they should exercise direct censorship when dealing with children—those who were perceived to be most vulnerable to negative influences and therefore most in need of protection. Increased attention to the role and ideas of children's librarians significantly alters the evaluation of the American Library Association's similarities to moral reform groups in the Progressive Era by demonstrating how librarians employed arguments about the morally impressionable nature of youths. The moral guardianship of youths became a site of cultural struggle between professionals and laypeople, and the censorship and regulation of books inside libraries became librarians' primary means of control.

The American Library Association refused to engage in political censorship of books or in political debates for or against legislative censorship, barring several significant exceptions. The most dramatic exception was its display of patriotic fervor during World War I, when the association created a Library War Service Department. World War I marked the high point of *political* censorship by public librarians. American Library Association members removed all literature deemed socialistic, revolutionary, or even pacifist in orientation. Participating for the first time in systematic political censorship, librarians voluntarily removed from library shelves books by Germans, books about socialism, or about other alternative forms of government and politics. Historian Dee Garrison explains that beginning in 1918, "the War Department issued orders to the ALA that forbade the stocking of certain books in the [military] camp libraries"; these and other books were frequently destroyed. After the war ended, the ALA became ambivalent about its recent collaboration with the government and disavowed further political censorship.[7] Subsequently, the association returned to its prewar focus on librarians' right as professionals to regulate books for their *moral*, not political, content.

In contrast to the American Library Association, the Woman's Christian Temperance Union ignored the focus on political censorship during World War I and continued to focus its censorship efforts on questions of morality.[8] During the war, state unions that had previously taken "good literature and pictures" to prisons, reading rooms, and poor families now began to channel this energy into sending reading materials "to the soldiers over the seas and in camps in this country."[9] WCTU members put aside their earlier calls for pacifism and, as patriotic citizens, often subscribed to "good" magazines in order to send them off to American soldiers. This project interested them in the content of magazine fiction. One department superintendent, for instance, "protested against obscene and vulgar stories in 'Snappy Stories.'"[10]

Just as the American Library Association generally avoided politically motivated censorship, the organization did not formally support any of the pro-censorship legislation designed to regulate reading matter that was sponsored by moral reformers at the state and federal levels during the nineteenth or twentieth century. As with the case of political censorship during World War I, there were exceptions to this rule. In particular, individual members of the association argued in favor of governmental intervention and citizens' actions because they were frustrated by the fact that young readers often supplemented the "good" books provided by the public library with "absolutely worthless, trashy, immoral" books available from circulating libraries and book stands. A librarian stated: "I make open war on a class of novels which are boldly displayed in shop-windows, which also disgrace the counters of many respectable book-stores, the contents of which outrage good taste, and decency. . . . And it seems as if the proper time had arrived to put such books under rigid censorship."[11]

One librarian entered the public debate about censorship on the side of organizations like the WCTU. He argued, "it is not only our duty to buy good books, but also to prevent the sale and distribution of bad and poor books. The same thing is true of the penny dreadfuls and the *Police News* and *Police Gazette*. I think it is the librarian's duty to suppress the sale of the *Police News* and the *Police Gazette*; especially in New York State, where there is a good law." Pointing to crime-story papers as the lowest form of "sensational" literature, this librarian argued that a modicum of action on the part of librarians as citizens—rather than as professionals, where the ability to act politically was restrained—could lead to their effective suppression. Raising the dilemma of librarians' public versus private actions, he explained that he acted as an individual not as a government employee: "I simply sent to the Secretary of the State of New York for copies of the law, and then took the District Attorney by the hand, and went from book store to book store and said the *Police Gazette* shall not be exhibited here hereafter. . . . I bought it myself and had the salesman convicted [using the power of the law to make a citizen's arrest]."[12] Worrying that children would not come to the libraries to read "pure" fiction when "trash" was available at such a cheap price, this librarian had a broad view of his responsibilities. In fact, he focused his efforts on a genre of literature that was outside of the official purview of librarians (the *National Police Gazette* and all other crime-story papers were summarily excluded from all libraries and despised by most members of this profession). Other professionals encouraged librarians to take direct political action by supporting an expanded definition of "obscenity" that would allow governmental regulation of crime-story papers and dime novels. A *Library Journal* article written by a teacher singled out the *Police Gazette* for particular condemnation because of its popularity with youths: "We have a [national] law against the sale of that which is obscene, and it is worthy of consideration whether the law should not go one step farther—not a long one—and include such papers as the *Police Gazette* and those other forms of degrading literature known as the dime novel."[13]

Barring these scattered instances of individual librarians who favored political censorship laws, the American Library Association, from its inception, distanced itself from the legalistic, governmentally imposed coercive censorship promoted by reform groups like the Woman's Christian Temperance Union. Instead, the association favored professional guidance and control of reading. Most librarians suspected that official legislation would transform the government into a centralized caretaker of morals, delegitimizing professionals' claims to responsibility for moral guardianship of the public. Sanctioning librarians' regulation of morality in literature, a Cleveland, Ohio, librarian explained: "It is only when we come to books which affect the question of morals, the question of conduct, that we feel that we have the right to draw the line of exclusion. . . . I believe that we have a perfect right to exclude from our shelves books which seem likely to prove harmful, no matter with what reputation as classics they come to us."[14]

The ALA's dominant approach to censorship was based on the idea that regulation could be done effectively and efficiently *without* public discussion or legislation. Although librarians freely discussed censorship among them-

selves, most were reluctant to have their views and tactics made public by
the press: "Newspapers sometimes try to draw us into a statement that a
certain book has been rejected or excluded. Usually able to dodge."[15] Librarians feared that newspapers would give negative publicity to their regulatory efforts or portray their censorship of books as "arbitrary," at which point
librarians might lose what they perceived to be their professional mandate
to exercise "a certain legitimate and proper censorship . . . by which a large
majority, perhaps, of the books now in question may be excluded."[16] Librarians optimistically suggested that quietly and "gradually, most of those
books may be withdrawn, and the public taste may be led up to a rather
higher and better level."[17]

Debates among librarians about the validity of reading regulation demonstrate the contested state of their attitudes toward popular literature and
are directly related to their (insecure) assertions of professional autonomy.
To entrench their position as professional arbiters of taste and morals, for
instance, a *Library Journal* editorial warned librarians not to be swayed by
"abnormally sensitive" library patrons (possibly WCTU members), such as
the woman who demanded the removal of *The Admirable Adventures of Lady
Biddy Fane*, which, the editors declared, was not "bad," but rather a "delightful wild adventure." If the librarian in charge had been "indiscreet" and had
agreed to censor it, they warned, he could have risked losing the respect of
"public opinion."[18] Furthermore, the "ostentatious removal" of a particular
book might backfire by creating more interest in the book among those who
would otherwise have been "unaware" of its existence. Following this line
of reasoning, librarians feared publicizing which books they had withdrawn
and referred to them only obliquely: "There are certain books—it is not necessary to name them—which lie along the border line." Librarians may have
intuitively grasped that to talk about forbidden things is to promote a discourse one wishes to suppress. These precautions are comparable to moral
reformers' fears that controversy over "immorality" in specific texts would
encourage people to search out and read the condemned books.[19]

A few librarians did believe in making their censorship decisions public. They envisioned librarians to be educators engaging in public relations
efforts, explaining persuasively why they should be able to purchase books
selectively. ALA members invoked this role in debates over their right to
withhold or not order books that were paid for by taxpayers' money: "The
librarian's duty, it seems to me, is to come in and say, 'We cannot advise you
to read this book. We do not say it is a bad book. We simply say we do not
think it is a book which should be purchased by public money and used by
the people of the city as part of the equipment furnished them at government
expense.'"[20] In this case, librarians depicted themselves as public servants

entrusted with the responsibility of carefully allocating tax funds. Others publicly justified their refusal to buy "sensational" contemporary fiction by arguing that it was too expensive to purchase each popular novel that was published during the year and that these ephemeral publications should be sold or rented through the circulating libraries:[21] "These persons could then pay for what they wanted, or they could go without; but they could not have it at the public cost. The demand for the sentimental and more highly seasoned literature of the day,—the Southworths, the Ouidas, the Optics, and the Kingstons,—would then be measured and limited, as it should be, by the willingness to pay something for it, and not stimulated by a free distribution."[22] This pro-regulatory stance is complicated by the fact that by pointing to public funding, librarians also called attention to the fact that they were public employees and so were engaging in state censorship when acting in their capacity as acquisitions librarians.

If ALA members decided to publish their censorship decisions, they were advised to quote respected literary critics "in order that the public might see how these authors are estimated by a competent critic and not think that the librarian was acting arbitrarily in the matter."[23] Although this might seem like a site of potential professional conflict between librarians and literary critics, librarians found it useful to quote critics' reviews in order to justify their book censorship and seemingly to shift the weight of the decision to a "neutral" party. Librarians, moreover, carefully chose which reviewers to evoke. Caroline M. Hewins, librarian of the Connecticut Library Association in Hartford, regularly published reading lists of "Literature for the Young" in the *Library Journal* in the 1880s. Hewins's lists reviewed recently published books and warned readers of "impure" or sensational books by using selected quotes from book reviews by critics that were culled from respectable newspapers and journals.[24] To warn librarians against purchasing *Facts and Phases of Animal Life*, by Vernon S. Morwood, for instance, Hewins quoted the *Nation*'s negative review: "The anecdotes consist largely of obnoxious stories conspicuously silly, teeming with errors of fact, often superstitious or ludicrously credulous. It is a book which should not be put into the hands of any child."[25] Hewins also used book reviews from the religious press, such as the *Christian Register*, which cautioned readers as follows: "One closes this admirably written story with sincere regret that so charming a book should be deformed by two or three painfully sensational chapters. The characters . . . are brought into most undreamed of and tragic situations. . . . For younger children, it is too exciting to be wholesome reading."[26] Occasionally, Hewins herself wrote the criticism; her reviews emulated the style of established literary critics, but she was, perhaps, more critical of adolescent romances and books that celebrated rags to riches dramas. Reviewing the book *Elsie Dins-*

more, by Martha Finley, Hewins claimed: "Like the other books of the series, a compound of cant, twaddle, mawkishness and descriptions of fabulous wealth. The marriage of a girl of fifteen is alone enough to condemn the book and its predecessors."[27]

* * *

From the 1870s through at least 1930, librarians focused most of their regulatory energies on debates over what books should be censored, the definition of immorality, and whether to concentrate primarily on workers' or children's reading. Beyond their universal rejection of the *Police Gazette,* the American Library Association was unable as a group to clearly define "immoral" books. A standard definition, offered in the pages of the *Library Journal* in 1923, was presented as unambiguous but is in fact highly imprecise and subjective:

> The most widely accepted definition—certainly it is the most familiar to librarians—and most often used is that of Miss Corinne Bacon: *"The book which degrades our intellect, vulgarizes our emotions, kills our faith in our kind and in the Eternal Power, not ourselves, which makes for righteousness, is an immoral book."*
> ... He [the librarian] should be actuated by a desire to protect the immature and not by a desire to suppress a point of view or an opinion with which he disagrees.[28]

In its implication that morality entailed a respect for the "Eternal Power," the ALA echoed the WCTU's complaints about "ungodly" or blasphemous books. The two organizations also agreed that, at least, informal (professional) censorship was needed to "protect the immature." The (unacknowledged) amorphousness of this definition did not serve the ALA as well as it did the WCTU, since it led to internal disagreements among librarians rather than represented an attempt to make the term "immoral" cover a wider variety of literary forms.

Indeed, some librarians ignored this expansive definition. For them, the term "immoral" referred narrowly to "tabooed" books for adults such as Boccaccio's classic *Decameron,* Queen Margaret's *Heptameron,* the works of Rabelais, or the modern novel by H. Mathers, *Cherry Ripe.*[29] Books such as these were considered "unfit to read" and were usually locked up in restricted shelves that librarians referred to as "the Inferno."[30] Those who focused their regulatory efforts primarily on notorious "classics of pruriency" argued that such books had to be banned completely or at the least restricted to select adults, because "every school-boy is tempted sooner or later to try to secure" them.[31] "Sex-hygiene books" and medical texts were also kept in the locked shelves to guard against their use by "perverted individuals." A Chicago public librarian confidently explained that these books were only given to respectable adults of "normal tendencies."[32]

Others went to the opposite extreme, using the term "immoral" loosely and casually, indicating that they assumed a common professional consensus or definition of immorality, in spite of the fact that there was none. Confronted with rapidly changing standards of morality and propriety both in popular culture and in avant-garde literature at the turn of the century, librarians often supported and reinforced moral and societal standards that ostensibly could be easily evaluated in any given work.[33] Community standards, they reassured each other, were high: "Of course the community will demand no immoral and absolutely worthless books."[34] The librarian who casually suggested: "Every normal book and no abnormal one would be an excellent rule to follow in choosing," clearly assumed a level of agreement among her colleagues that did not in reality exist.[35] In spite of the slippery nature of such standards, little effort was made to define these terms. When attempting to justify their regulatory actions, librarians explained that "the public expects . . . to be denied the morally bad ones [novels]."[36] Disagreements over the basic definition of "immoral" books made it difficult for librarians to present a united front to the press when a controversial censorship case arose.

Historian Dee Garrison emphasizes librarians' self-stated mission as "apostles of culture," whereby they aimed to introduce more Americans to "higher" literature, thereby raising their aesthetic taste and literary standards. The phrase "apostles of culture" implies, on the one hand, a paternalistic aim to civilize, and on the other, a more democratic desire to distribute literature widely. Librarians' alternative and competing role as "guardians of public morals," however, was just as crucial to their professional identity.[37] In the latter case, librarians emphasized their role as protectors of American youths *from books*, especially those books that might challenge conventional morality or class distinctions. Judging content rather than literary style, many were often willing to sacrifice "classics" to a higher standard of purity. As censors, librarians focused on content over and above artistic form. Acting on their fear that few could read something "vulgar," yet remain "noble," some bluntly declared that "the question of classic or not is subordinate in importance to the question of dirty or not."[38] Others agreed that style alone could not determine a book's acceptability: "It is notoriously true that the most perfect form may be given to stories so sordid, vicious, or trivial that the knowledge therein acquired is knowledge to be avoided, and the effect on character can at the best be null, at the worst disastrous to the point of ruin."[39] By viewing literature as a tool for character development, librarians thus demonstrated a willingness—problematic in light of their conflicting role as "apostles of culture"—to modify their aesthetic standards when evaluating books: "A lower standard of literary merit might be admissible, with an absence of psychology in the delineation of character, but let there be no lowering of the moral standard."[40]

Whereas the American Librarian Association's rejection of national censorship laws constitutes its most significant difference from the Woman's Christian Temperance Union, its rhetoric against "immoral" reading constitutes its point of greatest similarity. Most strikingly, Josephus Larned, ALA president from 1893 to 1894, argued in favor of library censorship through an attack on proponents of the phrase "Art for Art's Sake." Larned's 1895 article closely parallels (surely quite unintentionally) an 1893 argument made by WCTU President Frances Willard that insisted upon a cultural hierarchy based on morals.[41] Entering the wider cultural debate over the primacy of morality versus aesthetics, Larned attacked the European modernist and avant-garde art that seemed to be gaining influence with American artists:

> All this which I am saying is straightly opposed to a doctrine much preached in our day, by a school of pretenders in art, who . . . are seriously dangerous. It first appeared, I believe, in France, among the painters. French literature took infection from it; then England became diseased, and America is in peril. It is the false and ignorant doctrine which phrases itself in the meaningless motto "Art for Art's sake!" . . . —"Enjoy Art for Art's sake!" say these aesthetic prophets of our generation, who have no comprehension of what Art is. . . . What they are really striving to do is to degrade the content of Art, and to persuade the world that it can be made the vehicle of low suggestions and mean ideals without ceasing to be Art in the noble sense.

Artists themselves did not know "what art is" but had to be taught by more knowledgeable and respectable experts, particularly librarians. Larned, like Willard, saw artists and novelists as having an obligation to engage in moral "uplift" precisely because of their power to influence behavior and ideas: "Art is a vessel, a vehicle, for the carriage and communication of something from one mind to another mind—from one soul to another soul. . . . Considered in itself and for its own sake, it has no existence—it is an imposture— a mere simulation of Art; for that which, duly filled with meanings and laden with a message, would be Art, is but the handicraft of a skilful mechanic."[42] The pro-regulatory position of some professionals in the American Library Association seems to represent an attempt, similar to the WCTU's, to create a middlebrow culture based on the nineteenth-century's genteel tradition. Larned did not draw the line between "high" art and popular culture, but between what is morally elevating and what is not; he, too, insisted upon a cultural hierarchy that privileged morally "pure" art.[43]

Larned asserted that professional librarians were morally and culturally superior to the general public they served. Librarians, he argued, had a duty to keep "low" writings from free public access: "It is for us who are among the custodians of good literature to set our faces against them."[44] Clearly, the stakes were high; librarians argued that their power and regulatory responsibilities were increasing together: "Libraries which are fast becoming such a power in the land are instruments of evil as well as of so much good."[45] The central issue behind censorship attempts was who would have the power to influence and direct the mental and moral development of America's young people.

In order to bolster their professional claim to the right to censor books, ALA members employed a medical/hygiene model and a rhetoric of moral contamination that was central to the popularizing of other reform ideas in the Progressive Era. Larned's argument, for instance, relied on metaphors of disease to describe the dangers of the spread of Continental literature to the United States. He condemned avant-garde art as a foreign "disease" threatening Americans' moral health and compared librarians to doctors whose primary professional duty was preventive care. Another librarian declared that novel reading so "enfeebles the mind" that it was worthy of "study as a new disease (which might be classed under the head of psychological physiology)."[46] Furthermore, the effect of reading "insipid or sensational fiction" was compared to a drug's negative effects on the nervous system; it "simply and certainly emasculates and destroys the intelligent reading power."[47] In a move the WCTU would have approved, an article in the *Library Journal* boldly connected the "dime novel business" to the "liquor traffic," saying: "There is money in it, and unscrupulous publishers, like manufacturers of intoxicants, are pushing their sales with all the energy and skill of the most shrewd and successful business men."[48] By equating fiction with drugs or alcohol, reading became a "stimulant" in need of control.[49] Most dramatically, if reading was a drug or a disease, professional librarians were obliged to act as physicians to carefully determine which books were safe for the public. If they neglected this duty, they would be serving as drug pushers or a "monster" pharmacist who would "pass out the drug over the counter on demand, not concerning himself with its fitness or unfitness for the prospective reader, not caring whether it will kill or cure."[50] By using a medical discourse and hygiene metaphors, librarians aligned themselves with those Progressive Era reformers who consistently wrapped moral questions in medical rhetoric, hoping to invoke its "scientific" authority.

Reports by New York City children's librarians also engaged the rhetoric and concerns of the Progressive Era's social hygiene movement and prioritized issues of class and ethnicity. Attempting to keep the books in good condition and participating in a hygiene campaign against spreading disease, children's librarians, for instance, sent reports of their battles against real dirt

to their superintendent: "More dirty hands than clean ones. Some children
are sent home to wash their hands before they are allowed to take books."[51]
Engaging in amateur urban anthropology, they attempted to observe the
patterns of cleanliness and of reading among various ethnic groups; they
cited as positive role models for other immigrant youths the intellectually
eager and curious young Italians, or Russian and Polish Jews who, they reported, voraciously read the classics of English literature: "We have come
to the conclusion that the Italians have a better and finer reading taste than
the Irish. Our Italian children seem anxious always to profit by their books
and one is frequently asked, 'Teacher is it a good book or is there a better one
just like it?' While the Irish children ask, 'Is it exciting missus?' "[52] The Jew-
ish children, they concluded, were "always cleaner during Passover holidays
than at any other time during the year."[53]

Librarians applied Progressive Era health concerns to the act of reading
sensational fiction; excessive reading was deemed to be physically and mentally unhealthy for youths. The desire to balance "the benefit of outdoor play"
with children's studies was particularly important to librarians who served
an urban population yet who generally believed in the superior wholesome
qualities of rural life.[54] On the one hand, urban librarians argued that the
library "has a special duty to perform for the city child. . . . For these the library must to some extent take the place of Mother Nature, for under present
conditions it is through books alone that some of them can ever come to know
her. . . . [The children's librarian] must find ways of attracting these children
to spend a healthy portion of their time among the books, always guarding
against too much as against too little reading."[55] By emphasizing "the recre-
ative function of the public library," librarians offered books to city children
as mental equivalents to fresh air.[56] On the other hand, following progressives' interest in playgrounds, calisthenics, and outdoor activities for youths,
others sometimes worried that children spent an unhealthy amount of time
indoors reading.[57]

Librarians also promoted a particular social-psychological model of behavior, arguing that audiences respond mimetically to literature or art. Like
WCTU members, they theorized that reading about adultery, for instance,
might inspire the reader actually to commit it. Larned employed this line of
reasoning: "Our minds are as sensitive to a moral force of gravitation as our
bodies are sensitive to the physical force, and we are as conscious of the
downward pull upon us of a vulgar tale or a vicious play as we are conscious
of the buoyant lift of one that is nobly written."[58] Fiction, as a carrier of moral
contagion, could lead to "injury to moral character . . . [and] bold or polished
villainy."[59] Caroline Hewins supplemented her lists of "Literature for the
Young" with a column that reprinted newspaper articles purporting to link

dime novels to boys' behavioral problems. Under the heading "Dime Novel Work," Hewins quoted, for example, the Hartford *Courant:* "People talk, and rightly, of the pernicious influence of yellow-covered literature upon the boys. It leads to all this runaway nonsense, to the buying of pistols, the thefts of property and the delusions of highway heroism that end in trampism."[60] Expert repression of these novels was readily justified by librarians, particularly when compared to the possible "immoral" actions of deluded child readers.

* * *

Questions about book selection in predominantly working-class and immigrant branch libraries engaged American Library Association convention speakers at the turn of the century. Librarians' debates about the necessary extent of censorship reveal their conflicted views on class relations, social order, and urban life. Samuel S. Green, ALA president in 1891 and head of the public library in Worcester, Massachusetts, argued that his clientele of working-class textile mill operatives had distinctive needs. He openly advocated a double standard of morality for literature. For a library in a small, rural town populated by native-born white Americans, Green claimed he "did not put on the list a single book by Adams, Alger, Kellogg, Mayne Reid, Fosdick ('Castlemon'), or any other sensational writer for the young." In contrast, for a town that included "a great shoe-shop or cotton factory" with immigrant workers, he advocated setting up "a branch library, supplied with a considerable proportion of exciting stories, in the factory itself, or in the part of the town where the operatives live, and keep the main library almost free from sensational literature."[61] Factory workers' sensibilities were less refined, he explained, and their branch libraries would have to be "sensationalized" to satisfy them. Citing the public library's obligation to cater to all taxpaying citizens, the author of "Fiction in Libraries: A Plea for the Masses" similarly reminded his readers that "the library is in existence by the grace of the public, and it is its duty to cater to *all* the classes that go towards making up the community in which it is established." (He added the familiar and ubiquitous caveat that "no one, so far as I know, defends the admission of impure or immoral fiction into the public library."[62])

Green's comments point to some problems with librarians' professional claim to the right to censor. Woman's Christian Temperance Union members could profess to represent society's interests as women; they believed and played upon nineteenth-century assumptions about women's greater moral sensibility. Because librarians were men and women and because they had to base their assertions on *professional qualifications,* they had only two choices: they could either serve the public taste, as Green argued, or they could make a case for their own special knowledge and role in selecting what the public read. Neither was entirely tenable. The first option meant catering to a public with "low" taste. Making the selection of books more difficult was the fact that there were, moreover, multiple publics with different tastes, as Green acknowledged. The second option was impossible to enforce because librarians had not managed to lay claim to an autonomous knowledge and authority as other professionals had, primarily because they were still seen as mainly caretakers of books. Both options, moreover, ignored the reality of widespread public access to print material and other forms of popular culture outside the public library. Librarians did not have a monopoly on sites for reading comparable to the courtroom's monopoly of resolution of certain kinds of conflict.

Based as it was on presumptions about class and ethnicity, Green's double standard was subject to a great deal of debate. One librarian condemned the proposal as paternalistic and elitist since it held the working classes to lower standards of morality and taste: "The children of factory hands should not be forced to read the vile stuff which they would find in their branch of the library, while the good, wholesome novels, which they perhaps would rather read, are away off in the main library, where they have not time to go and get them."[63] To others, the very assumption that most youths and workers favored "sensational" novels mandated stricter regulation by public librarians: "Is there, then, any good reason why this savage tendency should be fostered at the public expense? Shall we deliberately make criminals and prostitutes, that we may fill our jails and homes for the fallen?"[64] The last scenario was strictly gendered, with "sensational" novels leading boys to theft and girls to prostitution.

Class-based arguments could be used for opposite ends, such as to convince more reluctant colleagues of the need to control the quality of fiction in public libraries. A supervisor of the Home Library program for the Pittsburgh library, like Green, dwelt on the "pernicious" reading tastes of the poorest inhabitants of the city, but unlike Green, she did so in order to establish the need to suppress "cheap" literature and distribute "good" reading through a "home library" program: "It is a fallacy to think that the poorer classes are not reading. They are, how much we cannot adequately estimate; if we could, I think we would be startled out of our complacent inactivity in the matter. Go, as I have, week after week on Saturday evening to a stationer's in one of the crowded portions of the city and watch the steady stream of people who seek the tiers of illy assorted novels and the rows of cheap magazines and newspapers."[65] Charging that giving sensational novels to working-class youths was a "dangerous experiment" approaching "pandering," Charles Francis Adams, Jr., a trustee of the Quincy, Massachusetts, public library warned that librarians had to devise clever ways to teach about good literature because: "Taking the mass of those who use the public library, and especially the children in our public schools, who are born and bred in the habitations of labor . . . whom we especially wish to reach,—these cannot and will not read what, as a rule is recommended. What I like is to them incomprehensible; and what they like is to me simply unendurable. They are in the Sunday police-paper and dime-novel stage."[66] Adams complained that librarians expected working-class readers to switch easily, for example, from sensational novels to history with a simple recommendation. He argued that workers could only be interested in "better" fiction if they were given reliable catalogues of popular reading that judged the literature according to "unpretentious" standards.

In direct contrast to Green's permissive stance, the Society of Friends' Free Library in Germantown, Pennsylvania, excluded all fiction in an attempt to control the perceived problem of unruly working-class behavior:

> Do novels teach them contentment with their lowly but honest occupations? . . . [The factory girl's] mind is filled with false ideas of life, and she is prepared easily to be beguiled into an improper marriage, or to become the victim of some pretentious scoundrel. The boy reads of equally false deeds of daring—fortunes made by unjust dealings . . . —and his bewildered mind is unfitted for the hard duties of life, only by patient grappling with which he can reach that position which will lead him to competence and respectability.[67]

The Friends' librarian, William Kite, argued that fiction reading might lead youths to want more than their working-class backgrounds might otherwise have led them to expect. Although he represented a sectarian religious organization, Kite participated in ALA conventions, and his articles were published in the *Library Journal,* wherein his views represented an extreme, but not embarrassing or unacceptable, pro-censorship position. In fact, his concerns echo those of public librarians who worried about the impact of Horatio Alger novels because they could encourage working-class boys to dream of upward mobility.[68] Additionally, librarians such as Caroline Hewins agreed that fiction might disrupt the social order by weakening "the national standard of moral purity . . . and the sanctity of marriage."[69] The Society of Friends' censorship position highlights librarians' underlying fears that any and all fiction could have disruptive and transformative effects on readers.

Librarians who worked at private institutions also censored books but carefully positioned themselves as allies of the working classes. They implied that they shared workers' less debauched moral sensibilities: "The commonplace reader does not desire and will not tolerate so much immorality as will the person of highly-cultivated literary taste."[70] They argued that workers were more interested in "useful" books, such as technical manuals, than fiction. YMCA librarians, for instance, asserted that wage earners desired books that would help them master their crafts. This argument elided the issue of censorship and implied that the working classes sanctioned librarians' rejection of "light" fiction:

> The interests of industrial classes, and justice to brain-workers demand that there should be a limitation in the purchases of books of fiction for the higher purpose of meeting these wants [for trade and professional literature]. . . . The artisan and the student stand in far greater need of the last edition of a book on sanitary plumbing, or electricity, or an important work on history or literature, than the reader of fiction, who need never suffer for lack if the newest book is not at hand.[71]

A Stanford University librarian similarly argued that "immoral" literature by the "decadents" should not be available in libraries; the "professional man" could afford to buy it himself, while it "should be kept from the young, and the working people do not want it."[72] Although maintaining that workers would reject "immoral books" of their own volition, he simultaneously promoted the elitist notion that books could be justly kept, at the discretion of librarians, from those who could not afford to buy them.[73]

When their focus shifted from adult (often immigrant) workers to immigrant youths, more librarians stressed the need for a collection of "pure" books: "It is for the boy . . . the child of foreign parents, who, in the first blush of patriotism, inspired by the sight of the school flag, comes to the library for a United States history, that we want books, the right kind of wholesome joyous books, that shall bring sweetness and light into their lives, and ideals of virtue and civic morality to their minds."[74] Echoing the Americanization interests of moral reformers and industrialists alike, librarians believed that young immigrants—especially boys who would grow up to vote—needed to be trained "to become good and intelligent citizens." To the ALA, it followed logically that "patriotism, love of truth and beauty are best cultivated by the reading of good literature."[75] A school principal, Mary Comstock, emphasized the educational and language barriers that working-class immigrant youths faced. Writing in the *Library Journal,* she asserted that boys needed special direction: "There *is* material here of which to make future scholars, men of letters and statesmen, and it is our duty to discover these and speed them on their way. Their apparent stupidity arises principally from their inability to understand the English language, and it is for this class . . . that the library should come to aid us in our work."[76]

* * *

The majority of librarians accepted by the late 1890s the admission of youths in public libraries (a relatively new phenomenon) and thus the need for careful regulation of children's reading. They then began to outline and define the characteristics and training necessary for those who would carry out this work. Their ideas upheld and confirmed traditional notions of women's central role as caretakers of morals and youths. At the local level, those public librarians who were entrusted to carry out any and all regulation of children's fiction were women. As early as 1876, an article in the *Library Journal* explicated the essential attributes of the female assistant who would help *adults* to select proper fiction. This assistant to the male librarian should be a "cultivated woman." Moreover, "she must be a person of pleasant manners, and while of proper dignity, ready to unbend, and of social disposition." By the late 1890s, these traits came to represent the desired traits of children's librarians.[77] Anne Carroll Moore, who later became supervisor of children's rooms in New York City, began the task of defining the special traits and skills necessary for children's librarians in an 1898 *Library Journal* article. Moore envisioned a cultured woman with a good personality and social skills: "The children's librarian should be first of all well educated, refined . . . possessed of sound common sense, clear judgement, and a keen sense of humor, gifted, it may be, with that kind of sympathetic second-sight that shall enable her to read what is often obscure in the mind of a child."[78] Moore outlined a set of characteristics that emphasized "maternal" instincts and unabashedly mobilized gender stereotypes. She proposed a series of possible "examination" or interview questions for children's room job applicants based on the presupposition that the applicants would be women. Only the first question focused on work requirements; it suggested that children's librarians attempt to bolster their professional credibility as censors by personally reading all children's books, rather than simply relying on other critics or reading lists to determine their quality and acceptability.

All the other interview questions sought to discover personality traits in the applicants that were implicitly gendered as maternal or female. One inquired, for example, if the applicant had "some personal knowledge of children, based upon recollection of one's own childhood and upon contact with children." The question reflects librarians' appreciation of the social scientific approach to youths as a separate category, as adolescents, whose unique needs had to be recognized.[79] Moore also asked, "have you known any one child or group of children intimately within the past five years, and in what relation?"[80] One implication of this question is suggested by a report on "Special Training for Children's Librarians," by Frederick Crunden, printed next to Moore's article in the *Library Journal*. Crunden emphasized the importance of a "winning personality" and then exclaimed, "fortunate it is for the children's librarian, and for the young folks she serves, if she is aunt or godmother to several children whose mental development and reading tastes she can closely observe."[81] Concern that the librarian "know" children was directly tied to her ambiguous status as a single wage-earning woman who must still somehow embody the best maternal traits as part of her professional identity. This was especially true in city libraries with an immigrant or working-class population where, as another author put it, the "little woman who greets the boys and girls . . . is often in the place of father or mother."[82] Taken as a whole, the interview questions used prescribed gender roles and identified women as primary nurturers in order to bolster women's entrance into the library profession. Male and female librarians' acceptance of this gendered professional definition encouraged a predominance of women first in the children's and then in adult departments; by the 1910s, almost eighty percent of all librarians were women.[83]

A psychological model of child development formed the theoretical basis for Moore's questions. It emphasized early learning and reflected librarians' concern for regulating the reading of youths. She asked: "Did you have many friends as a child?" and, "Did you as a child care for nature? and were you taught to observe carefully . . . ?"[84] The applicant's suitability was based on her ability to put herself into a youth's place by remembering how she herself had felt as a child. This identification of empathy as a professional skill is compatible with progressive educators' ideas about child development that argued that children would respond and learn better in loosely structured, nonthreatening environments with teachers aiding them in less authoritarian roles. Moore's overall perception of librarians' need for academic training in the social sciences was ambivalent: "The relation of child-study and of experimental psychology to the problems of our work is yet to be determined. That a certain amount of practical psychology is essential to any successful work with children is beyond dispute."[85] Director of the Pratt Institute Free Library, Mary Wright Plummer, suggested that "scientific training" was not enough, explaining that library work with children was a true calling: "It [the calling] is quite as serious as one to the ministry, if not more so, and no amount of intellectual training will make up for the lack of patience and fairness and of a genuine interest in children and realization of their importance in the general scheme."[86] Plummer carefully formulated a stance toward social science and training in such a way as to valorize women's special role. She was aware that an emphasis on expert training could, in other hands, delegitimize and undervalue women. She suggested that "if there is on the library staff an assistant well read and well educated, broad-minded, tactful, with common sense and judgement, attractive to children in manner and person, possessed, in short, of all desirable qualities, she should be taken from wherever she is, put into the children's library, and paid enough to keep her there."[87]

Five years later, Anne Moore indirectly questioned the utility of her gendered characterization of children's librarians: If librarians were seen as, and perceived to be, surrogate mothers who loved children and instinctively knew how to fulfill their jobs (like unpaid mothers in the home), they would be less likely to receive decent wages or, importantly, professional respect. Moore's 1903 article on "The Work of the Children's Librarian" emphasized the word "work." Moore questioned the benefits of the "fact that there had been a good deal of sentimentalizing over the work" of children's librarians. In a shift from her earlier focus, Moore stressed work hours, wages, and job responsibilities. Practical experience and the increasing number of children's rooms in the early twentieth century now exposed the problems female librarians faced as wage workers.[88]

Unfortunately, Moore noted, women's wages in library work were lower than those of male librarians, and "the prospects [for promotion] are not bright in comparison with the prospects of teachers." Moore compared librarians' wages to the wages of another female-dominated profession, yet she did not attribute children's librarians' poor wages solely to sex discrimination. Instead, she explained that "the salaries in many libraries are disproportionately small, in view of the fact that the children's library is not recognized as a separate department, but is administered as a part of the general circulating department." In her view, work in children's room was marginalized because work with children held less status than work with adults, further compounding the problem that wage-earning women were paid less than men. Many difficulties, she argued, arose from the fact that children's librarians were often expected to divide their time between the adult library in the morning and the children's room in the late afternoon after school let out. Emphasizing health issues, Moore complained that the librarian was expected to fulfill all the responsibilities associated with the children's rooms in just two to three hours, producing a "very exhausting nervous strain" that "is to be labelled *dangerous*."[89]

The situation was so bad, Moore explained, that an experienced children's librarian found herself questioning the benefits for women of entering the library profession: "Can a young woman who is not only herself dependent upon her salary but who has others dependent upon her, afford to give the best years of her life for so inadequate material compensation as is represented by the average salary of a children's librarian? What hope of promotion or advancement does the work hold out to those who have served a term of probation?"[90] The children's librarian was now identified by her need to earn a decent living and support others. What in her earlier article Moore characterized as "routine work" was now described in detail as particularly burdensome; the "demands of the work . . . are very much more

exacting than has been commonly taken into account." The duties of the job
were more onerous than those of other librarians. To emphasize the point,
Moore provided her colleagues with a long list of children's librarians' responsibilities:

> The children's librarian is commonly accounted capable of recommending
> the books, stamping the books, teaching the children the care of the books,
> seeing that the books are not stolen, performing all clerical work connected
> with the issue of the books, furnishing information on all topics connected
> with the course of study in the public schools, watching the effect of bulle-
> tins on children and teachers, giving a great deal of help to teachers or re-
> ceiving help from them, welcoming interested visitors, and at the same time
> preserving in her crowded room the quiet atmosphere which should always
> be felt in a library and which is probably never secured save by the exercise
> of a commanding personality.[91]

Moore's description of the demanding work environment of the child's librarian owed little to her earlier account, although in its own way, it was also
sentimental: "What then must be the strain upon the poorly paid children's
librarian who is laboring . . . in a small, dark, ill-ventilated, poorly equipped
room, opening directly off the street with the easy transfer of an outside dis-
turbance to the inside."[92] Moore concluded her 1903 article with a series of
practical recommendations aimed at improving the working conditions and
wages of children's librarians. Specifically, she advised that the children's
section "be recognized as a distinct department of the library," that the children's librarian be able to choose the books for her department, and that "at
least two *morning* hours a week" be given to her to analyze and critique children's books. Advocating expanded rights and privileges for working wom-
en, Moore concluded with an overall recommendation for: "Better salaries,
longer vacations or more frequent short vacations. Shorter hours: no day
should exceed seven hours."[93] These concerns went largely unaddressed by
the American Library Association throughout (and beyond) the period under study, but the problems encountered by female children's librarians are
linked to the ALA's debates over professionalization and to its working relationships with other organizations.

* * *

The significance of the struggle for authority between "experts" and parents
(and among "experts") for control of the child is forcefully presented by
authors Christopher Lasch and Jacques Donzelot, who view the turn of the
century in both the United States and France as a pivotal moment of change.
Professionals presented an educative, tutorial model that relied on the "voluntary" or semivoluntary inculcation of their norms and expertise in par-

ents (usually mothers). This raises the question of how dependent the "students" were upon the "teachers"; Lasch and Donzelot answer that mothers became "very" dependent. In *Haven in a Heartless World*, Lasch argues that Progressive Era "experts" in the United States destabilized the family by usurping some of its important functions, such as replacing parental authority with professional authority. Ironically, Lasch contends that the "invasion" of the family by social science was facilitated and even sanctioned by "the housewife." To stave off this very invasion, she acquired her own training, hoping to become an expert herself in "domestic science."[94] Progressive Era feminists, too, were complicit in moving the locus of authority from parents and families, as they allied with "temperance advocates, educational reformers, liberal ministers, penologists, doctors and bureaucrats" to force bourgeois values on unsuspecting immigrants and the poor. Lasch presupposes an unlikely level of homogeneity, whereby professionals, feminists, reformers, and even ministers all actively cooperated to achieve cultural domination.[95] While this aspect of Lasch's argument may underestimate the tensions and conflicts between these various groups, his explication of a struggle for authority between experts and families is pertinent to my discussion of librarians and their alliances with laywomen and other professionals.[96]

Jacques Donzelot extends Lasch's argument to a Western European context in *The Policing of Families*. Donzelot finds that in turn-of-the-century France, reformers and experts also focused intensely "on the theme of the safeguarding and social control of children." The result was a "saturation" of the family by new professionals, who promoted "hygienic, psychological, and pedagogical norms." Donzelot argues that the incorporation of the family into the regulatory functions of the state made it "harder to distinguish the family from the disciplinary continuum of the social apparatuses," such as juvenile courts and government-run social welfare bureaus, thereby decreasing the family's power and status.[97] Like Lasch, Donzelot suggests that women became "students" of the new experts or "consumers" who identified their expanded and rationalized "knowledge" as a gain. Both authors conclude that the alliance between social science experts and mothers was an unequal one, where mothers ultimately ceded autonomous control over their children in order to have a symbiotically dependent part in the progressives' re-ordered society.

The American Library Association's working relations with female moral reformers and women's club members, with teachers, and with mothers demonstrate the tensions and ambiguities of its efforts as a professional group to cooperate with others while negotiating boundaries of expertise. Displaying territorial fears of encroachment, the ALA made gestures toward involving others in the responsibility for promoting good reading, while it ultimately maintained that librarians alone were capable of the task. The fact that members of library fiction committees and teachers were predominantly women compounded the difficulties of cooperation, because the male leadership of the ALA was fearful of being any more closely allied to women or "femininity" than it already was, due to the high number of female librarians. Regardless of the number of female librarians, ALA leadership was heavily male dominated; from 1876 to 1911 all ALA presidents were men, and even after 1911, the great majority of higher-paid jobs and other official positions went to men.[98] For these reasons, the ALA's efforts at cooperation with others were more openly antagonistic than those between the Woman's Christian Temperance Union and men's vice societies, teachers, or women's clubs.

Sites of interaction between librarians of both sexes and laywomen can illuminate the complicated dynamics between these groups. The most immediate site for struggles over authority between librarians and laywomen was the public library's fiction reading committee, also called the ladies' committee or purchase committee, that helped decide which of the thousands of newly published books librarians should order each year. Although some committees were made up of combinations of library staff members, trustees, and laywomen, many were staffed solely by volunteer women (often WCTU members) from the local community. Books were typically subjected to rigorous scrutiny. The "ladies' committees" were reputed to be harsher than librarians on "impurity" in literature, yet the following description of the screening process carried out at the Portland, Oregon, Public Library in 1922 suggests that librarians put similar demands on the literature they themselves reviewed: "Every book of fiction is read by some member of the staff, and its moral tendency commented upon. If the Librarian has reason to doubt the judgement of the reader, another review is requested. Even after a book is passed upon, the cataloger considers it; and if she has reason to believe that it should be restricted, the matter is brought up further. Often, after a book is on the shelves, it is removed because of complaints from the public." Although some historians have argued that book censorship by librarians declined dramatically by 1910, my evidence, including this quote from 1922, suggests otherwise.[99]

Fiction committees composed entirely of volunteer women, such as the committee for the Boston Public Library, received extensive guidance from librarians. Its fifteen to twenty members were asked to report, in writing, on every book "under consideration for purchase," using as standards for evaluation a series of questions including:

> Is the book suitable for child or for adult? Is it historical or purely romantic? narrative, or does it deal with some contemporary social problem? if histor-

ical, what period of history does it depict? its merits and defects: as to accuracy (if historical), temper (if touching social problems), apparent sincerity (if treating religious problems), morality and style; and an outline of the plot sufficient to render intelligible the information above described.[100]

These questions, formulated by librarians, simultaneously assumed and promoted uniform standards for the evaluation of everything from the "temper" of a book's treatment of social issues to its "morality." This fiction committee reviewed 548 books in 1898, obviously saving librarians a great deal of time. The trustees, however, felt defensive about their use of female volunteers, for they hastened to assure concerned persons that the committee "does not *select* books for the library. . . . It indicates . . . an opinion whether, on the whole, the book is worthy. But this opinion does not finally control." The trustees further explained that a committee composed of laywomen was a good way to anticipate and forestall future controversies since the committee members' relatively conservative opinions represented "the average instinctive judgement of the general public."[101]

Other libraries hoped to counter charges of conservatism by creating seemingly "scientific" evaluation systems. The New York State Library's "fiction slips" had columns with various titles, such as *"Character."* The "character" column had eleven categories: "Style, English, Slang, Vulgarity, Profanity, Trustworthiness, Partizan, Moral tone, Objectionable tendency, Immoral, Weak." Evaluators were instructed to "indicate opinions by underlining words or using the letters *a* to *e* as follows: a = recommended, very good; b = allow, good; c = doubtful; d = undesirable, poor; e = exclude from libraries, bad."[102] There was no space given for a full written explanation of the evaluator's *a* to *e* choice, indicating that librarians believed that all involved knew exactly what an "objectionable tendency" was and that women volunteers approached literature with similar standards. The use of lettered choices also reflects a social science faith in the systematic collection of data into quantitative; seemingly objective categories.

Not all fiction committees were organized by librarians; some ladies' commissions were originally created by Christian women, such as WCTU members, to evaluate children's fiction for Sunday-school libraries. These committees gained a positive reputation among librarians for supplying the general public with useful lists of "good" reading for youths. Librarian Samuel Green praised the Boston committee members as "highly cultivated young ladies" and suggested that:

> One of the most valuable aids which the librarian may avail himself [*sic*] of in selecting books for the young, seems to me to be the different catalogues issued by the Ladies' Commission here in Boston. The ladies who compose this Commission read all the books for the young that they think will prove

suitable reading, and base their recommendations upon actual knowledge of their contents. They are women of high culture and good judgement, and the results of their work are very valuable.[103]

Importantly, Green qualified his support by adding that some books chosen by the Ladies' Commission were possibly a trifle too refined and that "perhaps, also, the fact that gentlemen do not aid in making out the lists, limits somewhat their value."[104] Green implied that women might be too conservative and that men had a range of knowledge that women lacked.

Green's hesitant qualifications anticipate an 1899 article by Boston librarian Lindsay Swift, the author of *Brook Farm,* the novel about the communitarian living experiment associated with the transcendentalists. His *Library Journal* article, entitled "Paternalism in Public Libraries," contains a scathing indictment of the well-established reading committees.[105] While acknowledging the members' devotion of time and energy to a cause "pointing in the direction of good public morals" and conceding that they were "responsible members of the community," Swift charged, however, that they represented only an elite "portion of society rather than its various interests." Worse, the committees were "apt to be composed of women." Swift attributed this to the possibility that "no man could be found who had leisure enough to attend to the matter. . . . As a rule, heavily burdened people are the best to fulfil an obligation. I have my doubts of the utility of those who have time on their hands." Following this delegitimization of the volunteer work of middle-class women, Swift continued with a more generally misogynistic condemnation of women's intelligence. The committees, he declared, were vested with powers beyond their abilities; their evaluations were "flippant" and "uncritical." He challenged those female library volunteers who believed that "many poor and half-trained young men and women, with the sharp problem of bread-and-butter existence before them, are better off without glowing pictures of wealth, splendor, social ease and comfort, and all the allurements which would naturally tend to make them dissatisfied with their own condition." Instead, he argued that "dissatisfaction is a holy thing; it is the greatest possible incentive to progress."[106] Implying that only women could hold such narrow and prejudiced views, Swift ignored the fact that large numbers of male librarians also feared "sensational" literature (including the quintessential tales of upward mobility by Horatio Alger) for its potential to disrupt the social order. He also charged that these women had other political or reform group affiliations (as did most men, for that matter) so that the "Purity League woman," for instance, was sure to have a narrow agenda and to show her prejudiced and "warped mind." Swift only digressed from the topic of reading committees to lambaste a related phenomenon—women's clubs' involvement in self-education programs and traveling libraries, such as those created by the WCTU:

> Let me instance the late prevailing enthusiasm for women's clubs . . . a great rush for culture. . . . Well do I recall the invasion of one large institution a few years since by one of these women's clubs. Apparently hundreds of large, square, dominating ladies, with square, inexpressive visages and ponderous tread, filled the corridors and staircases. As one of a timid and weaker sex, a sense of helplessness came upon me. They were all red-hot and sizzling for culture; but as individual seekers after learning, I have never beheld one of these good women since.[107]

Not surprisingly, Swift favored the abolition of the reading committees, stating: "Amidst these manifestations of a tendency nowadays to meddle publicly with other people's business instead of working out one's own salvation with fear and trembling—in the midst of these paternally (*or shall I say maternally?*) minded outsiders—the librarian ought to stand unshaken."[108] Swift's criticisms of women reviewers, while atypically vehement, suggest an underlying preoccupation among male librarians with the ever-growing entry of women into wage-earning white-collar work, especially theirs. These fears coincided with an increasing public dialogue about the virtues of strong living and masculinity advocated by important public figures like President Theodore Roosevelt.[109] It is possible that this popular discourse heightened male librarians' defensiveness about the feminization of their profession. Swift's complaints did not translate into a rejection of women's committee work by the American Library Association as a whole, but they indicate the potential for conflict between professionals and voluntary women reformers over the control of morality.

Whereas Swift's article positioned the American Library Association in an antagonistic relation to women reformers, other *Library Journal* articles and editorials pointed to some reasons why the ALA might benefit from alliances with laywomen. Beginning in the 1880s, women's clubs and organizations like the WCTU developed "home libraries" and traveling libraries. These libraries usually consisted of fifteen to twenty-five carefully selected books; "several volunteers assist in this labor, which involves reading and critically examining many books, as only the best are accepted."[110] The books were intended for rural children who had no access to public libraries and for the poorest city children, "whose ignorance keeps them from understanding their own need" to go to the library.[111] Each week, a "volunteer visitor," whose role combined the duties of evangelical home visitors with the educational agenda of the settlement house worker, went to the tenements or country schoolhouses, exchanged the books, and perhaps discussed them with the children in a "reading circle." Her role was quite active, for she also: "Arranges pleasant outings, teaches home games, induces the children to save their pennies and open accounts at the savings-banks, and enters in a hundred ways helpfully into the lives of the youthful readers."[112] Public librarians supported these home libraries as a means to reach more children and as an antidote to the "lawless excitement" of the poorest urban neighborhoods: "The rescue of children from moral ruin requires above all the purification of the moral atmosphere in which they grow up, and the home libraries bring a fresh, strong, and varied influence for good to the home and the neighborhood."[113]

The 1900 convention of the General Federation of Women's Clubs (GFWC) featured exhibitions by club women who had organized traveling libraries of books on American history for rural districts in midwestern states such as Missouri, Kansas, and Wisconsin (children who read the books also received study outlines and "historical pictures"). The ALA set up a Bureau of Library Information at the GFWC's convention and praised the women's efforts. More particularly, it hoped that the federation's members would build on this experience and lobby government representatives to create public libraries in their communities: "Pamphlets showing how to obtain library legislation, state library commissions, etc., were eagerly sought for by the delegates."[114] Clearly, the women's activities greatly assisted librarians, as members of an emerging profession, by lobbying for funding for public library buildings and jobs. With the benefit of historical hindsight, critics of the alliance between laywomen and the "helping" professions have observed that volunteer women did not gain anything comparable for their efforts.[115]

Bypassing organized women's clubs, librarians frequently focused directly on mothers as their point of entry into the family, hoping to use them to influence the development and training of children. Librarians first approached mothers by paying lip service to the ideal of parental responsibility for the regulation and control of children's reading.[116] Like other members of the "helping" professions, they assumed that because of the "nature of things," mothers would reach children first and were therefore sure to acknowledge the significance of this role: " 'On them, as mothers and sisters, rests a great responsibility . . . [as] childhood's first teachers. . . . A well-read mother can direct her *son* to adventures, as marvelous as those of the cheapest fiction, in the chapters of Dr. Livingstone and kindred writers."[117] *Library Journal* articles usually referred to the mother, even when using the word "parent," and her child was almost always imagined to be a boy, suggesting that most librarians were more invested in influencing boys' moral and intellectual development but expected mothers to do much of the work.

An article written by a librarian praising the role of mothers in choosing children's literature suggested that for them, special "knowledge" was unnecessary: "The unerring instinct of the mother has seized upon those ditties and jingles which were best suited to the awakening senses of the child, and without knowing that she was obeying a great psycho-pedagogical law, she has for centuries been stimulating the sense of rhythm and exciting the wonder, fancy, and imagination of her babe with the material which awakens the best response and which has the greatest educative value at this early stage."[118] This construction of motherhood idealized the mother's role as natural and instinctual. This was not a good strategic argument for a professional seeking clients to make. In fact, most parental advice literature promoted professionals' interests, disparaged maternal instinct as a guide to child-raising, and believed in the superiority of experts' knowledge and in "learned" techniques for child raising.[119] Having upheld the mother as the child's best teacher, librarians usually reversed themselves and criticized mothers for being too lax and for failing to live up to this ideal.[120]

Library association members asserted that most parents did not, in fact, understand the need for vigilance over their child's reading: "A great deal of fault is to be found with parents in this connection. Intelligent people will complain that their children read too many stories, and yet they do not take any trouble to prevent it."[121] According to librarians, the problem was twofold. First, parents had been advised by social scientists and librarians to encourage their children to read. Those who followed this advice were then charged with ignoring another piece of "expert" advice that insisted upon strict regulation of content: "Many parents are satisfied to see a child with a book or paper without inquiring what is the character and effect of the literature which is being read. . . . When, as is natural, the child has fallen into bad reading habits they do not realize that they themselves are largely responsible and are powerless to assist in a recovery."[122] Parents did not see the harm in children's fiction reading, treating it simply as a positive stimulation to their imaginations, not as a stimulation to criminal tendencies.[123] Second, librarians claimed that some parents and adult relatives more actively discouraged their children's good taste in reading by asking them to bring home from the library "semi-demi-novels," rather than the nonfiction "charming little book on natural history" that they supposed the child would otherwise have chosen. Children's librarian Mary Wright Plummer noted "the difficulty in keeping 'hands off' in a case where grown people are thus influencing children injuriously can be fully appreciated only by one who knows and cares for children."[124] Thoughtless and irresponsible parents required librarians to train them properly to be good parents.

Thus, although parental responsibility was ostensibly the ideal, librarians argued that it was not a reality: "This missing element of parental influence is the one sad lack of the cause we plead."[125] Librarians justified their authority to censor books by promising that they would cede responsibility as soon as mothers became more aware of the need for regulation: "The time will come when *parents* will be more alive to their responsibilities than they now are. Many of our larger towns now have clubs and schools for the training of *mothers*." Note that by the second sentence, "parents" became "mothers"—the real target of librarians' directives. By discrediting instinct, parents (mothers) became clients in need of training by expert librarians (often women).[126] Pointing to mothers' flaws, librarians then claimed the authority to teach them to fulfill properly their obligations. The ALA regaled mothers with hints and warnings, such as "children are always glad to read a book which has been recommended by their parents" but would read "sensational and trashy books" recommended by their friends if they did not have proper guidance.[127] Defending his choice to exile "from the shelves of our public library the story of 'Tess: A Pure Woman,'" one librarian recalled his encounter with a "clever critic" who highly praised Thomas Hardy's novel but then recoiled involuntarily when the librarian suggested that the critic's own seventeen-year-old daughter Ethel read it. Triumphant, the librarian gloated: "I am quite sure that you did not want Ethel to read the book. And we, upon whom the responsibility for the selecting of books in public libraries rest, have other Ethels to think of, whose parents may not guide their reading as wisely and judiciously as you."[128]

The unwise parent was likely, in librarians' minds, to be an immigrant. The association of the indifferent parent with the figure of the working-class mother who produced wild or immoral children was, in fact, a dominant stereotype around the turn of the century in social science discourse about immigrant children and their families.[129] Librarian Linda Eastman advocated the use of Mother's Clubs in Cleveland, Ohio, to train "mothers to a serious interest in child study." The mothers she referred to were uneducated "wives of workingmen, largely German and Irish." In connection with a session "devoted to the questions, What shall I read? and What shall my child read?" this library sent the mothers: "Simple and practical books on the care and training of children, household economy and sanitation, home nursing, family ethics, house planning, flower gardening, some sweet, wholesome stories of home life, and a little choice misselany [sic] in the shape of poetry, history, and a bright book of biography or travel."[130] Most of the books focused on social hygiene and domestic science, with virtually no adult fiction. In contrast, native-born women also needed expert advice, but not at such a rudimentary level. A "wise mother" (I read this phrase to mean educated, white and middle-class, for librarians never referred to poor immigrant women as "wise"), should encourage her child's "love for truthful stories." She should not read only for her own pleasure, but to help her children study and learn well, and finally she should read "to her *boy* . . . to impart useful lessons in morality."[131] Librarians assumed that middle-class women simply needed to apply their education to the task at hand.

* * *

The 1907 to 1910 monthly reports on children's reading rooms in the New York City public libraries provide us with a case study of how the various alliances, proposed or contested in the *Library Journal*, worked at the local level. The reports were written by children's librarians to Anne Carroll Moore, the supervisor of work with children. These children's librarians, all women, wrote to Moore about their concerns, detailing their attempts to guide children's reading.[132] The monthly reports indicate that children's librarians identified as a primary professional duty their regulation of reading and worried more about the practical success of their interventions than about the abstract principles of regulation and censorship.

Librarians in New York City recorded a notable minority of parents who took a forceful role in directing their children's reading, contrary to the *Library Journal*'s criticism that parents generally had irresponsible attitudes regarding their children's reading habits and choices. In some cases, parents reinforced librarians' efforts to push youths toward nonfiction reading at what might now seem like a very early age. Specifically, parents were allowed to sign applications to check out books for children aged "about six or seven." This system worked well, according to one librarian, because "in most cases the parent selects a non-fiction book, which pleases me very much."[133] One mother seems to have taken quite seriously a WCTU Mother's Meeting-type insistence on maternal responsibility over youths' reading: "One mother said that she had begun by not allowing her daughter to read anything which she herself had not read first but she was very busy and as she understood that all the children's books were carefully selected, she allowed her to draw books without question."[134] To the librarian's satisfaction, this mother eventually convinced herself that she could lessen her vigilance since librarians had made regulation of reading their professional duty.

Ignoring *Library Journal* complaints about lax supervision by parents, New York City children's librarians sometimes found themselves in the unexpected position of enticing children to read fiction over their parents objections: "A girl of 11 . . . was accompanied by her mother who wished to know whether we had books on stenography as the child's father insisted upon her reading useful books." The librarian explained that they did not have vocational training books, but convinced them to check out "a copy of

Master Skylark [by Bennett] and one of Switzerland (Peeps at Many Lands)."
The librarian reported that "the mother was perfectly amazed at the kinds
of books we had. She had an idea they were all fairy tales and books on the
Elsie Dinsmore order, and concluded by saying her husband thought the
child should read something heavier than fairy tales and silly trash." Jock-
eying for authority over the child's reading, the librarian persuaded the
mother to bring the "respectable" fiction home to test her husband's restrictions. The librarian's success came the following week, when the mother and
daughter returned, pleased with the recommended books, and having
gained the father's approval.[135] Fathers did not always settle for instructing
their wives on the proper books for their children but also took a more direct interest, as when "one father [came] to see if we had any books which
would improve his son. He did not want him to read fiction."[136] Another librarian reported that "a father came into the library with his boy, and paid
a long-standing fine on the child's card, in order that his boy could obtain
the good literature he had always received at the library instead of the dime
novels he had been reading elsewhere."[137]

The activism of parents in New York City suggests that *Library Journal*
complaints did not accurately reflect the reality. In fact, Moore's librarians
were not always successful in winning over vigilant parents to their points
of view: "One little girl cannot join because there are novels in the library."[138]
More dramatically, one mother withdrew her child's reading privileges in
disgust at the quality of fiction her daughter was obtaining from the library:
"a mother came to us in great excitement to request that no more books be
given to her daughter, as the fairy tales, pirate stories, and St. Nicholas,
Chatterbones, had made her wild in the mind."[139] Curiously, the mother
denounced "St. Nicholas," probably a reference to a popular children's
magazine by that name that was consistently praised for its good morals by
members of the Woman's Christian Temperance Union. It is not clear why
this secular children's magazine was included along with undesirable "pirate stories." Another child showed the influence of her parents' teachings
when she refused to look at a book with an "indecent" picture in it: "A little
girl on being asked if she had read Frost's Wagner Story books said, 'No, there
is a picture of a nude woman in it and I did not think it was nice.' I think she
referred to the picture opposite page 200."[140] Articles in the *Library Journal*
generally ignored and marginalized these instances of parental moral vigilance and focused instead on bolstering their professional claims to the parental, regulatory role, substituting themselves for lax parents as better
guardians of the young.

The only genuine alternative perspective presented in the *Library Journal* on the role of the parent in the regulation of reading was an 1879 article.

Entitled "The Responsibility of Parents in Selection of Reading for the Young," the article was written by Mrs. Kate Gannett Wells, a prominent Boston club woman and anti-suffragist, not a librarian.[141] Like ALA and WCTU members, Wells wholeheartedly agreed that reading directly influenced behavior: "Many a girl's sentimentality or foolish marriage, and many a boy's rash venture in cattle ranches or uneasiness in the harness of slight but regular salary, is owing to books that fed early feeble indications of a tendency to future evil. Children must be guided till seventeen or eighteen, and only left free to choose for themselves as far as that freedom is necessary for growth." This observation led her, however, to affirm the primary importance of parents, rather than professionals or the government, in the training of children: "If, then, it is neither the exclusive duty of the library nor of the schools to maintain the proper use of its books, upon whom does the responsibility rest? *Upon the parents.*" Wells rejected librarians' claim that many parents effectively abdicated their responsibility by virtue of their lack of education. Such an argument, she claimed, "defeats its own end and fosters that socialistic view of the state which places education in its hands, rather than in the individual parent's, who alone is responsible." Wells's criticism of governmental regulation as "socialistic" is an interesting attempt by a woman's club representative to discredit governmental regulation by associating it with socialism, a political pariah in the United States. It also anticipates the later critique by scholars like Lasch and Donzelot of the alliance between the state and the nascent "helping" professions.[142]

Wells's argument demonstrates that not all middle-class women were comfortable with relinquishing maternal control over morality to either the state or professionals. Wells opposed legal censorship and was ambivalent about professionals' concern with youths because she wanted all aspects of moral education, including the selection and regulation of books, to be completely within the control of mothers. She proposed that mothers rather than librarians be in charge of preparing lists of "undesirable" books, for they would employ the most useful criteria, such as: "Books that make children cry; Books of adventure for unexcitable and unimaginative children; Un-love-sick novels."[143] In contrast, the Woman's Christian Temperance Union supported federal regulation, thereby admitting that mothers, even middle- and upper-class mothers, lacked the power and control necessary to influence their children for the better; this argument was obviously problematic from Wells's perspective. Wells explicitly rejected censorship as anti-republican: "Legislative interference with personal reading is not republican, so benevolence can only clothe itself with moral suasion and library associations. . . . Therefore, would I lay the responsibility more strenuously than before upon the *parents*, whether ignorant or well-taught; because no

American public library should assume direct, authoritative protection over all the details of an individual's reading."[144] Wells's belief that women should use "moral suasion" and philanthropy rather than governmental assistance or legislation is also reflected in her anti-suffrage position that rejected politics and the federal government as a possible source of power for women. The American Library Association's claim, as a professional group, to the right to censor reading materials for the young was challenged by Wells's association of it with the repressive tendencies of the state. Wells insisted that the library, as a public institution, should not be used as an instrument of state censorship and control that violated individual rights.

* * *

If alliances with mothers and reform-oriented women were problematic, perhaps there was hope for cooperation in the educational sphere. Many librarians advocated creating special alliances between public libraries and public schools. As public schools increased along with the number of immigrants to the United States, as more students (especially native-born Americans) stayed on for a high school education, and as literacy increased in the years after 1880, the role of the public library in the education of youths entered a period of experimentation and transition.[145] Librarians suggested that teachers should be able to check out greater numbers of books for longer periods of time and that public libraries loan large numbers of books each academic term to be placed in individual classrooms for students to use.[146] The ALA emphasized that teachers had potential to positively influence their students' reading: "From their teachers in the public schools, from the club associations, and from their books they must often get all they are to know of the good and beauty of life."[147] In conjunction with the developing field of child study, librarians allied themselves with public education: "a Free Public Library is an educational institution; a member in fact, if not in form, of the system of public schools."[148] By 1896, moreover, the professional organization for teachers, the National Educational Association, had established a library department, a move the *Library Journal* editors claimed "marked the formal recognition on the part of teachers of the bond that unites the library with the school."[149] Librarians conceived of this bond as part of a concerted effort to educate children: "The school trains the child in the use of his powers and faculties, teaches him *how* to learn; the library is the storehouse of wisdom."[150] In this spirit, librarians often referred to the importance of cooperation, celebrating the ideal of "the librarian and teacher, acting in concert."[151]

In spite of this ideal, librarians' relations with public schools and teachers were often as ambivalent as their relations with laywomen's library fiction review committees and mothers. Librarians berated teachers, like mothers, for a multitude of perceived sins. The "lack of successful accomplishment" in the fight against "impure" children's literature was blamed on "a lack of enthusiasm in the schools; and that, again, is due to indifference on the part of the teachers."[152] According to librarians, children needed to be asked intelligent questions about the books they read in order to help them define good and bad qualities in literature, but teachers could not adequately do so since "teachers are not, as a rule, well-read."[153] This criticism of teachers, made by a female librarian, suggests a possible rivalry between these two female-dominated professions, as well as an attempt to increase the prestige of librarians over teachers by claiming that the former were better educated and more culturally literate. Moreover, as librarians tried to limit fiction reading to two books per week, they alleged that teachers let "children read too much" and that "teachers, as a rule, have not yet developed the enthusiasm necessary for effectual work with their pupils in this direction. . . . Librarians must therefore continue to carry the war into the enemy's camp, and by their very intrepidity enlist parents and teachers to their standard until the day is won."[154] Here, mothers and teachers had become the "enemies" of librarians, whose role as moral custodians of the young increased proportionately to the failure of others.

Rather than bemoan this lack of cooperation, some librarians resisted the alliance of librarians and teachers, fearing interdependency and the duplication of efforts: "If the Board of Education would confine itself to the collection and maintenance in each school building of a good reference library . . . leaving the circulation of books for general reading to the public library, this duplication would be avoided."[155] Self-consciously worrying about issues of professionalization, others argued that the ALA's relation to public schools had pernicious effects on the organization's self-definition, threatening to erase or merge professional boundaries. Boston librarian Lindsay Swift, in particular, grasped the essence of professionalism: "If ours is really a profession it is, through this gradual reliance on external relations, doing something practically unknown in other professions. Law, medicine, or theology does not look outside its own domain for development or assistance, and these professions are not interdependent."[156] Librarians' relations with teachers, fiction committees, and mothers complicated their efforts to obtain a higher professional status.

The monthly reports from New York City children's librarians generally reinforce *Library Journal* complaints about ineffective teachers, unlike *Library Journal* complaints about mothers. The most positive reference in the reports to a teacher simply noted that one had come to the library for help "to interest her class of girls in history. This seemed a fine opening for a reading club."[157] This, at least, satisfied librarians by enabling them to intervene and assist the teacher's students. According to another children's librarian, some teachers reflected the worst ineptitude in that they were unable to create a genuine interest in learning or provide their students with the ability to learn. One teacher's class assignment struck her as particularly inept: "Many children have been sent by a teacher to find the dates of birth and death of *any* author. Most of the requests have been for dates of Alger, Optic, Otis, Henty, Ray, Richards, etc. There seemed to have been no attempt on the part of the teacher to give the children any real knowledge of the life of a writer worth knowing."[158] An alliance between teachers and librarians in the early twentieth century seemed unlikely to succeed at the local level.

Confusion over how to increase their professional prestige also led to librarians' conflicted stance on several new movements of the Progressive Era, including child study, kindergartens, settlement houses, and the increasing use of questionnaires, or poll taking. One male librarian implied that a more systematic exclusion of women volunteers would give movements like child study more clout with professionals like himself: "It is to be looked for that a movement like child-study, which has broadened out into a wide, popular current, should take on something of shallowness here and there. The ill-prepared amateur has been rather too prominent, the scientifically trained student not prominent enough."[159] Professional librarians feared that scientific rigor might be lost in a movement that had gained the interest and participation of so many "amateur" women, especially mothers. Children's librarians thus needed to approach progressive movements cautiously: "Without identifying itself with any of the movements such as the kindergarten, child-study, and social settlement, without losing control of itself and resigning itself to any outside guidance, the children's library should still absorb what is to its purpose in the work of all these agencies."[160] The ALA tried to be current on Progressive Era reform and social science issues yet viewed the popularity of these movements as problematic.

The fact that a number of librarians enthusiastically adopted the languages and techniques of other disciplines and professions was a point of contention. In particular, many librarians eagerly adopted surveys and questionnaires, an information-gathering methodology that gained popularity early in the rise of the social sciences. Librarians sent questionnaires to each other to find out how and what they censored; they also distributed them to children. Children were asked, for example, how often they read "cheap, flashy, inflammatory literature," and when and why they stopped reading it. When immigrant youths were asked if they shared their library books with other family members, librarians displayed their bias and reported that "the large number who shared their reading was a pleasant surprise to us, evincing a companionship at home that we had hardly anticipated."[161] Those librarians who worried about professional boundaries questioned this enthusiasm for borrowing techniques from other professions and suggested that "the common mode of inquiry by setting questions to numbers of children and young persons, and collecting the answers can have but little if any scientific value."[162] Yet even here, while disputing particular techniques, they did not dismiss the social science ethos per se.

* * *

The American Library Association aimed to professionalize librarians through its claims to specialized tasks and responsibilities. Central to this effort was its acceptance of careful censorship. By identifying themselves as "guardians of public morals," librarians justified their intervention into the private realm of reading and limited the types of books available at the public library. Although librarians can be considered members of a cultural elite that might be expected to object to censorship on grounds of artistic freedom they were generally sympathetic to a middle-class critique of "impure" literature. While they had qualms about regulating adult fiction, librarians agreed that children's reading was a special case, open to considerably more control. Linking their professional identity to censorship enabled librarians to see and present themselves as superior parental figures, as careful teachers, and as doctors protecting youths from harm. Yet librarians failed to achieve the prestige and autonomy awarded to other professions, in part because they had not managed to establish rigorous academic professional training or other claims to expertise.

Librarians' regulatory activities and debates reveal subtle conflicts over issues of gender and professionalization. Censorship posed a special problem for librarians. Although librarianship became increasingly female dominated, male and female librarians sought to distance their approach to censorship from the type of women's social action characterized by voluntary organizations and fights for national reform legislation. Librarians instead moved toward a treacherous new terrain of expertise, although librarians as professionals had not made effective claims to a monopoly of authority. More than laywomen reformers, members of the American Library Association struggled with the issue of censorship. They tried to balance their strong antipathy and fear of sensational and popular novels with their sense of obligation as public servants to supply what the public itself demanded. Moreover, whereas laywomen in the WCTU purposefully used an amorphous definition of "immorality" in order to expand what could be censored, the ALA had problems arriving at a clear, uncontested definition of "immoral" books. These problems jeopardized librarians' professional role as censors by leading to fundamental disagreements among ALA members about the necessary level of censorship.

Librarians' regulatory actions dealt only with postproduction issues, such as withholding or directing reading at the point of consumption. Professional rationalization also meant that librarians dealt solely with the medium of books at a time when other cultural forms were assuming more and more importance. There were also, of course, other points of consumption and sources of reading materials for youths and adults, such as bookstores and barber shops. If librarians kept public libraries too free of "sensational" literature they risked losing their clientele entirely. In contrast, volunteer activists in the Woman's Christian Temperance Union comfortably maintained a dual strategy of producing their own "pure" literature while fighting for censorship laws. As the following chapters demonstrate, the WCTU, as a volunteer reform organization, had more flexibility when challenging and trying to regulate not just literature but art and commercial films.

CHAPTER 4

Amateur Censors and Critics

Creating an Alternative Cultural Hierarchy

The Woman's Christian Temperance Union's initial interest in censoring the written word through a Department for the Suppression of Impure Litera-ture almost immediately expanded to include a broader range of popular culture, from sculptures, paintings, dance, and plays to movies. The WCTU's regulatory interest in art included items of popular or mass culture such as advertisements and "indecent" postcards, as well as paintings and statuary. Important early issues, such as the WCTU's condemnation of novel reading as a waste of women's potential for full participation in the public political world, remained an important part of the department's evaluation of other cultural forms, such as burlesque, as degrading and belittling to women. Its campaigns to regulate "impure" art were consistently presented as part of the WCTU's overall maternalist agenda and emphasized its belief that all cultural forms could influence youths' behavior. Concern for children's moral development allowed for women's greater involvement in the different realms of politics and art criticism.

In the five decades from 1883 to 1933, Woman's Christian Temperance Union members actively resisted imposition of a cultural hierarchy based on a distinction between high art and popular culture. They aimed to maintain their role as amateur critics who could accept or reject what they would.[1] Cultural historian Lawrence Levine states that by 1900 a newly formed cul-tural elite had claimed and defined "high art"—consisting of European avant-garde painting, realism and naturalism in literature, the ballet, and symphony orchestras—for itself. In contrast, a "low" or mass popular culture—identified as amusement parks, crime-story papers, movies, and dance halls—functioned outside of "high" art in an attempt to create a cultural free space for working women and men.[2] I argue that significant portions of the middle classes were uncomfortably positioned between these two notions of culture that were promoted at the turn of the century. The Woman's Christian Temperance Union exemplifies the ambiguous position of the middle classes vis-à-vis the "sacralization" of culture, for it fought against high art as well as against popular culture.

Rejecting cultural heterogeneity, the WCTU believed that there ought to be a homogeneous "middle" culture that its members would have a role in creating.[3] This ideal "middle" culture had several key characteristics. It was to be a culture that all Americans could share, a culture that reinforced and valorized a particular Protestant-based morality that privileged purity, social responsibility, and piety. It had to be accessible to average people, not just to elites or to the lower classes. Stylistically, it had to be realistic, in the sense of not engaging the imagination in fantasy, but also *not* as realistic as works dealing with prostitution or "fallen women" by authors such as Theodore Dreiser or Thomas Hardy. Equally important, the "middle" culture's locus of control was not to be with professional critics, artists, or the market. It was to be with morally informed laypeople, primarily women.

Determined to be an active force in the cultural process, the WCTU opposed the "new cultural authority," variously represented as artists or as arbiters of culture (including critics, fair committees, and museum professionals). Denouncing artists who placed "cultural perfection" above morality, accessibility, or public responsibility, the WCTU rejected the notion that unique art objects created by a "genius" were inherently superior to mass-produced forms. Promoting art as a tool for moral education, the department advocated, for example, the wide distribution of photographic reproductions of certain "pure" paintings.[4] The WCTU produced its own "pure" children's literature, and later, its own pro-temperance movies. Its members were less concerned with cultural status than with championing morality through culture. In effect, the WCTU contested one emerging hierarchy—that of high art and popular culture—while substituting another hierarchy based on a distinction between "pure" and "impure" cultural forms.

Asserting their right to *be* the arbiters of culture themselves, the middle classes did not wholly or willingly become part of the audience for either "high" art or for popular culture. Joan Rubin argues that a "middlebrow" culture first developed in the 1920s. While acknowledging the new dominance of commercial entertainment and the avant-garde, her definition of middlebrow culture stresses the persistence in the twentieth century of a Victorian "genteel tradition." This genteel tradition was characterized by a privileging of personal moral "character" and "public spirit," an interest in self-improvement and education, a wider general knowledge of literature and art (in the face of specialization and professionalization and a burgeoning of cultural production), and a popularization of "high culture" to a wider public.[5] The stance of the WCTU suggests that from the 1880s through 1920s many middle-class Americans adopted, or maintained, "genteel" notions that insisted upon a tie between culture and morals, whereby culture "which was not morally sound could not be aesthetically pleasing either."[6]

Lawrence Levine summarily allies the "new middle classes" with new industrialists and upper-class elites, claiming they all looked to "arbiters of culture" to give them a sense of security and superiority in a turbulent society destabilized by increasing numbers of immigrants, economic instability, and labor unrest. He argues, however, that this quest for cultural order did not translate into a pro-censorship position characterized by a desire for authority over conduct or morals exhibited by the WCTU and its "old middle-class" reform allies. The backgrounds of WCTU leaders in the nineteenth century have been examined to determine their class status and national representativeness. These studies suggest that most national and state (but not necessarily local) WCTU leaders were white, native-born members of the middle- and upper-middle classes who had a relatively high level of education compared to the general female population. Studies of local leaders have been less systematic and more difficult to conduct, but Ruth Bordin argues that there was significantly greater diversity in the professional background of local leaders' husbands in comparison to those of national leaders. Whereas many national leaders had husbands who were businessmen and industrialists and clergymen, local leaders' husbands were also store clerks and skilled artisans.[7] This suggests that there was a greater diversity in the pro-censorship coalition than Levine's analysis allows.

* * *

The WCTU department's title was changed in 1889 from the "Department for the Suppression of Impure Literature" to the "Department for the Promotion of Purity in Literature and Art." This change reflected the fact that the department had already been focusing as much energy on art as on literature. The new name was also intended to emphasize the positive, productive nature of the department's goals—the promotion of purity—not just the reactive suppression of impurity.

In many of the WCTU's campaigns for "pure" art, the female body became a powerful site for cultural contestation: WCTU members objected to images of women created or displayed for commercial purposes, as well as to what they interpreted as the gratuitous sensuality of female nudity in paintings and statuary. Nineteenth-century American painters seem to have acquiesced to (or perhaps agreed with) their society's suspicion of nudity in art, for the nude was not a favored subject. The American art scene was dominated by landscapes, painters of the Hudson River school, and the practitioners of luminism (namely Fitz Hugh Lane and John F. Kensett), along with painters such as George Caleb Bingham, who depicted frontier experiences. The female nude was infrequently portrayed by American artists for several reasons. Most simply, those artists who were particularly interested in the themes and painterly modes used in Europe often became expatriates abroad. When artists painted from live nude models in art studios or schools in the United States, furthermore, they risked censure from the general public, whose standards of propriety equated nudity with "immoral" activities. Significantly, it is strikingly difficult to locate paintings of female nudes in standard art history texts on nineteenth-century American art. Painter Thomas Eakins had been forced to resign from the Pennsylvania Academy in 1886 for allowing female art students to participate in life drawing sessions with nude male models. Eakins's 1908 painting of *William Rush and His [Nude] Model* was intended as a critical commentary on turn-of-the-century "prudery."[8] Even in 1908, this painting was subject to the public's disapproval. Finally, Americans with the means to buy paintings often purchased "unexperimental traditional paintings" from Europe, attempting, perhaps, to impress others with their respectable yet cosmopolitan taste.[9] Comparable art history texts on nineteenth-century French painting reveal a considerably different situation. Although certainly controversial, many famous French paintings prominently featured female nudity, from Ingres's *Odalisque* (1814) to Manet's *Olympia* (1865).[10]

A New York court ruled in 1884 that "mere nudity in painting or sculpture is not obscenity." WCTU members were unwilling to accept this new sanctioning of nudity in art. As legal routes became blocked, the WCTU relied on social pressure to force art gallery exhibitors of paintings and sculptures of nudes to modify their displays.[11] Even art with religious or biblical themes was not immune to its criticism. The department's national superintendent objected to an 1889 book by a Reverend Talmage (before it went into print) because it included a nude painting of Eve; another painting of Cleopatra was also condemned as "shameless," and "embarrassing" to the average woman. Upon receiving the WCTU's objections, the publisher removed both reproductions.[12]

WCTU activities against "immoral" fine art, both paintings and sculptures, peaked in the early 1890s. The department, under the new leadership of Emilie Martin, undertook a concerted campaign to eliminate all depictions of the female nude from the art pavilions of the World's Colombian Exposition to be held in Chicago in 1893.[13] National Superintendent Martin anticipated a problem with "impure" artistic representations of the female form because several similar works had been displayed—with some controversy—at the Philadelphia Centennial Exposition of 1876. Works by important contemporary European artists would be gathered together in the exhibition halls. Most disconcerting was the prospect of what would be on view, to children as well as adults, in the French pavilion—paintings by Edouard Manet, Auguste Rodin, and Edgar Degas. These artists were associated with the rebellious Salon des Independants and depicted the naked female form with a startling, often unromanticized honesty. The female nude had been a traditional subject of French art, but within that cultural context, its presentation had changed dramatically. Prior to the Impressionist era, nude women had typically been depicted in allegorical settings. In contrast, a painting such as Manet's *Dejeuner Sur L'Herbe* (1863) placed a nude woman among fully dressed men in a picnic scene otherwise marked by bourgeois respectability. The ideas of critics and the public changed more slowly in the United States, for even the paintings of nudes by popular French Romantics like Bouguereau were considered by many Americans to be "indecent" at the turn of the century. By the second decade of the twentieth century, idealized nudes had won the approval of conservative art critics like Kenyon Cox, who now supported figure painting, even as he vigorously courted the American public to join his protests against avant-garde painting (represented in and by the Armory Show of 1913) because it was not beautiful and was degenerate.[14]

To WCTU members, the mere idea that Impressionist and other avant-garde art might again be open to examination by American youths at the Chicago World's Fair made them shudder—and organize. Superintendent Emilie Martin rallied her department with the xenophobic exclamation, "God deliver us from copying after the lowest and vilest of Parisian indecency!"[15] The WCTU marshaled its large forces to inundate the directors of the exhibitions with letters demanding "purity" in art. Almost every state union was effectively organized for this campaign. The managers, advisory committees, jurors, commissioners, and chiefs of the Departments of Fine and Liberal Arts were each sent thousands of letters and petitions "protesting against nude subjects, paintings, pictures, marble and casts of a shameful character."[16] In its attacks on nudity, the WCTU rejected attempts by artists and some professional art critics to define "high" art as unique and inviolable to criticism. This great campaign was only moderately successful; the WCTU received the cooperation of some curators who "issued an order excluding all nude studies" from galleries they controlled. The most cooperative curators included the fair's female managers (mostly the wives of important industrialists), who may have considered it their duty as women to promote "pure" art from within their elite social class. Mrs. Bertha Potter Palmer, director of the Board of Lady Managers, wrote to Emilie Martin assuring her that "there will be nothing in the Woman's Building objectionable to the most refined taste."[17] In contrast, the director of the French National Pavilion initially refused to remove one particularly "impure" painting from his gallery.[18] Public reaction was so strong, however, that the recalcitrant director was forced to compromise and cover the painting, hiding it from public view.[19]

During and after the World's Fair of 1893, the WCTU employed two strategies to fight nudity in art. First, it argued against the avant-garde's valorization of "art for art's sake"—Frances Willard termed it "this selfish rallying cry"—and second, it advocated a "pure art education," centering on the mass distribution of "uplifting" images to as many families as possible.[20] An 1894 series of articles in the *Union Signal* entitled "The Nude in Art" insisted that art must have a moral purpose. Arguing against what she termed the "new criticism," the author dismissed the assertion that artists should prioritize aesthetics over morality. Tracing the downfall of the Roman empire to the nude statues of ancient Greece, she stated: "First, a pure art; then a nude art; then a sensualized people . . . then sure decline and at last complete downfall."[21] A later editorial made the stakes of the pro-censorship position explicit: "we all as a nation are running no small risk of becoming . . . completely ruined, in the sacred name of art."[22]

The WCTU searched for exemplary artists whose "pure" art could replace the "impure." Frances Willard praised in 1887, for example, the work of the sculptor Joel Tanner Hart:

> The sculptor Hart told me, when I visited his studio in Florence, that he was investing his life to work into marble a new feminine type which should express the twentieth century's womanhood. . . . His statue, purchased by patriotic ladies of his native state, Kentucky, adorns the city hall at Lexington. . . . She has strength and individuality, a gentle seriousness; there is more of the sisterly, less of the siren; more of the duchess, and less of the doll. Woman is becoming what God meant her to be and Christ's Gospel necessitates her being, the companion and the counselor, not the incumbrance and toy of man.[23]

Although literally on a pedestal, this sculpted ideal of womanhood rejected the notion that woman's power lies in her weakness and celebrated her "strength" and "seriousness." This paragon of womanhood asserted her equal role in both individual relationships and in politics. Placing the WCTU's regulatory activities into a woman-centered progressive framework, Willard declared that "the WCTU is doing no work more important than that of reconstructing the ideal of womanhood."[24]

The Department of Purity in Literature and Art engaged in a spirited public debate with contemporary American artists. The WCTU appealed directly to artists "not to make nude portraits" and pointed to Jean-François Millet as an ideal role model for other artists, claiming that he had stopped painting in the "modern French style" when he saw some youths examining—too eagerly—his "suggestive" work in a gallery window.[25] In an 1893 address delivered at the Art Institute Building at the World's Columbian Exposition, Frances Willard outlined the WCTU's position on art:

> It is a principle that we are responsible to humanity in exact proportion to the power of which we are the custodians, and men and women of the pen [and brush] who in this day of humanity's unequal struggle for its own betterment do not turn the pictorial and dramatic art of the novelist to the higher uses of socialism, temperance, the woman question, the advocacy of peace and other living issues that most intimately touch the life of the race, have by no means measured up to the ideal standard.[26]

The production of culture invested artists and other producers of culture with power *and* responsibilities. Artists should accept their responsibilities, Willard insisted, by privileging moral reform and activist politics above all else, especially above abstract notions of beauty.

Responding to the arguments of the WCTU, the Society of American Artists disagreed, placing "cultural perfection" above morality, accessibility, or public responsibility. It argued that the artist rather than the moralist should be in charge of "questions of taste." As New York Superintendent Harriet Pritchard put it, "the Society of Artists blame us for trying to circumscribe art by morals."[27] Modern and avant-garde artists insisted that pure beauty or aesthetics should be the artists' goal rather than art with a prescribed moral meaning.[28] They refused to be beholden to the artistic tastes of the public. Determined to follow their individual inspiration, they would then "educate" the public to appreciate the final product. The WCTU retorted that the law was on the side of the common person rather than the artist ("unregenerate genius"). It cited as proof a court of appeals decision that "it does not require an expert in art or literature to determine whether a picture is obscene, or whether printed words are offensive to decency and good morals. These are matters which fall within the range of ordinary intelligence."[29]

As laywomen critiquing "high" culture, WCTU members vociferously objected when the Boston Public Library purchased in 1898 the sculptor Frederick Macmonnies's controversial *Bacchante*. They condemned the statue because they interpreted it as a three dimensional representation and celebration of the god of wine and drunkenness. The Boston Library Board of Trustees received many public protests against the statue's central place in an educational institution and reluctantly (and ironically) agreed to give it up to the Metropolitan Museum of Art.[30] Macmonnies managed to elicit the protests of the WCTU once again, almost twenty-five years later, when he designed another statue for New York City. I have not yet found a clear description or illustration of the sculpture that was the focus of the 1922 protest, but it seems to have represented a far different theme. WCTU literature described it as follows: "The statue represents the degradation of womanhood as the passionate center figure *appears to have his feet almost on the necks of his beguilers,* although Matthew Henry declares, 'God made woman, not from man's head, to rule over him; Nor from his feet to be trampled upon by him; But from his side to be equal with him; And near his heart to be beloved.'"[31] Willard's earlier ideal, as represented by the Hart sculpture, helps place this later WCTU critique of Macmonnies into perspective; woman should not be "trampled upon" or compositionally subordinated, but should be glorified as a representation of female "strength and individuality." The New York union exclaimed: "The statue designed and executed by Frederick Macmonnies challenges our bitterest opposition. The mayor of New York gave two hearings that the women might express their opinions about it. If the women of other societies or clubs had turned out as our W.C.T.U. women did, led by Mrs. Boole, we would have had the statue refused a position in our metropolis, but they had many excuses to give for their absence."[32] The WCTU was clearly bitter over the lack of support it received from other women's groups. Even as it cited the virtues of women's equality, by the mid-1920s it apparently found female solidarity to be elusive. This reflects the unwillingness of other women's groups to be affiliated with the WCTU on the—by 1925—potentially prudish subject of a battle against nude or suggestive statues. The WCTU found willing allies in its fight for movie censorship in the 1920s and 1930s, however, so this incident does not indicate the organization's real loss of power, which did not really occur until 1933.

Throughout its arguments favoring the production of a "pure" middle culture, the WCTU positioned itself as anti-elitist. In her 1890 Presidential Address, Frances Willard characterized censorship debates as "the great controversy now being waged between so-called fashionable circles and the circle of women reformers."[33] Superintendent Martin also used a democratic argument against the professional claims of the Society of American Artists. In a curious formulation, she claimed that all great artists come from the people rather than the elite, and that "of all the muses, there is none so truly democratic as that of art." Martin rejected the notion that artists could work without any thought of the final product's moral implications. Martin's ideal artists of the people, it seems, could be trusted to give more thought to the moral and social consequences of their work. She emphasized the importance of "public sentiment" in creating a change, whereby artists would see they had been wrong and selfish and would voluntarily reform.[34] The problem with this position is that it was untenable for the WCTU when applied to popular culture, rather than to "high" art. When confronting "immoral" popular culture, the union did not dare vest moral authority in "the people" and saw God's higher moral laws as the ultimate standard. This inconsistency was a logical one for a group in the middle—when criticizing the professional claims of artists and their supporters, it appealed to the masses; when criticizing popular culture, it appealed to God's moral law, as interpreted by the godly.

* * *

The United State government's first legal action against the "obscene" in the nineteenth century was not directed against "high" art such as the sculptures and paintings of nudes discussed above but was an 1842 ruling against imported French postcards with seductive photographs of women on them.[35] Legislators considered the postcards to be a harmful foreign influence and targeted them, in particular, because they were mass produced and easily available. By defining obscenity in terms of accessibility rather than any specific topics or inherent characteristics, this ruling allowed imported French novels, in contrast, to escape regulation until the Comstock Act of 1873 because it was assumed that only an elite group of Americans could either afford or comprehend them. By the last three decades of the nineteenth century, all forms of art and literature proliferated as cheaper and quicker methods of reproduction, transportation, and communications technology allowed popular images from the mass media to pervade the public space.[36] These changes increased the WCTU's fear that the United States would lose its treasured innocence and become like Europe, thereby spurring its censorship activities. Moreover, all culture, not just sexuality, was being packaged and standardized by advertisers and marketers in the late nineteenth and early twentieth centuries. Women reformers deplored the exploitation of the female form that was part of a larger process of cultural commodification. The pro-censorship movement thus illuminates an important phase in the evolution of consumer capitalism by pinpointing early moments of resistance to commodification. The reformers' incomplete critique of the new world of mass consumption reflects a viewpoint that later radical critics, such as Herbert Marcuse and Marshall McLuhan, would more fully elaborate.[37]

WCTU censorship efforts against "suggestive" images of women on mass-produced billboards, posters, and postcards represent a strategic use of the law combined with community pressure, as well as a program of outreach to local governmental authorities.[38] Surviving state annual reports from 1894 through 1923 emphasize that individual women and local unions could, at least temporarily, remove "impure" images by protesting immediately against their appearance. In New York, for instance, the state and local superintendents went "to the police commissioners concerning life size pictures exhibited on fences, and . . . wrote to the newspapers who used the same for advertising medium. Nothing of the kind has appeared since and the police commissioners promised to co-operate."[39] The WCTU took up the fight against "indecent" mass produced postal cards, just as it had lobbied for "pure" paintings and sculptures at the Chicago World's Fair. Under pressure from the pro-censorship movement, in 1907, the postmaster general pledged to interpret the postal laws of the United States more strictly. Subsequently, WCTU members could personally turn in postcards (as well as books and papers) they deemed to be "obscene" and "unmailable," and the postmaster general could have them destroyed. The department claimed that "under this law thousands of indecent postal cards have been destroyed."[40]

Censorship activities took union members farther into the realm of politics; WCTU state annual reports provide numerous accounts of local cooperation between the mayor, the police, and WCTU members to have "unmailable" postcards removed from stores. In most instances, the WCTU member(s) would enter the store, find the objectionable items, state that they were illegal and ask the proprietor to remove them voluntarily.[41] If the owner refused, the WCTU member would visit the mayor or the police chief, who would order an officer to examine the merchandise or display and have it removed if it failed the "test" of "whether such pictures or shows had a demoralizing or uplifting influence on those who daily and in largest numbers looked upon them." When an officer examined at the WCTU's prompting a graphic picture postcard of the "electrocution of Chester Gillette," for instance, he instantly had all those cards withdrawn.[42] Many citizens' actions were recounted with praise in the annual reports. As a grassroots organization, the WCTU appealed to women by arguing that even disenfranchised individuals could successfully initiate political change.

The WCTU's commitment to regulating billboards and advertisements went beyond a narrow concern for purity and arose principally out of a demand that women's bodies not be used as a marketing tool to sell products or theatrical events. Frances Willard's presidential addresses at the WCTU conventions set the tone for the department by discussing "purity" in literature and art not as a means for repressive control over cultural forms, but as an issue of woman's self-respect. One formal resolution of 1887, entitled "Faces and Forms of Women as Trade Marks," argued against the use of images of women to sell commercial products, including alcohol and cigarettes: "*Resolved,* That we protest with righteous indignation against the growing tendency to exhibit the faces and forms of women as trade-marks and advertisements of liquor dealers and tobacconists; and also against obscene language and pictures in and on cigarette boxes. That we regard such exhibitions as the 'Belle Bourbon Sour Mash' whiskey pictures, as a degradation to womanhood, and call upon all respectable journalists to refuse such advertisements."[43] Members of the Young Woman's Branch of the WCTU (for high school and college aged women) signed a resolution asking that an advertisement for alcohol that pictured "a figure of a young woman holding a glass of liquor" be discontinued since it was inconsistent with the "purity of young womanhood." A look at other WCTU resolutions suggests that their goals went beyond an interest in regulating images of women in connection with alcohol and temperance.[44] A 1910 resolution, circulated among the state unions, argued that an image of a woman holding an unobjectionable loaf of bread, for instance, would be deemed offensive—and therefore unacceptable—if she, rather than the product for sale, was the focus of attention and was scantily dressed in "tights and excessively abbreviated skirts."[45]

More profoundly, department Superintendent Emilie Martin claimed that this was an issue of respect: "We all unite against the desecration of woman's form."[46] President Willard also strove to teach women that they were being wrongly used and to reject their formerly willing participation in their own degradation.[47] A 1902 WCTU national resolution against representations of women on billboards and posters stated:

> Resolved, That the innocence of youth, the purity of middle life and the sanctity of age are alike shocked and degraded by illustrations of the female figure *unclothed, or partially and suggestively clothed,* upon bill boards and in other public places; we will use every proper means by striving to awaken public sentiment, by appeals to city or state authorities and by legal measures if need be, to have this menace to public morals and stumbling block to clean manhood and womanhood removed.[48]

The resolution provides an interesting clarification of the turn of the century use of the word "nudity"; the WCTU used the term nudity to highlight the erotic nature of images, rather than as a description of what was actually depicted. In this case, the word "nude" was not meant literally but rather referred to sexual display or a calling attention to the female body. Women depicted in corsets, or even wearing dresses with décolleté necklines, might be called "nude."[49]

* * *

Regulation of other forms of popular culture such as the theater, living pictures, and burlesque was, arguably, part of an overall trend within the WCTU toward focusing more attention on visual images and the spoken word (especially motion pictures—a topic for a later chapter) as agents of vice. While burlesque exhibitions and living pictures were clearly forms of popular entertainment aimed at the widest possible audience, the case of the "legitimate" theater is more complex. Historian Lawrence Levine documents changes in theater audiences, ticket prices, and standards of behavior to prove that early nineteenth-century rowdy mixed-class audiences had been replaced by the turn of the century. In their place were more homogenized audiences willing to pay higher ticket prices and to sit quietly, passively acquiring culture from the artist or artistic director. Levine argues that by the early twentieth century, the "legitimate" theater gained elevated status as "high culture" and became a respected form of "cultivated" entertainment for the middle and upper classes.[50]

Like "fine" paintings and sculpture, however, the theater's ostensibly "high" status did not save it from some reformers' critiques. The WCTU continued to present the theater as the site for immoral liaisons and the mixing of classes. Theaters were characterized as "low" places where youths would be exposed to crime and impurity. A *Union Signal* article quoted a secretary of the Pennsylvania Prison Society, for instance, who claimed he interviewed boys in prison and found they had met at the theater "improper companions and immoral girls" who led them into their lives of crime.[51] According to New York's department Superintendent Harriet Pritchard, Americans had mistakenly "put their dependence in culture, education, and civilization, which alone can never save a nation. Righteousness as represented in God's Son and Word alone will save us."[52] Pritchard suggested that the problem with art at the turn of the century was that it was divorced from and did not serve religion or God.

The department sought to "save" the theater from the worst elements within it, explaining that "the drama, as interpreted today does not meet with the approbation of the general public, leading drama critics, and many of the profession."[53] As proof, the department announced in 1898 that the actress Mary Anderson and the celebrated singer Jenny Lind had renounced their public lives in favor of communing with nature and God: "They left the stage while yet at the zenith of worldly honor and glory, Mary Anderson publishing a warning to young girls against leading such a life and its surrounding temptations."[54] Casting itself as the leading voice of (and for) the people, the WCTU called for "pure" theater: "When we find that any play or spectacle is dull or coarse, we should promptly condemn and array public sentiment against it."[55] The WCTU argued that the theater and its actors "should show its spectators an ideal to be emulated—in character, life, and manners, making them happier than before seeing it, leaving their hearts uplifted and minds refreshed."[56] The organization again denied the right of the actor/

artist and director to uncontrolled freedom of expression. Union members desired the power to regulate the theater because they recognized, however reluctantly, that real power was located outside of the protected domestic sphere at the sites of cultural production and consumption.[57]

Reformers attempted to regulate the theater by banning or closing certain plays on a city-by-city basis. Together with the local clergy, WCTU members visited both the editors of the local newspapers and theater owners to try to persuade them to sanction and produce "none but clean plays."[58] In some areas, theater managers had extra incentive to book only "safe" plays, for they personally could be levied with fines by the city government if a show was closed down.[59] The governor of New York signed a bill in 1909 that made "it a misdemeanor to advertise or present any obscene, immoral or impure drama, play, exhibition, show or entertainment, which would tend to the corruption of youth or others."[60] Boston also officially outlawed the production of "questionable" plays. But continued protests by reformers in both areas indicate that state and local theatrical censorship laws were, at best, inconsistently enforced. Certainly, municipally based censorship led to uneven results; a play with a long run in one city might show only one night or a week or not at all in another before it would be closed in response to community protest.[61] During an 1894 campaign against living pictures, or *tableaux vivants*, Frances Willard suggested that local WCTUs work to create community review boards: "I do not see why the local WCTU in any town or city should not combine with all the other societies of women to secure, by means of a petition bearing the names of 'the best people' in the best sense, a local ordinance declaring that no play shall be put upon the stage which has not first been passed upon by a committee of reputable men and women." A Michigan union took initiative and created its own unofficial review board and visited the theaters, explaining that "where there was reason to believe that immoral plays were upon the boards, such exhibitions [were] denounced and a demand made of the mayor that they be suppressed."[62] By visiting those plays with the greatest potential for immorality, WCTU members acted as tough critics who would endure offensive displays to save others from having to, but their actions also suggest that these shows might have had a transgressive, even titillating appeal.[63]

Typically, reformers could anticipate a fight even before the play arrived in their locale. With a play such as *Salome*, for instance, they knew the story to be about "one of the most abandoned creatures in history" and deemed it to be inherently offensive.[64] Moreover, the "Salome dances," or belly dances, within the play were specifically objected to. In some cities, the surveillance of plain clothes police officers, together with negative public opinion, forced performers "to don respectable garments" and change the dance itself.[65] Clearly, plays of this sort could not fulfill the demands the WCTU had put on culture as an "uplifting" influence. The appearance of certain actors was "resented" by local people, who encouraged officials to prohibit performances of "[Olga] Nethersole as 'Sapho,' [Lillie] Langtry in the 'Degenerates' and [Mrs. Leslie] Carter as 'Zaza.'"[66]

The controversy and suppression of the play *The Thaw Trial* points to the many interconnections between the types of cultural media the WCTU tried to regulate. The play was based on a real murder trial that implicated "respectable" elites in a scandal involving murder, divorce, and adultery. The famous architect Stanford White, of the firm McKim, Mead, and White, was known for his designs of important buildings from 1880 to 1906, especially in New York and other east coast cities. At the peak of his career, White was shot and killed during the spring opening of the Madison Square Garden roof restaurant and theater on June 25, 1906. His murderer was Henry Thaw, husband of Evelyn Nesbit, a former chorus girl, who may have had an affair with White before she married. (Thaw accused White of raping Nesbit.) The murder of White—a member of the upper class, a representative of taste and fine art in America, and a well-known person—by a working-class man from Pittsburgh generated an enormous amount of interest in the press. Harry Thaw and Evelyn Nesbit became household names all across the country as people followed the investigation and subsequent trial in 1907. In the course of the trial it became clear that whatever White may not have done, he had frequented (although married) the Tenderloin district in New York City to pursue affairs with women there. The first trial produced a hung jury; a subsequent jury judged Thaw insane.[67] The WCTU originally protested the graphic recounting of the murder trial by the daily press in 1906–7. Later it found itself protesting and closing down a theatrical version and then a movie version in 1913.[68] This progression represents in much compressed form the WCTU's gradual shift during the early decades of the twentieth century, away from campaigns to censor the written word and toward campaigns to censor visual forms.

* * *

In Karen Halttunen's study of post-bellum middle-class American culture, *Confidence Men and Painted Women*, she discusses *tableaux vivants*, or living pictures, as a form of parlor theatrical whereby middle-class families and their friends turned themselves into "still lives" with themes such as "Papa's Birthday" or "Winter and Summer."[69] By the early 1890s, living pictures moved out of the middle-class parlor (and the working-class concert saloons) and into mainstream theaters, where diverse audiences looked at living pictures that were more suggestive than "Papa's Birthday." Many offered audiences scenes of Turkish baths, for instance, as an excuse to show partially clothed female models (some women wore "shocking" flesh-colored body suits).[70] The provocative quality of living pictures is captured in fiction by Edith Wharton's 1905 novel, *The House of Mirth*, wherein the main character, Lily Bart, earns herself the censure of respectable high society when she appears at a private party in a revealing *tableaux vivant*, wearing only "pale draperies." She is immediately derided as cheap—"damned bad taste, I call it," says one gentleman—and her beauty is degraded.[71] Wharton's use of living pictures as the pivotal moment that leads to Lily's downfall powerfully illustrates their challenge to respectability at the turn of the century.

Tableaux vivants were not unique to the American scene but were also appearing on stages in Great Britain. In fact, the WCTU's 1894 campaign against living pictures was initiated by Britain's WCTU under the leadership of Lady Isabella Somerset. Somerset's "open letter to the women of England" received great publicity and appeared in a wide variety of British newspapers. As a member of Britain's aristocracy and as a defender and consumer of "high" art herself, Lady Somerset was most careful to contrast the "impure" *tableaux vivants* to tasteful and artistic *paintings* of nudes, which she deemed acceptable:

> It will be said that the artistic merits of these presentations are their *raison d'etre*. I absolutely deny that they are artistic. They have nothing in common with the treatment of the nude in art. Go to the South Kensington Museum and look at Mr. Watt's Psyche, and then go the "Palace [Theater]" and wait for the "Moorish Bath." The one is a glorification of womanly form. . . . But the other—! These "tableaux" *violate every artistic canon*. It is sham nudity, not spiritualized and made ideal by the hallowed creating hand of genius, but palpably gross and disgusting in its suggestive flesh-colored skin tights.[72]

Somerset accepted a cultural hierarchy whereby paintings made by "the hallowed creating hand of genius" were inherently elevated above unaesthetic, common displays such as living pictures. Her distinction between fine art and its imitators was important because it delegitimized theater managers' and promoters' attempts to copy their subject matter and poses from "fine art," as a justification of their displays of the female form. Somerset's arguments, combined with social pressure, ensured that the British WCTU quickly succeeded in removing the "offending" tableaux from London's Empire Theater.[73]

While perhaps appropriate for her upper- and middle-class British audience, Somerset's argument contradicted the American WCTU's massive campaign against nudity in art at the World's Exposition in Chicago of the previous year, 1893, when it had argued that nudity degraded women and denied their purity. In that battle, the WCTU had rejected the very privileging of the artist as genius that allowed for and justified artists' control over aesthetic and moral judgments and had demanded that all representations of the nude be excluded from the fair's exhibition halls.

Upon the easy success of the British effort against "living pictures," American WCTU members immediately took heed and began their own campaign in New York and other cities such as Chicago.[74] Department Superintendent Emilie Martin mobilized WCTU members against these displays by playing on their ethnocentrism and reminding them of the origin of living pictures in the Parisian "students' quarters," thus tying living pictures directly to French "filth."[75] The WCTU began its official United States campaign of 1894–95 by distributing copies of Somerset's galvanizing letter for publication in the press. More importantly, in speeches and articles tailored to the American context, WCTU President Frances Willard ignored the artistic and aesthetic questions pursued by Lady Somerset. Explicitly rejecting her elitist argument, Willard presented the WCTU campaign against the living pictures as one that was in harmony with the needs and desires of the working classes:

> Before the crusade closes the people will find out that no class of women so much desires a decrease in their hours of work or an increase in their opportunities of recreation as the white ribboners. This has been testified for years by our sympathetic action toward the labor movement, the eight hours day, the Saturday afternoon closing, the "pleasant Saturday evening," and in other ways too numerous to mention, but we are crippled in our efforts by lack of capital. If rich people who desire to increase the sum of human happiness would help us to establish places of resort for the wage-worker, we would soon demonstrate our appreciation of amusement, harmless fun and a good time generally, in which all classes could meet on terms of mutual enjoyment and good will.[76]

Rejecting the notion that its censorship campaign was an elitist attack on working-class amusements, Willard emphasized the WCTU's promotion of a hierarchy based on a distinction between "pure" and "impure" cultural forms, not on a class-based hierarchy of "high" and "low" culture. Willard carefully positioned the predominantly middle-class WCTU as different from "rich people" and as in a natural alliance with labor for a "pure" popular culture. As proof of her organization's sincerity, Willard reminded her newspaper and lecture hall audiences of the WCTU's support of the Knights of Labor, as well as its early participation in progressive campaigns that united reformers and workers around the issue of improved working conditions for wage-earning women and men.[77] More radically, Willard suggested: "No single change in our social life would be more wholesome and elevating than the *nationalizing of our amusements*. . . . The State ought to have and some day will have a department of recreation, with a Cabinet Minister as its representative, and it should be enforced by law in all our cities and towns that a committee of men and women should pass upon the decency, not to say elevating influence of all public spectacles."[78] Willard's unique call for the "nationalizing" of amusements radically challenged capitalist presumptions regarding the right to free market production of commercial leisure culture. The WCTU's readiness to use the state as an instrument of reform and its support for federal control over culture and leisure activities is compatible with progressives' approval of a strong central government and a national legislative agenda.

Whereas Somerset and Willard disagreed on issues of class and elitism, they agreed on issues of gender. Their central thesis was that living pictures were demeaning to all women. Somerset declared that "no one who sees [the living pictures] but must agree here is the gravest insult and dishonor that has been put upon women in our time; for that at last we have, in letting women make public merchandise of the beauty of their bodies, surpassed even the Oriental standard of female degradation."[79] Somerset's comparison of the living pictures to allegedly degraded "Oriental" standards most likely referred to the threatening sensuality that Westerners associated with the Turkish culture as represented by the "Moorish bath" scenes in *tableaux vivants*.[80] Somerset did not link *paintings* of nudes exhibited in museums with monetary exchange or public display, but she did associate the living pictures with crass commercialism, partially because here the display of women's bodies was real and unmediated. Condemning the public unveiling of the female form, Somerset charged that women performers were, in effect, prostituted by making their bodies available for viewing for the price of a theater ticket.

Similarly, Frances Willard characterized living pictures as "that organized disrespect toward women" and argued that their popularity exemplified "the actual contempt [with] which a certain class of men look upon women."[81] She warned of the threatening power of the male gaze to dehumanize women by treating them as marketable and consumable products. Willard described living pictures as having, "as their cardinal attraction, posed in the middle of the stage, as the focus of ten thousand eyes, a representative of the mother sex so set forth that if a man's own mother, sister, or daughter stood thus revealed to the unpitying protuberant eye of the pleasure lover as he would never again recognize her as having in her veins the same blood that now flows in his."[82] Willard also emphasized the violence inherent in the objectification of women by men: "God never meant that the relations of one-half the human race to the other should be to either one the cause of pain, of shame, of cruelty."[83] The WCTU's campaign against living pictures was presented as a way to redeem women's dignity and humanity.

At the beginning of its campaign, in September of 1894, Willard announced the WCTU's introduction of a bill in the New York legislature restricting "demoralizing" living pictures:

> The white ribbon women of the state of New York have taken advanced
> ground concerning living pictures. The bill that has been introduced by a
> leading senator at their request is *aimed directly at the women who exhibit them-
> selves* in such dress or attitudes as tend to corrupt the morals of the young,
> and at those who employ them for this purpose. The object of the law is stated
> in these words: "To better protect public morals, defend the health and hap-
> piness of youth, prevent the degradation of women and girls, and preserve
> the honor and respect due to woman." It is inevitable that women should
> condemn public amusements that involve a moral taint in their sons and
> daughters.[84]

The wording of the bill defined as a major problem the possible presence of
young people in theater audiences. Appeals to protect the morals of youth
were especially important to WCTU members, who justified much of their
political and public activism by identifying themselves as mothers or potential mothers.[85] WCTU members condemned and tried to suppress deviant
female sexuality through their proposed law, whereby the women performers themselves, as well as their employers, were liable to prosecution. As in
the analogous case of social purity demands that prostitution be illegal, moral
imperatives could not be pushed aside out of concern for their "fallen" sisters.[86] This bill passed the New York legislature in 1896 but was repealed as
unnecessary (the popularity of living pictures had reportedly subsided) and
unworkable within two years.

In other cities, living pictures and billboards that advertised them were
also intermittently repressed through police control. A Chicago newspaper
reported on a successful WCTU campaign against advertisements for living
pictures in its city: "The first fruits of the crusade in which the union has been
engaged were realized . . . when Chief Brennan ordered the police raid which
resulted in the removal of the obscene and indecent signs." His actions were
based "on the strength of a letter addressed to Mayor Hopkins by Mrs. Mary
A. Woodbridge, corresponding secretary of the Woman's Christian Temperance Union." This sympathetic article in the *Chicago Mail*, "Make War on
Nudity. Woman's Christian Temperance Union gives Battle to a Fad. Living
Pictures must go. Committee of Three Members has Seen the Evil in All its
Hideousness," suggested that women must see "the evil" in order to fight
against it. The article did not criticize the women's activism and termed the
tableaux vivants a "fad."[87] In one bizarre instance, the WCTU's *National Minutes* reported that "living pictures cannot be seen in Danbury unless the living pictures wear skirts."[88]

* * *

In contrast to living pictures, where most performances were limited to theaters in American towns and cities, even the most rural area was likely to have a county fair with burlesque dancers. The 1893 Chicago World's Fair introduced "obscene dancing in the Midway Plaisance"—namely, the belly dance and its variants performed by exotic dancers such as "Little Egypt." Anthony Comstock and five women on the World's Fair Committee of 1893 stopped some of the dancing at the Midway: "No earnest effort for God ever fails to do good, as was shown when two white ribboners [WCTU members], Mrs. H. M. Barker, of Dakota, and Mrs. R[ebecca Latimer]. A. Felton, of Georgia, together with three other managers of the Woman's Board, in company with Anthony Comstock, visited the Midway Plaisance, saw some revolting exhibitions, and made complaint to President Davis, who at once had the most conspicuous nuisances removed." The WCTU referred to this partial victory in many of its later attempts to close similar exhibitions at local fairs.[89] Subsequent state and county fairs (as well as smaller street fairs and carnivals) increasingly featured similar dances in their own "Midway" sections, providing many small-town and rural American men with the opportunity to see erotic displays of women's bodies. The *Police Gazette* promoted the sexually titillating belly dancers through articles describing how their "bosoms heaved with tantalizing irregularity." Its descriptions of the dancers' "writhing bodies" were accompanied by illustrations that further emphasized their bare midriffs and legs (see figure 3).[90]

Contrasting burlesque to the ballet, Robert Allen claims that "what would be condemned as depraved if it emerged from the lower social strata is celebrated as art (or, at least, condoned) if its provenance is upper-class." Ballet had indeed won the tolerance of the upper classes by the 1840s or 1850s, but the WCTU does not fit this pattern, for it supported attempts to suppress the ballet as "indecent" entertainment. The organization reprinted articles from Christian journals by religious reformers such as the Reverend Josiah Leeds that condemned the ballet. Leeds asserted that the ballet was "immoral" because the dancers in tights looked nude. The department's middle-class members were unwilling to help elites sustain what they perceived to be a false differentiation between the ballet and other "indecent" theatrical productions such as burlesque dance shows.[91]

The WCTU tried to regulate the midway sections through its strategy of community-based campaigns. Some unions circulated petitions to forbid traveling caravans the right to participate in local fairs and asked "that the fair board consult with the State College of Agriculture and Farm Bureau, requesting that a constructive plan be worked out that would make this aspect of the fair as representative of the county as are its other features."[92]

Figure 3. Left: "Little Egypt and Anita dancing for the senators"; right: "Little Egypt and Anita. Agile and beautiful exponents of the graceful, sensuous Oriental danse du ventre." According to the accompanying article, the "wicked man" who arranged the evening for the senators "can now get any bill passed that he likes." (*Police Gazette,* Dec. 21, 1895)

Members pressured mayors to deny temporary permits or annual licenses to offending promoters, as well as to forbid any billboards advertising "impure" shows.[93] The *Police Gazette* parodied reformers' efforts to ban the show bills by illustrating other advertising techniques, such as having the dancers themselves carry the show bills while visiting factories to lure potential customers, working-class men, to their shows (see figure 4). Finally, respected social groups such as the Elks (some of whom were the husbands and friends of WCTU members) often organized and profited from these fairs, in which case the WCTU relied on peer pressure to discontinue "corrupt shows."[94] WCTU members were most successful at achieving locally based censorship and regulation of cultural forms, anticipating the Supreme Court's 1973 decision basing definitions of "obscenity" on local "community standards."[95]

Figure 4. "Come Early, Old Man. The Lockport, N.Y., authorities would not permit a burlesque company to bill the town, but they got there." (*Police Gazette,* Apr. 9, 1892)

Between its 1894 campaign against living pictures and its 1921 work against burlesque shows, the WCTU moved away from condemnations of the women performers for sexual display (and deviant female sexuality) to a view of the female performers as "victims" of male sexuality. This is a significant shift in understandings of sexuality and the sexual order. It is most likely that the organization changed its interpretations of women's sexuality in response to what it perceived to be an increase in the exploitation of women's sexuality in the burlesque shows. Most importantly, during the first two decades of the twentieth century, the content of these performances had become far more sexually explicit. A 1921 *Union Signal* article entitled "The Show 'For Men Only'" discussed the fact that as burlesque shows proliferated, they became striptease acts where the female dancer often removed all of her costume. Burlesque dances of the 1920s certainly put into a new perspective Frances Willard's 1889 condemnation of the relatively innocent waltz as an "evil . . . dance-delirium"![96] WCTU editors claimed that a written description of the burlesque shows would be "too obscene to be sent lawfully through the United States mails." Implicitly, if the shows were too obscene to write about, then they were too obscene to observe. Unlike the

1894 WCTU-sponsored bill against living pictures, wherein the female participants could be charged as well as the male producers, in this case the organization presented a united, if condescending, front as women. It decried the increased exploitation of the female performers in the shows and pitied them as "the misguided victims of our social order."[97]

Most unfortunate about these burlesque shows, in the opinion of the WCTU's special correspondent, was that young boys as well as grown men were often drawn by the barker's cry, encountering therein ideas and forms of sexual expression and display that often violated social norms and obscenity regulations.[98] More dramatically, the WCTU contended that the shows were: "Of such a nature as to pollute the minds, degrade the morals and endanger the health of those taking part in the orgies, communicating disease to innocent wives and helpless children."[99] WCTU women linked the shows directly to sites of Progressive Era social hygiene reform efforts, such as prostitution and V.D. In this way, the "for men only" tents became not merely sites for the unacceptable scopic act of men viewing an unknown woman's naked body but also directly initiated sexual urges that would end in the men having sex with prostitutes, spreading social diseases to their "innocent wives."[100]

The WCTU's concern with the danger inherent in the male gaze on the female body reinforced its support of regulatory control. In an interesting role reversal, moreover, the WCTU attempted to try to place women in the conventionally male position of judge and viewer. In 1922, WCTU members bid to be "placed on the board of judges" for local beauty contests. As judges, WCTU women could potentially modify the prevailing notions of female beauty. Most important, they could attempt to redirect the male judges' gaze away from the "full outlines" of the women's bodies toward a less eroticized standard of female beauty.[101]

* * *

While the WCTU worked to regulate many specific cultural forms, from paintings and the ballet to living pictures and the burlesque, one particular site runs through these examples: the female body. The WCTU purposefully contributed to the development of regulatory practices around sexuality in advertisements, paintings, and the theater. WCTU reformers intended, of course, to create an ever more inclusive notion of "immorality." Yet, despite their anti-nudity "purity" position, they seem to have inadvertently contributed to the culture's volubility and multiplication of sexuality as well. Recent cultural theorists have suggested that attempts to point to "immorality" in order to suppress it can lead instead to a multiplication of the condemned images.[102] Nudity symbolized to the WCTU a disrespect for and a depoliticization of women that transformed them into the sum total of their physical appearances. Yet female nudity also symbolized a threatening sexuality and eroticism, as well as a new generation's rejection of the Victorian values of female purity in favor of a more heterosocial, eroticized public world of leisure.

A new cultural medium was developed in the late 1890s that became the most important manifestation of this new public world of leisure and commercial culture: moving pictures. Questions about the exposure of women's bodies and the invasive (male) gaze intensified with this new medium. The WCTU's response was, not surprisingly, to call for new and stronger censorship laws. Eventually, the WCTU even tried to sponsor and make its own "pure" movies that would make use of exciting technological developments without sacrificing its emphasis on moral content.

CHAPTER 5

Mothering the Movies

Women Reformers and Popular Culture

The Woman's Christian Temperance Union's movie censorship campaigns reveal a significant aspect of the middle-class response to the development of film in the twentieth century and to other perceived changes in American popular culture. The WCTU waged its battle for movie censorship with the rhetoric of child-saving. Its members fought for federal censorship, promoted and created "educational" films, and strictly controlled their own children's access to movies under the rubric of safety for youths. The organization supported federal regulation in part because it believed that the impact of motion pictures, especially on impressionable children, was too strong to allow the emerging movie industry to remain unregulated.[1] Perceiving a spatial and moral threat to their role as guardians of youths, WCTU members made concerted attempts, from the 1890s through the 1930s, to fight for censorship of motion pictures.[2] The height of WCTU movie censorship campaigns fell between 1925 and 1933, when the great popularity of movies and their increasingly sexualized content led to a broad pro-movie censorship movement led by Christian organizations.

This chapter analyzes the federal movie censorship agenda of the WCTU and evaluates its implementation on the national, state, and local levels. The organization attacked the problem of the proliferation of "impure" films at the point of production, as well as just prior to consumption. Charting youths' overwhelming movie attendance rates, WCTU activists argued that youths were in greater danger of becoming "addicted" to watching movies than they were of becoming addicted to alcohol. Like Progressive educators, the WCTU concluded that movies now served as "the greatest factor in the education of youth."[3] The union's complaints against movies had social power inasmuch as they represented a coherent synopsis of public fears concerning the "evils" of film. This critique gained the support of many Americans at key moments of crisis for the industry, finally forcing it to agree to stricter self-censorship in 1934. Its desire to offer a "pure" version of American culture to replace the "impure" made the WCTU's dual goals quite complementary. It advocated censorship on the one hand, and the promotion of educational and "pure" movies for youths on the other.

In the late 1890s, one of the first popular moving pictures made for the kinetoscope was a representation of a boxing match between the fighters James Corbett and Bob Fitzsimmons. Boxing films provided the organization with both a metaphor and an opportunity to point to movies as a source of social evils. Kinetoscopes and early motion pictures often featured prizefights, events that would otherwise have been inaccessible to most children. The WCTU opposed prizefighting as a sport that encouraged male brutality and illegal betting, incited violence in its audience, and worse, resulted in an "ungovernable spirit" in youths. Film historian Miriam Hansen suggests other reasons why boxing films represented a new type of transgression and elicited calls for censorship. Hansen points to the erotics of spectatorship in these films, where exposed male bodies were available to women's independent gaze.[4] (Early films in nickelodeons were also part of a more general reconfiguration of public space into heterosocial arenas where men and women sat together in these new movie theaters.) One of the first historians of film, writing in 1925, lamented that the films of boxing matches doomed early motion pictures to be stereotyped as "low-brow, and entertainment of the great unwashed commonality." Movies could thereby be subjected to middle-class reformers' protests and legislative regulation on the grounds of protecting youths.[5]

The Department of Purity in Literature and Art did, in fact, quickly single out boxing films for censure and called for regulation. President Frances Willard sent out an appeal to all WCTU state presidents asking them to work for laws against prizefight movies. Several states successfully passed such laws in the late 1890s, but most state legislatures and local officials remained unmoved until prizefights threatened to increase racial tensions in the United States.[6] Specifically, in the famous 1910 Johnson-Jeffries fight in Reno, Nevada, African-American boxer Jack Johnson beat the "Great White Hope," heavy-weight champion Jim Jeffries. Violence occurred as African-Americans celebrated and white Americans vented their anger and took revenge. The WCTU analyzed the riots as a class as well as a race issue. Citing "unwonted elation among the more ignorant negroes" as the cause of the violence by "the lower element of the white people," it immediately reissued a call to Congress to prohibit films of prizefights as inciters of race riots.[7] Officials in at least nine states quickly barred prizefight films, including the governors of Maryland, Montana, Georgia, and New Jersey and the mayors of Cleveland, Ohio, and Salt Lake City, Utah.[8] Further agitation by southern legislators in favor of a law prohibiting prizefight films ensured the passage of a federal bill in 1912.[9] The continued popularity of prizefights suggests that these laws did not effectively halt the distribution of prizefight films, but the laws do indicate that they were not received by either the public or legislators with complacency.

The problems encountered with prizefight films on kinetoscopes were magnified, or so it seemed, by motion pictures projected onto large screens in "nickelodeons."[10] News of the moving picture theaters and their wares reached middle-class reformers early; the Woman's Christian Temperance Union published articles about the need to reform the five-cent theaters in 1906, only one year after they opened. Until about 1910, movie theaters were welcomed by some hopeful reformers who believed that local movie theaters could vanquish the neighborhood saloons.[11] The General Federation of Women's Clubs, for instance, claimed that saloons "have found the competition of the motion picture a more serious foe than the W.C.T.U. or any anti-saloon or anti-cigarette league." Yet the WCTU, not surprisingly, rejected this view of commercial movies, pointing instead to their potential to corrupt youths as surely as alcohol would.[12]

The WCTU's first published condemnation of movie content demonstrates the continuity of its fundamental concern for the morality of all cultural productions, from literature and art to the new motion pictures.[13] A *Union Signal* editorial of 1906 emphasized the "sensational" aspects of movies that undermined traditional values: "Natural modesty receives its first shock. Crime is made 'interesting,' 'romantic,' 'exciting,'—everything but criminal. Deformities of the human frame are made laughable. Age is represented as a target for youthful scorn and laughter."[14] The focus on crime and immodesty was a consistent part of the WCTU's definition of "impure" cultural forms. Observations regarding ageism were specific to the new genre and highlight the appeal of movies to youths; it is possible, however, that the popular appeal of slapstick humor owed more to the immigrant audience's lack of competence in English.[15]

The Department of Purity in Literature and Art noted in 1907 a disturbing increase in the number of children in movie theater audiences, as well as unwelcome new theater locations.[16] *Union Signal* editors observed that increasing numbers of young girls went to the movies right after school and that wage-earning girls came when they got off work; boys ("hoodlums") often frequented the theaters in the evening as well. Citing the importance of control over children's activities, the editors solemnly declared that "eternal parental vigilance is the price of unsullied young womanhood and manhood."[17] Not only were children increasingly attending the movies, but "from the downtown districts and cheaper business streets, these nuisances are invading the better class residence portions of the city."[18]

WCTU activists often entered local campaigns for movie regulation using rhetoric consistent with Progressive educators' and social scientists' commitment to reforming children's health and hygiene. This focus on popular "progressive" issues such as health and safety rather than morals provided yet another argument in favor of regulation. The issue of health and safety was a serious one in the early nickelodeon years; historian Douglas Gomery concludes that theaters were indeed dangerous places, especially because of the risk of fire.[19] Concern for the physical safety of movie viewers, particularly children, locates the WCTU and like-minded reformers squarely within Progressivism. Some early state laws regulating movies focused specifically on youths because, as labor protection laws of the era exemplify, it was easier for the courts to accept regulations based on protecting children or women, thereby excluding adult men from consideration. By 1909, for example, New York and New Jersey had passed laws making it illegal "to admit to a kinetoscope or moving picture performance or to any place of entertainment injurious to *health or morals,* any child under the age of 16 years, unless accompanied by parent or guardian."[20] As late as 1939, the New York director focused on health-related issues, contending that children's physical health could be harmed by watching long programs that included previews, two feature films, and news reels: "Most theater exhibitors would like nothing better than to return entirely to the showing of single bills. Long hours in a movie are detrimental to the health of children, so from a standpoint of health your state director urges you to work for single bill features."[21]

While arguing for the legal censorship of movies, WCTU members became critics and developed "theories" of how children, in particular, respond to film. Various rationales for censorship appeared in WCTU publications. Subjects appropriate for adults and cultivated people might be "obscene" when seen by youths or the uncultivated and should thus be banned altogether. Any layperson, moreover, had the ability and responsibility to judge all movies as either "moral" or "immoral." Alternatively, the department focused on the issue of movie "realism" and praised any serious movie dramas that demonstrated moral lessons. Movie plots derived from respectable novels or from the Bible were recommended as superior to "unrealistic" Westerns, comedies, or gangster movies with sensational action, crime, or sexually titillating themes. Portrayals of urban crime could be praised by the

WCTU, however, if they "documented" and condemned the evils and dangers of alcohol use. Drunkenness, seduction, or even violence might be acceptably portrayed in motion pictures in order to teach youths the danger of such activities, as long as the terrible fates of wayward characters were consistently emphasized throughout. In the mid-1930s, the WCTU produced its own films, with titles such as *The Beneficent Reprobate*, that purposefully showed the worst results of drinking and smoking in order to dissuade people from engaging in these activities.

For the WCTU, the power of film resided in its status as a visual medium that made people, especially children, vulnerable to suggestion. Watching movies could produce in children "unwonted elation" and an "ungovernable spirit."[22] The WCTU reported in 1910 that a child arrested on burglary and assault charges told a judge that he had learned how to break into homes from watching the movies and that a boy copied a "self-murder" by gas asphyxiation that he had seen at a motion picture show.[23] The judge's account suggests that the WCTU's discussion of the impact of movies on youths' behavior was part of a larger discourse of social science, subscribed to by juvenile court judges as well as evangelical laywomen.

WCTU directors cited studies by social scientists and reformers to demonstrate that the movie industry had consolidated its monopolistic power and gained large, passive audiences full of youths. "The Motion Picture houses of this Country," they insisted, "are frequented daily by great numbers of people, including boys and girls of whom it has been estimated 75% are under twenty-four years of age."[24] They believed that in the hands of the consolidated movie industry a medium with much positive educational potential was instead teaching the evils of cultural and moral relativism, thereby alienating youths from the older, Victorian generation. "You are disgusted and stay away from the movies," they warned, "but your children and grand-children are becoming perhaps oblivious to the degrading tendencies of the movies and cease to distinguish good from evil."[25] At best, movies were creating an amoral, if not wholly immoral, rising generation. State Motion Picture Department reports asked suggestively, "to what extent are 'movies' responsible for the 'crime wave' and the wet political situation?"[26] Through the 1930s, WCTU department directors cited increasing "evidence" of the movies' responsibility for inducing youths to anti-social behavior, such as six "well authenticated cases of crime, misdemeanor or delinquency due to influence of motion pictures," and "four runaway marriages resulting from the influence of motion pictures."[27] To women moral reformers, the evidence suggested a significant loss of maternal control over their children's behavior.

Apart from a general examination of WCTU theories about the impact of movies, an extensive analysis of the WCTU's negative response to any particular film is made difficult by the fact that its condemnations were usually so broad and inclusive that specific titles were rarely mentioned. The 1917 New York annual report, therefore, provides us with uncharacteristically specific information regarding the movies it both approved and opposed: "Appreciative letters [were] sent to the Worlds' Film Company commenting on clean, wholesome pictures shown, especially, 'The Man Who Taught.' Protested against the film, 'Intolerance,' and other vulgar films. . . . Mrs. Lindsay, Mrs. Dennison and others of the county [Albany] called up the mayor and chief of police and protested against the exhibition of 'Twilight Sleep,' in the actual birth of a child. This latter part was omitted."[28] In the case of the film *Twilight Sleep,* a WCTU director atypically took the time to specify that the reason for the union's protest was a relatively graphic portrayal of childbirth. The question of realism thus re-emerged, as WCTU members implicitly made distinctions between "good" realism and "bad"; the latter included such things as glorification of urban crime and prostitution and the invasion of women's privacy in childbirth. Another account described the nature of the cuts made in the offensive scene in order to satisfy the WCTU: " 'Twilight Sleep' was advertised greatly but owing to strong opposition from county union instead of an actual birth being shown with nurse and doctor in attendance, only the faces of two mothers were shown, one in quiet sleep, the other showing traces of suffering."[29] WCTU members interpreted the movie scene as disrespect toward the sanctity of motherhood and demanded that it be eliminated. Respect for women's purity as mothers could be jeopardized by a voyeuristic ability of men and youths to watch an honored and private female act. Its protests against *Twilight Sleep* were based on scenes it interpreted as disruptive of social conventions. WCTU complaints against D. W. Griffith's *Intolerance* owed less to scenes of decadence than to his belittling and critical portrayal of female social purity reformers (so similar to WCTU members). Within the film, the interference of women reformers destroys the life of a woman and her child.[30]

Historians who discuss Progressive Era rhetoric about the morality of movies assert that reformers' emphasis on youths masked their prejudice against immigrants who entered the United States at an unprecedented rate in the early twentieth century. Larry May, for instance, suggests that Progressive reformers wanted to manage and control immigrants' introduction to American culture, while simultaneously halting a perceived "revolution" in morality. Robert Sklar contends that the pro-censorship "moralists" (as he deridingly refers to them) focused on youths as a way to disguise their class-based agenda.[31] The WCTU's regulatory stance was, indeed, partially motivated by its desire to assist immigrant youths in becoming law-abiding citizens. In this context the WCTU framed its requests for pro-censorship activism in terms of citizenship. "You are asked to help mobilize public sentiment," a Kentucky report beseeched, "until all motion pictures will reflect a wholesome attitude toward life and will help to make patriotic citizens instead of creating false ideals and helping to nullify respect for law and order."[32] This aspect of the WCTU's interest in youths as citizens can be tied to class-based fears of immigrants who often symbolically represented the poorest and most alien of the urban classes.[33]

Yet the WCTU's intentions were more complex. In focusing upon youth, the WCTU was putting on its traditional maternal mantle as protector of children, displaying a tangle of gender, ethnic, and class concerns and was legitimizing women's participation in the political public sphere. WCTU activists identified their movie censorship goals as the salvation of youths and referred to their censorship efforts as campaigns to " 'mother the movies.' "[34] In fact, some local unions actually targeted mothers by "sending out 5,800 pages of motion picture literature to seven hundred new mothers."[35] Most unions publicized statistics regarding children's high movie attendance patterns to dramatize the urgent need for all women (as nurturers and mothers) to take action. Censorship demands appeared as part of women's unselfish desire to help children, not themselves, yet the WCTU's focus on youths was also an integral part of its justification of women's activism in politics.

The WCTU's pro-movie censorship political style was a mix of local action and calls for state and national regulation. At the local level, WCTU members relied upon peer pressure and legislation to regulate films. Agreeing upon the dangers of movies to youths, the WCTU's Department of Purity in Literature and Art organized a series of campaigns designed to convince local theater managers to show better movies, to close on Sundays, and to schedule special children's matinees. The department often targeted theater managers, since they were most vulnerable to community pressure. The WCTU recognized that even though exhibitors were locked into nationwide movie distribution contracts, they could be flexible regarding what types of movies they showed during those hours and days when the largest numbers of children attended the movies: "Isn't it time to demand of local theater managers that pictures shown on Friday nights and Saturday afternoons be chosen carefully? A committee representing the General Federation of Women's Clubs, and similar organizations found that of 800 feature pictures only 39 were fit for children to see, and only 80 fit for any person under twenty to see."[36] Agreeing that only a small number of Hollywood films were suitable for children's viewing, the General Federation of Women's Clubs and the WCTU, among others, attempted to regulate more closely children's access to commercial leisure activities. In New York, the WCTU noted that, after protesting, it "received fine cooperation from local manager in showing better pictures for the children's matinees."[37]

WCTU members also influenced town and municipal officials and elections. Like their earlier work against plays and living picture expositions, locally based movie censorship attempts often involved investigations of "doubtful" movies followed by complaints to local authorities, such as the chief of police or the mayor.[38] Local union members joined with churches to campaign for restrictions on movies by distributing hand bills and attending town and city council meetings en masse in attempts to influence legislators and the community and win these elections.[39] For instance, WCTU records show that as the result of special elections, Sunday movies were forbidden in various communities in North Dakota, New Jersey, Ohio, Florida, Illinois, and Pennsylvania in the late 1920s and early 1930s.[40]

From 1914 through the 1930s, the state and local WCTUs heeded the national union's call for federal regulation of motion pictures and put tremendous energy into lobbying national congressmen and senators for a series of laws ranging from restrictions on block booking to bills demanding full federal movie censorship. Most historical attention on the involvement of women's reform groups in motion picture censorship debates has focused to date on the General Federation of Women's Clubs. In particular, the federation's early cooperation with the movie industry for "better films" and then its reversal, by 1918, in favor of state censorship has been examined.[41] There has been less attention to other women's organizations, including the WCTU, that favored national movie censorship from the start and joined with religious and moral reform groups to call for strict regulation. WCTU departmental reports indicate that its national campaigns often took priority over campaigns for local or state censorship: "This department has made its major work along legislative lines, principally flooding the United States legislators from California with resolutions and through them urging both houses of Congress to support the Motion Picture bills H.R. 2999, H.R. 4757 by Culkin and H.R. 6472 by Pettingill and later when introduced in the Senate, S-3012 by Neely."[42] A 1938 comment by the New Jersey WCTU points to a serious problem with state and local regulations—they were often ignored and unenforced: "Much would be accomplished if the state law which forbids children under twelve years of age unattended by an older person [to] be admitted to the motion picture theatre, was obeyed."[43] Motion picture censorship at the federal level was never achieved, but the WCTU's persistent dedication to such a difficult national campaign makes sense in the context of its participation in other national legislative battles. One director sanguinely explained, "that is the way we gained the 18th and 19th amendments."[44] The department argued that in light of the large number of movies produced and distributed each year, national censorship would be most efficient.

The WCTU's Department of Purity in Literature and Art supported the first proposed federal movie censorship law, the Smith-Hughes Picture Censorship Bill of 1914, in order to affirm its interest in maintaining children's good morals. Written by Reverend Wilbur Crafts of the International Reform Bureau, this bill mandated the creation of a Federal Motion Picture Council as a part of the Bureau of Education, "whose duty it will be to censor all films, endorsing the good and condemning those which come under the specifications of what is 'obscene, indecent, immoral, inhuman, or those that depict a bull-fight, or a prize-fight, or that will corrupt or impair the morals of children or incite to crime.'"[45] The department was confident that educators, appointed as censors, would have a moral reform agenda similar to its own and that the above list of taboo subjects—including anything "inhuman"—was broad enough to improve the movies. The WCTU urged its members, as well as other reform and religious organizations, to endorse the bill by sending letters, telegrams, resolutions, and petitions to Washington.[46] Four months after their initial calls for action, however, union leaders reported that "very few petitions" had been received in Congress and that the bill would probably be indefinitely held up in the House Committee on Education.[47] At this early stage, it seems, the WCTU could not successfully rally its large membership to the movie censorship cause, even with a technique—petitioning—at which it had become so adept. The extraordinary effort WCTU members were giving at that time to woman suffrage and the passage of national prohibition diverted their attention from the movie issue, on which, they judged, it would take years of further public agitation to create a consensus.[48]

The WCTU interpreted as a victory for children the Supreme Court's first ruling on censorship and motion pictures in 1915. The judges decided that movie censorship was not in violation of the First or Fourteenth Amendments of the Constitution because movies were not art but were merely commercial products made for profit and open to regulation as "a business pure and simple." This ruling was important because it legitimized prior restraint, allowing a movie to be evaluated by a governmental agency or representatives before it was seen by the public.[49] Subsequent WCTU reports reiterated and supported the Court's decision: "[Movie producers'] goal—self stated, is 'profit.' 'Does It Pay' is their slogan. All is grist that comes to their mill—children, youth, foreigners who are trying to learn the meaning of Christian civilization, as well as the thronging adults who are ever looking for the latest thrill." (The WCTU's image of the movie producers as obsessed with profit may have been part of a veiled anti-Semitism that was sometimes directed at the movie industry.[50]) The movie "problem" was compounded by the perceived commercial corruption of the magnates and the movie industry system. The movie industry's status as a money-making business was used to suggest that it had no regard for the moral ramifications of its products. Ironically, this attack on the profit motive constituted a critique of capitalism that came from within the very middle classes that promoted it.

Agitation for federal regulation of the movie industry gained momentum in the early 1920s, after World War I had ended and Prohibition and woman suffrage had been achieved. A series of scandals over the dissipated life styles of famous actors and actresses—accompanied by a noticeable proliferation of "sex pictures"—helped precipitate the first of two major crises for the movie industry. A noticeable decrease in middle-class movie attendance and more calls from the public for national movie censorship forced a response from the movie industry. In 1922, the Motion Picture Producers and Distributors Association (MPPDA) hired the former Postmaster General Will Hays to oversee the upgrading of morals in the movies.[51] Reform groups such as the WCTU, the General Federation of Women's Clubs, and the National Congress of Parents and Teachers were initially optimistic that Hays would stand by his pledge to make "progress in 'ESTABLISHING AND MAINTAINING THE HIGHEST POSSIBLE MORAL AND ARTISTIC STANDARD OF MOTION PICTURE PRODUCTION.'"[52] Indeed, fearing the real possibility of federal censorship, movie producers temporarily improved the "purity" of the images placed before movie viewers. When movie theaters tried to show films starring Fatty Arbuckle in 1923 (after he was barely acquitted on a murder charge), the WCTU organized local petition drives against them. WCTU activists subsequently stated, "no law is necessary to keep Fatty Arbuckle's figure off the screen. Public sentiment has done that." The department announced: "The drinking pictures are very rarely seen now, because the public demands a change, and the theatre manager will give the people what they want. The loose, sensual picture now is not tolerated, and the clean, bright picture is becoming more and more in demand. If a picture is not what it should be, a word to the Mayor is usually sufficient, and as a rule, the theatre manager is willing to co-operate." This report emphasized the department's success at gaining the cooperation of local officials and theater managers, so that even if movies were not adequately censored at the source of production, "clean" pictures might be exhibited in local communities. Nevertheless, the WCTU generally downplayed the industry measures as temporary and noncompulsory and insisted, "we feel impressed with the need of a Federal law for the control of the motion picture business of the whole country."[53]

While they worked toward the ultimate goal of federal regulation, WCTU members and their pro-censorship allies continued to lobby hard for the creation of state and local censorship boards. In a strategy of building the organization and its political strength from the bottom up, WCTU members believed that state and local movie censorship laws, like local dry laws, served as a first step toward their ultimate goal of federal censorship just as they had for constitutional prohibition. Citizen's boards of censors, the most common regulatory alternative to federal censorship, were eventually implemented in the states of Kansas, Maryland, New York, Ohio, Pennsylvania, and Virginia and in approximately one hundred cities including Chicago, Memphis, Detroit, Denver, and Pasadena.[54] State censorship boards could remove drinking scenes or scenes of female seminudity and yet pass the film as a whole, giving the censors, in effect, a line-item veto over movie content.[55] Overall, state-controlled censorship was relatively effective because the industry made the required deletions and then—in an effort to cut costs—distributed the expurgated version of the film to the entire distribution region that included the censoring state.[56] The WCTU considered the regulatory boards to be allies, and its relations with both state and local censors were quite good. Indeed, WCTU state reports contain many examples of cooperation for "clean pictures" and of collaborative campaigns for censorship laws.[57] In Colorado, Pennsylvania, and Kansas, the state unions reported cooperation with censors to eliminate "drinking scenes."[58] When the movie industry cleverly introduced a bill to "exempt 'talkies' from censorship" in Pennsylvania, the WCTU and the State Board of Censors fought together to save the state's censorship system. Obviously, neither could accept the industry-proposed bill that "would practically have destroyed all of our Pennsylvania censorship and flooded the State with rankly immoral pictures."[59]

* * *

The National WCTU's increasing belief that movies had become the central cultural influence for youths prompted it in 1925 to officially rename its pro-censorship department. That year, its name became the "Motion Picture Department" in order to emphasize its ongoing fight for movie censorship laws. This renaming reflected the department's steady shift of focus away from concern with books and paintings and toward movie censorship efforts. Harriet Pritchard explained that the new name did not indicate an altogether new focus. The Department of Purity in Literature and Art had not only supported movie censorship, it had worked to produce and support acceptable "pure" temperance movies since 1914: "We believe the respectable shows [anti-alcohol and other educational movies in schools] will counteract the desire in the hearts of the children for the sensational and dangerous pictures that are now being presented to them in the public movies. It is ten years since we made arrangements to have moving pictures used, knowing that they would be helpful in Scientific Temperance Instruction."[60] Although local and state unions continued to protest against "immoral" burlesque shows or "bad" magazines, the national work of the former department had decreased by the late 1920s.[61]

The final 1925 report of the national Department of Purity in Literature and Art, written by Director Harriet Pritchard, emphasized the WCTU's growing conviction that "the movies constitute much of the education of many." She offered a dramatic vision of the power of movies over youths that not only justified but demanded the creation of a motion picture department: "Shall this [movie industry] education produce graduates of the type of the 14 year-old girl murderers, of the Leopold-Loeb super-intellectuals criminal breed, of the flapper who is a potential mother and may reproduce more of the same, of the foreigner, the fool and the traitor who consider the 18th Amendment a joke and laugh at the Stars and Stripes?" These rhetorical questions affirmed that much was at stake in the WCTU's support for movie censorship. Indeed, the regulation of literature and art, and even of popular journalism, seemed far less important than that of motion pictures, for "an evil incident in a newspaper does not have, perhaps, one-tenth the bad influence upon human conduct as would ensue if the same story were depicted in motion pictures."[62] Equally important, after the passage of Prohibition, movie censorship came to be seen by WCTU leaders as a cause that might provide the national organization with a new and broader justification for its existence.

The new motion picture department's national work began with its leaders testifying to Congress about self-regulation by the movie industry. The national department director, Maude Aldrich, reported that she and Mary Caldwell, the state director for Tennessee, attended the 1926 hearings on federal regulation held by the House Committee on Education where Caldwell "gave a very convincing testimony as to her efforts to co-operate along lines suggested by the Motion Picture Industry, and of her failure to get better pictures, or to check the showing of the worst ones by the co-operation."[63] The WCTU observed that the movie industry's power was now far greater, aided by reformers' patient attempts at cooperation: "During these years in which the public has cooperated with the Motion Picture Industry and awaited reform from within, the solidarity of the Industry and its wealth and influence have increased many hundred fold and the situation is far more serious and difficult than ever before."[64] In the early 1900s, prior to the development of the Hollywood industry, stars, and feature-length films, the movie producers had fought among themselves for greater power. By the late 1920s (the period of transition from silent to sound), the movie industry had become an interlocked oligopoly with a star system. As a unified organization, the Motion Picture Producers and Distributors Association effectively fought against censorship and could ensure that no major movie companies would sign a resolution in favor of federal censorship, as some had done as recently as 1916. WCTU directors in 1916 had publicized an unusual brief filed in favor of federal censorship by a few prominent film companies, including the Paramount and Equitable Motion Picture Corporations, to prove that "respectable" members of the movie industry had similar regulatory goals. Not surprisingly, most other film producers did not support censorship.[65]

As the WCTU's voice on this issue, National Director Maude Aldrich became a nationally visible pro-censorship leader. This visibility gained her positions as a lecturer for and member of the board of directors of the Federal Motion Picture Council in America, an organization instrumental in working for censorship both nationally and internationally.[66] Leadership roles in both organizations put Aldrich in a strong position to publicize the WCTU's stance in favor of federal movie censorship. In 1926, for instance, Aldrich gave "some 300 addresses," more than five per week, to various organizations.[67] She also published her views in periodicals such as the *National Grange Magazine, Woman's Missionary Friend,* and *Twentieth Century Progress,* as well as the *Union Signal.*[68] Hoping for overlapping membership and strong support for their pro-censorship agenda, WCTU state unions encouraged their members to join the Federal Motion Picture Council: "The fee is one dollar. May we show our interest in this great work by our generous contributions?"[69]

The Department of Motion Pictures organized its pro-censorship fight around an attack on the motion picture industry's purported predominance in American popular culture, in effect, its cultural hegemony. The department's campaign included a series of articles by Aldrich in the *Union Signal* that addressed such issues as "What the People Want," "What the Exhibitor Wants," "Moral Standards of Motion Pictures," and "Endorsing Motion Pictures." Each article explained a different aspect of the industry's increasing control of motion pictures, such as the block booking and blind selling of twelve to fifteen films at a time to local exhibitors. This practice compelled exhibitors to order several movies together without a chance to preview them or send one back, thereby making difficult local censorship of any particular film.[70] The *Union Signal* educated members about the movie industry, stressing its stronghold on both distributors and the public: "About 90 per cent of the producers and practically all of the distributors are organized into one gigantic monopoly."[71] Aldrich also explained that because the Motion

Picture Producers and Distributors Association kept prices significantly higher for ordering individual films, local distributors often could not afford to show films separately.[72] This practice particularly hampered potential cooperation between sympathetic local distributors and pro-censorship groups.[73] WCTU activists stressed that federal censorship laws were imperative because the motion picture industry was now "a great trust" that had to be controlled centrally to ensure effective regulation in the public interest. Desiring the government to oversee and participate in the production of culture, the department argued that "only the United States is bigger than the motion picture industry, therefore we must have federal control of production of motion pictures according to a high moral standard—NOT censorship after production."[74] By distributing concrete information about the economic power of the movie industry, Aldrich galvanized WCTU members to join in the motion picture department's crusade.

The movie industry's Hays Office became adept at deflecting reformers' critiques by promising with great fanfare to "clean up the industry." These announcements assured many reformers and the larger public that their protests were making an impact.[75] The Hays Office carefully maneuvered to diffuse criticism. In response to the WCTU's protests during Prohibition against films that showed people drinking with impunity, it issued—and widely publicized—guidelines requiring the industry to "make Certain that into no picture there be allowed to enter any 'shot' of drinking scenes, manufacture, or undue effects of liquor." Hays claimed that the movie industry was determined not to "promote the slightest disrespect for any law."[76] Although these guidelines were not systematically observed, the Hays Office's apparent acceptance of them served in the short term to dissipate the force of the WCTU's complaints. In attempts at co-optation, the motion picture industry learned how to foil its external enemies, such as pro-censorship foes, by seeming to meet some of their objections. Indeed, hiring Will Hays was a brilliant public relations move by the movie industry rather than a real commitment to the reform of the moral content of motion pictures.

A 1928 article submitted to the *Union Signal* by Jason Joy, industrial relations director for the Association of Motion Picture Producers, illustrates the industry's public relations maneuvers.[77] Joy's article, entitled "How Women Can Help for Better Films," began with a flattering statement about how the industry was "eager" for the WCTU's opinion and dependent on its support. Next, he presented WCTU members with a "plan of co-operation." This plan mimicked the industry-approved National Committee for Better Films' strategy of 1916–20 (sponsored by the National Board of Review of Motion Pictures); the plan called for the WCTU to publicize those films it approved of, while remaining silent about those films of which it disapproved.[78] Joy took the opportunity to chide WCTU activists' practice of making vocal protests against particular films: "Therein lies the greatest obstacle to successful club work with motion pictures—this eternal looking for flaws."[79] Whereas other women's groups affiliated with the Committee for Better Films had refrained from fighting for local censorship, focusing instead on inducing exhibitors *voluntarily* to schedule proper movies for children, the WCTU had repeatedly forced the issue into the legal and political spheres by fighting for regulatory laws.

The national WCTU responded sardonically to Joy's letter: "This would, indeed, be a most excellent cooperation in their own interest, for if we will advertise the good pictures they will advertise the bad ones and in this way get the largest possible gate-receipts from both."[80] Explaining that since its members were particularly interested in helping "neglected" children "who most need protection from undesirable films and . . . are the ones who receive the least protection through indorsed [*sic*] lists of films," the utility of such endorsements was limited.[81] Endorsed lists would only be read by responsible parents and so would not help those children who attended movies without guidance; censorship before distribution was necessary. In spite of Joy's attempts, legal censorship remained the national WCTU's goal.

Remaining unconvinced of the virtues of the movie industry, department officials claimed that, as the public waited patiently for self-regulation, the industry had produced "hundreds of the most artistic underworld films which the mind of man can devise."[82] By negatively characterizing Hollywood productions as representing the "artistic underworld," they obliquely identified the movie industry with a drug culture, as well as with a bohemian culture that ostensibly subverted America's moral and aesthetic standards through an obsession with sensuality, an overexposure of the female form, and a reliance on romantic plots that included adultery. Hollywood producers were charged with manipulating young audiences into a dependency on the cheap thrills of films: "Low standards of life and conduct and excessive dependence upon thrill tend to empty a human life and the emptier a life is the more dependent it is upon stimuli from without." In criticizing unregulated movies of the 1920s, the WCTU characterized motion picture viewers as dependent, soulless addicts, devoid of any true aesthetic sensibility, and movies themselves as suppliers of empty thrills rather than of "pure" ideals.[83] This image of the viewer as addict was common among progressive academics and reformers. The WCTU took for granted, however, that its own members would not become addicts; they could objectively view and then critique any movie without suffering from its otherwise harmful effects.

* * *

The surviving state annual reports allow us to see more precisely how the department's national goals and resolutions translated into state and local work.[84] Records of union activities at the state level indicate that the decentralized, localized structure of the WCTU encouraged local independence. Significantly, it appears that some renegade state unions actually supported the movie industry and de-emphasized or ignored the national organization's calls for federal censorship. Perhaps not surprisingly, movie industry representative Jason Joy encountered the least resistance from the Southern California Motion Picture Department director, Elizabeth Ussher. In her department's campaign literature, Ussher identified herself as a partner with the industry's chief public relations representative: "Col. Jason Joy and your director [Ussher] have worked *hand in hand* to carry out the wishes of the people. They are willing to hear from you, so please make the most of your opportunity for Better Films. Our slogan is as forceful as ever: 'Boost the best and ignore the rest;' otherwise you will fail to help us 'Make the best pictures pay the best.'"[85] Located in the heart of movie production territory, Ussher adopted as her department's goal a plan that seemed more fair, or "even," than censorship. Her state's department would reward the industry for producing "good" movies by increasing its profits on those films through greater attendance by WCTU families and supporters. This is precisely the technique that the national department ridiculed when it was proposed by Jason Joy. Ussher celebrated Hollywood's twentieth anniversary (in 1930) and then announced: "A questionnaire has been arranged for you that you may air your views on every film you see. Suggestions have been asked for, approval or otherwise to the films you see, and if you co-operate with your director, clean pictures are bound to result."[86] A questionnaire approved by the movie industry was not, of course, the preferred regulatory technique of the national Department of Motion Pictures. However, there was never any apparent condemnation by national WCTU leaders of southern California's censorship efforts. This suggests their willingness to allow states to fight for "purity" from a variety of perspectives, as well as their inability to control the agendas of those state departments with independent-minded leaders.

At least one other state director urged WCTU members to work toward the moderate program of "boost the best, ignore the rest." Jessie Leonard, a professional journalist and leader of the Motion Picture Department of Massachusetts, reported that as a member of the National Editorial Association, she had been invited to enter a script-writing contest:

Carl Laemmle, president of Universal City, sent the offer of a prize of five thousand dollars. His movie must have ten episodes, and must be written by at least ten members. The fortunate ones whose episodes are accepted are offered the opportunity of acting in them at Universal City, when the National Editorial Association meets next May in Los Angeles. Naturally all of Hollywood will be thrown open to the convention. Mr. Leonard and I are already working on our scenarios and trust we may be winners; you may be sure that liquor scenes are to be taboo in our story.[87]

Laemmle's offer was intended to interest the print media in the movie industry; if Laemmle involved as many of them as possible as contestants and as winners (ten writers, ten episodes), he might be able to have their sympathy when they reported stories of reformers' censorship attempts or when they wrote reviews of specific movies. Writing and acting in movies was a pleasing notion to Jessie Leonard; her mention of forbidding "liquor scenes" seems to be an afterthought. Leonard explicitly acknowledged that there were differences between the stated goals of the national department and the priorities that she had chosen for her state's department: "National stresses: 1, Federal regulation for motion pictures; 2, *New members* because interested in this subject and desiring to better the movies. Massachusetts stresses: 3, Constructive interest in motion pictures to help secure 'Better Pictures for Better People,' especially let us contend for morality, law observance and right ideals."[88] Leonard identified movie censorship legislation as part of a national WCTU strategy to increase membership by highlighting this popular reform issue of the 1920s and 1930s, but she rejected those goals for her own state.[89] In light of the scathing denunciations of the movie industry coming from the majority of WCTU movie department directors and members, Ussher's and Leonard's unique state agendas provide examples of both the success of Motion Picture Producers and Distributors Association's appeal and of the possibilities for the independence of state and local unions from the national WCTU's official agenda. Most unions, it should be emphasized, embraced the national agenda and worked for federal movie censorship laws.

* * *

The national WCTU's fight for the safety and purity of the child viewer was carried on at an international level, as well. The WCTU's commitment to international reform more generally first began in the early 1880s when it established the World's WCTU to spread the evangelical temperance movement. It was also intended to promote abroad other social and political reform issues such as women's rights and social purity. The World's WCTU sent emissaries to create new unions in countries as diverse as Australia and

Japan; these representatives functioned as both traveling Christian missionaries and as WCTU organizers.[90] As Christian women, union members gave
great import to evangelical proselytizing and fought against cultural productions that might present a competing, negative image of the United States
to people in other countries.

The WCTU was prompted to expand its movie censorship campaign to
other countries by the fact that by the 1920s, the United States produced "85
per cent of the pictures shown around the world."[91] Noting that complaints
about American movies had been heard "in the Orient," Mexico, Canada,
and Europe, the organization called for regulation of all films for international commerce.[92] The WCTU's negative view of the American domination of
the global film market is also linked to its advocacy of pacifism. It condemned
films that made war seem exciting to young people, especially after the horrors of World War I. WCTU reformers characterized American movies as
"one of the greatest obstacles to World Peace, inasmuch as they create international misunderstanding."[93] The WCTU established a Peace and Arbitration Department after World War I and, like many other women's groups,
believed in the importance of international alliances in preventing another
war. In the 1930s, the department protested against newsreels and feature-
length films with jingoistic themes: "By inculcating the war spirit through
news reel episodes which glamorize the use of military force as the solution
of international problems and through numerous feature pictures which
make war seem a glorious adventure, the screen continues to present war
as an honorable phase of present-day life."[94] Those forms of popular culture
that made war seem exciting to young people were consistently condemned.
(During both world wars, the WCTU discarded its peace rhetoric in favor
of patriotism and work for soldiers on the front.)[95]

In 1926, New York's director of motion pictures, Helen A. Miller, explicitly warned her colleagues about the impact of American movies on colonialism and imperialism. Colonial rule (especially British rule) was threatened, she claimed, by the destabilizing impact of the multiple and often
negative images of whites in American movies. This situation did not satisfy the need to bolster imperial control through a unidimensional portrayal
of whites as competent rulers who should be obeyed and respected:

> Will Hays said in a recent speech in Berlin "the world-wide distribution of
> films fill an important part in making people in different lands understand
> each other," but Sir Hesketh Bell [former Governor of Uganda] says, "Noth-
> ing has done more to destroy the prestige of the white man among the col-
> ored races, than these deplorable pictures." . . . Our missionary magazines
> are full of the subject and our church bodies are continually calling our at-
> tention to the enormity of it.[96]

Returning from a 1930 national convention of the Federal Motion Picture Council, department Director Maude Aldrich added a race-based reason for censorship: "The films that are undermining the ideals of the youth of all lands, causing the colored races of the world to distrust the leadership of the white race, and spreading international misunderstanding, are made in America."[97] If the "colored races of the world," she claimed, saw evidence of lynchings, vigilante justice, adultery, and crime, they might judge white Americans to be hypocritical, immoral racists. Asserting the need to maintain the prestige and power of North American leadership over South America, the WCTU argued that the United States could not convincingly assert its moral and political influence if its popular culture pictured a society whose people disregarded its laws—including, of course, the WCTU's prized Volstead Act.

Articles in the *Union Signal*, such as one entitled "Recent Publicity Concerning Film Censorship," reported on the foreign response to Hollywood films. It was important, it argued, for America to present a consistent moral image in order for American religious missionaries to succeed in gaining converts abroad: "Countries we have long characterized as 'heathen' have taken active steps against the American movies. Even Turkey has forbidden children under fifteen years of age to attend the movies 'to protect young Turks from the demoralizing effects of American-made films.' The infidel nation is aroused to save its children against the Christian nation."[98] American women reformers tried to increase pressure for censorship at home through their focus on children around the world. For Miller, heathen Turkey's need to censor American movies revealed Will Hays's pro-movie propaganda as superficial and false.[99]

A reporter accompanying President-elect Herbert Hoover to South America in 1928 quoted a Uruguayan editor who claimed that American movies were a "main obstacle to the proper understanding and esteem between the United States and the South American countries" because they showed only the "cabaret life, the sins of society and crime. The news is filled with bank robberies, Hollywood divorces, gunmen and lynchings."[100] Reports such as this reinforced the claim that popular culture produced in the United States threatened to jeopardize the prestige and dominant position of the nation and to destabilize international relations. The fact that movies had become a source of international concern is demonstrated by the 1926 convocation of an "International Motion Picture Conference, called by the child welfare committee of the League of Nations to consider the problems created in all lands by the Motion Picture."[101] The Federal Motion Picture Council of America, a national pro-censorship coalition of ministers, reform, and educational groups including the WCTU, sent a representative to this important meeting. The Federal Motion Picture Council of America believed that successful censorship laws in the United States could help avoid these problems with the country's international image.

* * *

The WCTU's Department of Motion Pictures achieved its greatest credibility and political and organizational strength in the late 1920s and early 1930s. Its most sophisticated national pro-censorship campaign of 1930 grew out of the movie industry's attempts to increase audience attendance during the early years of the Great Depression, when movies again became more openly "impure." Another noticeable increase in "sex pictures" such as those featuring the sexual innuendos and "loose" morals of the bawdy Mae West, reflected the movie industry's attempts to boost profits. West's on-screen independence challenged old values, as did the fact that, off-screen, she was one of the highest paid performers in the United States. Her growing notoriety and popularity, stemming from her starring roles in the new "sex pictures," generated a backlash within large segments of the public that threatened to result in federal censorship.[102]

To initiate its largest campaign for national censorship, the department issued a national resolution asserting that the motion picture industry had been given ample time to demonstrate its dedication to "clean" films and had failed to do so:

> WHEREAS, Present-day methods have proven entirely inadequate to meet the situation, and many pictures shown on the screen depict crime and immorality, scoff at Prohibition and establish false standards of social life, thus signally *failing to transmit the best, Therefore Be It Resolved,* That we respectfully request that your honorable body enact a law for the federal supervision of motion pictures, establishing higher standards before production for films that are to be licensed for interstate and international commerce.[103]

Emphasizing the necessity of preproduction intervention, the resolution was then distributed in triplicate copies to state directors by national Director Maude Aldrich "with a request that they not only encourage the unions to send in these resolutions but that they enlist every other organization possible to assist in the task."[104]

The political savvy and organizational skills of WCTU members produced results. Aldrich noted with satisfaction one newspaper article that reported that, within a few weeks of the campaign's launching, "resolutions were reaching Congress from many organizations. The article said, 'apparently some organization is back of the movement.' Our WCTU leaders were actually mobilizing the organizations of the nation."[105] Demanding federal censorship of motion picture production, WCTU activists asked for, and received, signed resolutions from a wide variety of middle-class clubs and organizations: "Churches, Missionary Societies, Bible study groups, Sunday schools, Men's Forums, Brotherhoods, Parent-Teacher Associations, D.A.R.'s, Daughters of Confederacy, Women's Clubs, Mother's Circles, Legion Auxiliaries, Rebecca Lodges, Business Men's organizations, Granges, Epworth Leagues, Y.P.B.'s [Young People's Branches of the WCTU], Girl's schools, and many other groups."[106] In spite of the WCTU's professed concerns about "race hatred," Aldrich unproblematically reported that among the approximately two thousand resolutions sent to Congress in 1931, the "Women of K.K.K." had registered its approval of censorship along with the Rotary Club and the Girl Scouts.[107] As national director, Aldrich was clearly pleased by the widespread response of state and local WCTUs and other organizations to the pro-censorship resolution. The WCTU saw itself—somewhat grandiosely—as the leading organization within the broader pro-censorship movement. In 1931, so many religious organizations "enlisted in the movement for federal supervision" that Aldrich modestly stated: "We would not as an organization claim credit for enlisting these great and influential groups in this vitally important movement, but we rejoice in their fellowship together with us and find renewed courage and inspiration in their action."[108]

The 355,000 member WCTU still commanded enough strength to organize another national petition drive for censorship, even in the year of its greatest failure—the revocation of the Eighteenth Amendment in 1933.[109] Aldrich presided over this pro-censorship campaign when she "turned in to the United States Congress with personal letters to Congressmen over 100,000 names of persons petitioning for federal supervision."[110] Unwilling to acknowledge that much of its power had indeed ended with the repeal of Prohibition—yet recognizing a need to shift priorities after this defeat—the WCTU tried to de-emphasize the importance of alcohol to its existence as a women's reform organization: "Motion pictures are having a far more injurious effect upon public morals in general than the saloon ever had. The saloon touched a few millions of people directly and these were in the main adults. The motion picture touches every man, woman, and child in the whole country directly and its character molding effect is appalling."[111] This position reflects both an intellectual shift and an organizational strategy that emerged in the 1920s, whereby movies became the union's new leading enemy and a new reason for being. Alcohol, the WCTU explained, had indirectly affected the child through the actions of a drunk parent, but movies directly affected each child's character. Moreover, the "scoffing" at Prohibition in movies helped provide the WCTU with a scapegoat for its failure to enforce Prohibition and provided a spur to its new campaign. While after 1933 the WCTU was certainly an organization in decline, the very next year

2,817 local unions (translating into thousands more individual signatures) sent pro-censorship resolutions to Congress.[112] As late as 1938, Pennsylvania's WCTU was able to send 1,047 personal letters to senators, representatives, and members of committees, along with 675 resolutions and 8,100 names on petitions.[113]

The period 1925 to 1933 was in retrospect the period of the WCTU's greatest strength as an organization working for movie censorship. The censorship efforts of the WCTU and other Protestant organizations, however, were overshadowed in 1934 by the Catholic Legion of Decency, an organization created by American bishops to force the movie industry to regulate itself. Although the Legion of Decency receives most of the credit for bringing a religious sensibility to bear on film, Protestant groups, including the WCTU, clearly paved the way for its efforts. What differed was strategy. While the WCTU pushed for federal regulation, a measure that was completely unacceptable to the movie industry, the Catholics, perhaps out of greater concern for the separation of church and state, advocated consumer boycotts. To spur Catholic parents into action, the legion used tactics familiar to WCTU members, such as focusing rhetorically upon the dangers movies presented to youths: "What a massacre of innocence of youth is taking place hour by hour!"[114] The increasing political influence of Catholics during the period, along with the organizational power behind the Legion of Decency's threat to decrease film attendance significantly through a national boycott, made the movie industry fearful of the power of the Catholic church.[115] More important, the Catholic strategy of focusing on voluntary measures seemed reasonable and acceptable, in contrast to the more radical national censorship position of the Protestant-led groups.

While insisting on the importance of Protestant support, Aldrich acknowledged the legion's role in forcing the movie industry to strengthen its self-censorship mechanisms:

> The year [1934] has been notable for the creation of the "Legion of Decency," which has given unusual publicity to the character of the films being exhibited and to the need for more wholesome motion pictures. The immediate effect of this movement, originated in the Catholic church and *now equally shared by Protestant denominations,* has been to cause considerable activity among the Motion Picture Producers in selecting a number of splendid books and dramas as motion picture themes. They have also made deletions or stopped production in the case of a few films.[116]

Aldrich acknowledged the positive results of the industry's increased efforts toward self-censorship, specifically its commitment to produce movies based on "splendid books," but she also emphasized the WCTU's difference from the Legion of Decency. The WCTU insisted upon its continued determination to passing a federal movie censorship law: "If the present movement is to result in permanent good it will have to be continued thorough the years with unabated determination. The need is . . . that federal supervision may bar . . . all films which fail to measure up to minimum standards of whole-someness."[117]

Fearful of the Protestants' calls for national censorship legislation, the movie industry perceived that the demands of the Legion of Decency offered it a way out. It could (partially) comply with the legion's moral concerns by taking voluntary action toward regulation. The movie industry inaugurated stricter self-censorship in creating the Production Code Administration in 1934. Lea Jacobs's thoughtful study of movie industry self-censorship, *The Wages of Sin*, argues that 1934 marked a decisive turning point in the operation of the Hays office. The Production Code Administration demanded more thoroughgoing revisions of plot and narrative structure, rather than the mere imposition of facile moralistic endings that had marked the industry's earlier self-regulatory efforts.[118] The new restrictions enabled some WCTU directors to modify their view of the immediate danger presented by the movies.[119] Stating in 1938 that the "indecent picture is almost a thing of the past and drinking to some extent has been eliminated, as well as other undesirable features," the department's New Jersey director acknowledged improvements, yet even she immediately modified her approval: "However, the work must go on, and every woman at her post is necessary. We have our movie-mad children and the powerful influence of the screen with us, as well as block booking and blind selling, which has been an agitation for the last ten years and which has not yet been definitely settled at Washington."[120] The sheer number of young viewers, all "mad" about movies, signaled to her that the American public could never rely on the movie industry's self-control but rather must continue to lobby for federal legislation. Her insistence reflects a bias within the WCTU against the effectiveness of "self-restraint." Paradoxically, federal censorship was much less likely to win the support of politicians after 1934, for the industry could point with greater sincerity to its "cleaned up" films as proof that further regulation was unnecessary.

* * *

The phrase "mothering the movies" offered a justification for the activism of WCTU members who felt compelled to protect all children, their own and others. "Mothering the movies" is also a paradigm for WCTU members' entire conceptualization of the relationship between motion pictures and audiences and is therefore representative of their solutions to the problems of the movies. Concerns about children were consistently linked by WCTU reformers to their views of the moviegoer as addict. The WCTU's censorship activism was tied, therefore, to its temperance activism. Its members believed that moviegoers were, like children and "heathens," eminently corruptible; like drunkards (or moviemakers), they were incapable of self-control. The WCTU's lack of faith in self-restraint applied to all moviegoers, but especially youthful ones. "Immoral" movies, in effect, drugged them. The organization had consistently argued that neither the drunkard nor the drink seller could exercise self-control; there was, by extension, no reason to expect that either the moviemaker or the moviegoer could restrain themselves. Insisting "that every public amusement should be not only a pleasure but a moral uplift to humanity," the WCTU asserted that all movie viewers were in need of women's or mothers' protection and that reforming women could make all forms of cultural consumption safe.[121] Women's censorship activity was different from men's, moreover, because it emphasized to a greater extent maternal activism and the protection of children. The irony, or double-edged nature, of this maternalist ideology is that women gave up as much or more than they gained, as experts and governmental agencies or regulation took over the tasks outlined and fought for by laywomen reformers.[122] Its emphasis on the *creation* of "pure" culture distinguished the WCTU from other reformers, including the male vice societies that worked exclusively for censorship.

CHAPTER 6

The Production of "Pure" Children's Literature

The WCTU's Young Crusader

Beginning in the 1880s, the Woman's Christian Temperance Union developed a program to champion what it defined as "pure" literature, art and, eventually, movies. I have referred to these activities as the promotion or creation of an "alternative" or "pure" cultural hierarchy, meaning that it was counterpoised to, as well as offered as a positive alternative to, popular commercial culture and the avant garde.[1] In this context, "pure" culture does not necessarily refer to originality, for the WCTU used well-known reproductions of "pure" paintings and formulaic melodramatic plots for its children's stories. In most cases, the source of contention was the message, not the medium. At stake was not the originality of its vision, but issues of cultural dominance. The WCTU fought for attention against newer cultural trends, yet despite its claims to conventional values, its writings also espoused more subversive ideas, especially about gender.

In an 1883 article on children's literature for the *Library Journal,* librarian Caroline Hewins had wished aloud for "wholesome" books for girls: "One of the needs of today is a series of stories for girls of twelve or fourteen, telling of the wholesome, sheltered home life of American girls who are carefully brought up, but at the same time have plenty of fun and frolic."[2] Hewins's article addressed professionals in the American Library Association, yet her organization did not respond. It did not produce or publish professionally sanctioned children's fiction. Independent of Hewins's appeal, a laywomen's group, the Woman's Christian Temperance Union, did take the initiative. Its members wrote and published "wholesome" stories for youths.

Hoping to inculcate its values in the younger generation, the Woman's Christian Temperance Union published a monthly children's magazine, the *Young Crusader,* from 1887 through the 1930s. The WCTU reached a substantial number of young readers through its publications. The *Crusader* was aimed primarily at children aged six to twelve, but each month a variety of articles also addressed youths in their late teens and early twenties. By 1891, the magazine had 34,000 subscribers, many of whom were probably the children of union members. The group published another periodical beginning in 1887 called the *Oak and Ivy Leaf* that was directed at women under twenty-five who were active in the Young Woman's Christian Temperance Union. Within two years, the *Oak and Ivy Leaf* reported having 30,000 members and 10,000 subscriptions to the magazine. These circulation figures suggest that the union sold over 44,000 subscriptions to its youth magazines. Local WCTU youth groups, such as the Loyal Temperance Legions, purchased one subscription and shared the magazine among all their members. We may safely assume that some children shared their personal subscriptions with siblings and friends. A middlebrow culture was thus a feature of the lives of significant numbers of young people—the WCTU's intended audience. This is not to insist, of course, that these same children read only "pure" literature—some of them may have surreptitiously read the "sensational" dime novels and crime-story papers that union members fought against. These figures are simply meant to provide an estimate of the size and scope of the *Crusader*'s audience.[3]

The *Young Crusader*'s monthly cover story was typically a "pure" fiction story (often serialized in five to fifteen chapters) written for youths by authors who were either WCTU members or pro-temperance/reform sympathizers. Four of those serialized fiction stories will serve as case studies for an in-depth analysis of WCTU "pure" fiction. First, however, it is necessary to present an overview of the magazine as a whole, from its nonfiction articles and its short stories to its similarities and differences to other children's magazines of the time. *Crusader* editors emphasized the positive uses of their magazine's "pure" literature, particularly its potential to introduce children to a gendered style of politics and to the WCTU's favorite reform causes such as benevolence, temperance (as a health concern and societal/familial problem), other social reform projects, and activism in political campaigns.[4] The alcoholic and the city, moreover, figured as prominent targets in *Crusader* fiction, the latter as the site of corrupt politics, ethnic and racial divisions, saloons, and disease. Through the early decades of the twentieth century, *Crusader* fiction changed in response to important new movements and social problems, particularly Progressivism, immigration, and the intensified fight for national prohibition of alcohol.

The WCTU's *Crusader* published mostly fiction and poetry, assuming that young children would not respond as positively to nonfiction stories. In its first year, the editors announced that they would not publish "long, solid articles on scientific temperance" for fear of alienating the children but would instead try to attract youth's attention with stories and information presented in "short, crisp paragraphs." Temperance, of course, was an important motive behind creating a children's magazine, and pro-temperance appeals appeared consistently in its fiction. Each February, for example, the *Crusader* published stories in honor of Washington and Lincoln that lauded both as "total abstainers." Other stories glorified dedicated teachers who taught innovative scientific temperance instruction lessons, or a school superintendent who "told his teachers he wished them to teach temperance" in spite of the fact that his state legislature had not passed a temperance education bill.[5] Ambivalent about whether to include articles that might interest adults involved in child development and education, especially teachers, the editors occasionally experimented with the magazine's format and included special temperance instruction inserts for teachers.

Because children's developing characters were believed to be particularly impressionable, "pure" fiction could teach them good morals and protect them from immoral behavior, just as surely as "impure" fiction would ruin them. The WCTU's official organ, the *Union Signal,* openly discussed using fiction as a means to influence youths and identified literature as a medium in need of legal regulation and control. In contrast, after the first few issues, virtually no overt discussion of this agenda appeared in the pages of the *Crusader.* Of course, no story presented drinking or smoking in a positive light, and many presented intemperance as the main cause of a character's physical and mental damage or loss of popularity or social status. Each story expressed the WCTU's ideals of "pure" thought and behavior but was open to multiple interpretations by readers who, even within the confines of WCTU literature, had access to other perspectives such as the *Crusader's* nonfiction selections and the organization's national policies and actions. Created expressly as a "pure" alternative reading choice for boys and girls, the *Young Crusader* also avoided all discussion of "unwholesome" subjects such as crimes, guns, war, romance, or sexuality commonly found in crime-story papers, Westerns, "sensational" dime novels, or romance novels—all condemned as unacceptable for young readers because they purportedly taught deviant social behavior.[6]

Each month, the *Crusader* published "wholesome" articles in a variety of narrative forms including motivational stories, political lessons, didactic moral teachings, poems, and short stories. Editorials and other articles offered advice on behavior, career goals, pro-temperance activism, and information about WCTU "auxiliaries" for youths, such as the Loyal Temperance Legion. These various genres asked for and expected different reader responses; some editorials presented straight-forward political news about the fight for prohibition; whereas melodramatic stories were expected to elicit emotional responses against alcohol use. WCTU fiction generally used correct English, with a minimum of "slang" or heavy dialect, in the hope of training children to develop careful speaking skills and polite behavior. Assuming that a child's bad language (as well as reading) could lead to improper behavior, the *Crusader* warned youths against using "unpleasant words," "untruth," "slang," "bad grammar," or "gossip." According to cultural historian John Fiske, puns and slang are often purposeful "misuses" of language and forms of cultural opposition, so the WCTU correctly identified language as a site for intervention. The WCTU's children's magazine was not simply the product of grammatical purists (as some of the quotations of children's speech in the stories demonstrate): it was engaged in a cultural struggle, with language as its hostage.[7]

The first issue of the *Young Crusader* counseled children to spread the temperance message to others. The periodical's title used a medieval metaphor, "young crusaders," to identify its readers as members of the larger pro-temperance movement. They were Christian "crusaders" who would conquer alcohol, the evil enemy. This choice of metaphor was not arbitrary, for medieval metaphors appealed to a variety of organizations in the late nineteenth and early twentieth centuries. The Woman's Christian Temperance Union, the anti-tuberculosis public health movement, and the Ku Klux Klan each mobilized medieval metaphors to stress the need for individual, heroic action on behalf of various causes.[8] The WCTU hoped that every young reader would be converted to temperance by reading the magazine's persuasive "pure" fiction, would then pledge to abstain from alcohol and cigarettes, and would ultimately carry the "truth" to others through political and social activism: "Don't you suppose, if every reader of the *Young Crusader* gave or lent it to some poor child . . . a great many could be taught how much better it is to live clean, honest, good, useful lives, than to be drunken, smoking, swearing, idle loafers? I wish every boy and girl would try."[9] By promoting the periodical's circulation at schools and playgrounds, the editors hoped to expand the mostly middle- and lower-middle-class readership to reach poor and working-class youths. They also hoped to reform immigrant families through the children.

WCTU editors assumed an imitative or mimetic model of reading; readers would learn from its "pure" fiction how to behave and why such behavior was desirable. A short story tellingly entitled "The Danger of Too Much Liberty" illustrates the complexities of this goal. At the most obvious level, it implied that excessive geographical and personal liberty are dangerous: a puppy ignored its mother's warnings to stay safe in the barn, went out to explore the farm, and got lost and afraid. The puppy ultimately returned to the cozy barn, but "doesn't talk so much about 'personal liberty' as he formerly did."[10] This genre of the "fortunate fall" also suggests that autonomous experience, even misjudgment, is necessary, that the goal is moral autonomy—the ability to internalize distinctions between legitimate freedoms and excesses. Another short story called "Doing As You Please" also aimed to teach children a moral lesson in fictional form; it featured a mother who convinced her child "that it is not possible to separate the actions of one person in a community or a home, in society, from those of others in such a way that what one does will not affect another."[11] The story's lesson, that all members of society are interconnected and are responsible for the general welfare, articulates the progressivism of the "new" middle class yet also represents maternalist values in its assertion that mothers, not professionals, must teach these lessons to children.[12]

Crusader authors often assumed that the problems and interests of boys and girls were different and so addressed each sex separately. One article, for example, discouraged boys (not girls) from leaving their small towns or rural areas for the largest cities: "No doubt this first number of the Young Crusader will be read by many boys whose thoughts turn with eager and intense longing to . . . Chicago or New York. . . . Don't come to a city, though, if you believe . . . city fun to be your just dues. . . . Thousands of homeless young men and boys; they have boarding houses with small, cheerless sleeping rooms, for homes."[13] "Cheerless" cities lacked the warmth and protection associated with the ideal middle-class haven, the home; boys should not leave maternal comforts for the lonely cities. The WCTU's anti-urban bias was echoed by many progressive reformers, who viewed the city as the site of health and hygiene problems, political corruption, and, of course, increasing immigration.

The Crusader's nonfiction offered optimistic, encouraging, even feminist advice to girls. In particular, it de-emphasized the sanctity of the private domestic sphere by celebrating the entry of women into public, wage-earning work. Carroll Smith-Rosenberg identifies the "New Woman" as a member of the new middle class, "most frequently a child of small-town America," who attended college from the 1880s to the 1920s. Smith-Rosenberg excludes WCTU members from this category, terming them "True Women." In fact, the WCTU encouraged women's higher education and their entry into careers, including business and medicine, and some young WCTU members were themselves New Women.[14] Advice columns, such as "Safe Business Openings for Girls," praised wagework for women as "good for everybody."[15] An 1892 column, "What Our Girls Think," listed and described white-collar jobs that women could have if they planned ahead and pursued the proper training and education. One girl intended to be a stenographer after she finished high school; another wrote of visiting an "Industrial College" where many young women were "learning to be doctors! Don't you think doctors is a good business for girls?" Elsewhere, the *Crusader* editors pridefully noted that young visitors to WCTU publishing offices saw proof that women could train to become business managers and publishers who "knew all about money and big printing presses."[16]

As it celebrated their accomplishments, the *Young Crusader* encouraged its girl readers to expand their opportunities and options further than had their mothers or older sisters. *Crusader* biographies celebrating seven young women who were prominent leaders of the Senior Loyal Temperance Legion in 1905 hint at the periodical's readership and at the types of wage-earning jobs they pursued. Many young women in the WCTU were wage earners; the majority (mirroring overall employment trends in the United States) worked in sex-segregated fields such as teaching or stenography.[17] Four of the seven young WCTU members can be described as New Women. One Swarthmore College graduate, Alice Linvill, became a teacher affiliated with a New York City college settlement house—a haven for progressive, college-educated professional women (see figure 5).[18] A second WCTU woman rejected the domestic ideal, daring as an independent single woman to leave teaching to become a missionary in India. Two other women left kindergarten teaching to become paid Loyal Temperance Legion organizers in Wisconsin and Connecticut. The Bridgeport, Connecticut, organizer Bessie Lee Clink is identified primarily as a Christian whose early conversion influenced her career choice (see figure 6). In contrast, Alice Linvill's biography only briefly mentions that she was a Quaker (American Society of Friends) and emphasizes instead her secular and scholarly endeavors. As the WCTU expanded in the first three decades of the twentieth century, its organizational work was no longer solely the realm of married middle-class volunteer women but now constituted a possible paid career for dedicated members. Some young women had been active in the legions since a very early age (often six years old) and seem to have gone straight from high school or normal schools to work for the WCTU. These biographies suggest that women's culture—from settlement houses, WCTU organizing, and continuing options in missionary work—provided independent career opportunities for young WCTU women in the first decade of the twentieth century.[19]

Crusader articles pushed young women further into the public sphere and gave explicit attention to questions of public policy that went far beyond temperance politics. An 1892 article, for instance, discussed United

The Senior Loyal Temperance Legion

SENIORS WHO HAVE WON SUCCESS
Alice Roberta Linvill

MISS ALICE ROBERTA LINVILL

Although born in one of the farm homes in Chester county, Pa., Alice Linvill spent eight years of her early life beside a beautiful lake in Florida, where, with her young sister, she ran along the white beach or swam in the sparkling water, as best pleased her fancy.

Of English, Irish and Welsh ancestry, Friends in religious belief, Miss Linvill has inherited those strong traits of character that make for success. Her school life began in the public schools of Kennett Square, Pa. Always a careful student, she was graduated from Martin Academy, and completed a four years' course in Swarthmore College. Her fondness for cooking and recognition of the open door of opportunity, led her to specialize in Domestic Science, taking a two years' course at Drexel Institute, whence she was graduated in 1904.

Even before graduation a position had been secured in New York City to teach in the Hartley district on the College Settlement plan, with basketry added to her teaching. She also passed the examination under the Board of Public Instruction, which makes her eligible to teach in the New York city schools.

Miss Linvill is a graduate of the Kennett Square L. T. L., where she was a most faithful worker in the Flower Mission department and a valuable aid to the W. C. T. U. on social and other occasions. For three years she has been treasurer of the Pennsylvania State Loyal Temperance Legion.

SENIOR NOTES

Rouseville, Pa., has a thriving Legion of sixty members.

During his recent trip in Ohio, Mr. Floyd Starr organized three promising Senior Legions in Wood county.

The Sidney (N. Y.) Legion was greatly helped by the visit of Mr. Howard Smith of Ithaca, whose addresses were much appreciated by large audiences.

Detroit's (Mich.) new Senior Legion gave a very successful Silver Medal contest. There were eight contestants, and the medal was won by Hazel Frence.

Rushford (Minn.) Legion with a membership of twenty-eight pledged members, has an attendance of fifteen. It meets at the houses, where refreshments are often served.

The annual banquet of the Rochester (N. Y.) Senior Legion was voted a great success. The tables were prettily decorated with chrysanthemums and carnations, and after a sumptuous repast, several toasts were given.

Since the National Convention, Mr. Richard L. Evans, president of the Massachusetts State L. T. L., has been actively strengthening the work in his state. He has visited four Legions, addressed two Y and two W. C. T. U. meetings, besides having charge of two Legions.

Through inadvertence the name of the writer, Miss Addie A. Andross, was not appended to the article on "Duties of a Treasurer," which appeared in the Superintendents' Round Table in the February issue of THE CRUSADER MONTHLY. Miss Andross, as the able treasurer of New York Legion, is a competent authority on all that pertains to the duties of the office of treasurer.

An up-to-date promising Senior Legion of twenty-four members has been organized at Doster, Mich., by Miss Charlotte Barnum, vice president of Michigan's state Legion. The following departments have been adopted: Press, Flower Mission, Physical Education, Parliamentary Law. Leaders have been appointed for the social hour, and with a competent instructor for Manual work and a gifted Musical director, this new Legion bids fair to succeed.

Bedford (Pa.) Legion, organized with few members November 13, 1903, now has an enrolled membership of 109, with an average attendance of forty-five, most of whom are boys. The Legion has rented a library. Scrapbooks of colored pictures and short stories are made and distributed in the hospitals. Arbor Day will be observed by planting a tree from Valley Forge or some other historical place. Through public entertainments money has been raised to meet all expenses and leave a surplus in the treasury.

NORTH CAROLINA
By SALLIE BLALOCK, Corresponding Secretary

Albemarle Legion meets every Sabbath afternoon at the Englewood Seminary, and with fifty-five pledged members, it has an average attendance of ninety-five per cent. Great interest is taken in the meetings of this, the largest L. T. L. in the state of North Carolina.

Twenty-two L. T. L. honorary members have paid five-cent state and National dues, and the Legion is gaining in members every Sabbath. From use of mite-boxes during the summer, and dues paid by members since the middle of September, the work was reopened with money in the treasury.

We subscribe for ten copies of THE CRUSADER MONTHLY.

The Junior Legioners take great delight in bringing new members, and very often frankly announce that Miss Ufford has given a "member prize."

Local Rally
"Bim, bim, bim, boom, bum!
"Saloons, saloons, saloons can't come!!"

Eager to secure a large attendance at their state convention which is to be held in DuBois, Pennsylvania Legions have inaugurated a savings bank system, whereby weekly deposits of ten or twenty-five cents will be made by the members desirous of attending the convention, the deposit to be withdrawn if attendance is impossible.

Figures 5 and 6. The short biographies of successful seniors were frequently accompanied by outlines of Senior Loyal Temperance Legions' activities, from annual banquets to planting trees. (Courtesy of the National Woman's Christian Temperance Union, Evanston, Ill.)

The Senior Loyal Temperance Legion

SENIORS WHO HAVE WON SUCCESS

Bessie Lee Clink

"I consider her a remarkable girl," writes one who has known Bessie Lee Clink ever since her parents moved to Grand Rapids, Mich., when the little girl was two years of age. Blessed with a mother who is not only a devout Christian, but a strong temperance woman, the young girl united with the church at the age of twelve, and we are told that ever since it has been a stormy night indeed that failed to find her at prayer meeting.

Miss Clink is a charter member of the Big Rapids L. T. L., having joined the Junior Legion at the age of six. Later she was graduated into the Senior Legion, from which she was one of the earliest to win a diploma. Always at her place, her work is characterized by faithfulness, whether as superintendent of Flower Mission, as recording secretary or president, or whether circulating petitions, visiting councilmen and officials to prevent the establishment of a beer parlor for women, training the little ones in the Junior Legion, or performing the work

MISS BESSIE LEE CLINK.

of a state superintendent of the Michigan L. T. L.

The completion of her public school course was followed by kindergarten training at the Ferris Institute.

It was a higher ruling than mere coincidence that opened for her the door of opportunity;—that a W. C. T. U. in an eastern city should seek to find the salaried L. T. L. worker through a notice in the columns of a recent number of "The Union Signal," which notice should reach Michigan's General L. T. L. secretary about the time a letter came telling of the young girl's desire to spend her life in service for the Loyal Temperance Legion.

Not yet twenty years of age, standing at the threshold of womanhood, Bessie Lee Clink has won the highest success, the opportunity of service, and the Loyal Temperance Legion of Bridgeport, Conn., has gained a worker whose ability and sweetness of spirit is rivaled only by her loyalty and devotion to the work.

PENNSYLVANIA

Excellent Literary Features at Bucks County Convention

By HATTIE M. JOHNS

The initial number of the literary program was an excellent paper on "Methods of Temperance Reform in Germany." It was shown that in spite of the prevalent opinion that beer drinking in Germany is not discouraged, for several centuries the German people have been struggling against intemperance. As early as 1517 there was a moderation society, called the "Order of Temperance," designed to put an end to the custom of pledging health, and to reform the so-called higher classes which were fast becoming ruined by intemperance. In 1600 Maurice of Hesse established a society, the fundamental rule of which was that its members should never become intoxicated. The conditions required that no member should be allowed more than seven goblets of wine at one meal, and that not oftener than twice a day. Count Frederick V. established another league, whose members were pledged to observe its rules for two years. In that time there

were allowed 5,000 goblets of wine to each member. The next movement for temperance reform came two hundred years later when, under royal auspices, the German Templars were formed. Later still, came the Scholars' societies, Women's societies, and Bands of Hope, but these workers, unlike their forefathers, foresaw that in dealing with the liquor problem temperance alone is unavailing, and that nothing short of total abstinence is of enduring value.

Today German scientists declare that moderation is undefinable, and that every popular movement against alcohol based upon moderation must fail. Deep concern is felt among official circles in Germany at the alarming increase of alcoholism reported by the investigation of the conditions of the army.

The paper, "Temperance in Literature," traced through poetry the change in public sentiment concerning the ruby wine cup. The ancients who were adoring devotees of the flowing bowl were worshipers of Bacchus, and much of their literature consists of odes to their god of wine. Nevertheless, even here we read traces of doubt, little suggestions of lurking dangers in the midst of pleasure. Later came the rollicking drinking songs, and even these, though careless and reckless in words, yet breathe dissatisfaction between the lines. As the centuries pass and man becomes more perfectly educated, we find less and less of the spirit of intemperance in the poetry of the times. While there is cause for regret that the conditions are such that the modern realistic novelists must make such frequent use of the intoxicating beverage, we have cause to rejoice that we may search long in a volume of our beloved bards, Longfellow or Whittier, before we find an ode to Bacchus.

That "prohibition does prohibit" is shown by the report of the Commissioner of Internal Revenue for 1904, who names three prohibition states, Maine, Vermont and North Dakota, as paying the smallest amount of internal revenue taxes.

States policies toward Native Americans and informed its young readers of the broken promises of "land, horses, tools, schools and money" made by the United States government to the Ute tribe in Colorado. The government, it explained, wanted to move the Utes from Colorado to Utah because "white men want the land. . . . It is a shame!" This position was based partly on a civilizing impulse within the WCTU, expressed as its concern that the Utes would again be forced to live "by their old savage habits of hunting."[20] A July 1898 article entitled "A Patriotic Message to Girls" was written by Susan B. Anthony, the prominent woman suffrage activist and friend of WCTU President Frances Willard. Anthony urged each girl to take good care of her body, to have "strength and vigor," and to acquire "the power of self-support by the best education she can possibly get." Even with the power of a decent living wage, Anthony argued that girls could not be full citizens without the right to vote: "But to be truly free themselves and best able to serve their country our girls must have the ballot, and there is no girl who cannot help to speed the day in some way if she chooses."[21] Although Anthony's message was addressed to girls, it is likely that boys read the periodical's many articles about voting rights and careers for women. These articles were probably also intended to raise the political awareness of the *Crusader*'s boy readers.

Asking girls as well as boys to think of themselves as full citizens, *Crusader* editors urged them to become directly involved in politics. A series of articles published in 1909, written by Margaret Dye Ellis, national WCTU lobbyist and Washington, D.C., correspondent for the *Union Signal,* explained the political system to girls and boys. The first article, "What Our Young People Can do For Temperance Legislation," suggested that youths circulate petitions, making sure that "voters' signatures should be on one blank, non-voters on another."[22] Other articles detailed the workings of the legislative bodies, the Supreme Court, the U.S. Treasury, the Library of Congress, and the U.S. Post Office, among others.[23] Ellis's series introduced girls to the terminology of politics and government, a language that most females were excluded from. Young women who were taught the procedures of government would be better able to enter this conventionally forbidden territory. Knowing that educated and politically aware young women represented the potential for a more democratic United States, as well as the future growth of the WCTU, the *Crusader*'s nonfiction challenged traditional gender roles by encouraging girls to be politically engaged.

In order to see if and how the WCTU's *Young Crusader* differed from other children's magazines of that era, I will provide here, as a basis of comparison, a brief sketch of *St. Nicholas Magazine,* the best respected secular children's magazine of the turn of the century. Frequently praised by both the

WCTU and the American Library Association, *St. Nicholas* became nationally known in the 1880s and 1890s under the editorship of Mary Mapes Dodge, a writer of children's stories including *Hans Brinker, or The Silver Skates* (1865). Half of the magazine was composed of nonfiction articles that were intended to inform and educate young readers. The various types of nonfiction articles have been categorized by historian Fred Erisman as travel, biographical, historical (mostly United States and British history), and scientific articles that explained phenomena in the natural sciences and technology.[24] The *Young Crusader* also featured nonfiction articles, but its articles focused on topics such as politics, current events, and advice on career options. The *Crusader* featured fewer historical and travel articles, and its biographies focused on reform and temperance leaders (young and old) or on famous writers such as Louisa May Alcott. Scientific articles in the *Crusader* rarely described new mechanical inventions and focused instead on the physiological effects of consuming alcohol or smoking cigarettes.

Serialized and shorter works of fiction, often by famous authors including Louisa May Alcott, Jack London, Frances Hodgson Burnett, Mark Twain, Rudyard Kipling, Kate Douglas Wiggin, Bret Harte, William Dean Howells, and Edward Everett Hale, composed the other half of *St. Nicholas.*[25] Erisman classifies *St. Nicholas* fiction into four categories. The least common, "technical fiction," was designed to teach children science in a fictional format. Similarly, the *Young Crusader*'s story "The King and His Wonderful Castle," written in 1911, was a fictional form of health education and provided the WCTU with a way to discuss the harmful physical effects of alcohol on the body.[26] *St. Nicholas* also published "fantasy" stories about dragons and elves. These stories taught children to appreciate qualities desired in humans: "love, politeness, optimism, contentment, generosity, and industry."[27] Historical fiction made up another small part of the fiction offerings. In these stories, a youth "comes in contact with notable events or personages and learns something of himself, his time, and the world."[28] Few of the *Young Crusader* stories were either fantasies or historical. WCTU publishers favored instead the same type of fiction that was most frequently published in *St. Nicholas:* Domestic fiction stories with moral lessons that were set in the contemporary world among mostly middle-class characters.[29] The editors of *St. Nicholas* were dedicated, it seems, to imparting certain ideals to children— "the basic values of middle-class America." The magazine also "implied that these values are desirable, and worthy of perpetuation for all time."[30]

In its fundamental commitment to teaching moral lessons, *St. Nicholas* did not differ substantially from the *Young Crusader*. Each magazine was dedicated to instilling proper character-building values in children. The WCTU's *Crusader* had another agenda, however: To teach abstinence from alcohol and cigarettes to its child readers. This other agenda, in addition to its less noteworthy contributing authors, might make the *Crusader's* fiction more didactic or less compelling, but questions of literary value are not at stake in my analysis. What is significant is that the *Young Crusader* differed more in emphasis than in kind from the best-known children's magazine of its time. Unlike some Sunday school books like *Elsie Dinsmore*, the *Crusader* did not contain unadulterated preaching or frequent references to God or religion.[31] Reform-oriented parents probably found the *Crusader's* format and content to be fairly representative of the other respectable middle-class children's magazines of the day and were simply pleased to have pro-temperance messages highlighted for their children.

* * *

My review of fiction in the *Young Crusader* begins in 1887 with a serialized story called "Three Children and How They Amused Themselves," a fictionalized autobiographical account of Frances E. Willard's own childhood on an isolated farm in rural Wisconsin in the 1840s and 1850s.[32] This story will be the base line from which to judge change in the WCTU's fiction, for it will be followed by an examination of three other *Crusader* stories from the second decade of the twentieth century. This fiction was not radical in most senses of the word, but Frances Willard's claims about gender were. Of the four stories analyzed here, Willard's story offered the most specific challenges to women's restricted role in American society.

Written by the revered president of the WCTU, the story may have carried extra authority and meaning for child readers and their mothers, who most likely explained to their children that the main character, Kate, was in fact Frances Willard, a character whose life's tale might be emulated. In any event, Kate Hill was a likable character who could be seen as a role model and heroine without this explicit knowledge about her similarity to the WCTU president. Willard's story of the Hill family contained important messages about child rearing, gender roles, child development, urban and rural life, and women's career ambitions. Furthermore, the details of the Hill's amusements provided an object lesson in wholesome, productive entertainment in contrast to the commercial urban culture WCTU members opposed in their Department of Purity in Literature and Art.

Willard's story described how the three Hill children—the older brother Atherton, the middle sister Kate (Frances Willard), and the youngest sibling Nell—"amused themselves" in their isolated rural house by creating a make-believe city. Willard called it "Fort City," thereby evoking the family's Western pioneering spirit and metaphorically placing Kate in an unconventional setting for girls, a center for military battles and defense. Militarist images of the "Fort City" complemented the WCTU's use of medieval metaphors of the "crusade" to describe the temperance movement. In Willard's story, Fort City was an almost idyllic place in childhood fantasy and was the site of female liberation in adulthood. Given the evils associated with the city in WCTU literature, it is interesting that Willard chose a "city" as the site of wholesome recreation. In fact, Willard's story redeemed the city as a benevolent, skill-building place; all games associated with the Fort City were constructive and of necessity had an educational purpose since there was no nearby school house for the children to attend.[33]

Although some *Crusader* fiction reinforced traditional values and conventional gender roles, Willard's story, which ran for a year, challenged conservative preconceptions by rejecting the notion that gender is an essential category and by offering uniform models of play for girls and boys, thereby making the *Crusader* subversive in at least one crucial way. As a play activity and pedagogical tool, Fort City provided the children with an opportunity to become familiar with and adept at "masculine" and urban professions such as finance, the ministry, and construction. One of their first tasks, for instance, was to open a bank and outline to imaginary customers the benefits of "investing in coin."[34] Discussions of investments and banking reflected WCTU notions of child education that emphasized the power of learning by doing; if girls played at banking, they might be able to imagine being bankers as adults, at ease making business transactions and financial manipulations. Willard's model of at-home socialization stressed the need to make girls feel at ease in a male-dominated public world.

Believing in the power of words to influence action, Willard expected to educate girl readers to be unintimidated by public speaking. When the Hill children organized a church for rainy Sundays when the roads were impassable, Kate alternated preaching in turn with her brother and a neighborhood boy, Jamie.[35] Kate was not optimistic about her own prospects in the adult world and sighed discontentedly, "'I can never be a preacher—folks won't let women do *that*.'" In the meantime, however, Kate would not accept sex-determined limitations; acting as the local carpenter, she "set to make herself a pulpit." Beginning in the 1880s, the WCTU encouraged women to speak in front of their local church congregations as religious leaders in their own right, and union members broke traditional barriers by preaching simultaneously from as many church pulpits as possible in those cities that hosted WCTU annual state and national conventions.[36]

WCTU members were also encouraged to give public speeches, even on unpopular political topics. This agenda appeared in Willard's fiction when one evening, for instance, Kate stood on a chair before her assembled family and neighbors and read "her 'views,' which were not applauded as her brother's had been, for she said that if women who had endured more misery because of the liquor traffic than anybody else on earth, could only have a hand in the voting they would soon set this whole matter right."[37] This passage reflects the WCTU's linkage of pro-temperance activism to women's direct participation in national politics. Kate's friends expected that she would continue to defy social convention and be a public speaker as an adult; they even suggested topics for her future speeches that were conveniently compatible with a career in the WCTU: "You could tell mothers in a temperance speech, that if they didn't take a great deal of pains to teach their boys never to smoke, or chew, never to swear or use impure words, never to touch a drop of drink, or to play cards, and tell the reason why, each time, they couldn't expect the boys to have good habits, because good habits are not born, but made."[38] Willard's own speeches at WCTU conventions were so eloquent that she often convinced more conservative members to accept liberal proposals. Most importantly, through a discussion of the need for a "Home Protection Ballot," Willard had successfully propelled the WCTU into a pro–woman suffrage position by 1881.[39] Kate and Atherton also took a great deal of interest in politics. Their own weekly paper, called the Fort City *Gazette*, was decidedly partisan and favored "the third party, now despised, but which, being devoted to the best interests of the people, is sure to succeed in the long run."[40] This political commitment mirrored WCTU President Willard's insistence that in the 1880s her organization endorse the Prohibition Party.

   Crusader editors used other genres, such as poetry and songs, to inculcate pro-suffrage ideas in young girls. An 1887 poem called "Just Before Election," written "By a Little Girl," encouraged girls to expect the right to vote as adults:

> I'm going to be a woman
> And vote as well as you.
> I'll learn while I am growing
> What voters ought to do.[41]

A "Motion Song" printed in 1915, called "Women's Votes," set up a dialogue between girls and boys about gender roles, temperance, and politics. The girls sang about leaving the kitchens for the voting booths:

> I've good news for you, my dear,
> Women's votes shall soon be here,
> And the men shall mind the kitchen,
> By and by!

Women's votes would transform the public space, too:

When the ballot we can cast,
The saloon will go at last,
Yes, we'll vote for prohibition
Everytime![42]

Highlighting for *Crusader* readers the gendered implications of language, Willard explained that members of the Hill family consciously worked to employ a more neutral, inclusive language: "Atherton was not one of those youth who are forever talking about 'a man;' he preferred to include the whole human race in that fitter phrase, 'a person.'"[43] Believing in the need to initiate social change at the levels of the individual and the family, Willard encouraged brothers to treat their sisters as equals and pointed to Atherton as the model boy, praising atypical traits such as his use of gender neutral language. Identifying language, moreover, as a source of power and knowledge, Willard implied that women needed to be adept at the male-dominated parliamentary language of politics. All official dealings in Fort City, therefore, were conducted by a chairperson who called upon members to make and second motions. When the youngest child interrupted, "Kate whispered, 'That's very unparliamentary, for you must wait your turn.'"[44] Several descriptive passages served as brief guides to parliamentary conduct: "Mr. Hill arose and said, 'Mr. Chairman.' Atherton, with a courteous nod, said 'Mr. Hill' (that is, he 'recognized' him and he was then entitled to the floor)."[45] Other *Crusader* articles, such as "Talks on Parliamentary Law," had similar lessons, including the tip "Caution: Please address a young woman president as Madam President, not as Mr. President."[46]

As author and narrator, Willard clearly rejected prescribed gender roles. Expanding upon the tomboy character popularized by Louisa May Alcott's "Jo" in *Little Women,* Willard's main character Kate is even more daring and adventurous. For Jo, being a tomboy is a phase; she marries and becomes a mother, while Kate (Frances) does not. Kate is a strong and active girl with a "love of out-door sports," in spite of the fact that she was raised in the 1840s and 1850s when calisthenics for girls were still anathema to some educators and women were deemed to be prone to fainting and constitutionally weaker than men.[47] Kate whittled her own arrows and then honed her skills with her sister's help: "The girls used to shoot at a mark with arrows and became very good at hitting, so much so that at Kate's request, Nell, whose trust in her sister was perfect, stood up by a post with an auger-hole in it, and let Kate fire away and put an arrow through the hole when her young sister's sweet blue eye was just beside it. But this was wrong, and when they rushed in 'to tell mother,' she didn't smile, but made them promise 'never, no, never,' to do such a thing again."[48] Although Kate was chastised, Willard clearly delighted in the daring incident.[49]

Just as females needed to have access to male's skills and traits, Willard argued that men should learn from women those characteristics conventionally coded as feminine, such as compassion, spirituality, aesthetics, and cooperation.[50] As a contemporary commentator on sex roles, Willard opined: "It is good for boys and girls to know the same things, so that the former shall not feel and act so over-wise. A boy whose sister knows all about the harness, the boat, the gymnastic exercise, will be far more modest, genial and pleasant to have about. He will cease to be a tease and learn how to be a comrade, and this is a great gain to him, his sister, and his wife that is to be."[51] In this passage, Willard equalized the relations between brother and sister and then reconfigured the conjugal pair, basing marital relations upon mutuality. The girl's greater knowledge and skill was not just a benefit to her but an advantage to the boy, and not only because he gained a better wife and sister, but because *he* became a better person for her independence. Importantly, Atherton was praised by Willard, as narrator, for his "tolerant spirit." He let his younger sisters imitate him and join in as he played with his friends: "He had a cross-gun; they got him and Loren to help fit them out in the same way, and Kate painted in capitals along the side of hers its name, '*Defiance.*' "[52] Boys gained positive female qualities in part by sharing their knowledge with girls.

When communicating controversial ideas to her readers, Willard shifted her authorial voice from that of omniscient narration to personal address. Digressing from a description of Atherton's room, Willard addressed part of her audience personally and placed herself in the rooms of her middle-class boy readers: "How is it in your room, my manly young reader? What should I find if I ventured there as a committee of examination?" She doubted she would find "a hundred pretty contrivances" but added, "I don't say this is entirely your fault, for I think that your mother and sisters ought, at least, to share the blame . . . of this forlorn looking apartment." Here, she moved from addressing the boy to indirectly speaking to his mother and sister who took great interest in decorating their own rooms yet, unfortunately, "take it as a matter of course that yours shall be the dingy place it is."[53] Willard argued that beauty and decoration should be available to males, too. In this way, men would appreciate women more and learn to be more like them; if both sexes shared each others' most positive attributes, they would reach a position of greater equality and mutual respect and be better individuals. Having presented her controversial opinions on contemporary expectations about gender, Frances Willard as WCTU president receded into the background, returning to her position as omniscient narrator.

Willard's favored model of child raising was characterized by Mrs. Hill's gender-blind technique; she divided up chores based on each child's developing personality rather than on a dogmatic sense that all girls must embody a domestic ideal: "Their mother did not talk to them as girls, but simply as human beings, and it never occurred to Kate that she ought to 'know housework' and do it. Nell took to it kindly by nature; her sister did not, and each one had her way." Willard emphasized that Kate did her fair share around the house but was allowed to choose her chores according to her inclinations rather than her gender, without being made to feel odd because of it: "Their mother never said, 'You must cook, you must sweep, you must sew,' but she studied what they liked to do and kept them at it with no trying at all. There was never a busier girl than Kate, and what she did was mostly useful. She knew all the carpenter's tools and handled them: made carts and sleds, cross-guns and whip-handles."[54] Kate chose to do woodwork, a hobby usually associated with boys; she also made conventionally masculine items, such as cross-guns. Mrs. Hill herself combined traits usually attributed to men with women's skill at "quiet" nurturing: "Mrs. Hill had the brain of a man and the courage of a major-general, it was always her plan to put her children forward and then help them by her quiet counsel."[55] As "major-general," Mrs. Hill was the overseer of Fort City. Here, Willard used a masculine military metaphor to emphasize Mrs. Hill's strength and intelligence, thereby endowing her with qualities rarely described in conventionally feminine imagery.

Willard intimated that the children preferred Mrs. Hill's unprejudiced and thoughtful method of child raising over their father's more disciplinarian approach. Mr. Hill forbade the girls (but not Atherton) to swim, go boating, ride on horseback, or hunt. These restrictions prompted Willard to comment in another personal aside that, "at this distance, it looks to this narrator . . . a pity," asserting that if Kate's parents were so afraid of her drowning, they should have taught her to swim rather than kept her from the water.[56] Mr. Hill was strict and "severe" in his demands that no weekday activity be done on Sundays. Mrs. Hill "did not interfere with all this by any word, but the children all felt a difference, and had a sense of greater 'elbow room' with her." When Christmas day fell on a Sunday, for instance, the children were not allowed to play with their new toys; Kate ingeniously avoided her father's stricture by asking and receiving her mother's permission to draw meeting houses on her new slate.[57] Mrs. Hill took good advantage of Kate's childishness to instill discipline and socialization in a less overt, yet ultimately more effective way. In this instance, Willard also depicted as a positive good a wife's subtle undermining of her husband's authority.

In the Hill family, the ideal of equality for boys and girls broke down around the issue of education; the girls' education was more restricted than their brother's, for he attended school while they stayed at home: "Atherton had already been two winters in the 'Academy' at Janesville, walking in and out each day. Of course he was to go to college, but the fate of his sisters was more misty in those days. Kate looked upon him as a prince, and only wished, although she dared not say it, that she had been born to a boy's chances in the world—she never really wished she was a boy."[58] The idea that "boy's chances" could be separated from the boy was part of Willard's degendering of human characteristics. Kate coveted privileges and opportunities equal to Atherton's; she did not desire to be a male.[59] Kate "was persuaded in her own mind that something out of the common lot awaited her in the future. [But] women were allowed to do so few things, that her ideas were quite vague." Willard commented that, in comparison, girls in the 1880s were privileged, for they could dream of and plan for many more specific careers and could look to a wide variety of female role models.[60] Throughout her life, Frances Willard was a prolific writer and lecturer; her own story certainly provided a model of female ambition for *Crusader* readers. Willard stressed authorship as an important means of communication, as a skill women could learn at home, and as a career they could pursue from home, too. Moreover, women's groups like the WCTU fostered and promoted women writers through their own periodicals, such as the *Union Signal* and the *Young Crusader*. Willard explained in an 1888 nonfiction article called "Hints About Authorship" that success as a writer would only come after "the most steady, quiet, earnest work." Willard asserted that with dedication, any young woman could be "an authoress—though I would leave off the ess—why, then, go to, and be one."[61]

Viewing rural life ambivalently, Willard both idealized its nurturing qualities, such as open space, safety and purity, yet recognized its limitations, such as its inability to provide talented young women with specific career goals, or even educations, thereby necessitating creation of a make-believe "city" that provided them with a broader education and experience. These issues may have been particularly relevant to those among the WCTU's middle-class readership who had rural roots or lived in smaller towns and cities. Perhaps "Fort City" represents Willard's creation of a temptationless city, a blending of the urban and rural ideal. In its favor, according to Willard, country living taught youths to balance their needs against those of the plants and animals around them.[62] As president of the state horticultural and agricultural societies, their father assured them that nature could be "managed"; he "always carried his little spy-glass, folded foot measure, and pocket thermometer, and taught his children how to use them and to make careful observations on the weather."[63] Rural life was a vehicle for temperance lessons as well, for although Willard's story differed from the average *Crusader* story by subordinating temperance to the overall plot, she directed several abstinence messages to her young audience.[64] In one passage, Mr. Hill challenged Loren, a stubborn neighborhood boy, to sign Nell's temperance pledge, offering him material incentive in the form of a new pair of ice skates for Christmas:

> This announcement caused much hand-clapping and delight, for Loren was a smart, good-hearted fellow, and the three children felt that he must be brought into the temperance fold *before he left the farm and struck out into the world of temptation that lay beyond*. . . . He had not formed the [alcohol] habit, and had declined to give his name before from simple prejudice and a foolish dislike "to be bound." . . . When Nell hastened to bring the pledge from its place on the wall, he put his name down . . . and the evening closed with "Guide me, O thou great Jehovah."[65]

Loren's earlier refusal to sign the pledge was dismissed as foolish prejudice, especially in light of the fact that, according to Willard, his pledge to abstain from tobacco had noticeably improved his health.[66] In this context, Willard valorized rural America as a good place to raise innocent children, removed from the worst sources of temptation.

Oscillating between the view of rural life as good and clean or as constricting and oppressive, Willard ultimately revealed her own fundamental problems with it. Her ambivalence is clearest in a passage where her voice and perspective as narrator again slipped as she remembered an important trip "East." In this passage, all pretense of fiction disappeared as Willard abandoned the fictional Hill family and lapsed into an entirely autobiographical account of her own childhood. Willard's oscillation between fiction and nonfiction seems to parallel her oscillation between valorizing and criticizing rural life. The reader is informed that Kate's best role model was her friend and cousin, Charlotte Gilman, another young woman who promised to have a brilliant "literary career" and had great "gifts of heart and mind and pen."[67] Interestingly, Gilman's life symbolized the better educational opportunities available to girls in the East, for Gilman planned to attend Oberlin. From the time of their visit, the Hill children focused on cities and "the East" as a "wider" world of opportunity, where Kate, in particular, wished that she could live in order "to learn—to do—to achieve."[68] Inconsistently, Willard noted Kate's chafing—"I want to see the world," yet dismissed it in the following paragraph, asserting that, "this country life had been the making of them all, and of none more than Kate, who was the most fragile, physically, of the three."[69] This might not have convinced Willard's readers, however, for throughout the story, Kate ran and played hard.[70] Willard did not resolve the tensions about the fact that cities were the sites both of temptation and opportunities. Perhaps readers tended to interpret the story as ultimately favoring urban life because in the last chapter, Kate

(Frances) moved to a suburb of Chicago, the biggest midwestern city, in order to achieve her own educational and career ambitions. Indeed, as president of a national reform organization, Willard's career required the city to succeed.

Willard's story was open to multiple interpretations, for it could be read primarily as a feminist tract or, alternatively, as a paean to "feminine" virtues of piety and nurturing. Knowing that her reading audience included dedicated WCTU mothers who viewed their activism as social housekeeping, Willard balanced her challenges to convention with scenes that reinforced the importance of the mother in child rearing, especially in the instilling of "proper" religious and social values.[71] The WCTU's tactic of glorifying women's purity generated great activism among its members and echoed social purity ideas. In particular, women affiliated with the WCTU looked to Victorian notions regarding women's greater religious piety as justification for their secular activism.[72] As president, Willard was careful not to alienate this strong WCTU contingent; thus, Mrs. Hill's innovative gender-neutral child rearing notions were balanced by "feminine" traits celebrated in the Victorian era, such as her saintly, religious nature. Depending on their own priorities, readers could come away from the story with competing interpretations of Willard's true emphasis and interests.

Willard portrayed Mrs. Hill as the spiritual leader of her family. Accordingly, at their improvised church services, Mrs. Hill led them in prayer: "they all knelt, while that deep, motherly heart carried to the Heart that 'mothers' all the world, its love, its trust and adoration." Presenting a maternal and female model of religion that was independent of organized religion dominated by male ministers, Willard characterized Christ as the nurturing "mother" of all humanity. Kate drew strength from her mother's religious nature, "she was never afraid while her *mother's* soul was lifted up to God."[73] Willard revealed that Kate herself was not particularly religious and thought her mother pious enough for two:

> They did not insist that the children read the Bible for themselves, and Kate seemed very shy about it, so much so that her mother playfully called her eldest girl, "my little infidel," for when, at a very early age, the Testament was specially read to her on Sunday, she had asked, "How do you know God sent it?" . . . Her mother had the good sense never to seem shocked by this bit of bravado, but patted the busy little head with her kind, steady hand, saying "My little girl will be a missionary, yet." She knew these symptoms were not of ugliness, but just a little prancing about of a nettlesome steed before it settled to life's long and difficult race. She knew the more she argued and reproved, the worse the case would be, so she just lived the gospel right along and taught its precepts and *prayed much.*[74]

Kate was an "infidel" who did not want to be pushed into religion. As WCTU leader, Frances Willard herself represented a new type of Christian "missionary"—one less religious and more interested in social reform. Mrs. Hill was right about Kate (Frances) becoming a missionary, but she did not become exactly the kind of missionary her mother had in mind. Willard did not quite secularize the term missionary but moved in that direction. This is similar, perhaps, to the WCTU's use of the term young "crusaders" to motivate youths to fight for a broad political agenda. In Willard's adult life, religion was a means but never the final goal of her work. When Willard became president of the WCTU in 1879, she broadened its focus beyond its original role as a Christian temperance union toward becoming a more inclusive women's organization, one dedicated to bringing about a whole series of profound social changes to American society. In fact, while she was president, Willard's elderly mother acted as the surrogate for Frances on religious matters; she was celebrated, for instance, as "Saint Courageous" in Willard's articles and speeches.

Willard's competing narratives regarding both the virtues of country life and the need of greater opportunities for women ultimately favored the urban environment, where more freedom and career options were available to adult women. Mrs. Hill's life of rural isolation did not provide a direct role model for Kate, who wanted to be an agent of change. In fact, Mrs. Hill's life was full of regret and sacrifice; she herself vowed that her children would lead more productive lives: "Mrs. Hill . . . never complained of the loneliness from which she had so keenly suffered, except to make her children feel these words: 'I had many ambitions, but I've buried myself on this farm—disappearing from the world to reappear, I trust, in my children at some future day.' "[75] Mrs. Hill's mobilizing narrative for her daughters is an early "feminist narrative" of white middle-class women's oppression, although located in a rural, rather than a suburban setting. Willard's narrative anticipates and parallels Betty Friedan's 1960s narrative of the oppressive and isolated white women's domestic sphere. Mrs. Hill's own life was stifled for the sake of her husband, a would-be gentleman farmer. Whereas Mrs. Hill lived though her children, Kate lived for herself, something that could only occur, it seems, in the city. Willard's organization was obsessed with the evils of the city, yet she idealized it as a possible site for women's liberation, recognizing that it perpetuated certain evils yet eradicated others. Willard's story is most significant for its insistent, destabilizing focus on women's place in family and society, a focus designed to make readers question and confront societal norms and conventions, including ones that Mrs. Hill appeared to uphold.

* * *

Three *Young Crusader* stories written between 1911 and 1916 highlight the changes and continuities in the WCTU's priorities over a decade after Frances Willard's death. I have chosen for analysis three long serialized stories that were similar in format to Willard's "Three Children and How They Amused Themselves." Two have male protagonists, and the third features a girl like Willard's main character, Kate. These stories show how male and female characters and gender roles were represented by *Crusader* writers other than Willard. The following stories were also chosen to reflect the various themes and concerns of the *Crusader* staff, especially their continuing interest in political and social reform. The story by a southern writer complements Willard's focus on the Midwest, points to some interesting regional differences, and reminds us that the WCTU had a national constituency and was not simply restricted to the East Coast. Each story highlights a different set of issues about which the WCTU wanted to influence children in the twentieth century, from temperance and politics to immigration and the role of children as social reformers. Willard's 1887 treatment of gender issues complemented the magazine's nonfiction articles of both earlier and later periods. The *Crusader* consistently advocated that girls become politically aware activists, reformers, and career women. These three later stories also subvert preconceptions about gender but in more subtle, less overtly challenging ways. In one story, we will see, the main character becomes a hero only when he adopts the moral values of his mother and his aunt as his own.

I have argued in previous chapters that Willard's death in 1898 did not represent a key point of departure for the WCTU from its activist "Do Everything Policy." The content of the WCTU children's fiction published twelve to sixteen years after Willard's death supports this conclusion. Even stories that featured stronger pro-temperance appeals also encouraged youths to engage in diverse types of moral and political reform, as well as benevolent work among the poor and immigrants in America's urban areas. Gender issues figured in the following stories in more subtle ways, suggesting some possible retreat from Willard's advanced feminist position. The post-Willard *Crusader* fiction both challenged convention and reinstituted it in new contexts.

A 1911 story, "The Little Captain," by Lynde Palmer, was a true temperance melodrama, creating an interplay between the WCTU's substantive positions on morality and temperance, and aesthetic considerations. Of the three post-Willard stories under examination, this one focused most exclusively on the social and familial effects of alcohol. It explicitly detailed the seamiest sides of city ghettos, and even family violence. WCTU editors expected its unrelentingly miserable content to be so unappealing to youths that it could act only as a deterrent.[76] The "fallen" character in the melodrama, James Grey, was a father of four young children who was ruined by alcohol and destroyed his family in the process. An early chapter focused on the necessity of the temperance pledge to secure abstinent behavior. Awakening from a drunken stupor with a "blinding headache," Grey, ashamed and temporarily repentant, declared, "I shall bring no more misery into this pleasant home. . . . I shall never drink again."[77] His wife, Margaret Grey, immediately asked him to sign a pledge promising to be an abstainer, but he rejected it with disdain, saying that to sign would be a "positive disgrace" and would put him in a "strait jacket." Grey wanted to retain his masculine prerogative to continue to "take a social glass now and then." According to the WCTU, real manliness lay in promise keeping and following one's written commitment. On New Year's Eve, Grey participated in the "wild orgies" of the saloon, where he gambled away all his pay and lost his job in the process. He returned home less than a man—a "beast" and a "pitiable object."[78] Margaret Grey's earlier plea that he sign the pledge had gone unheeded, an action that doomed him to continued alcoholism. One must sign the formal pledge in order to become a true abstainer; in no piece of fiction published in the *Young Crusader* did someone sign the abstinence pledge and subsequently break it. This was not a possibility, for the power of the pledge was predicated upon reformers' will to believe the bourgeois ideal that a written contract is inviolable.[79]

In contrast to Willard's story, the city figured in Palmer's tale as the site of saloons, disease, immigrants, and Grey's destruction. Forced to auction off their cottage in the wooded suburbs and move to a tenement apartment building at the city's center, Margaret Grey feared that the city and its inhabitants would corrupt—both physically and morally—her innocent children: "The sultry, unwholesome air rose from the steaming streets, and she sighed heavily, remembering that around their old cottage home swept the pure breezes. . . . Alas! how would her delicate little human flowers thrive in this foul air? Or, even if they escaped sickness and physical waste, how could they remain pure and innocent, exposed to the contamination of intercourse with the almost heathenish children in the row."[80] Metaphors of contamination melded moral and health images, linking Progressive Era hygiene reform to temperance. The "sickness and physical waste" of the city were contrasted to the "pure and innocent" country. Although not explicitly stated, the "heathenish children" in the tenement were probably immigrants, those perceived by reformers to be in particular need of instruction in matters of health and hygiene and a source of social contamination to innocent rural and suburban children.

Although this story did not engage gender issues as directly as Willard's, it offered to *Crusader* readers an unusual boy hero whose saintly, "feminine" qualities dominated. Ignoring or perhaps rejecting the era's cult of manliness, the author presented Jamie as spiritually and morally strong but physically weak.[81] With James Grey consigned to the role of a doomed alcoholic, the story shifted its focus to his sons, Harry and Jamie (aged about twelve and seven). Each child represented a distinct possible response to life with an alcoholic father. The oldest boy, Harry, reacted with powerless rage.[82] Young Jamie responded differently to the crisis, becoming a nonviolent temperance crusader, modeling his behavior on female WCTU members.

Jamie's desire to stop his father's drinking led him, with his little sister Kitty, to enter a saloon in the city center frequented by his father. Unnoticed at first, they overheard a debate about the constitutional prohibition of alcohol. This scenario provided the author with the opportunity to present prohibition in the best possible light. A "bloated" man declared: "I say this is a free country, and no one has a right to say to me, You shall, or you shall not drink. A man has a perfect right to go to the devil, if he wants to. . . . As for all this nonsense about a prohibitory law, it was just got up by a set of meddlers and fools."[83] The defender of alcohol did not deny the WCTU's main argument—that alcohol is debilitating and character altering—he simply, and weakly, argued that "a man has a perfect right to go to the devil." For the pro-prohibition side, a "gentleman" abstainer (who just happened to be in the saloon to preach his cause) argued: "My friends, you get this poison in your heads, and you become wild. You go forth to steal, to ill treat your wives and children, and sometimes—sometimes—to murder. My friends, has not society a right to protect itself against such enormities? Has it not a right to aim at the root, the cause, of all this evil?"[84] Covering as much ground as possible, the gentleman identified alcohol as a poison that had direct physiological effects but then proceeded to emphasize that alcohol was also a women's and a family problem, a social problem that demanded a national solution.

The "Little Captain" presented a model of temperance activism based on mobilizing urban children to participate in the WCTU's Loyal Temperance Legion. In spite of the hostility he faced, Jamie vowed that he would eventually convince all the tenement youths to join a "cold-water army." Jamie's use of the term "cold-water army" referred to teetotal campaigns of the antebellum era, while his actions echoed progressive reformers' resolve to remodel the family (especially the immigrant family) through the child.[85] Mobilized into action by the sight of a drunken woman lying in the street being tormented by the "young vagabonds" of the neighborhood, Jamie gave an eloquent and extended pro-temperance appeal. Passages like the following seem to have been included as a practical guide to "crusaders" on how best to appeal to other children and successfully form a Loyal Temperance Legion:

> "Oh, boys," said Jamie, with a quick, gasping breath, "you all know what it is to have some friend a drunkard. . . . Very near my dear old home there is a little wood, and right in the midst of the thick of trees there is a little stream as cool as ice. . . . Oh, that's the kind of drink God meant us to have. . . . We can be wise, and good, and respected. We can come out of this dirty little street, and live in clean, healthy houses. We can earn money, and take care of our little brothers and sisters; and there is no reason why we shouldn't, some day, get to be judges or governors, or even (who knows?) presidents of the United States. Come, boys," said Jamie, seeing his young audience were with him, "I've been thinking of getting up a cold-water army."[86]

The phrases "dirty little street" and "healthy houses" demonstrated the need for both a temperate, "pure" family life and a literally clean, disease-free house. Although the Grey's new neighbors initially tormented and ridiculed the boys for going to church on Sundays, they were converted through preacher Jamie's eloquence to the Christian temperance crusade and enthusiastically signed the very pledge that Jamie's own father still refused to sign.[87]

Jamie returned home jubilant, only to encounter the most recent victims of alcohol's destructiveness—his dead baby brother and his grieving family. The "Little Captain's" plot is melodramatic, in the sense that it is "characterized by sensational incident and violent appeals to the emotions," for it was structured on a series of family tragedies caused by Grey's alcoholism and relied upon new tragedies to maintain its momentum.[88] The tragic sight of his dead baby brother reinforced the moral rightness of the cold-water cause: Sufficiently stirred and yet "subdued by sorrow," the army of boys marched the city streets in "orderly array," stopping to shout "Death to King Alcohol" in front of each saloon. Although in other contexts, the WCTU fought against literary sensationalism, Palmer wrote in vivid, almost sensationalist prose. If melodramatic tragedies could mobilize readers to moral action and reform, then WCTU editors and parents were willing to expose children (properly armed) to the negative aspects of cities and alcoholism, such as saloons, poverty, and death. As with the WCTU's favorite industry-produced movie, *Ten Nights in a Barroom,* the worst effects of alcohol could be represented, *had* to be represented, in order to deter effectively youths from drinking.[89] This dual emphasis on both excess and "realism" is characteristic of WCTU literature as a whole, including the reports and press releases of its Department of Purity in Literature and Art that pointed to the dire consequences of consuming "impure" culture. The WCTU could, and did, stylistically represent its cause by balancing realism—the threatening horrors of an "impure" life—with piety and a sense of high drama. Realism was determined by a standard based on whether the portrayal of "immoral" activities served as an enticement or a warning to the reader.

In a voluptuous scene replete with violence and pathos, James Grey returned home to find that Margaret Grey had sold the clock—their last "nice" possession and symbol of middle-class respectability—to feed her starving children. Ignoring their plight, Grey demanded the money. When his wife refused, he violently threatened her:

> "Then I'll kill you." Mrs. Grey stood fearlessly before him; the brutal arm was raised; but Jamie, with a wild cry, threw himself between, and the ill-directed blow fell heavily upon his upturned head. The child dropped as if he had been shot, and there was a moment of death-like silence. Then, with a wail whose horror thrilled every nerve of the wretched father, Mrs. Grey cried, slowly. "You have killed him—your little son! killed Jamie—our little Jamie!" she repeated, with a wild tenderness, lifting the helpless child in her arms.[90]

Wife abuse, murder, and uncontrolled anger were vividly and unrelentingly recounted for the child-readers of the *Crusader*. Dwelling on the scene's pathos, Jamie did not die immediately but instead suffered "unconscious ravings" full of "revelations of sufferings" that forced his father, James Grey, to recognize the extent of his wrongdoings. After exhorting that "no drunkard can inherit the Kingdom of God," Jamie finally "raised his beautiful eyes, full of a wonderful light" and died.[91] The chapter's title, "The Captain's Promotion," refers to Jamie's "promotion" from earth to heaven, a term that the WCTU used in the *Union Signal* to announce the deaths of its members. His death, although tragic, confirmed his "angelic" nature and was designed to steel the resolve of the story's readers to resist the temptations of alcohol.[92]

"The Little Captain" is structurally similar to what Judith Walkowitz describes as a "transformed melodrama, complete with stereotyped characters, extreme states of being and danger, rapid action, and the vindication of virtue over vice."[93] Melodrama, however, usually features a female victim/heroine, but in this case, the boy Jamie was the story's principal victim/hero. This reversal is similar to Willard's desire to change conventional gender roles; a boy, not a girl, was the religious saintly reformer, a moral "feminine" hero rather than a hero who performed acts of physical prowess. The role of the saintly child was typically reserved for female protagonists, such as little Eva in Harriet Beecher Stowe's *Uncle Tom's Cabin*.[94]

Those readers who interpreted the death of the virtuous hero as a signal of defeat for pro-temperance forces could find some reassurance in the final chapters. Jamie's providential death set the stage for moral action and regeneration, thereby justifying Jamie's martyrdom. James Grey's guilt and suffering led to permanent change in his behavior and to the family's escape from the city, a city depicted quite differently from Willard's utopian "Fort City" or from the Chicago of her adult life. This change began the day of Jamie's funeral, as the father endured and overcame "that fearful disease— delirium tremens."[95] Jamie was buried amid the healthy sunshine and fresh air he had missed, for "they carried little Jamie away from the dark city, out to the old country burying ground, where the violets grow, and the robins come in the spring."[96] Two years later, the Grey family was back in the suburban countryside. James Grey entered their old cottage with a "manly tread," home from a temperance meeting he attended with his surviving son, Harry. Telling Margaret Grey of the many city people from the tenement building and surrounding saloons who had been saved by Jamie's death, he concluded, "Well, Maggie, God has brought good out of the evil. Our little Jamie began a great work in that wretched lane, and now, many a poor creature, whom the world regarded as utterly lost, is bravely struggling back to life and hope." Margaret Grey, holding their newborn baby in her arms, had the last words as she concluded, "He that overcometh shall inherit all things."[97]

Leaving melodrama for a courtroom drama and a narrative of political reform, a 1913 story entitled "Roger Hillman's Honor," by Jennie N. Standifer, from Gulfport, Mississippi, is notable—and atypical among *Crusader* stories—for its southern author (prominently identified as such), as well as its southern perspective on populism and race and on progressive issues such as political corruption and reform. By 1913, several southern states had passed, by landslide margins, statewide Prohibition statutes, primarily by playing up fears that alcohol use among blacks was furthering crime and political corruption.[98] Standifer's complex story wove prevalent racist stereotypes into a populist tale of reformers' triumph over a political boss. "Roger Hillman's Honor" is also one of the first long, serialized *Crusader* stories that focuses on abstinence from cigarette smoking as well as drinking, reflecting the WCTU's growing concern in the 1910s that more and more young boys, and even some girls, were taking up smoking. Beginning in 1910, the *Crusader* devoted anywhere from two to six full pages (out of about 12 pages) per issue to anti-cigarette warnings, stories, chants, and lessons. A 1911 article, for instance, attacked the young woman who smoked as "a cheap, unwomanly being, and be she rich or poor, mansion-dweller or street-walker, she is a blot on woman's honor, always and everywhere."[99]

The story began as fifteen-year-old Roger Hillman faced a familiar temperance challenge—his aunt's will left him $5,000 to use for his college education with the stipulation that he sign a pledge promising not to smoke or drink until he became twenty-one. The plot hinged upon whether Roger would be able to resist temptation, stop smoking, and sign the pledge. With "deep humiliation," Roger informed his widowed mother that his smoking habit had caused him to fail his tenth-grade algebra and Latin courses and to play poorly on his school's baseball team. Roger's mother's widowhood seems designed to elicit the sympathy of the reader and to explain her difficulty in controlling her son, as evidenced by his smoking habit. She responded with skepticism to his reluctance to stop smoking: "That will not do, Roger. I am confident that it is the habit you have formed of almost incessant smoking that is injuring your eyes and making you nervous. Sign at once the pledge requested in Aunt Louisa's will; then your eyes will improve, and you can easily finish your tenth grade work this summer." Echoing the character James Grey in "The Little Captain," Roger resisted, saying, "I thought I would leave off gradually."[100]

Encountering a series of urban temptations on his walk to his first day of summer school classes, Roger's inauspicious plan to stop smoking gradually was immediately threatened. First, he passed the church deacon—a would-be role model—smoking a cigar, then alluring billboards "proclaiming the merits" of tobacco, and finally, a shop's window display advertising pipes and cigars. The shop, tellingly, was owned by "a leading church member." Upstanding members of the church community were implicated in placing profits and their own pleasure over virtue and responsibility, thereby leading young Roger further astray.[101] The issue of the corruptibility of the church is an intriguing one for a southern WCTU member to be addressing and suggests that Standifer wanted to shame churches and church members into taking a greater responsibility for civic reform and community regeneration.[102]

Roger was also thwarted in his attempt to study quietly in ostensibly the safest of places, the church yard. Instead of peace and quiet, he overheard the church janitor, Bill Hall, threatening a young boy, "little Rastus," to keep silent about a secret: "Ef you lets drap one word bout dis . . . dar won't be room in dis town for you. . . . You mind nigger?" Hall threatened the youth, who illegally delivered alcohol for him, to keep their activities a secret and even threatened to send Rastus's father to jail on a false murder charge if he disobeyed. Roger discovered that Bill Hall's secret was a basement full of boxes of alcohol—illegal in their dry town. Both Hall and Rastus were black; the author gave each character a heavy dialect and interspersed terms like "nigger" and "pickininny" throughout their talk, thereby mobilizing and making use of culturally available stereotypes about supposedly ignorant and unlawful black people.[103]

With the introduction of Bill Hall's customer, United States Senator John Holder, racist fears about corrupt black people merged with fears about the power of white politicians who illegally used alcohol to win elections.[104]

Upon seeing Roger in the church yard, the senator tempted him with visions of easy profit and power by offering him a job in his office and suggesting that he reject his aunt's will: "'Ha!' laughed the politician as he lighted an expensive cigar and handed one to Roger. 'Here, have a smoke, old fellow, and get the cobwebs out of your brain. Well, so she wanted to put you on a prohibition diet, did she, until you are twenty-one? You'd better let that legacy pass on to the orphans, Roger, and make your own money.'"[105] The janitor, Bill Hall, embodied stereotypes of the dishonest, immoral, black men who illegally sold alcohol. Senator Holder, in turn, embodied stereotypes of cigar-smoking, white politicians who willingly corrupted youths and bought votes to gain power.[106]

With little internal coherence, the story became a courthouse drama in which reform, corruption, and race played out in interesting ways. Roger was served with a summons to appear in court as a witness in the trial of "Bill Hall, colored," who was charged with running a "blind tiger" (i.e., illegally distributing alcohol in a town or municipality). As Roger waited in the courthouse, he looked through the window to the county jail where he could see little Rastus's father being questioned. Roger wondered if political corruption was behind it and "if Bill had meant what he said when he threatened to send Rastus' 'daddy' to the penitentiary." Here, the author suggested that political alliances between blacks and politicians lead to corruption and abuse of power. In the courtroom, "much to Roger's surprise Senator Holder appeared as the old janitor's attorney" and led the impressionable Roger to testify falsely that Hall was a "harmless old man." Roger then stepped into the hallway only to overhear some police officers voice their disappointment with his testimony: "Several meat markets [houses of prostitution?] get their booze from Bill, and he furnishes the club rooms, and the Senator himself, when drinks are need[ed] to clinch a voter." The senator's politically motivated self-interest, his desire to keep Hall in the business of supplying alcohol to buy votes, led him to be Hall's defense attorney. Another added, "the negroes are committing crimes every week while drunk on Bill's whisky."[107] Politicians and blacks were charged with ruining the town by creating and supporting a criminal underworld of gambling and prostitution. Feeling disgraced, Roger approached the police officers with his information regarding the alcohol stored in the church basement. Roger's new information prompted the judge to give the police permission to raid the church and confiscate the alcohol.

With a new spirit of openness, Roger came home and eagerly told his mother of these events:

> Under the basement of the church in which you worship every Sunday Bill Hall has been running a [blind tiger]. I was a weak, cigarette-smoking cow-

ard when I found it out the other day, Mother, and I was afraid to tell. Today things have happened that have made me wake up. As my father's son—as a Hillman—I feel that I must make a stand for what is right and have the courage to help in the downing of evil. I am proud of being of real help in freeing our town of the unlawful sale of liquor.[108]

Roger Hillman's triumph was in rising to a standard of reform and temperance set by a woman, his aunt. He became a reformer and an abstainer as he went to the lawyer's office and signed his aunt's abstinence pledge. The male authority figures—except for the police and perhaps the judge—were corrupt in one form or another, including the minister. The church itself rested on a foundation of sin. Redemption came from fidelity to a standard set in the home and by women, both his aunt and his mother. This locates the beginning of reform in the private and personal realm (in good nineteenth-century fashion), but the result is civic action and political change. The story, for all its confusion, neatly straddled Victorian and Progressive modes of reform.

Young readers of "Roger Hillman's Honor" were provided with more than one moral or message, for abstinence changed Roger's character and also led to a crusade to eliminate political corruption. On the level of personal reform, Roger's new, cigarette-free life led to important improvements at school: He did well in his classes, "organized a football team, and soon total abstinence from the use of intoxicating liquors and tobacco was very popular in the Bankston High School." Later, he did well in college, too.[109] On the level of political reform, Roger explained to his mother, "the men and boys of the town are going to organize a league to keep a clean, law-abiding community," and he would be among them. Furthermore, Senator Holder withdrew from the race, defeated by the drys, thereby foiling the alliance between politicians and blacks. Standifer's racist representations in the *Young Crusader* reflect the WCTU's uneven commitment toward improving race relations or gaining adult black members. The WCTU began a Department of Colored Work in the 1880s but bowed to local prejudice by organizing both integrated and segregated local unions. Ruth Bordin praises the department for its unusually progressive and inclusive stance (for its time), particularly when it was headed by an African-American woman, Lucy Simpson Thurman, in the 1890s.[110] This story suggests, however, that WCTU members were not uniformly sensitive to racism or to their own participation in the creation of racist stereotypes.

The final *Crusader* story to be analyzed here, "The House of Goodwill," by Jessie E. Wright, was written in 1916 and featured a girl heroine and echoed Willard's gendered themes, including her interest in promoting women's role in reform. The story addressed political and social issues that were current during the World War I era such as immigration, citizenship, and Americanization. As with their conflicted ideas about racial equality and integration, members of the WCTU exhibited ambivalence toward immigrants and continued immigration. In the 1880s, the WCTU targeted newly arrived immigrants for missionary evangelizing work and hoped to organize immigrant women into the WCTU, thereby encouraging them to reject their husband's use of alcohol as un-American. This work reflected progressive reformers and industrialists' concerted campaigns to incorporate and assimilate immigrants into the United States just before and during World War I. In 1914, Henry Ford began the best known of these programs, proudly labeling it a plan for "Americanization." It encouraged immigrants to learn the English language and to adopt American customs; it taught the foreign born lessons in United States history, and it aided these newcomers in applying for citizenship.[111]

Ruth Bordin argues that by the 1890s, the WCTU was influenced by another strain of Americanization, nativism, whose adherents claimed that the United States could not withstand the diversity represented by the millions of people entering the nation and called for stricter restrictions on immigration.[112] Nativist woman suffrage advocates resented the fact that foreign-born men could vote upon gaining citizenship, whereas native-born American women could not exercise that right. By 1895, the national WCTU officially supported educational requirements for voting, a plan explicitly aimed at restricting voting by immigrants and, in the post-Reconstruction South, blacks.[113] Affirming Bordin's analysis, the WCTU magazine for young women, *Oak and Ivy Leaf,* printed early nativist and racially based arguments for women's voting rights: "Foreigners come here, their habits different from ours, unused to our laws, with no education to enable them to learn, but they are considered capable of citizenship in a short time; if they can become eligible so quickly, certainly the American woman who has spent her life here can. If the negro could be taken from servitude and given the ballot, certainly our educated women will know how to exercise the same rights."[114] The *Young Crusader'*s fiction stories diverged from the WCTU's national policies by advocating a comparatively benign program of "helping" immigrants to become "good" American citizens. "The House of Good Will" differs from earlier stories in that a fascination with the foreignness of immigrants is a central theme in the story, as is the explicit desire to make the "others" familiar, to Americanize them. Jessie Wright's 1916 story mingles benevolence, ethnic stereotyping, and a naive sense that assimilation could be readily effected through "good will."[115]

Wright's story presented a strong female heroine similar to Willard's character, Kate. In this story the heroine, Jean, takes after her WCTU-member mother and is an activist who does what needs to be done for others, with a minimum of fuss or effort. By setting the story in a city suburb rather than in an isolated rural area, Wright could pass over Jean's need to develop, educate, or reform herself (as Willard's Kate had to do) and focus instead on her work for others. Throughout the story, her actions went beyond what is typically expected from adolescents, but Jean was never identified as being of stronger character than others—any girl could be like Jean if she so desired. Although the story was ostensibly about two native-born Protestant teenage twins, Jean and John, it was Jean and not her male sibling who was the main character and whose actions drove the story. By featuring the twin sister and not the brother, Wright prioritized gender and women's activism. The twins were left at home one weekend day to entertain themselves when their mother left town for a WCTU meeting (where she was having "the time of her life") and while their father was at work.[116] Instead of entertainment, they found a reform cause of their own in the appearance of "a Jew peddler . . . a bearded, bent, depressed looking little man."[117] The peddler was accompanied by his wife, baby, and a son and daughter, David and Zeelie. Invested with adult capacities, Jean questioned the family regarding their welfare. In response to Jean's inquiries, Zeelie (not her brother, David) explained that her parents' native language was Italian ("we speak dago") and that her father had been working very hard but had been cheated of his salary, could not pay the rent, had been evicted, and felt compelled to move with his family to a new town. Zeelie described their eviction as a racially motivated, anti-Semitic attack; the men who came to evict him had said "Here you dago! Here you jew! . . . You get out of Here!"[118]

Concerned about their lack of shelter and the fact that the children were leaving school a month before summer vacation, Jean decided—without consulting her parents or her brother—to let the family stay in a small house adjacent to her family's house. Jean's "house of goodwill" became a site of reform and education, a mini-city that was just as utopian and reform oriented as Willard's "Fort City." Coincidentally, Jean had recently purchased this house, a former caretaker's cottage, from her father with the promise that she would fix it up and find a renter for it. This information is imparted to the reader without any hint that adolescents do not usually buy houses, not even small ones. Although Jean sometimes followed dutifully in the footsteps of her WCTU-member mother, as when she appealed to her mother for help preparing a temperance slide-show and willingly received it, Jean often acted without adult supervision. When the twins' father arrived home, Jean precociously explained, "As soon as John told me you had the deed for me I—I rented it!"[119] Jean expressed her excitement at finding suitable tenants through the language of possession, transforming Zeelie and her family into veritable *ob-*

jects of reform: " 'Oh John,' began Jean, barely able to keep the dance out of her feet, 'isn't it perfectly lovely—I have an immigrant—I have an immigrant—*five* of them!' " Again using proprietorial language, Jean decided to hire Zeelie's mother to clean her parents' house: "I am going to see if Zeelie's mother can't come and work. You see, mother didn't have her cleaning woman come today, as I had to be in school, and she couldn't come tomorrow, so I'll just take the dollar and pay it to our Mrs. Foreigner if she will work."[120] Stories featuring characters like Jean—a precocious girl with articulate reform interests and projects—were criticized by librarians in the *Library Journal* as sanctimonious, unrealistic, and as granting too much authority to youths, thereby denigrating the parental role. Two children's librarians in 1901 outlined the proper way to evaluate children's literature for libraries and gave as an example of a rejected book one that sounds strikingly like this WCTU story: "Raymond, Evelyn. *Reels and Spindles.* Story of good but self-sufficient young girl whose mastery of financial and moral problems ranges from the sale of her pet burro (without the consent or knowledge of her parents), to the conception of costly philanthropic schemes to be carried out by a selfish, but finally repentant, rich elderly cousin, won over, of course, through the heroine's influence. Exceedingly improbable and sometimes tiresome. Rejected."[121] WCTU members not only approved of such fiction; they wrote it themselves.

Leaving none of the immigrant family's housekeeping to chance, Jean mused, "Mary Antin [an adult advisor] said they needed *showing*. Perhaps they are not used to that sort of house; perhaps they haven't bed-clothes enough."[122] Accordingly, Jean led Zeelie and her mother through the small house, explaining where she thought things should go, making sure that Zeelie's mother was disabused of her "improper" desire to make the living room into a bedroom, for "Jean regarded the point as a serious one." The narrator's stance is not ironic, for a floor plan of the house accompanies the story and makes it clear that each room has only one proper middle-class function, such as living room and hall (see figure 7). Additionally, the family's lack of "proper" possessions is the butt of several jokes; Zeelie's proud announcement that they owned "a dish" led John to ridicule the family's primitive state, yet Zeelie's comment also suggests that this family wants to be civilized.[123] The family's gratitude for Jean's benevolent concern and generosity was not dampened by her interference on the issue of room arranging. Zeelie translated for her mother: " 'She says,' said Zeelie proudly, 'that you are a queen—that your riches are like the sands of the sea. . . .' She added hesitatingly, 'United States not so—' "[124] Zeelie's gratitude was mingled with fantasy and the desire to have and to give as Jean could. Furthermore, Zeelie explained that Jean was the exceptional American, for Zeelie's family had met with overt hostility and resistance up to that point.

THE HOUSE OF GOOD WILL

JESSIE E. WRIGHT

CHAPTER IX

"Mother," said Jean, in her usual ingratiating way, "when you and father go to that banquet Tuesday night, may John and I have a party?"

"A party!" exclaimed her mother dubiously, "why on earth should you have a party—especially when I can't be here?"

"Oh, it's not so very much of a party; we only want to have—let me see," counting for a moment, "we only want to have eight people; and perhaps only five can come, and we will take care of the refreshments ourselves."

"Now, Jean," said her mother, "perhaps this is possible, but you might as well be more explicit. Let's talk it over."

"All right," laughed Jean, "I just wanted to sound awfully mysterious. Saturday when we were working on our little House of Good Will John said that David thought beer drinking and smoking, and I don't know what else, were quite proper—and I told John I would find a way to give him a chance to know such things are not all right, and I don't want to lose any time about doing it."

"Yes!" encouraged her mother.

"Of course we couldn't do anything over here that would spoil the evening for you and father; and we can't get their family together any other 'ime—the Yoes I mean—and so I thought as long as you and father were both going to be away this very Tuesday we might have the family over and I could make a beginning."

"I see. Surely that part would be easily arranged—but what good would it do you? How could you teach David anything?"

"I have it all planned out—just the best—and John will help." Jean's eyes shone in a way already familiar to her family when she had something particularly novel on foot.

"Who are the other three you spoke of?"

"I thought perhaps it would be a good chance for our principal to get acquainted with the Yoes. You see Mary Antin said if we only knew these strangers who aren't used to our ways we might find them really worth while, and not so awfully undesirable after all, and I do think the Yoes are the nicest people I ever saw in my life."

Jean's enthusiasm made her mother laugh, but she agreed with the idea of having the principal over if she could come. "But who are the other two?"

"Why, David's teacher and Zeelie's teacher. If they could see Mr. and Mrs. Yoe they would know so much better what such children have the most trouble to understand. I don't believe those teachers ever before spoke to any one just like they are—and those three teachers are all down here together in the same boarding house, and could come just as well as not."

"Of course, it would be nice to have them—but what are you going to do?"

"I am going to make a cake, if you will let me, and John is going to make ice cream."

"I didn't mean that part, although that will be fine, too, but how are you going to bring understanding to David and his family on the points you mentioned?"

"Oh, just as easy! I am getting up the grandest show—and so is John. We are going to use the screen and the reflector; and I have lots of pictures and things cut out already."

"Like what?"

"I'll show a nickel—big, you know, on the screen—and show the glass of beer, it will buy, and the loaf of bread it will buy. And then I will show how many glasses of beer it would take to equal the nickel's worth of bread in food value, and what an awful lot they would cost."

"Why, Jean, that is fine!" exclaimed her mother enthusiastically. "I have lots of charts and things you could use along the same lines."

"Yes'm," giggled Jean. "We've been using them some already, I guess."

"That is what they are for. I will help you get up some things that will show, through pictures, the foolishness of using beer and tobacco. I suppose they feel as though those things are actual strength producers."

That very night Jean and John and their mother cut pictures from colored advertisements of different sorts of foods, of clothing, furniture, and everything that people feel are necessities. They made a fine set of pictures with scales showing the way food and clothes outweigh, in value, beer costing the same money. John was partic-

(Continued on Page Ten)

THE HOUSE of GOOD WILL

Figure 7. The campaign to bring respectability to the immigrant Yoe family is the focus of "The House of Good Will." In chapter 9, the author ties respectability to the immigrant family's acceptance of temperance as well as to the life-style and values associated with the idealized bourgeois home. (Courtesy of the National Woman's Christian Temperance Union, Evanston, Ill.)

One passage anticipates and seeks to dismiss criticisms that American-ization efforts like those organized by the WCTU were meddlesome and offensive to the immigrants themselves. Jean's friends, called the "Jolly Six," came to share an interest in Zeelie and her baby sister, for whom they de-cided to make some baby clothes. One friend asked, "will her people mind?" but another responded, "I don't believe so if it isn't just giving things, but being friends—'United States' friends," implying that Zeelie's family would accept gestures of equal friendship but not charity. Jean agreed, suggesting, "we won't make a nuisance of ourselves, but I will explain it to Zeelie, and she can make her people understand; and we will just do what will be kind, a help, and not a bother."[125] The girls remained confident that Zeelie's "peo-ple" would be properly grateful if approached with a modicum of sensitiv-ity. In this spirit, Jean rejected John's suggestion that they simply give the family some furniture stored in their attic, "the Yoes are pretty nice people, I think, and I know Mrs. Yoe would feel lots more as if they were hers, if she sort of earned them." The family's last name, Yoe, is revealed to the readers for the first time here in chapter seven; knowledge of the family's full name was only important, it seems, after they began to assimilate themselves into the United States. Whereas charity might have robbed Mrs. Yoe of her self-esteem, belongings that she earned through wagework would be more le-gitimately hers. Jean proved to be right, for Mrs. Yoe was, indeed, glad to work to earn the furniture and "tackled her job with radiant enthusiasm."[126]

In a subsequent chapter, extraordinary for its condensed presentation of domesticity, consumption, and Americanization ideas, the "Jolly Six" decid-ed to help the Yoes decorate their home like respectable Americans, putting up curtains and framed prints.[127] Zeelie was pleased with the changes and produced a "curious" bed spread "from her chest—a relic of housewifely enterprise that was in itself a guarantee of self-respect." The author tied self-respect not only to women's craft traditions but also to middle-class posses-sions that were equated with status and stability. Most significantly, Zeelie was "almost dazed by the idea of having a room like Jean's own, for *Jean had been very careful to create a desire along that line* by several times showing Zeelie things in her own attractive room." Zeelie's "dazed" desire was directed at achieving a middle-class American status and was not based solely on ma-terialistic desires. What makes Zeelie American is not the having but the wanting. Jean's determination to create these fantasies self-consciously linked consumption and goods to an American myth in which even immi-grants could succeed and where hard work was valued over class rank or inherited background. Moreover, the primary consumers in this story are female, thus fulfilling gendered patterns of women's commercial consump-tion and males' market production. In a nonfiction article, one WCTU leader directly connected home decorating to developing a child's "pure" character; the mother influences her children "with the art of holding those whom she loves, and second, with the art of so arranging her home in regard to color and furnishings that they shall give a sense of rest and harmony to those who enter."[128] From another perspective, this explicit creation of desire for consumption reflects a worldview very different from a critique of alcohol that denigrated it as a symptom and symbol of decadence and luxury.

Zeelie revealed that her father had made both the bed spread and a seat cushion and that his true profession was that of a tailor. Rewarded, in effect, for her display of her possessions, Zeelie was informed that a father of one of the Jolly Six "employed more tailors than any other shop in town"; he hired Mr. Yoe, who became the now properly producing male.[129] As the family entered into working-class respectability, Jean continued her Americanization campaign by asking her mother for permission to have a temperance party. Jean had discovered that Zeelie's brother, David, "thought beer drinking and smoking, and I don't know what else, were quite proper." She asked her mother if she could invite the Yoes to her party, along with the school principal and the children's teachers. The teachers, Jean explained, were not yet properly sympathetic to the learning difficulties the language barrier posed to the Yoe children; "I don't believe those teachers ever before spoke to any one just like they are." Jean added that she believed that "if we only knew these strangers who aren't used to our ways we might find them really worth while, and not so awfully undesirable after all, and I do think the Yoes are the nicest people I ever saw in my life."[130] Jean's remarks "combined sympathy and social distance," as Judith Walkowitz so nicely puts it; *Crusader* readers were asked to go beyond reactive, nativist prejudices against immigrants and to learn tolerance and appreciation while, of course, helping them to change their "ways."[131]

Entertainment at Jean's party would have a didactic purpose, so she asked her mother if she could borrow her WCTU charts and slides for a pro-temperance show. Her mother enthusiastically agreed, saying "I will help you get up some things that will show, through pictures [because the Yoe parents could not read English], the foolishness of using beer and tobacco. I suppose they feel as though those things are actual strength producers." Jean's mother alluded to alcohol's damaging physiological effects but, perhaps influenced by the new generation of progressive educators, Jean focused on its social impact, explaining that she had thought of many ways to express visually the wastefulness of alcohol: "I'll show a nickel—big, you know, on the screen—and show the glass of beer it will buy, and the loaf of bread it will buy. And then I will show how many glasses of beer it would take to equal the nickel's worth of bread in food value, and what an awful lot they would cost."[132] Jean's lecture provided the new Americans with a lesson in proper consumption. David and his family were converted to abstinence by her slide show and lecture and thus continued on their way to becoming good citizens of the United States.

The story concludes with the Yoes participating proudly in a Fourth of July celebration, learning what the holiday meant to "patriotic people."[133] Addressing her readers, the author of "The House of Goodwill" argued that immigrants had come to the United States in order to advance themselves and their families and should be given the opportunity to do so:

> They had come over the ocean on a great adventure. Nothing but the absolute belief that they were going to a country where they would have a chance to work and where the harder they worked, the better they would get along, would ever have made the uprooting possible. And at first it had seemed that there was not work enough to go around, and that hard work was not correspondingly rewarded. . . . But their chance, and friendly help had come in time. And a passion for work, begot of right ambition, was indeed theirs.[134]

"Right ambition" consisted of the will to work as hard as possible to achieve. A product of assimilationist rather than nativist thought, the story declared that immigrants should be treated with benevolence, respect, and concern rather than indifference, hatred, or fear.[135]

* * *

An examination of the WCTU's literature for children tells us a great deal about the goals and agenda of the WCTU, as well as about how its members conceived of the job of child rearing and of child development. For at least forty years, from 1887 through the 1930s, fiction in the *Young Crusader* consistently focused on temperance and reform, broadly defined. Although gender as a theme or a subject for analysis as such did not appear in each story after Willard's story of 1887, a gendered style of politics was promoted in and influenced each *Crusader* story. In Lynde Palmer's "The Little Captain," for instance, temperance was portrayed as the ultimate woman's issue by focusing on alcohol's disruptions of the home and its possible effects on mothers' children. Just as Willard's Kate combined "masculine" and "feminine" characteristics, Palmer's hero, Jamie, was nurturing, saintly, and brave. Moreover, the stories taught both boys and girls that their personal actions could make a difference. Just as WCTU members acted in the political arena even without the right to vote yet still gained various reform victories, so could girls and boys do the same. "Roger Hillman's Honor" taught children the larger ramifications of their actions; if they acted selfishly and without honor, they might doom their town to crime and corruption and themselves to physical degradation, but if they acted honorably, they could initiate broad political reforms *and* succeed personally. Similarly, in "The House of Goodwill," Jean took on a project of benevolence (a common and accepted role for middle- and upper-class women in the nineteenth century) and Americanization (a newer concern of the twentieth century), refusing to leave these matters in the hands of male experts. Youths would learn to be good citizens and reformers through WCTU fiction stories that featured children as active instigators of social and political change.

By producing its own "pure" children's fiction, the WCTU expected to counteract the negative influence of widely available commercially produced "impure" literature. The *Crusader* sympathetically portrayed girls and boys successfully employing a style of politics and reform conventionally coded as female. WCTU activists expected this "pure" fiction to be powerful enough to reconfigure girls' and boys' ideas about heroism and their own potential role in the political or public spheres. Clearly, the repressive censorship laws supported by the WCTU could not alone transform (or reform) American culture. Moral transformation and political regeneration could only occur through the positive influence of a "pure" culture produced, in this case, by the Woman's Christian Temperance Union. On the one hand, *Crusader* stories looked backward to nineteenth-century modes of feminine action rooted in volunteer organizations, writing, and notions of woman's nature and the home. On the other hand, the organization and many of its members looked forward to a new world of state power and professionalization and to a prominent place for women within it.

CHAPTER 7

Hearts Uplifted and Minds Refreshed

Promoting and Producing Pure Culture

Support for censorship is usually seen as wholly repressive, yet those groups that supported regulation were actively engaged in reworking the available cultural media and in creating their own "pure" culture. Both the American Library Association and the Woman's Christian Temperance Union accompanied their support for the regulation of "impure" reading and art with programs to promote or produce "pure" culture. The ALA created safe spaces for children in public libraries and championed "good" books. The WCTU encouraged, endorsed, and even produced "pure" art, literature, and moving pictures. The WCTU's enthusiasm for new technologies, from cheap reproductions of paintings to the production of motion pictures, is suggestive of its complex relationship to cultural change. As social actors and cultural propagandists, WCTU members had a subtle grasp of the connections between moral vision and the culture of the commercial market. They rejected any idea that the market conditions that generated such images should be considered immune from moral distinction or restraint. Librarians were removed from the site of production—their professional organization did not publish its own children's literature—but they relied on the strength and effectiveness of careful book selection to improve children's reading. WCTU members pursued a dual strategy of fighting for censorship laws while supporting and producing "pure" culture, including literature, art, movies, and radio programs. That WCTU women saw such arenas as amenable to moral distinctions and cultural improvement is at the core of the complexities of the late nineteenth and early twentieth century censorship movement. Having previously examined the regulatory efforts of the American Library Association and of the Woman's Christian Temperance Union, this chapter analyzes each organization's promotion and/or production of "pure" culture.

* * *

The arguments of male and female ALA members in favor of professional regulation and the promotion of "good" children's literature place them on a continuum with the WCTU members' support of purity and morality in literature. Concerns for the stability of immigrant and working-class boys and girls, especially in urban areas or factory towns, generally reinforced librarians' pro-regulatory perspective. ALA members looked at regulation and the promotion of "good" literature as part of their professional duty and as a prerogative of theirs as "guardians of public morals." In contrast, WCTU members looked at regulation as part of their protective role as mothers and as the reason behind their political fight for legal, governmental intervention. The production of culture was an important component of the WCTU's pro-censorship program. At the same time, its volunteer membership, composed mainly of laywomen, enabled it to take a more activist role. Librarians were constrained by a sense of professional boundaries that kept them separate from reformers and authors at a time when the WCTU was willing and able to reform, produce, and mediate cultural forms.

The American Library Association's debate about the quality and types of children's reading suitable for public libraries provides insight into how their promotion of "pure" reading served as a focal point for questions of class, ethnicity, and gender.[1] Both male and female librarians participated vigorously in debates about the extent of book censorship for children, giving special consideration to the needs of youths in cities and in factory towns, especially the children of immigrants. For the ALA, the initial question was simply whether or not to admit youths into libraries, a site that could clearly become an important source for children's reading. Once children were admitted, the issue became one of guiding their reading. An examination of librarians' views about children's literature, and their creation of a hierarchy of literary genres—particularly the emphasis on nonfiction over fiction—sheds light on Progressive Era views of child morality and socialization and reveals what librarians perceived their own professional role to be. Moreover, at the local level, children's librarians—all of whom were women—chose "good" books as part of their own professional self-identification.

Initially, librarians could not promote good books for children because children were excluded from public libraries altogether out of a concern for the condition and care of books and out of a fear that inappropriate adult fiction might reach young patrons. The American Library Association's "Yearly Report on the Reading of the Young" of 1885 indicates that most libraries did not admit children; many prohibited children under twelve or fourteen and limited any older students to one volume per week. Attempting to break this pattern, one librarian complained that even "the pupils in the highest classes [at school] were too young to hold library cards"; he convinced his trustees to issue "pupil cards," allowing them to check out non-fiction "but not permitting them the use of story books."[2] The ALA's 1890 yearly report recorded the first changes in this system. The pioneer children's reading room in the country was established, and a number of librarians modified official restrictions against children under fourteen. One librarian explained that he granted children reading rights on an individual basis, "provided they allow me to guide them in their reading."[3]

As progressive reformers paid more attention to the special needs of youths, most restrictions against children in libraries were successfully challenged as counterproductive. Reformers pointed out that children in school had the most need for the public library's expensive reference books, subject guides, and wide selection of books. They lamented that the "largest proportion of our children leave school at the age of fourteen, and but little before that time are they admitted to the use of the library." Reformers argued that children who developed the "habit" of using public libraries while in school would continue to use them after they began working.[4] A Milwaukee librarian took a different tack and challenged restrictions against youths by pointing to the proliferation of "poisonous" printed materials available to children elsewhere:

> In this age of trash and printed wickedness, when a professor in one of our western universities feels tempted to say that the youth of this country would grow up to better citizenship and stauncher virtue, were they *not* taught to read. . . . when we hear all this, and see for ourselves, bad literature on every hand, is it not a pitiful spectacle to see this sign conspicuously displayed in one of the circulating libraries in this country—"CHILDREN NOT ALLOWED IN THIS LIBRARY."[5]

Together, these arguments prompted wider change. In 1898, an ALA survey indicated that "of 125 libraries 31 have children's rooms, or will have them within three months." By the 1910s, separate children's rooms were common.[6]

The presence of younger children, not surprisingly, strengthened librarians' arguments in favor of careful book selection. The challenge was to create reading rooms that would supply children with "moral" fiction and non-fiction books. As one librarian explained, "if the age-limit for readers is withdrawn . . . all argument for the lowest grades of literature falls to the ground."[7] Anne MacLeod, a historian of children's literature, argues that "within the highly successful public library movement, the also successful drive to establish specialized services for children was equally a crusade to direct children's reading to 'the best.' "[8] Turning their attention to their own collections, librarians worried that careless book selections might harm youths' scholarly abilities, leading to "inattention, want of application, distaste for study, and unretentive memories." *Library Journal* editors opined that the popular juvenile fiction available in many public libraries—"a mass of maudlin twaddle, morbid, unhealthy, and entirely unfit to give proper views of life"—could seriously damage a child's mind. "In these days the flood of weak fiction is so great and children are allowed to read so much that the natural result is incoherence and flaccidity of mind."[9] Impressing upon their peers the need for vigilance, some ALA members argued that these problems were "directly traceable to the influence of that ill-directed and inordinate use of light literature which is fostered by the present library system."[10]

Librarians devised as many means as possible to improve youths' reading, referring to them as the "baits by which we may allure" young readers. They carefully organized bulletin boards and book displays: "New books, *except fiction*, are placed uncovered on book shelves accessible to the public."[11] They also enforced restrictions on the number of fiction books a child could check out each week and used reading lists to help guide youths to the "best" books.[12] Denying that their objections to "sensational" children's literature derived from "minor morals" or "squeamishness which would emasculate literature of all its virility," they argued that their objections were "part of a larger question—that of civilization itself."[13] Ostensibly concerned that reading low quality fiction would lead to permanent mental damage, this male librarian's choice of metaphors suggests that they were also afraid of producing "weak" or "feminine" young men.

Librarians who wanted to change children's reading tastes were presented with significant difficulties and pondered the questions: "How are we going to reach the boy who has read every one of Optic's books 'straight through,' who has nearly finished the Alger series . . . or his sister, whose ideals of girlhood are Elsie Dinsmore and Little Prudy?—Are these children to be led to read, and to prefer to read, the children's books which may have a strong influence for good on their characters?"[14] They usually objected to books such as *Elsie Dinsmore,* by Martha Finley, because, as one historian puts it, "the overriding fact of the novel is that Elsie is the clear winner in every contest between child and adult, even (or especially) when the adult is her parent."[15] Many concluded that a careful analysis of the individual child's reading interests needed to be followed by the librarian's personal intervention: "The change must not be made sudden or abrupt. . . . If the boy has delighted in red-handed tales of Indian border wars, coax him into the realm of history by means of Custer's books. . . . And there are quite a number of similar books sufficiently sanguinary to conceal their strictly historical character which will keep him in reading until his taste is formed for the historical."[16] WCTU members did not approve of "sanguinary" books, even as a technique to interest children in history books, but librarians believed that they were useful. Children were still malleable and teachable: "The aim of the children's room, like that of the main library, is to induce people to read better books, but the field is a far more hopeful one. With children we have no such fixed and inflexible habits to break, no such suspicion of attempts to direct reading."[17] Thus, they admitted adult resistance to censorship but assumed that they could gradually regulate and re-educate young readers.

As late as 1923, even as librarians divorced themselves from censorship of adult fiction, they continued to regulate books for youths: "On some points all of us can agree. For example, that the librarian is responsible for the reading of the young, the immature; that the librarian is responsible for discouraging a low quality of reading and for encouraging a high."[18] Anne MacLeod argues that censorship of children's books continued until the mid-1960s: "The community of adults engaged in bringing children and literature together [including librarians] endorsed, apparently without much real dissension, an implicit code of values which was observed virtually unbroken in thousands of children's books published between 1900 and 1965."[19]

* * *

To rationalize their efforts to promote "good" reading, librarians created a hierarchy of unacceptable and acceptable children's literature. It was based, in part, on genre considerations that prioritized nonfiction books over fiction and then ranked some types of fiction as better than others.[20] As we have seen, ALA members (and WCTU members) consistently described the *National Police Gazette* as the lowest possible reading material available to youths and banned it without debate from all public libraries. It was the worst form of fiction because, according to librarians, it was so dangerously unrealistic that it would encourage youths to indulge in "artificial excitements" as they grew older.[21] The next level of fiction was the "sensational" or "borderline" children's fiction, often termed the "Alger-Adams kind," referring to the authors Horatio Alger and William T. Adams (also known as "Oliver Optic").[22] Librarians agreed that their works were of low quality but disagreed on whether this meant that they should be prohibited from public libraries.[23] Although scholars now see Horatio Alger's novels as quintessentially American because they encouraged virtues such as pluck, determination, and hard work, librarians, acting as middle-class critics, disparaged his writings. What they did not like reveals that their aesthetic standards and their moral standards were deeply intertwined: his stories were not "real"; they upset the social order by conjuring dreams of upward mobility, and the heroes did not live in families and hence were free from female supervision and guidance. Their devotion to "realism" identifies ALA and WCTU members as cultural critics who applied moral standards to cultural products.

Librarians derided Alger-Adams books and other sensational dime novels for children as those "which are either false to nature, or to morals, or to art, or to all of these, and therefore are injurious to those who read them. They are untrue."[24] Although all fiction was inherently a product of the imagination, they believed that children would be better off if they avoided "sensational" fiction and read, at least, "truth *like* little stories."[25] Thus, a major factor in librarians' evaluations of children's novels was whether or not they seemed "true" to life: "These books [Alger, Adams, Southworth, and Hentz] are not condemned, however, because they have an interesting plot, but because the incidents are startling and unnatural, and the sole reliance of the writer for attracting readers. They have little literary merit, and give us incorrect pictures of life."[26] Proper children's fiction would present natural and correct "pictures of life" that would not challenge the (working-class or immigrant) child's class background, filial responsibilities, or job expectations. The rigorous standards that favored realism for children were abandoned for adult literature, where the stark naturalism of Thomas Hardy or of Emile Zola, whether in depictions of prostitution or coal mining, were condemned and the books restricted.[27] Librarians, like WCTU members, relied on a highly selective notion of what comprised "reality," thereby acknowledging that realism was a problematic aesthetic. Excluded from their aesthetic standard of "reality" were, for instance, crime, prostitution, and even upward mobility. While always claiming to support books that presented reality in a transparent fashion, librarians' promotion of nonfiction was in practice a way of masking their aesthetic and moral principles, which favored stories of class stability, education, and hard work over luck.[28]

Children were expected to find nonfiction inherently more interesting than fiction once properly introduced to it at the public library. Miss Jenkins, of the Boston Public Library explained: "The indefatigable reader of Adams and Alger is often diverted from these books, by a tempting display of some attractive, illustrated volumes, combining stories of history and travel, and when you assure him that *these stories are true*, he often goes to the other extreme and demands persistently 'true stories.' "[29] Like many reformers, ALA members believed that children should be content with their status in life and noted with displeasure that the "contrast between rich and poor children appeals to boy-and-girl readers, and wealth and material success play a large part in their estimates of books."[30] Accordingly, a boy's critique of Horatio Alger's fiction pleased one children's librarian. "This is a conversation and criticism of some books we over-heard among some boys the other day," she reported: "Another boy spoke then, saying 'Oh! You make me tired about Alger, he always writes about the same "feller" only under another name, who gets rich quick and you know that's impossible.' "[31]

Those who favored withdrawing Alger's and Adams's books echoed and then went farther than judicial "obscenity" decisions that were based on the notion that children needed protection and "moral teaching."[32] Youths' characters were not yet fully developed and were thus more open than adults to negative influences; librarians posited young readers as weak victims and easy recipients of evil suggestions. Condemning Oliver Optic-type books as "addictive" to the average boy with a "limp mind," who "settles down into it and does not rise above it," librarians suggested, "fill your town library with *real* books, and then teach people to read them."[33] ALA members and reformers denied that they were motivated by class bias, claiming that the problem of "sensational" fiction reading went beyond class boundaries, for any child could be vulnerable to the excitement the books offered.[34] Children's librarians stressed that their regulatory efforts were also attempts to bolster the authority of adults: "The school-boy takes his first initiative in insubordination to teachers and parents from the lawless career of "Jack Harkaway," or some one of the boy-heroes of the "Wide Awake Boys of America."[35] Other adults should, therefore, show greater appreciation for librarians' promotion of "good" literature.

American Library Association members were conflicted on how to regulate "sensational" or "borderline" fiction; they watched for minute variations in circulation of the Alger-Adams type novels and then interpreted these variations in widely divergent ways.[36] While some officially banned Horatio Alger-type books, others took a more informal approach and simply "discourage[d] applications for stories of street-life, poor-house boys who become millionaires, etc.," in favor of wholesome and "homely" stories.[37] A librarian in Lancaster, Massachusetts, for example, monitored the circulation of Oliver Optic books: "We try to be especially careful in our purchases of juvenile works. We have bought none of Oliver Optic's books for eleven years, but the twenty-eight volumes which were in the library in 1872 have been allowed to remain and they form 2 per cent of the fiction circulated."[38] One female librarian worried that sensational reading was preventing the development of the next generation's great men. She noted, "In a catalog of books for young people, issued by one of our leading libraries last year, may be counted 90 titles of Oliver Optic, 48 of Alger, 49 of Fosdick, 11 of Susan Warner. This is only one of many similar catalogs. It is to be feared that even the brains of a Lincoln, a Gladstone, a Darwin or a Spencer, would have softened on such literary manna."[39]

Others withdrew "sensational" literature without public announcement and without concern for consumer demand; the "Alger and Finley books are constantly asked for, but have been eliminated from the library." Another asserted, "The boys take to them [better books], and do not forsake us because we have neither 'Optic,' 'Alger' or 'Castlemon.'" Similarly, the head of the Fletcher Free Library in Burlington, Vermont, categorically stated: "I have withdrawn permanently all of Alger, Fosdick, Thomes, and Oliver Optic."[40] A public school librarian declared that parents' complaints and his own reservations brought him to the conclusion years before that he should not replace any worn out copies of the "Optic class."[41] Alternatively, some reported purchasing those books, only to regret the decision: "I consider that Alger and Castlemon have done irreparable injury to our boys, in their taste for more solid reading. Since their purchase, solid reading for children has fallen off ten per cent."[42] Yet another librarian insisted to the contrary that there was "a decided falling off in his [Oliver Optic's] devotees, as well as of many other writers of his stamp, for which we are truly thankful."[43] Circulation figures were used to bolster their discussions about "sensational" literature, yet their lack of consensus suggests that librarians' evaluative criteria were inconsistent and ambiguous.

To those who kept Alger-Adams novels in circulation, they seemed "merely entertaining" when compared to the National Police Gazette. Few librarians were willing to praise the books, but they did suggest that these books had the potential to "keep users from worse literature" or even had the potential to lead young boys to "a higher class of reading" simply by gaining their interest and attention.[44] An ALA conference member asserted: "If . . . nothing takes hold of a neglected Irish boy, for instance, like Oliver Optic's stories, then I would give him Oliver Optic in copious draughts, and give it at the public expense; he will be all the less likely to supply himself with the Police Gazette at his own cost."[45] In his view, exciting books could keep immigrant boys (who lacked watchful parents) from worse reading materials and so, ultimately, from "idleness and vice."[46] A librarian who openly defied the negative characterizations of Alger-Adams books explained, "I don't consider some books bad that other librarians do. I put Oliver Optic into the library freely" to attract young readers.[47] Another permissive ALA member associated Alger-Adams books with ambition, independence, and the frontier and argued that, overall, the books were not "impure" or censorable because they reflected the American boy's "love of adventure" and pioneer spirit, as well as his love of reading about "real boys and their success."[48] This liberal minority still felt compelled to add the familiar caveat that their ultimate desire, as professional custodians of books, was to "try to lure him away from his idols."[49]

In light of the difficulties encountered when evaluating the effect of "sensational" children's fiction, many librarians tried to direct youths away from all fiction reading. New York City children's branch reports of 1907–9 provided Superintendent Anne Carroll Moore with the names and ages of important conquests. Each youth represented a possible convert to nonfiction reading, and each hard-won convert was celebrated, with his or her conversion retold in splendid detail: "Rose Levy, a child of about 10 years of age was looking at the picture book 'Joan of Arc.' She was so interested in the pictures that I told her Joan was a *real little girl*, who lived in France years ago. Shortly afterwards she came up to the desk and asked for a book about 'Joan of Arc.' Rose usually takes fairy tales and nothing else."[50] A picture book, in this case, became a positive inducement to good reading because it lead a child to a higher, more "realistic" level of reading. This librarian believed that Rose's request for a biography signaled a new direction in her reading interests. Another recounted with pleasure how her earlier gentle suggestions had proven to be successful: "I felt quite gratified the other day when one of the boys coming to the desk to have his book stamped, called my attention to the fact that it was non-fiction whereupon I told him how glad I was to see he was reading books of that kind. He said, do you remember, Miss Conway, one time you asked me if I ever read books from the other side of the room (meaning non-fiction) and I told you no? Well, he said, I'm getting so I love those books."[51]

Believing that reading clubs could improve youthful habits where other attempts had failed, New York City children's librarians organized clubs and "special classes" and carefully chose, of course, nonfiction or historical novels for the children to read. Reading clubs and traveling home libraries were popular tools for urban reform and the Americanization of immigrants in the Progressive Era. As we have seen, the Woman's Christian Temperance Union promoted "Anti-Dime Novel" reading clubs for boys, and the General Federation of Women's Clubs and YWCAs organized traveling libraries.[52] The Rivington Street librarian speculated in September 1908 about the benefits of reading clubs: "The refreshing and ennobling qualities inherent in good literature might be felt by the children if we had reading clubs of various sorts with *not too much self government* and some imperceptible guidance from the children's librarian."[53] By January 1909 she had successfully formed several clubs to improve children's reading: "The large increase in special classes such as history and literature certainly shows that the children are not wholly devoted to fairy tales."[54] Librarians' promotion of a hierarchy of reading—beginning with the best (nonfiction), and moving down through various types of fiction—played an important role in debates about what types of books were suitable for youths and the immigrant working classes.

* * *

Children's librarians often based their generalizations regarding youths' good and bad reading patterns and preferences on gender, just as they conceived of some of their professional duties in gendered terms. As their debates about working-class and immigrant readers indicate, concerns about the quality of boys' reading often took precedence, and librarians focused most of their practical regulatory efforts on boys. This is not surprising, for throughout the nineteenth and twentieth centuries, the majority of children's fiction was written about boys and addressed the reader as if he or she were male. The notion that books about girls could not hold boys' attention was, and is, prevalent.[55] Indeed, librarians agreed with publishers' estimations that it was financially safer to publish books with boys as the main characters and assume that girls would read them, too: "If boys' books are mentioned to the excess of those intended for girls, it is only because boys' books chiefly abound, and that a good boys' book is not a bad book usually for a girl to read."[56] A study reprinted in the *Library Journal* suggested that boys' and girls' reading tastes diverged in their midteens: "From 9 to 15 most of the reading of boys and girls belongs to the class of juvenile stories; after that age fiction takes the lead with girls, and general literature (biography, history, science, etc.) with boys. . . . While some of the books mentioned by the girls were stories about boys alone, not one mentioned by the boys were merely in regard to girls."[57] By compiling and distributing recommended reading lists, such as "Books that Boys Like to Read" and "Books that Girls Like to Read," others acted on the notion that gender (as well as class and ethnicity) was a criteria in youths' reading selections.[58]

Often, female librarians noted and recorded youths' book selections as gendered but did not think that they themselves had either encouraged these choices or held a priori assumptions based on the child's sex. Library director Mary Wright Plummer stated, for instance, that "boys proved to prefer history and books of adventure, travel and biography to any other class of reading; girls, books about boys and girls, fairy stories and poetry. The tastes of the boys on the whole were more wholesome, and the girls need most help here."[59] Although all agreed that more boys read the *Police Gazette* and "sensational" dime novels than girls, ALA members confidently asserted that even those boys who read only crime-story papers had more innate potential to become readers of serious nonfiction than girls.

Generalizations of this type often encouraged librarians to "save" the boys first, since they were ostensibly more open to nonfiction reading. In contrast, girls were thought to have a seemingly inborn interest in fiction, especially romances. Accordingly, children's librarian Elsie Otis focused her reform efforts on boys aged eleven to sixteen who liked adventure stories. She chose and recommended to them nonfiction books that had parallels to the fictional adventure stories they already enjoyed; these "better" books included histories of pirates and sailors such as "Dana's *Two Years Before the Mast,* Custer's *Boots and Saddles,* and Stockton's *Buccaneers and Pirates of Our Coast.*"[60]

When they did pay attention to girls, children's librarians disregarded Victorian idealizations of the inherent purity of females and made sweeping generalizations about girls' "bad" reading habits. Mrs. Sanders of the Free Public Library in Pawtucket, Rhode Island, noted, for instance, "I find more satisfaction in directing the minds of boys than girls, for though I may and do succeed in interesting them in the very best of fiction, it is much more difficult to draw them into other channels, unless it is poetry."[61] Another agreed that "the boys are always more easily influenced to like useful reading; the girls rarely take anything for amusement but stories."[62] Female librarians asserted that girls' reading habits were more ingrained and difficult to change than boys': "We have doubtless all met the little girl of twelve years coming for a good book, a story, and a book for her brother of fourteen, please. 'What does he want; a story, too?' 'Oh, no! A history.' So off she goes, with her story for her, *his*story for him."[63] These generalizations could either encourage librarians to spend more time directing girls' reading or justify the resignation implicit in the phrase, "off she goes." Resignation is absent from their more admiring descriptions of boys. One concluded, "taken altogether, boys are more definite than girls in their attitude."[64]

Not all librarians gave up on girls as a lost cause. Those who tried to reform their reading habits, like Dayton, Ohio's Linda Eastman, charged that children's librarians ignored girls and were therefore responsible for their ostensibly poor choices: "It is for the girls, however, that we would make a special plea; so much pain is often taken to interest the boys in biography, history, travel, and science." She further charged that most librarians willingly gave girls the sorts of "pretty stories" that they were unwilling to give to boys. To rectify this pattern, Eastman recommended guiding girls first to the novels of Louisa May Alcott, Mrs. Burnett, and Laura E. Richards and then to biographies of these famous female novelists: "An interest aroused in the personality of the writer of 'A New England Girlhood' [Alcott] will in turn carry her into poetry, a never-ending delight to the child who has found it out. History, too!"[65] These recommendations reinforced librarians' promotion of a hierarchy of literary genres that privileged history and other nonfiction over fiction.

Struggling to promote good reading and to regulate girls' access to a wide variety of "bad" books, two children's librarians, Evelyn Lane and Ida Farrar, wrote a 1901 *Library Journal* article that provided information regarding the preferred "Methods of Evaluating Children's Books." The authors gave examples of the proper types of comments that should be written on appraisal blanks for new books. One such sample evaluation indicates that librarians worked in alliance with mothers to protect their children without any indication that they feared competition or a loss of professional authority from this cooperation. "Blanchard, A. E. *Her Very Best.* In two parts. (1) A pleasant, wholesome story adapted to girls from 14 to 18. (2) A love story. Objection has been made to love stories by mothers of girls who use our library. Such parents would have good reason to object to this. Rejected."[66] Librarians' desire to bolster the authority of parents and other adults is revealed most clearly in their negative evaluation of the book series featuring the "Five Little Peppers," by Margaret Sidney, in contrast to another series, the "Prudy" stories: "The best that can be said of the Pepper books is that the Peppers were cheerful in spite of their poverty. . . . [Yet] the younger children, Joel particularly, are self-willed and often disobedient. . . . [In contrast,] the Prudy stories are simple but they are not weak. . . . There is always a firm hand at the helm. . . . The children are never allowed *in command.*"[67] Another librarian revealed similar priorities in her comments about the characters in children's novels. "The children of the present [1900] are very far away from those of Mrs. Sherwood and Miss Edgeworth," she noted. "If these latter seem dull and priggish, at least they did not consider themselves the most important actors in the drama of life—their elders merely supernumeraries."[68] Contemporary children's fiction lacked the proper moral values, such as respect for the authority of adults that could be found in earlier fiction. Children's librarians' preconceptions about what girls were inclined to read also influenced their book evaluation system. Caroline Hewins commented that, " 'Little Women' is Miss Alcott's best book, but even that has too much slang and love-making." Her critique assumed that girls would be particularly drawn to inappropriate romances and clarifies her assertions that girls were more vulnerable and that they should read only "sheltered" stories.[69]

Girls often resisted attempts to redirect their reading. Indeed, as they tried to direct them toward nonfiction and keep them content with juvenile literature for as long as possible, New York City librarians' regulatory efforts and the older girls' desires came into conflict. Irma Horak noted that "girls of thirteen to fourteen years say that they have read all the nice books upstairs and would like to get downstairs [adult's] books."[70] Once in the adult section, she complained, the adolescents were given no attention or supervision by the busy adult librarians, "the consequences are that soon these girls are clamoring for the latest [romance] novel by McCutcheon etc."[71] Horak tried to appease teenaged girls by adding carefully selected books to the children's room appropriate for slightly older readers. She hoped that the older ones would "read them and by the time they are old enough to use the adult department they will have acquired a taste for worthwhile books."[72] Another complained that conflicts and resistance were widespread among seventh and eighth grade girls, who were "again troubling us for adult fiction. They will take nothing but fiction, the latest questionable novel if possible." Adolescent girls had this librarian quite concerned about issues of authority and control; in one case, she asked Supervisor Moore for advice: "What can one do when the girl presents her mother's card or an adult card and says the book is for her mother when you are quite sure it is for herself?"[73]

The prominent children's librarian Caroline Hewins argued in 1883 that the real solution to the proliferation of "impure" literature would be to produce new, higher quality books that would meet the needs of young readers and their protectors. Hewins suggested that authors of children's books should write new, "wholesome" novels designed to counter girls' negative reading tendencies and preferences. Centered in the home, these stories would offer playful but unproblematic plots that would not challenge the ideas of "sheltered" girls. Hewins complained about the various book series then available, pointing out, for instance, that "Miss Douglas' Kathie series is improbable. The little heroine, who begins in poverty and by the sudden appearance of a rich uncle is transformed into a little heiress and Lady Bountiful, has a tendency to make children unhappy and discontented." Hewins feared that this fiction series could, by showing alterations in the status quo, lead youths to expect or want more from their lives, including money and the power that accompanies benevolence.[74] Attempting to explain what this ideal good literature should be like, Hewins resorted instead to outlining what it should not be like. She quoted a review of W. O. Stoddard's *Among the Lakes* from the magazine *Good Literature:* "There are no villains, no mysteries, and no sudden acquisition of wealth. Mr. Stoddard never preaches, never moralizes, and never sentimentalizes—three negative qualities always praiseworthy in writers of juvenile books. But the lessons of the book are none the less effective because they are not obtruded on the reader's attention."[75] Hewins's suggestion that authors should write better stories was limited by the fact that writers of children's books were not a significant part of her *Library Journal* audience. In contrast, when the Woman's Christian Temperance Union wanted new "pure" fiction, it organized its publishing division and solicited stories from its own members and from other sympathetic reformers who then wrote and produced its children's magazine, the *Young*

Crusader. Interestingly, while Hewins and others were opposed to stories about assertive girls who became "Lady Bountiful," the WCTU's children's magazine presented just such stories with plots in which young girls were indeed benevolent heiresses (such as Jessie Wright's series, the "House of Good Will"). The WCTU intended these characters to motivate middle-class girls to act as reformers.

* * *

Believing that suppressing and condemning impurities in "high" and "low" art was not enough, the Woman's Christian Temperance Union acted on the stated objective of its department's title—the *Promotion* of Purity in Litera-ture and Art. In addition to its production, beginning in 1887, of the children's magazine the *Young Crusader,* the department initiated a program to promote "pure" art and to create "pure" movies. In 1899, for example, its leaders began a plan of "art education," or "the gospel of pictures," arguing that viewing fine reproductions of "pure" paintings would actively inspire good behavior. Interpreting this idea most literally, Carolyn Leech, associate na-tional superintendent of the department, developed a plan of work where-by local unions would donate reproductions of paintings of Christ to hang in every room in jails, hospitals, and other government institutions. Leech, working from her home base of Kentucky, believed that the reproductions she selected would inspire moral behavior, even in condemned criminals. A notion of Europe as the center for respectable high culture (instead of the WCTU's more typical demonization of Europe as the center of avant-garde art) is revealed in a WCTU notice that "State Superintendent and Associate, Miss Carolyn A. Leech, has spent ten months in study abroad to make the art section of this work effective."[76] Other WCTU leaders embraced this plan, exclaiming that "the Christ pictures mounted on gray cardboard for the State Prison and others are really so beautiful that it is hard to believe them prints."[77] Advances in technology made high quality facsimiles of fine art readily available so that it could have a civilizing effect on a broad spectrum of American society, ranging from adult prisoners to middle-class families, not just on those wealthy elites who collected original works of art.

Saul Zalesch has recently documented the popularity of "millions of in-expensive, mass-produced oil paintings" in the 1880s. Zalesch astutely spec-ulates that middle-class and working-class purchasers of cheap oil paintings were resisting the claims that "art and its appreciation [were] for the exclu-sive benefit of elite circles." His judgment that consumer interest in cheap oil paintings can be attributed to a middle-class desire to attain "gentility" and "cultural standing" is only part of the story. These purchasers had to flout elite assertions that the only true quality paintings were originals created by well-known or respected artists. The paintings described by Zalesch were produced, in contrast, by work teams in factories or by poor women churning out paintings at home for piecework wages.[78] The distribution and popularity of these paintings is similar to the WCTU's promotion of inexpensive reproductions of famous works of art. The authenticity or originality of the prints was likewise not the primary concern. By ignoring elite prescriptions on the purchase and appreciation of fine art, those who ordered cheap paintings and prints through the mail helped to create a separate middlebrow culture while also asserting their own respectability.

The department's promotional work was multi-faceted: WCTU traveling libraries for children were henceforth accompanied by "travelling picture libraries" of the Virgin Mary, birds and animals, and Sir Galahad, so that even those children who could not read could be introduced to an appreciation of religion, natural science, and medieval role models. Public schools and young people's clubs would be given twenty-five reproductions of paintings of "different subjects" from "copies of famous paintings . . . [and] pictures of historical scenes, portraits of authors and their homes, artists and musicians and views of noted buildings in various countries." The reproductions were intended to assist the students in their studies of history and foreign cultures and facilitate their overall academic development, while also ensuring that they would develop proper morally based aesthetic standards.[79]

The art education campaign encouraged families to purchase, mount, and frame cheap reproductions of inspiring paintings that were selected by the WCTU and available at a low cost. An article entitled "Art Education in the Home," by Jeanhette M. Dougherty, noted that in earlier eras people could only see paintings by visiting the homes and palaces of wealthy people. She noted that changes even more radical than the establishment of museums had since occurred: "the present day brings us choice reproductions of the world's great paintings. . . . There is no longer excuse for any home being without art representation." Technological innovations that made high quality reproductions widely available could be used to help spread moral messages. This was not simply an attempt to emulate the tastes of the wealthy, for Dougherty insisted that "the day is past when anything will do to hang upon the wall, simply to fill space. We now demand pictures that mean something."[80] That meaning was to be primarily moral and religious. The department recommended, for instance, that a reproduction of Johann Hofmann's *Head of Christ* be hung in living rooms in order to inspire family members to emulate Christ's piety and righteous behavior.

The department's "art education" plan did not recommend the same reproductions for boys and girls. WCTU activists offered copies of a painting of Sir Galahad specifically to boys, for example, because they believed that viewing it could actively inspire in them "manly" and chivalric behavior. They chose a representation of Galahad by Watt that portrayed the moral image they most wanted to convey. Galahad's pose represented a combination of piety and dedication that the WCTU valued; members interpreted the standing hero as "half praying and half studying" beside his white steed. The department reasoned that when each boy had his own reproduction of the saintly and gallant knight hung above his bed, he would inevitably be influenced by his "clean and pure" life. It asserted that Sir Galahad had led the "fight against evil" and so was a perfect role model for young temperance "crusaders" who could join the organization's youth group, appropriately called the Loyal Temperance Legion. Historian Anne MacLeod's work on children's literature supports that the WCTU's attraction to medieval metaphors was part of a broader cultural trend: "Medieval myth and legend, reshaped to nineteenth-century sensibilities, came in floods: . . . as children's fare in Howard Pyle's buoyant versions of Malory and the Robin Hood legends, and Sidney Lanier's *Boys' King Arthur*, dense with Victorian renderings of medieval English."[81] The irony of choosing the medieval Sir Galahad as a role model in an age of technological reproducibility is striking. Yet Sir Galahad is a good representation of turn-of-the-century America's cultural fascination with the chivalric Middle Ages. The medieval Galahad was idealized as an individual who dared all for his king and for Christianity—or, translated into the WCTU's contemporary language, for the state and morality. He was no selfish renegade but rather a citizen activist in knightly garb.[82]

Both boys and girls would learn moral messages and gain role models through viewing pictures of, primarily, religious figures and pastoral scenes. In addition to Sir Galahad, boys were to receive reproductions of paintings of animals by Anton Mauve and Rosa Bonheur as well as paintings of Christ and the Madonna. For girls, Dougherty stressed the value of these reproductions but added some other possible subjects, explaining to parents that, "A girl's room would be incomplete without a few choice pictures, such as the 'Sistine Madonna,' which is called the greatest picture in the world; 'St. John,' by Andrea del Sarto, said to be the most beautiful head in all the realm of art; and some charming picture of Isreal's Dutch peasants . . . or Rosetti's 'Blessed Damosel.'"[83] Instead of Sir Galahad, girls would receive pastoral images or a painting of a romantic figure—Rosetti's *Blessed Damosel*.

The WCTU's suggestion that *both* boys and girls have paintings of the Madonna in their bedrooms was more compatible with the ideas of WCTU leader Frances Willard, who had recently died in 1898. Willard had not been interested in inculcating fixed notions of proper gender roles and was intent upon challenging those conventions. She encouraged WCTU members to do likewise: "Of all the fallacies ever concocted, none is more idiotic than the one indicated in the saying, 'A woman's strength consists in her weakness.' . . . What we need to sound in the ears of girlhood *is to be brave,* and in the ears of boyhood *to be gentle.* There are not two sets of virtues, and there is but one greatness of character; it is that of him (or her) who combines the noblest traits of man and woman in nature, words, and deeds."[84] Willard's children's fiction stories, published in the *Young Crusader,* suggested that men and women needed to acquire the best socially acquired traits of each sex.

WCTU members adopted some of the tactics that Lawrence Levine claims the cultural elite employed when it tried to impose a cultural hierarchy based on a distinction between high art and popular culture at the turn of the century. The department approached its program of art promotion from the perspective of a group trying to educate and uplift the masses. In this respect, the WCTU resembled those who promoted museums and symphonies. By bringing moralistic and religious art to the majority of American citizens, the WCTU hoped to create social order out of cultural chaos. It asserted: "Art brings into the home a refining and elevating influence that moulds character, and the demand for good pictures in the home is one of the delightful phases of modern culture." The fact that WCTU members promoted a "gospel of pictures" did not, however, signal their conversion *into* the cultural elite. The department did not adopt the exclusive vision of an acceptable "high" art of painting and opera versus a distasteful "low" art of popular songs and illustrated magazines. Most tellingly, it persistently rejected the celebration of aesthetics represented by French impressionism and other more avant-garde European art movements in favor of upholding morality as the ultimate critical standard.[85] The propaganda and cultural production of the WCTU reveals its energetic efforts to promote the ideals of moral culture and consumption.

Fusing Progressive Era faith in science and technology with Christian reform goals, the WCTU also embraced the new technology of motion pictures and dedicated itself to creating and producing "pure" movies to be used for educational and moral reform. Pro-censorship reformers have often been characterized—even parodied—as reactionaries who were unable to accept popular culture in the form of technological innovations such as motion pictures.[86] But as the complex history of censorship in the United States suggests, movie censorship was not simply a matter of modern versus anti-modern. For the first three decades of the twentieth century, the Woman's Christian Temperance Union complemented its censorship campaigns against the products of the movie industry with its own efforts to support and produce "educational" anti-alcohol and anti-tobacco films. The WCTU's promotion and production of motion pictures—the very medium of which it was so afraid—is a fascinating indication of the profound influence of Progressivism's faith in technology as a tool for reformers and as a symbol of progress. While fighting for purity and the proper moral education of youths, the WCTU used and advanced certain movies.

The WCTU's official organ, the *Union Signal,* reported in 1910 the first meeting between Thomas Edison (a fellow abstainer from alcohol) and members of the WCTU to discuss making pro-temperance or "Scientific Temperance Instruction" movies. Meeting with the WCTU Committee on Moving Picture Films, Edison spoke of his plan to develop educational pictures for the public schools on a variety of topics such as science, nature, and history.[87] The WCTU Committee was impressed with this educational approach and requested that Edison make movies that would complement its Scientific Temperance Instruction programs that had been in place in every state public school system since 1903.[88] The committee suggested that his movies show "the preparation of grain until it is manufactured into pure food" as well as "the evils arising from the use of alcohol and tobacco." Heartening the committee members greatly, he agreed to their request. As the secretary recorded his response, "Mr. Edison intends to show the evil effects of alcohol and tobacco on the human system, even on the blood corpuscles and the various organs of the body, nerves, etc. Every phase of what we now stand for and teach in scientific temperance is to be fully dealt with."[89]

An article in the *Union Signal* predicted that Edison's educational films would win children away from the movie industry's popular productions. "With such an attractive and carefully censored exhibit in schools, the glaring and cheap looking shows that are a disgrace to our city streets will lose most of their charm for children."[90] Harriet Pritchard, the department's national superintendent rhapsodized, "We should praise God for this wonderful advance in educational methods, and for the splendid prospect held forth that scientific temperance will be regularly taught in such an attractive and practical way to every child in the United States."[91]

When Edison, the famed inventor, grandiosely—but prematurely by seventeen years—announced to WCTU Committee members his invention of talking pictures, they had no reason to doubt his claim and immediately began pondering the impact of speech on motion pictures. On the one hand, they anticipated that there would be an even greater need for regulation in order "to see that the language is above censure."[92] On the other hand, they believed that talking movies would be much more powerful than silent movies, so that a talking film on the negative effects of tobacco, for instance, "would prove so startling that no girl or wife of the future could be induced to take up cigarette smoking."[93] Other state directors speculated that talking pictures would actually improve and purify the formerly silent genre since "people cannot say what they might picture."[94] The addition of words, they suggested, would force a certain self-consciousness upon the medium and act as a restraint upon movie directors and actors. These questions would have to wait, however, until the first talking pictures were actually produced in 1927.[95] In the meantime, when Edison released 102 silent educational films in 1913—none dealing with temperance—the WCTU doubted whether temperance films would ever be made by him yet magnanimously offered a resolution at its national convention praising him for "his magnificent work for children."[96]

Not content to wait for further action from Edison, the WCTU noted with interest the use by religious societies of "the motion picture to demonstrate Scripture and moral truths" and decided to sponsor showings of films that supported temperance and purity crusades.[97] By 1914, like churches and middle-class social clubs, the WCTU worked locally to show youths respectable educational films at a low cost or for free. Most Americans in 1920 still lived in small cities, towns, or rural areas; many acted as, or at least accepted the wisdom of, conservative Protestant critics of industry-produced films. They distrusted the "sensational" aspects of commercial culture but did not stand in opposition to all movies and were in fact an important part of the middle-class movie audience when noncommercial "educational" movies endorsed by respected civic groups were shown in schools, churches, or community halls.[98] Religious, reform, and social groups all promoted films with "moral" messages in order to counteract mainstream productions. The WCTU's use of educational films is similar to its advocacy of Scientific Temperance Instruction, for it represents an effort to move toward "positive" reform and to educate people *before* they sinned. As WCTU leader Maude Aldrich noted in 1928, "More use has been made of nontheatrical films to carry the message of prohibition, law enforcement and moral progress. Among these films 'Deliverance,' 'Lest We Forget,' 'The Transgressor' and 'Safeguarding the Nation' are most prominent."[99] The term "nontheatrical" refers to movies produced by reformers and educators that were not usually shown at the commercial theaters. The movie industry became unhappy with this trend toward independent productions between the midteens and the 1920s and characterized it as unwanted competition; the Hays Office condemned free movies as a "menace" and a threat to the industry's business.[100]

The WCTU began to contemplate such independent efforts in 1919, when the Department of Purity in Literature and Art produced leaflets such as "Making Our Own Motion Pictures."[101] Accordingly, new technological inventions that made amateur film making easier were welcomed by the

WCTU as a way to assert its own vision of social morality, without having to convince the resistant movie industry of the soundness of its demands: "One of the most marvelous developments noted is that of the movette, a large camera capable of taking pictures of either still or moving subjects with a projector that can be used in any sized hall or church. By this means our temperance hosts are made independent of the film people. A complete outfit costs but $100."[102] Such ambitions point to two important goals. First, the WCTU conceived of censorship as a means to help parents rest assured that their children could attend movies—the most popular form of all cultural entertainments—without putting in peril their moral development. By promoting and creating films, the WCTU offered the general public a "pure" cultural product, tailoring that product to impressionable children rather than focusing on either aesthetics or profit. Second, its efforts at film production demonstrate that the organization was committed to the championing of "pure" culture, not just the regulation or repression of the "impure."[103]

Local WCTUs helped youths to develop discriminating standards in movie selection by presenting " 'The Stream of Life,' a motion picture showing to young people the value of good pictures," at children's camps and churches.[104] The WCTU thereby relied upon the film medium to teach youths how to discriminate between good and bad movies, a strategy that may have instead reinforced young people's desire to consume any films. As early as 1915, a WCTU leaflet, "Motion Pictures as Educators," provided members with information on renting and buying temperance films: "If temperance films are wanted requests must be made to the manager [of the local movie theater] for their exhibition. For instance: Some schools request the exhibition of 'John Barleycorn' at a given time, and the request is granted if enough of an audience is promised to meet the expense."[105] The WCTU's educational films were usually pro-temperance films presenting themes in either a dramatic or scientific format and did not include the "scenics" and "industrials" sponsored by local social groups.[106] The department sponsored, for instance, screenings in many localities of *John Barleycorn* and *Charlie's Reform*, two movies warning against alcohol and tobacco use, for it hoped that temperance films would dissuade youths from drinking and smoking.[107]

In the 1920s, the WCTU worked with public schools and teachers to show other anti-alcohol and anti-tobacco films, produced mainly by doctors and health care professionals.[108] These films are the immediate precursors of educational films still shown in health classes today. National director Maude Aldrich recommended that local unions buy copies of *Safeguarding the Nation* and *The Tobacco Plague* for the Departments of Visual Education in their public schools so that the movies could be distributed to local high schools and to community groups.[109] *The Tobacco Plague*, produced by Dr. John Harvey Kellogg, superintendent of the popular health resort Battle Creek Sanitorium, was an anti-cigarette film. When promoting the film, the WCTU referred to the fact that Kellogg was a doctor by training, implying that he could therefore be trusted to have made an impartial scientific film.

The WCTU worked with other groups to try to give *The Tobacco Plague* a mandatory place "in the regular course on Hygiene" for both normal schools and single-sex religious schools.[110] This law successfully passed in Kentucky in 1927 and inspired the Massachusetts union to seek the same in its state.[111] Like Dr. Kellogg's film, WCTU promotions for the movie *Deliverance* focused on the writer's professional credentials: "We appeal to every county . . . to show 'Deliverance' a picture based on the book, *Prohibition at its Worst* . . . by Prof. Irving Fisher of Yale University. He declares Prohibition the best method yet tried of dealing with the liquor traffic."[112] The Pennsylvania union arranged for 22 showings of *Deliverance* to a total of 7,000 people in 1929.[113]

The WCTU argued that the showing of these educational movies in schools could increase students' interest in learning and present scientific knowledge so powerfully that "unrealistic" films produced by the movie industry would be superseded. "The pupils [of the eye] absorb the meaning of what they see while they might get exceedingly little out of a book or discussion. . . . The vividness of impression is important. What seems to be real and life-like will be remembered longer because it is more convincing."[114] In the WCTU's theory of how film works, its impact is stronger and more immediate than a book because its images are so realistic. A *Union Signal* article promoting educational movies announced that Yale University Press had launched an important film project on United States history called "Chronicles of America."[115] The same page in the *Signal* prominently featured an advertisement sponsored by the National WCTU for " 'Safeguarding the Nation,' a five-reel motion picture showing the effects of alcohol upon the body by means of the laboratory process, is a picture such as educators advocate."[116] In the context of a report on educational films, it suddenly seemed possible that a few movies of excellent quality might counteract the effect of the many "sensational" films produced in Hollywood. Promoting educational movies made WCTU members proud of their efforts and reluctant, temporarily, to focus on the negative impact of mainstream motion pictures.

When and if children and adults attended the public movie theaters, the department suggested that they not go on impulse but that they go only after careful consideration of the recommendations of a reform magazine called *The Educational Screen* that provided estimations of the moral quality of films.[117] Recommended films included *Ten Nights in a Barroom*, with William Farnam as the leading man. This movie was a rare Hollywood production that drew extensive praise from the WCTU for its anti-alcohol story. A WCTU reviewer claimed, "An unusual situation presented itself this year [1931] when a truly great film portraying the old saloon days and the alcoholic liquor peril was available in the regular theaters. This was enthusiastically heralded by WCTU leaders and workers. . . . The picture itself was of great value and played to packed houses."[118] State and local unions were encouraged to contact their local theater managers and request that the film be brought to their communities or else to rent it themselves directly from the distributors.[119]

The department cited academically respectable studies that reaffirmed the WCTU's focus on children as particularly impressionable for it was eager, moreover, to appropriate knowledge from the natural and social sciences to advance its "pure" movies and scientific temperance work. According to Aldrich, "the investigation by educators, psychologists and sociologists under the Payne Fund, now being published in ten volumes, brings to the study of the motion picture question authoritative facts never before available."[120] The Payne Study and Experiment Fund had awarded a grant to William H. Short's Motion Picture Research Council in 1929 to conduct a series of investigations into the effects of movies. The studies were done by social scientists from a variety of academic disciplines, including psychology and sociology. The research took four years and focused on topics such as the impact of motion pictures on the social and racial attitudes of children, on conduct, delinquency, and crime.[121] Film historian Lea Jacobs succinctly summarizes the Payne Fund's pro-regulatory conclusions. "The cinema," claimed the 1933 report, "had the capacity to undermine social norms as yet imperfectly interiorized by children and other groups defined as potentially deviant."[122] Woman's Christian Temperance Unions across the country eagerly studied a published summary of the Payne Fund written by the journalist Henry James Forman, *Our Movie-Made Children* (1933), and reviewed it for their meetings and for the press. WCTU praise for the Payne Fund was accompanied by the practical suggestion that its members actively support "the new Motion Picture Bill, H.R. 6097, introduced by Congressman Wright Patman of Texas, [which] furnishes an immediate opportunity to do something definite and constructive."[123] The scientific language and impressive research conducted by progressive social scientists and experts was embraced and appropriated by the WCTU and other members of the lay public who advocated federal intervention and aspired to mandate a "pure" presentation of social norms in popular culture.

During the 1920s and 1930s, WCTU members hoped experts would agree with them and approve of their methods, but they often went beyond citing "experts" and claimed scientific research as their own domain. They wanted unproblematically to unite scientific expertise and democracy and appealed to democratic sentiment with their use of "scorecards," for example, which were ostensibly "scientific" but could be filled out by any interested laywoman. By using scorecards to evaluate movies, the WCTU made an effort to provide the public with more "objective" evidence of the need for censorship. The department director in Illinois "bought 260 scorecards, and put one with a tract in an envelope, also a name and a date for a picture show, distributed these among the various churches, clubs, and organizations in the county to secure an opinion as to the need of local censorship."[124] Scorecards proved most useful as "a good way to tabulate their findings."[125]

State directors apparently felt that any explanations of methodology or terminology were unnecessary when presenting "scientific" tabulations and simply reported the raw data: "Members viewed 199 pictures, 25 of which were reported wholesome throughout; 19 wholly unfit; 21 attacks on Prohibition; 15 showed ridicule of law; 19 unlawful acts; 7 attacks on purity; 115 expressions of approval of good pictures; 26 disapproval of bad films."[126] Scenes of law breaking rendered at least fifty-five of the reviewed films objectionable, whereas only seven were specifically condemned for sensuality or "attacks on purity." In fact, the majority of the films were approved by WCTU members, confirming their willingness to discriminate between good and bad commercial productions rather than condemn them all. The WCTU's use of relatively neutral or scientific language in the scorecards surely met with an easier reception among the general public in comparison to some of their more dramatic and subjective evaluations. In the latter mode, Pennsylvania WCTU leader Alice Mann proclaimed, "The films for 1931 and '32 offer a continuous procession of kept women, gamblers, gangsters, murderers and morons. Could you name ten pictures the subject matter of which was wholly free from drinking, adultery, divorce, infidelity or violence of one sort or another?"[127] What mattered most to the department was less the existence of such scenes but whether such conduct was being condoned or condemned.

WCTU members also adopted "scientific" techniques associated with academic and professional research in order to legitimize their advocacy of movie regulation and to increase the respectability of their own department's work. The members of one local union, for example, were praised by the department for conducting their research on movies as if they were sociologists or psychologists who were "most alert to the necessity of finding out what our children see at the movies and how they re-act to what they see."[128] Claiming, moreover, that reformers' movies were "in line with the most advanced ideas in the educational world," the WCTU explained, "Educators concede the 'Eye Gate' as the most important factor in training of mind and pattern of conduct. 87%

of our impressions come through our sense of sight."[129] The phrase "educators concede" implies that science was conveniently confirming and lending its prestige to the WCTU reformers' intuitively held suppositions.

* * *

Just as the Motion Picture Department focused on a dual strategy of promoting "pure" movies and censoring the "impure," the WCTU's new Department of Radio operated on the same principle during the late 1930s and 1940s. The national director, Helen Green, briefly explained the purpose of her department:

> No one group of people can expect radio, which is meant for all . . . to cater wholly to its particular tastes or needs. But we can reasonably expect it to be kept clean, to be free from vulgarity and from the dangerous propaganda which tends to corrupt the minds and morals of childhood. . . .
>
> A little thought, a little time, and a three-cent stamp will carry a protest against any program straight to its sponsor, its master-of-ceremonies, or its station of origination.[130]

Green's emphasis here is on creating groups of "trained listeners" to act as censors.[131] The rationale for such vigilance over radio shows was similar to that for regulating the moral content of motion pictures—"With a radio in nearly every home, and with some time being devoted to listening by almost every person . . . our program of home protection must of necessity include the study of how to secure and maintain excellence on the air."[132] One WCTU report quoted Joy Elmer Morgan, "editor of the Journal of the National Educational Association," as confirming that "the influence of radio on the masses of the people is immediate and intimate."[133]

The Department of Radio's plan of "home protection through radio" consisted first in emphasizing the strength of listeners as consumers who could act together to change the product. The department's national director explained that WCTU members had "something to say about those parts of [a] program which seem to us in poor taste, harmful, or in any way a violation of radio's own code of excellence. We have the power of protest."[134] The most common type of WCTU radio protest was the use of letters to express satisfaction or dissatisfaction for a particular radio show or advertisement. State annual reports made a point of counting the number of letters that were sent annually by members in each county and reminded them that sponsors could cancel a show if enough protests were made against it. Stations, for example, received "many letters protesting use of radio for advertising liquor and tobacco."[135] Letter writing could also be used to praise radio stations, especially those, such as the National Broadcasting Company, that decided to refuse all liquor advertising.[136]

In addition to its work monitoring radio shows and advertisements, the WCTU's national radio department mandated that state and local unions create their own "pure" programs for broadcast on independent local stations. The southern California director reported that local leaders had succeeded in putting 133 WCTU programs on the air in California in the year 1938. She calculated that:

> Fifty-four weekly fifteen minute broadcasts have gone out over KGFJ, Los Angeles. . . . Considering radio as advertising, our 133 talks, at the minimum price of a dollar a minute, means we have had nearly $1500 given to us through these various stations. . . . Bearing in mind this free time has been given us for educational rather than for propaganda purposes, your director has carefully prepared all . . . material going over the air, seeking to make it conform to high educational standards in telling "the truth about alcohol— what it is and what it does."[137]

While the above WCTU radio programs publicized the dangers of drinking, others were "devotional" or were described as "symposiums [*sic*] on Youth."[138] Pennsylvania's radio programs, for example, included talks by state leaders and a "special Thanksgiving program" that included "some young people, all giving their reasons for being thankful."[139] In these instances, the organization took on the role of cultural producer in order to be certain that its values were represented in public discourse. WCTU members had to lobby hard to get free airtime and succeeded in doing so by making "personal visits to several radio stations soliciting time for WCTU broadcasts."[140] In the case of promoting its own shows, letters of support for WCTU broadcasts were also important. "Did you know," asked New York's radio superintendent in 1941, "that the value to a station or network of a non-commercial program is gauged largely by applause (fan mail)?"[141]

In order to encourage WCTU programs in every county, the radio department sent local unions "sample scripts" of its programs including one regular show called "Woman's Temperance Work." For the WCTU's national convention in 1941, "the state presidents and radio directors of New York, Pennsylvania, New Jersey, and Delaware were asked to collaborate in a broadcast from Birmingham [Alabama] on the topic, 'Freedom of Speech and Assembly,' from the Bill of Rights, one of a series on the subject, 'The Blessings of Liberty.' "[142] Here, patriotic WCTU members praised the freedom of speech available to Americans, thereby emphasizing their interest in cultural expression and production, rather than censorship. Excerpts of state WCTU conventions, especially presidential addresses, were also often broadcast over local stations. WCTU members were proud of their radio broadcasts, and sent letters documenting their successes to the state radio department. Lillie Shultis of Ulster County, New York, wrote, for instance, to say that "a man who heard my broadcast from a Kingston hotel remarked afterwards to my husband: 'I heard your wife on the radio and I tell you that was as good as any sermon I ever heard preached.'" Shultis seems to have presented an explicitly Christian perspective on her temperance work.[143]

The WCTU's participation in and creation of radio broadcasts during World War II points to its use of patriotic themes to promote its messages. New York's department created its own radio show with the title "The War-Time Program of the WCTU." Additionally, three WCTU members "were interviewed on 'Women at War' program in regard to work of WCTU for soldiers and sailors." Its wartime programs point to its continuing cooperation and collaboration with other organizations. Other WCTU members, for example, "broadcast weekly on Salvation Army's 'Songs at Eventide' program." The New York state radio director also "conducted [a] series of programs for The Woman's Club" during World War II.[144] Northern California's radio department spent most of its energy on "watching the air for excellence" rather than on producing many of its own shows. "Few stations," its director declared, "are now giving [free] time for broadcasting except to 'defense' programs. For this reason, it is difficult for us to get our message on the air. Two counties, Fresno and San Francisco, have kept their regular broadcasts, presenting our program to large audiences." She urged her members to "be sure to write and thank" the stations for their support of WCTU programs.[145] From radio and movies to art and literature, the WCTU committed itself to producing acceptable alternatives to the objectionable mainstream products. This commitment in such a wide variety of media suggests that WCTU members shifted easily between a vision of themselves as producers of culture and as cultural critics.

*　*　*

The WCTU's commitment to promoting its vision of a "pure" American culture is important because it distinguishes the organization from its pro-censorship allies in the male vice societies. The latter's activities (if not their ideological goal of a single standard of sexual morality) were seldom directed at creating "pure" alternatives to "immorality" but rather focused more narrowly on maintaining legal repression. The WCTU's determination to show educational movies, write radio programs, and publish its own children's magazine, the *Young Crusader,* demonstrates its commitment to the production of culture. WCTU women made crucially important contributions to shaping the public arena of cultural and social life in the United States at a point when critics see the rising dominance of commercial culture closing off some cultural debate.[146] Its focus on children reveals, moreover, the importance of a rhetoric and a plan based on maternal activism and the protection of children as a justification for its political work.

A belief in children's impressionable nature also mandated a program of regulation and promotion of reading by professional librarians. Their duties and responsibilities were conceived of in gendered terms that transferred, in effect, the regulatory role from the (WCTU member) mother to the female librarian, who would be a more reliable "guardian" in place of the child's potentially irresponsible parents. In this regulatory role, children's librarians worked to change youth's reading patterns and preferences but did so only fitfully with girls, whom they characterized as more difficult to engage in the intellectual excitement of nonfiction books. Librarians' presumptions about children's reading preferences led them to privilege boy readers in debates about the effects of "immoral" reading and as the site of their most consistent regulatory efforts. Concerns about professional autonomy constrained female children's librarians from the political avenue of regulation available to laywomen and concentrated their efforts on promoting "pure" reading in children's reading rooms. WCTU laywomen, in contrast, fought for national censorship laws, asserted their authority as real (not "surrogate") mothers to regulate children's reading, and produced their own acceptable "pure" literature. These efforts, far from suggesting the antimodernist character of temperance advocates, demonstrates the innovative and creative aspects of their reform programs.

Conclusion

The acceptance of censorship marks the existence of a strong regulatory impulse in American society at the turn of the century. Its impact can be seen in Boston's main public library, for instance, which offered children's books that had been selected for their moral qualities by laywomen volunteers and then approved and ordered by the librarians. Even the artworks inside the library had been carefully examined for moral purity—for example, women reformers had protested and won the removal of the Macmonnies sculpture *Bacchante* from display in the library. School programming, too, felt the impact of the regulatory impulse as laws were passed in every state that required teachers to include anti-alcohol and anti-tobacco units in their curriculum. The WCTU ordered and sometimes paid for showings of pro-temperance educational movies to be shown at schools—in some states they successfully passed laws mandating the showing of these movies. Public librarians also intervened and sent teachers instructive books for their students, including carefully selected "pure" fiction. Museum curators and other art exhibitors, sometimes against their will, had to bend to public pressure. They hid or eliminated those paintings that represented the nude human form. Even distributors of crime-story papers found it harder to find vendors once reformers initiated public censorship campaigns. Producers of both "high" and "low" culture felt the impact of the pro-censorship movement. From 1873 to 1933, attempts to narrow the definition of "obscenity" and to lessen the impact of censorship regulations met with limited sympathy from U.S. judges. The grass-roots pro-regulatory movement was bolstered and confirmed by most court decisions during that era.

How do we explain middle-class women's involvement in a social reform movement based on calls for increased governmental censorship? First, it is important to understand what they were *not* doing. They were not targeting overtly political writings or ideas such as workers' revolutionary literature, "subversive" anarchist pamphlets. With the exception of their critique of anti-Prohibition literature, they were not trying to censor other competing political groups. Their targets were forms of entertainment—literature, art, and shows—destined to be consumed by the public as a leisure activity. WCTU women called for federal censorship of a broad array of cultural products without involving themselves in the divisive partisan politics associated with, for instance, the organization's endorsement of the Prohibition Party.[1] The WCTU did not aim to restrict workers' political debates, nor did it aim simply to control the leisure activities of the working classes and the elites. According to its ideal, *all* culture would be regulated, including that consumed primarily by the middle classes. WCTU members were willing to subject their own forms of entertainment (which obviously overlapped at most points with those consumed by the lower classes and the wealthy) to government appointed censors. They were willing to subject themselves to censorship as a conscious act of sacrifice on behalf of all children.

By choosing to censor culture rather than politics, reformers avoided most charges of inhibiting or restricting free speech, particularly since commercial entertainments were not then guaranteed protection by the courts under the First Amendment. Calls for this form of censorship could be conceived of as genuinely nonpartisan. Censorship was not particularly associated with one political party over another; the Comstock Act passed in 1873 with bipartisan support. In addition to moral reformers, the courts, and Congress, professional groups like the American Library Association accepted book censorship and regulation as an important public service and a duty.

Middle-class women's call for and use of legal censorship regulation was a tactic that departed from previous modes of benevolent and charity-oriented social action, yet it was based on a vision of themselves as protective mothers. Censorship was both a tool for women's political empowerment—inviting a concerted involvement in governmental affairs—and a means of directing the future "rising" generation." The pro-censorship movement thus melded women's increasing interest in participating in the political sphere with their strong identification of themselves as maternal/nurturing beings.

A gendered style of politics has been identified by scholars such as Suzanne Lebsock and Nancy Cott to describe the rationale for activism adopted by women in, for example, the antebellum female moral reform movement.[2] Later, the WCTU's Department of Purity in Literature and Art employed a similar rhetoric, framing most of its pro-regulatory arguments around concerns for the welfare of youths, thereby identifying its members as maternal figures caring for children through any means necessary. Other feminists rejected a maternalist, or explicitly gendered, entry into politics. Frances Wright's radical public speeches of the 1820s insisted on women's full political and social equality with men.[3] This gender-neutral style appealed to some wage-earning women who demanded their inclusion into labor unions or, later, to those who resisted protective labor legislation by eagerly taking on "men's" jobs during World War I.[4] Estelle Freedman's study of women's prison reform demonstrates that women activists tried to unite these different approaches by advocating separate women's prisons on the grounds that the prisoners were their "fallen sisters" who needed special care and treatment designed to train them to be true domestic women. In order to effectively do this, however, the women reformers had to leave their homes to take over a previously "masculine" role and become jail wardens, guarding their sisters.[5] This ambiguous balancing act is apparent in the WCTU's approach to politics. Its members desired to enter the public sphere as equals to men, adopting and exploiting men's political and professional languages and men's laws, to achieve their goals. This entry into male-dominated spheres demonstrates their reluctance to be held apart, as women. Overall, WCTU members acted within a maternalist framework but co-opted the language of male-dominated realms such as politics and the social sciences, in order to demand legislative action, as women, on behalf of children.[6]

Paula Baker argues that with the exception of WCTU temperance campaigns, women in small towns eschewed local reforms in favor of national and international projects, a tendency that led to an increased reliance on the state and federal legislation.[7] WCTU members were indeed interested in reform goals so encompassing as to almost demand national regulation (a "dry" town would be more effective if the county was also dry, and so on). By examining small New York towns of about 3,000 inhabitants, Baker's research focuses on a type of rural life that is too restricted and atypical to work as a more general guide to patterns of women's activism in the nineteenth century. Moreover, my research into WCTU women's local activism for the Department of Purity in Literature and Art at the level of towns and cities reveals a different phenomenon.[8] WCTU women tried to pass numerous types of local laws, ranging from "Blue Laws" that were designed to keep saloons and movie theaters closed on Sundays to anti-spitting ordinances to ward off tuberculosis to bills against "indecent" advertisements of the burlesque shows featured at county fairs. WCTU members entered the offices of mayors, police chiefs, and other local officials, demanding that they enforce whatever laws were on the books. They also presented resistant officials with petitions for new laws and frequently confronted neighborhood shopkeepers who sold "sensational" crime-story papers and dime novels or displayed risque cigarette and alcohol advertisements. The accumulated evidence of women's multiple local actions, encompassing many more is- sues than temperance, demonstrates women's commitment to the necessity and rightness of their full participation in the local reform process. State action and local action were not mutually exclusive. It is less consequential whether they succeeded in passing particular bills or acts; what is consequen- tial is their conception of themselves as political, social actors. WCTU mem- bers based their calls for legislative solutions and a strong federal govern- ment on their right to participate fully in the democratic system as moral mothers. This allowed them to enter the political sphere yet appear to be disinterested and above the corruption typically associated with politics. By expanding their political involvement, WCTU members insisted that disen- franchised women were a crucial part of the American democracy who must not be kept out of the democratic process.

The WCTU's Department of Purity in Literature and Art entered the cultural debate at a crucial point in American history, when scholars such as Lawrence Levine see the emergence and quick solidification of distinct "high" and "low" cultures. The WCTU did not accept this hierarchy based on a division between either a "high" culture, defined by its insistence on aesthetic beauty and on the financial support of the upper classes, or a "low" culture, defined by its widespread accessibility and popularity—a commer- cial culture created for consumption by the working classes. The middle classes found themselves drawn to and repelled by both cultures as they were courted by the founders of museums and symphonies as well as by movie producers and amusement parks. Levine concludes that the middle classes aligned with the upper classes by the beginning of the twentieth century, becoming the paying audiences at the "legitimate" theater, the opera, and other forms of "high" culture.[9] The middle-class WCTU, however, resisted the imposition of this cultural hierarchy. It upheld a different critical stan- dard based on a mid-nineteenth century "genteel tradition" that emphasized morality above aesthetics, status, or profit. This fundamental disagreement with the two dominant cultural trends of its day contributed to the WCTU's support for censorship and to its attempts to create an alternative cultural hierarchy that valorized purity and morality.

Acting as well as reacting, the WCTU created its own "pure" culture. Purposefully disregarding a hierarchy based on aesthetic concerns, the WCTU's children's fiction in its *Young Crusader* magazine combined, for in- stance, melodramatic plot structures with "realistic" portrayals of alcohol- ism, in order to present what amounted to a surrealist portrait of urban life that was designed to convince children to become temperate, reform-oriented adults. Moreover, the department's sale of cheap color reproductions of paintings by famous "Old Masters" disrupted the aesthetic standards of "high" art by focusing on the uplifting subject matter rather than on the quality of the object—a quality that connoisseurs and museum directors had a vested interest in claiming existed only in the original works of art, not in reproductions. The WCTU invented its own canon of inspiring chivalry for boys and pastoral charm or religious beauty for girls. WCTU women showed a vigorous independence in their construction of the cultural hierarchies that should guide artistic choices. This aspect of the department's program is different from the attempts of later book-of-the-month clubs, described by Joan Rubin, to interest the middle classes in literature, especially the classics, by trying to make "high" culture accessible.[10] Most significantly, the department's production of "pure" culture offered women in the pro-censorship movement the opportunity for work that went beyond repression or regulation toward a more creative attempt to change culture at the point of production.

Efforts to produce and promote "pure" literature, art, and movies turned WCTU members into producers of culture and demonstrate their ultimate unwillingness to become passive members of an audience, or to accept what they perceived to be the "impure" standards of the professional art critics and artists. WCTU members even became creative writers and independent movie makers and used those media they believed most directly influenced the character and behavior of youths, thereby usurping control from commercially oriented producers and publishers. Keeping their own moralist, maternalist political agenda foremost, they hoped to remake American culture. As producers of culture, WCTU members demonstrated a flexibility that belies stereotypes about closed-minded and reactionary censors. WCTU members were not retreating from modern entertainments such as film so much as proposing alternative formulations of them. These alternatives include the numerous community venues for exhibition of nonindustry produced movies that are often neglected by historians who focus on the dominant meaning of the urban commercial cinema as the symbol of a modern popular culture. Reformers were willing to experiment with new media, to adopt the vocabulary and emphases of progressive reform movements, and to accept the advice of social science experts and support their points of view. They moved back and forth from the local to the national sphere in order to embrace a wide variety of solutions to the problems they perceived in their society. Ironically, even as they exploited for their own ends the new technologies of mass reproduction, by producing and distributing their own "pure" literature and then its own movies, WCTU members eagerly participated in expanding the range of cultural products available. They clearly were intrigued and inspired by what they understood to be the "eye oriented" character of twentieth-century culture.

The WCTU focused its regulatory attention on urban problems such as drinking, disease, immigration, and various forms of urban culture—including movies and dance halls—all problems and sites of progressive reform efforts. As a part of progressivism and a participant in the politics of public discourse, the WCTU advocated a series of national legislative solutions, all designed to increase the federal government's regulatory role. Frequently, the WCTU acted on the local, state, and national political levels simultaneously as it proposed various legal regulations. It did not make a distinction between a state's rights position versus a federalist position and was content to pursue its issues in several arenas simultaneously. From the perspective of some women's clubs as well as the members of the American Library Association, federal censorship legislation threatened to take regulatory powers away from the individual parent in the first case and from the professional in the latter. When faced with the happy prospect of curtailing alcohol consumption or the production of "impure" movies, the WCTU did not see this as a terrible risk. When they were hard at work for a national law, WCTU members never considered themselves, as women, to be relinquishing control to central authorities or to experts but rather to be gaining knowledgeable and capable allies. Indeed, at the local level, "Mothers' Meetings" continued to impress upon women their personal, daily responsibility to care for, regulate, and protect their children, even as they urged women to fight for federal and state censorship laws.

The WCTU's Department for the Promotion of Purity in Literature and Art accommodated a wide variety of interests and priorities. Its work combined a maternalist perspective that focused on the needs and vulnerability of children with progressive social scientists' determination to study every problem and create a group of experts to fix it, often with the help of the federal government. Its departmental reports discussed issues of "purity" and "immorality" but also employed the languages and issues of the social hygiene movement, progressive education, and child development theories. Furthermore, its discussions of the "degradation of woman's form" in advertisements offered a feminist perspective from which to critique new cultural trends and ideas. The WCTU's membership included representatives of the old and new middle classes, from professional women to married housewives. It accommodated those women who wanted to focus solely on temperance by regulating portrayals of alcohol consumption in movies as well as those who were involved with concerns such as woman suffrage and the advocacy of world peace.

I emphasize pro-censorship reformers' role as political activists and cultural producers over that of cultural repressors because the latter is the predominant historical characterization of pro-censorship activists and allows them to be discounted, ridiculed, or ignored. By mistakenly conflating contemporary and historical attitudes about cultural censorship, scholars have inaccurately characterized pro-censorship reformers as marginal figures when in fact they represented relatively *uncontroversial* opinions at that time. The WCTU was just one of a series of large organizations that worked for and supported pro-censorship legislation at the turn of the century, including the National Congress of Mothers, the General Federation of Women's Clubs, male vice societies, and other Christian reform organizations. Their pro-censorship demands represented mainstream middle-class reform goals. For a more accurate historical understanding of the Gilded Age and Progressive Era, it is important to establish how average these women and their ideas were within American society during the period from 1880 to about 1930.

Earlier censorship efforts resonate strikingly with current debates over the diminishing capacity of public discourse to locate political and economic relations that shape and skew moral categories, and over the standards by which our students should be educated. Significantly, today's pro-censorship campaign is not solely the domain of conservatives aiming to restrict the variability of cultural forms to that which is most banal or uncontroversial. It is also the domain of anti-pornography feminists whose concern for the physical and psychological safety of women mandates, from their perspective, the restriction of violent "pornographic" images of women. Responding to contemporary anti-pornography feminists, Judith Butler suggests that their pro-censorship position, like that of earlier women moral reformers, should be rejected because, "it is important to risk losing control of the ways in which the categories of women and homosexuality are represented, even in legal terms, to safeguard the uncontrollability of the signified. She argues that "it is in the very proliferation and deregulation of such representations . . . that the authority and prevalence of the reductive and violent imagery . . . will lose . . . the power to define and restrict the terms of political identity."[11] Today, moralized images similar to those mobilized by WCTU activists are being used to refute the very kind of focus on the social relations of production, consumption, and culture that they tried to import into the public sphere.

A history of the censorship activities of the WCTU provides another interesting historical parallel to today's pro-censorship movement, for it also embraces the dual role of cultural producer and of censor. Specifically, new right Christian evangelicals attack Hollywood and the mainstream media at the same time that they produce numerous cable television programs, videos, and publish their own literature that is explicitly designed to replace "impure" cultural forms. Although both sides of the contemporary pro-censorship movement are on the defensive and have, perhaps, already lost their battle to regulate cultural forms, the de facto alliance of conservative and feminist factions within it is curious, yet more comprehensible when viewed in conjunction with a complete history of the Woman's Christian Temperance Union's Department for the Promotion of Purity in Literature and Art.

As many Americans today contemplate pressuring or forcing the television networks to rate their shows and to cut down on violence and sex, as they pressure chain convenience stores not to sell *Playboy* magazines, and as they contemplate issues of "obscenity" and government funding of the arts, the turn-of-the-century censorship movement helps us to better comprehend the precedents, arguments, and powerful but problematic logic that pro-regulatory positions—especially those based on protecting children—still hold today.

Notes

ABBREVIATIONS

[Name] A.R.	*Annual Report of the WCTU of [Name of State or Region]*
LJ	*Library Journal*
Minutes	*Minutes of the National WCTU*
NYPL	New York Public Library Archives, RG8 Superintendent of Work with Children, B.L. Reports, 1907–10
O&IL	*Oak and Ivy Leaf*
Radcliffe	Radcliffe College, History of Women in America Archives, Arthur and Elizabeth Schlesinger Library
Signal	*Union Signal*
reel [#]	Microfilm edition, Temperance and Prohibition Papers, series 3, Woman's Christian Temperance Union, 1853–1939, University of Michigan, Ann Arbor
YC	*Young Crusader*

INTRODUCTION

1. John Higham, *Strangers in the Land: Patterns of American Nativism, 1860–1925* (1955; rpt., New York, 1963), 8.

2. James Paul and Murray Schwartz, *Federal Censorship: Obscenity in the Mails* (New York, 1961), chap. 2.

3. Edward De Grazia, *Censorship Landmarks* (New York, 1969), 5–11. For discussions of changes in the laws, see Ira H. Carmen, *Movies, Censorship and the Law* (Ann Arbor, Mich., 1966); Paul and Schwartz, *Federal Censorship.*

4. Paul and Schwartz, *Federal Censorship,* chap. 3.

5. De Grazia, *Censorship Landmarks,* 94–96; Carmen, *Movies,* 11–13.

6. Annette Kuhn, *Cinema, Censorship and Sexuality, 1909–1925* (New York, 1988),

113. For further discussion of issues of sexuality and censorship, see Lea Jacobs, *The Wages of Sin: Censorship and the Fallen Woman Film 1928–1942* (Madison, Wis., 1991).

7. For the most complete histories of the vice societies, see Paul Boyer, *Purity in Print: The Vice-Society Movement and Book Censorship in America* (New York, 1968); David Pivar, *Purity Crusade: Sexual Morality and Social Control, 1868–1900* (New York, 1973). See also Nicola Kay Beisel, "Upper Class Formation and the Politics of Censorship in Boston, New York, and Philadelphia, 1872–1892" (Ph.D. diss., University of Michigan, 1990).

8. Comstock's wealthy supporters included Morris Jessup and J. P. Morgan. P. R. MacMillan, *Censorship and Public Morality* (Aldershot, Britain, 1983), 362–63. For a contemporary's glorification of Comstock, see Charles G. Trumbull, *Anthony Comstock, Fighter: Some Impressions of a Lifetime of Adventure in Conflict with the Powers of Evil* (New York, 1913).

9. For early views, see De Robigne Mortimer Bennett, *Anthony Comstock: His Career of Cruelty and Crime* (1878; rpt., New York, 1971); Heywood Broun and Margaret Leech, *Anthony Comstock: Roundsman of the Lord* (New York, 1927). Similar interpretations have been offered more recently by Robert W. Haney, *Comstockery in America: Patterns of Censorship and Control* (Boston, 1960); James Jackson Kilpatrick, *The Smut Peddlers* (Westport, Conn., 1973); John D'Emilio and Estelle B. Freedman, *Intimate Matters: A History of Sexuality in America* (New York, 1988); Walter Kendrick, *The Secret Museum: Pornography in Modern Culture* (New York, 1987), chap. 5.

10. See, for example, Edward De Grazia, *Banned Films: Movies, Censors and the First Amendment* (New York, 1982); De Grazia, *Girls Lean Back Everywhere: The Law of Obscenity and the Assault on Genius* (New York, 1992). Both books are by a lawyer who is a prolific writer on the subject of the First Amendment. De Grazia himself argued against censorship regulations in several important court cases and presents one-dimensional caricatures of pro-censorship advocates in his books. See also Richard H. Kuh, *Foolish Figleaves? Pornography In—and Out of—Court* (New York, 1967). For a post–World War II focus, see Paul Blanshard, *The Right to Read: The Battle against Censorship* (Boston, 1955).

11. Lawrence B. Goodheart, "The Ambiguity of Individualism: the National Liberal League's Challenge to the Comstock Law," in *American Chameleon: Individualism in Trans-National Context*, ed. Richard O. Curry and Lawrence B. Goodheart (Kent, Ohio, 1991), 133–50.

12. Ruth Bordin, *Woman and Temperance: The Quest for Power and Liberty, 1873–1900* (Philadelphia, 1981), 3; Joseph Gusfield, *Symbolic Crusade: Status, Politics, and the American Temperance Movement* (Urbana, Ill., 1963), 162. The Woman's Foreign Missionary Society combined with other missionary groups to comprise the largest women's oganizations, according to Peggy Pascoe, *Relations of Rescue: The Search for Female Moral Authority in the American West, 1874–1939* (New York, 1990), xviii.

13. See Carroll Smith-Rosenberg, *Disorderly Conduct: Visions of Gender in Victorian America* (New York, 1985), 264–95.

14. For general discussions of these issues, see Nancy Hewitt, *Women's Activism and Social Change: Rochester, New York, 1822–1872* (Ithaca, N.Y., 1984); Mary

Ryan, *Cradle of the Middle Class: The Family in Oneida County, New York, 1790–1865* (New York, 1981). For critiques of the historical focus on separate spheres, see Carol Turbin, "Beyond Dichotomies: Interdependence in Mid-Nineteenth Century Working-Class Families," *Gender and History* 1 (Autumn 1989): 293–308; Susan Juster, " 'In a Different Voice': Male and Female Narratives of Religious Conversion in Post-Revolutionary America," *American Quarterly* 41.1 (Mar. 1989): 34–62.

15. For a relatively critical analysis of the WCTU's rhetorical approach to the ballot, see Ellen Carol DuBois, *Feminism and Suffrage: The Emergence of an Independent Women's Movement in America, 1848–1969* (Ithaca, N.Y., 1978).

16. See Bordin, *Woman and Temperance.*

17. Ibid., 150–51.

18. I put "impure" and "immoral" in quotation marks throughout this book to remind readers that the moral judgments of WCTU members do not necessarily correspond either to my own or to a fixed legal definition.

19. See Lawrence Levine, *Highbrow/Lowbrow: The Emergence of Cultural Hierarchy in America* (Cambridge, Mass., 1988), chap. 2. For other discussions of high and low culture, see John Fiske, *Understanding Popular Culture* (Boston, 1989); Joan Shelley Rubin, *The Making of Middle/Brow Culture* (Chapel Hill, N.C., 1992).

20. See, for example, Boyer, *Purity in Print.*

21. A shorter version of the *Young Crusader* was produced into the 1990s but is no longer being published.

22. D'Emilio and Freedman, *Intimate Matters,* 158–61.

23. Barbara L. Epstein, *The Politics of Domesticity: Women, Evangelism, and Temperance in Nineteenth-Century America* (New York, 1981), 129, 145; Boyer, *Purity in Print,* 12. See also Pivar, *Purity Crusade,* 182–84, 232–33.

24. Most historians of the Progressive Era, including Bledstein, Hofstadter, Trachtenberg, and Warner, do not even discuss the WCTU. See Robert H. Wiebe, *The Search for Order, 1877–1920* (New York, 1967), 57, 63, 90.

25. For these revisionist interpretations, see Bordin, *Woman and Temperance;* Epstein, *Politics of Domesticity.*

26. See Alan Trachtenberg, *The Incorporation of America: Culture and Society in the Gilded Age* (New York, 1982), 86; Sam B. Warner, Jr., *Streetcar Suburbs: The Process of Growth in Boston, 1870–1900* (New York, 1962), chap. 7.

27. Molly Ladd-Taylor, *Mother-Work: Women, Child Welfare, and the State, 1890–1930* (Urbana, Ill., 1994), 43.

28. See the discussion in chapter 3 of anti-suffrage activist Kate Gannett Wells.

29. Discussing Progressive Era vice societies, Boyer confirms that an agenda based on the welfare of children "proved highly appealing to a generation that worked for child-labor laws, applauded a White House Conference on children, and created a Federal Children's Bureau" (*Purity in Print,* 23). See also Pivar, *Purity Crusade,* 7.

30. Fanny G. Marshall, "The Importance of Child Study," *Signal,* Apr. 27, 1899, 4–5. See also Fred Erisman, "There Was a Child Went Forth: A Study of St. Nicholas Magazine and Selected Children's Authors, 1890–1915" (Ph.D. diss., University of Minnesota, 1966), 178–233.

31. Christopher Lasch, *Haven in a Heartless World: The Family Besieged* (New

York: Basic Books, 1977), chap. 1; Jacques Donzelot, *The Policing of Families* (New York, 1979), 18.

32. Ladd-Taylor, *Mother-Work*, 66.

33. Gusfield, *Symbolic Crusade*, 162.

34. See Francis Couvares, "Hollywood, Main Street, and the Church: Trying to Censor the Movies before the Production Code," in *Movie Censorship and American Culture*, ed. Francis Couvares (Washington, D.C., 1996), 129–58. For information on the Catholic Church, see also Frank Walsh, *Sin and Censhorship: The Catholic Church and the Motion Picture Industry* (New Haven, Conn., 1996).

35. To document the existence of widespread pro-censorship sentiments at the turn of the century, I describe WCTU and ALA regulatory attempts and their members' support of censorship. It is less important in this context to document the successful passage of specific censorship laws or the failure to enforce those laws. This will be a project for a scholar who wants to look more closely at censorship from a legal or governmental perspective. In that case, the fate and enforcement of laws passed by public consent and pressure would be the primary focus, but it is not the focus of this study.

36. For broad discussions of professionalization, refer to C. Wright Mills, *White Collar: The American Middle Classes* (London, 1951); Olivier Zunz, *Making America Corporate, 1870–1920* (Chicago, 1990).

37. For discussions of political and adult censorship, see Wayne Wiegand, *The Politics of an Emerging Profession: The American Library Association, 1876–1917* (New York, 1986); Esther Carrier, *Fiction in Public Libraries, 1876–1900* (New York, 1965).

38. Dee Garrison, *Apostles of Culture: The Public Librarian and American Society, 1876–1920* (New York, 1979), 75, 87. Evelyn Geller includes some discussion of censorship of children's literature in *Forbidden Books in American Public Libraries, 1876–1939: A Study in Cultural Change* (New York, 1984), 36, 85–89.

39. See Garrison, *Apostles of Culture*, 93.

40. Susan Gubar and Joan Hoff, eds., *For Adult Users Only: The Dilemma of Violent Pornography* (Bloomington, Ind., 1989), introduction, chap. 7. See also Susan Kappeler, *The Pornography of Representation* (Minneapolis, 1986).

41. See, for example, the debate in *Ms.* magazine: "Pornography: Does Women's Equality Depend on What We Do about It?" *Ms.*, Feb. 1994, 32–45. See also the various essays in Gubar and Hoff, *For Adult Users Only*.

42. The phrase is from Robin Morgan, "Theory and Practice: Pornography and Rape," in *Take Back the Night*, ed. Laura Lederer (New York, 1980), 139. For books that outline the position of anti-pornography feminists, see Diana E. H. Russell, *Against Pornography: The Evidence of Harm* (New York, 1994); Russell, ed., *Making Violence Sexy: Feminist Views on Pornography* (New York, 1993); Alice Walker, "Porn" and "Letter to the Times; or, Should This Sado-Masochism Be Saved?" in *You Can't Keep a Good Woman Down* (New York, 1971), 77–84, 118–23.

43. Catharine MacKinnon, *Only Words* (Cambridge, Mass., 1993), chap. 3; Andrea Dworkin, *Pornography: Men Possessing Women* (New York, 1979), chap. 6.

44. For books that outline the position of anti-censorship feminists, see Pamela Church Gibson and Roma Gibson, eds., *Dirty Looks: Women, Pornography, Power* (London, 1993); Lynne Segal and Mary McIntosh, eds., *Sex Exposed: Sexuality and the Pornography Debate* (London, 1992); Mary Caputi, *Voluptuous Yearnings: A*

Feminist Theory of the Obscene (London, 1994); Linda Williams, *Hard Core: Power, Pleasure, and the "Frenzy of the Visible"* (Berkeley, Calif., 1989). See also F. M. Christensen, *Pornography: The Other Side* (New York, 1990); Kendrick, *Secret Museum*. For two interesting articles, see Ellen Willis, "Feminism, Moralism, and Pornography," in *Beginning to See the Light: Pieces of a Decade* (New York, 1981), 219–27; Judith Butler, "The Force of Fantasy: Feminism, Mapplethorpe, and Discursive Excess," in *Differences: A Journal of Feminist Cultural Studies* 2.2 (1990): 106–11.

45. Joanne Meyerowitz has documented anti-obscenity campaigns in the 1940s and 1950s in "Beyond the Feminine Mystique: A Reassessment of Postwar Mass Culture, 1946–1958," *Journal of American History* 79.4 (Mar. 1993): 1455–82.

46. See Levine, *Highbrow/Lowbrow*, chap. 3.

47. Kuhn, *Cinema*, 123. For a critique of governmental regulation, see Broun and Leech, *Anthony Comstock*, introduction.

CHAPTER 1: WOMEN'S ACTIVISM AND ALLIANCES

1. See, for instance, brief mentions of the WCTU's censorship work in Epstein, *Politics of Domesticity*, 129, 145; Boyer, *Purity in Print*, 12; Pivar, *Purity Crusade*, 182–84, 232–33. Bordin (*Woman and Temperance*) does not list the Department of Purity in Literature and Art, its leaders, censorship, or Anthony Comstock in her index; nor does she discuss these in the text.

2. For a discussion of social scientists' theories of mimesis and of imitation, see Ruth Leys, "Mead's Voices: Imitation as Foundation; or, The Struggle against Mimesis," *Critical Inquiry* 19 (Winter 1993): 277–307.

3. Harriet S. Pritchard, "Purity in Literature and Art," *New York A.R.,* 1898, 190 (emphasis added). All WCTU primary source materials used here are located at the WCTU's Willard Memorial Library, Evanston, Illinois. The WCTU's official organ, the *Union Signal*, its *National Minutes*, and some of President Frances Willard's scrapbooks and speeches are also available on microfilm from the University of Michigan, Ann Arbor.

4. Leys, "Mead's Voices," 280. For other interpretations of the impact of movies, see Daniel Czitrom, *Media and the American Mind: From Morse to McLuhan* (Chapel Hill, N.C., 1982); Ellis Oberholtzer, *Morals of the Movies — Moving Pictures: Their Impact on Society* (1922; rpt., Philadelphia, 1971).

5. Harriet Pritchard, "Purity in Literature and Art," *New York A.R.,* 1923, 120. See the American Library Association president's quote of 1895 for a strikingly similar metaphor: J. N. Larned, "The Selection of Books for a Public Library," *LJ* 20 (Aug. 1895): 270–72.

6. Pritchard, "Purity," 1898, 189.

7. These words can be found throughout the *Union Signal* in any given year's reports from the Department for the Promotion of Purity in Literature and Art.

8. For an example of social purity literature, see Havelock Ellis, *The Task of Social Science* (Boston, 1915).

9. "'The Century of the Child': Fiftieth Annual Meeting of the National Education Association," *Signal*, July 18, 1912, 1.

10. "The Contagion of Crime," *Signal*, Aug. 29, 1901, 9. Elbridge Gerry, of the Society for the Prevention of Cruelty to Children, wrote to the WCTU depart-

ment superintendent: "An impure book is the devil's own hypodermic for injecting poison into the child's circulation" (quoted in Emilie D. Martin, "Promotion of Purity in Literature and Art," *Minutes*, 1898, 330).

11. Rev. B. W. Williams, "Vicious Literature," *Signal*, Oct. 3, 1889, 7. See also I. O. Dodge, "National League for the Prevention of Vice," *Signal*, Sept. 5, 1906, 6.

12. Anthony Comstock, "Purity in Literature and Art," *Signal*, Dec. 29, 1892, 4.

13. Belle H. Mix, "Immorality among Children," *Signal*, July 8, 1897, 6 (emphasis added).

14. Harriet S. Pritchard, "Purity in Literature and Art," *Signal*, Dec. 24, 1914, 12.

15. Harriet S. Pritchard, "Purity in Literature and Art," *New York A.R.*, 1925, 160. Further evidence was included in other annual reports: "The chaplain of Newgate prison in London . . . referring to many fine looking lads of respectable parentage in the city prison, said that he had discovered, 'All these boys without exception had been in the habit of reading cheap periodicals.' Such is the case in almost every prison" (Pritchard, "Purity," 1898, 190).

16. Pritchard, "Purity," 1923, 120.

17. Jane M. Kinney, "Purity in Literature and Art," *Michigan A.R.*, 1904, 140; Pritchard, "Purity," 1898, 191.

18. The feminist theorist Judith Butler identifies a similar belief in the power of cultural forms to effect behavior among contemporary anti-pornography feminists and the new right who define "fantasy" as an "injurious action" rather than as a substitution for action or a temporary release from reality. See Butler, "Force of Fantasy," 106–11.

19. Harriet Pritchard, "Purity in Literature and Art," *Minutes*, 1913, 339.

20. Emilie D. Martin, "Promotion of Purity in Literature and Art," *Minutes*, 1894, 460; Emilie D. Martin, "Purity in Literature and Art," *Minutes*, 1909, 337.

21. Emilie Martin, "Purity in Literature and Art," *Signal*, May 19, 1910, 11.

22. See the WCTU's magazines for youths, the *Young Crusader, Oak and Ivy Leaf*, and *Young Woman*, at the Willard Memorial Library, in Evanston, Illinois.

23. Lillie R. Stone, "Purity in Literature and Art," *Massachusetts A.R.*, 1923, 97; [Mrs.] Franc H. Palmiter, "Purity in Literature and Art," *Michigan A.R.*, 1899, 125.

24. Lillie R. Stone, "Purity in Literature and Art," *Massachusetts A.R.*, 1922, 78.

25. Stone, "Purity," 1923, 97.

26. Donzelot, *Policing of Families*, 21; Lasch, *Haven in a Heartless World*, 15–17.

27. Stone, "Purity," 1922, 78; Marian W. Wark, "Purity in Literature and Art," *New Hampshire A.R.*, 1908, 72. Using language suggestive of women's love of power, Lillian Stone described the ideal home as "a place where love and harmony reign. The mother, with her *power of love*, draws and holds her children; she has the purity in Art and Literature right there . . . choosing the books and magazines that will be helpful and interesting" ("Purity in Literature and Art," *Massachusetts A.R.*, 1924, 85).

28. "Forbidden Literature," *Signal*, Nov. 26, 1891, 8.

29. Emilie D. Martin, "Purity in Literature and Art," *Minutes*, 1893, 394; Harriet Pritchard, "Purity in Literature and Art," *New York A.R.*, 1921, 94.

30. Palmiter, "Purity," 1899, 125.

31. Bordin, *Woman and Temperance*, 151–55. For a similar assertion, see Cathe-

rine Clinton, *The Other Civil War: American Women in the Nineteenth Century* (New York, 1984), 177.

32. See Bordin, *Woman and Temperance*, 157–59.

33. See state annual reports from the 1930s, located at the Willard Memorial Library, Evanston, Illinois.

34. Bordin makes a similar argument in *Woman and Temperance*, 97.

35. Emilie Martin, "Promotion of Purity in Literature and Art," *Minutes*, 1896, 358.

36. Massachusetts and New York unions maintained separate departments. See Harriet Pritchard, "Purity in Literature and Art," New York A.R., 1926, 161–63; Helen Andruss Miller, "Motion Pictures," *New York A.R.*, 1926, 136–40, 161–62. See also Katherine L. S. Goddard, "Purity in Literature and Art," *Massachusetts A.R.*, 1927, 83–84; ibid., 1928, 91.

37. Louise J. Taft, "Social Morality," *Northern California A.R.*, 1924, 133–34.

38. Mrs. H. H. Hubbert, "Report of the Department of 'Purity,' and 'Purity in Literature and Art,'" *Pennsylvania A.R.*, 1905, 214–17.

39. Harriet S. Pritchard, "Purity in Literature and Art," *New York A.R.*, 1908, 211.

40. Gusfield, *Symbolic Crusade*, 162. According to Bordin, the WCTU's membership was well over 200,000 by 1892. She also says that the WCTU claimed "a half a million members in 1924," but that by 1910 "the Union had fewer than a quarter-million members." Although Bordin's claims are not well documented, it suits her argument to have the WCTU membership decline or remain the same in the twentieth century. See Bordin, *Woman and Temperance*, 3, 40, 94, 140, 198.

41. Jessie L. Leonard, "Motion Pictures," *Massachusetts A.R.*, 1928, 83–84.

42. A detailed exploration of the files of the local WCTUs that might have accompanied an institutional history of the WCTU was not attempted here.

43. For references to Kepley's impressively varied career, see "Editorial Note," reel 8, Sept. 1, 1892, 9; "Here and There," reel 17, Feb. 16, 1905, 11. See also Frances Willard, *A Woman of the Century: Fourteen Hundred-Seventy Biographical Sketches Accompanied by Portraits of Leading American Women in All Walks of Life* (Buffalo, N.Y., 1893).

44. Superintendent Ada H. Kepley, "The Suppression of Impure Literature," *Illinois A.R.*, 1887, 111–12.

45. See John William Leonard, ed., *Woman's Who's Who of America: A Biographical Dictionary of Contemporary Women of the United States and Canada* (New York, 1914), 280.

46. Willard, *Woman of the Century*, 434–35.

47. See Kepley, "Suppression," 1887, 112; Emilie Martin, "Purity in Literature and Art," *Minutes*, Oct. 28–Nov. 2, 1892, 9.

48. Willard and Livermore, *Woman of the Century*, 434–35.

49. Kepley's direct action in tearing down a burlesque poster anticipates today's radical anti-pornography feminists who place protest stickers on pornographic magazines and in some cases even destroy them. See Segal and McIntosh, *Sex Exposed*, 15–28; Frances Willard, President's Annual Address, *Minutes*, 1889, 128–29.

50. Lucy J. Holmes, "Suppression of Impure Literature," *Minutes*, 1886, p. cxxiii.

51. See Leonard, *Woman's Who's Who of America*, 274.

52. Mrs. M. D. Ellis, "Legislation and Petition," *Signal*, Nov. 7, 1895, 11.

53. Ellis was also a member of the Daughters of the American Revolution. See Leonard, *Woman's Who's Who of America*, 274.

54. Margaret Dye Ellis, "Cannot Deliver Spiritous Liquors," *Signal*, June 9, 1904, 2.

55. "The Passing of Mrs. Martin," *Signal*, July 20, 1911, 9.

56. This campaign is discussed at length in chapter 4.

57. Martin, "Promotion of Purity," 1896, 354.

58. Bordin, *Woman and Temperance*, 138.

59. Ibid. The obituary also noted that one of the largest donations for a new WCTU building was given by Mr. and Mrs. Martin.

60. Mrs. D. W. Ward, "Social Morality," *Michigan A.R.*, 1923, 70; Mrs. Franc H. Palmiter, "Purity in Literature and Art," *Michigan A.R.*, 1903, 139; Harriet Pritchard, "Purity in Literature and Art," *New York A.R.*, 1918, 85.

61. Palmiter, "Purity," 1899, 125. "An obscene advertisement of a theatre program was sent by Caroline P. Lindsay to the Commissioner of Safety who threatened the manager and notified the Chief of Police to instruct his men to watch and promptly report any infringement of the law" (Pritchard, "Purity," 1918, 85).

62. Pritchard, "Purity," 1918, 86.

63. Kepley, "Suppression," 1887, 111.

64. Mrs. E. A. Chambers, "Pure Literature and Art," *Washington, D.C., A.R.*, 1894, 30 (emphasis added).

65. Another commonly employed tactic was creating "memorials" signed by the president and secretary of the local unions in each state. Memorials were sent to important government officials asking for censorship laws. See Martin, "Purity," 1892, 191; "National Superintendents' Reports," *Signal*, Nov. 29, 1906, 12.

66. Wark, "Purity," 1908, 72; Mrs. H. H. Hubbart, "Report of the Department of Purity in Literature and Art," *Pennsylvania A.R.*, 1905, 214.

67. Pritchard, "Purity," 1921, 95.

68. Palmiter, "Purity," 1903, 140.

69. Ward, "Social Morality," 1923, 71.

70. Naomi Tomlinson, "Official Communications of the Department for the Suppression of Impure Literature," reel 4, Mar. 3, 1887, 12.

71. See Paula Baker, *The Moral Frameworks of Public Life: Gender, Politics, and the State in Rural New York, 1870–1930* (New York, 1991), xvi, 70–71.

72. "Editorial," *Signal*, May 11, 1893, 1.

73. Mary Sayers, "The Crusade for Clean Movies," *Pennsylvania A.R.*, 1930, 108. The New York Union distributed "two hundred and fifty copies of the *Christian Nation* containing an article by Anthony Comstock" to every "county superintendent and president in the state" (Martin, "Promotion of Purity," 1894, 461).

74. Williams, "Vicious Literature," 7 (emphasis added).

75. Rev. Wilbur F. Crafts, "Purity," *Signal*, July 15, 1897, 4.

76. Emilie Martin, "Purity in Literture and Art," *Minutes*, 1901, 301. After WCTU-led protests, nude statuary was even removed from a Boston public library. For other mentions of protests against nude art, see Emilie Martin, "Purity in Literature and Art," *Minutes*, 1907, 332; Jane A. Stewart, "The Golden Jubilee of the YMCA," *Signal*, June 27, 1901, 4–5.

77. "Indecent Theatrical Show Bills," *Signal*, Feb. 18, 1897, 9.

78. See "Library Problem," *International Messenger*, Apr. 1894, 1–2, at the National YWCA Library, New York City.

79. Martin, "Promotion of Purity," 1894, 462.

80. The Society of Friends banned all fiction from its library in Germantown, Pennsylvania. Josiah Leeds, "Pictorial Illustrations and Advertising that Need to be Condemned," *Signal*, Dec. 26, 1895, 4. See also Wilbur Crafts, "Clean the Streets for the Eyes," *Signal*, Aug. 31, 1899, 6.

81. Leeds urged that readings available at prisons and reformatories be scrutinized by WCTU members. Deborah C. Leeds, "Department for the Suppression of Impure Literature," *Signal*, Mar. 29, 1888, 12.

82. Rev. Wilbur F. Crafts, "Red Letter Days, 1895–1902," *Signal*, Nov. 13, 1902, 4. For another mention of blue laws, see Jane Kinney, "Purity," *Michigan A.R.*, 1904, 139.

83. Rev. Wilbur F. Crafts, "Reform Gains and Losses," *Signal*, July 6, 1899, 4–5.

84. Chase "published an outline of a proposed federal motion picture commission to be composed of the commissioner of education and six other commissioners, to be appointed, without party affiliation, by the secretary of the Department of the Interior" (Harriet Pritchard, "Purity in Literature and Art," *New York A.R.*, 1922, 98).

85. See Harriet Pritchard, "A Federal Motion Picture Commission," *Signal*, May 21, 1914, 10.

86. Dr. Jennie M. S. Laird, "Motion Picture Department," *Nebraska A.R.*, 1931, 51.

87. See, for example, D'Emilio and Freedman, *Intimate Matters*, chap. 7.

88. Anthony Comstock, "Crime Breeders," *Signal*, Nov. 12, 1891, 6.

89. Comstock, "Purity," 1892, 4.

90. Anthony Comstock, "Suppression of Impure Literature," *Signal*, Oct. 27, 1887, 4.

91. "WCTU National Convention," *Signal*, Dec. 3, 1896, 9.

92. "Purity in Literature and Art," *Signal*, Nov. 7, 1895, 11.

93. "Suppression of Impure Literature," *Signal*, Nov. 26, 1885, 2.

94. In one instance, "complaint was made to authorities about slot machines and [WCTU members] urged [instead] the establishing of playgrounds," a popular Progressive Era solution to youths' behavior problems. See Harriet S. Pritchard, "Purity in Literature and Art," *New York A.R.*, 1916, 175.

95. Kepley, "Suppression," 1887, 111.

96. Ada Kepley, "Suppression of Impure Literature," *Signal*, Mar. 3, 1887, 9.

97. "The Advertising World," *Signal*, Aug. 2, 1906, 8–9.

98. For a thorough discussion of Anthony Comstock, see Beisel, "Upper Class Formation," chap. 5. See also "Postoffice Investigation Progresses," *Signal*, June 16, 1904, 3.

99. D'Emilio and Freedman, *Intimate Matters*, chap. 7.

100. See Martin, "Promotion of Purity," 1894, 460; Katherine L. S. Goodard, "Purity in Literature and Art," *Massachusetts A.R.*, 1926, 87; Ward, "Social Morality," 1923, 71.

101. See Emilie Martin, "Promotion of Purity in Literature and Art," *Minutes*, 1897, 444.

102. Emilie Martin, "Purity in Literature and Art," *Signal,* June 9, 1904, 10. For a history of abortion in the United States, see Linda Gordon, *Woman's Body, Woman's Right: A Social History of Birth Control in America* (New York, 1974).

103. Emilie Martin, "Purity in Literature and Art," *Signal,* Jan. 9, 1908, 11.

104. Mrs. E. G. Greene, *Pathfinder for the Organization and Work of the Woman's Christian Temperance Union* (Vermont, 1884), 114–15, located at Willard Memorial Library, Evanston, Illinois.

105. Dora Webb, "How Can We Secure Purity in Literature and Art?" *Signal,* May 7, 1891, 12.

106. Beyond its attempts to work with and influence public school teachers, the WCTU was committed to an early type of university extension program. It recommended that the "working man or woman" participate in a "home school" or "self-education" program called the Chautauqua Literary and Scientific Circle that consisted of lists of readings upon various subjects with a certificate of graduation upon finishing the ten month long course. The course was run by the Chautauquas and had full support of WCTU members, many of whom participated by leading sessions over the summer in New York state. See Jane A. Stewart, "National Education Association Convention," *Signal,* July 21, 1910, 3; "Chautauqua Literary and Scientific Circle," *Signal,* Sept. 5, 1895, 4.

107. Jonathan Zimmerman, "'The Queen of the Lobby': Mary H. Hunt, Scientific Temperance, and the Dilemma of Democratic Education in America" (Ph.D. diss., Johns Hopkins University, 1993), 193–213.

108. By 1924, the name of the National Congress of Mothers was changed to the National Congress of Parents and Teachers.

109. Mary M. Coman, "National Mothers' Congress," *Signal,* June 6, 1907, 5.

110. "The Tendency to Specialize," *Signal,* Aug. 16, 1900, 8.

111. Emily Lee Sherwood, "The National Congress of Mothers," *Signal,* Mar. 2, 1899, 2 (emphasis added).

112. "The National Congress of Mothers," *Signal,* Apr. 18, 1898, 9.

113. Anthony Comstock spoke at the same convention on "immoral" literature. See "The Mothers Congress," *Signal,* May 12, 1898, 2.

114. "Promotion of Purity in Literature and Art," *Minutes,* 1897, 443. See also David J. Rothman and Sheila M. Rothman, eds., *National Congress of Mothers: The First Conventions* (New York, 1987), 271.

115. Coman, "National Mothers' Congress," 5.

116. Corinne Marie Allen, "What Should Be Taught to Children Concerning the Sex Relation," Utah Congress of Mothers, 1912, in the papers of Corinne Allen, A-5, A-42, folders 3 and 10, 1–2, Radcliffe.

117. "What Are Your Children Reading?" *Signal,* Mar. 13, 1913, 8.

118. Ladd-Taylor, *Mother-Work,* 62–66.

119. Butler, "Force of Fantasy," 106–11.

120. Mrs. Curtis Bynum, "Plans of Work of Committee on Standards in Literature," 1926, in the papers of Elizabeth Tilton, A-52, box 7, folder 224, Radcliffe.

121. Ladd-Taylor, *Mother-Work,* 64.

122. Bynum, "Plans of Work."

123. Ladd-Taylor, *Mother-Work,* 64 (emphasis added).

124. Ibid., 54.

125. "Report of Special Committee to Prepare a Statement of the Duties of Each Department and Standing Committee Chairman," *Minutes*, 1922, 1–3; "Minutes of the 27th Annual Convention of the National Congress of Mothers and Parent-Teacher Associations," Apr. 23–28, 1923, in Elizabeth Tilton papers, box 7, folders 222 and 223, Radcliffe.

126. See, for example, "Philadelphia Methodists Protest against Unclean Films," *Signal*, Apr. 13, 1929, 15; "Pictures Encouraging Lawlessness the Greatest Corrupter of Nation's Morals, Says Babson," *Signal*, May 25, 1929, 15; "Women Resent Lawlessness in Films, Says Mrs. Winter," *Signal*, Dec. 21, 1929, 14.

127. "Recent Publicity Concerning Film Censorship," *Signal*, Mar. 30, 1929, 14; Gabrielle Julien Koechlin, "International Motion Picture Conference," *Signal*, Nov. 20, 1926, 4.

128. "Parent-Teacher Congress Reaffirms Stand for Prohibition," *Signal*, June 11, 1927, 3. See also Miller, "Motion Pictures," 1926, 161.

129. Mrs. William [Elizabeth] Tilton and Mrs. Morey V. Kerns, "Attention All Who Are Interested in Motion Pictures," NCM Legislative Committee, Mar. 2, 1928, in the papers of Elizabeth Tilton, box 8, folder 237, Radcliffe.

130. Mrs. E. Hugh Morris, "Plan of Work of the Committee on Motion Pictures," Board of Managers Reports, 1930, 1–3, in the papers of Elizabeth Tilton, A-52, box 8, folder 230, Radcliffe.

131. Mrs. William [Elizabeth] Tilton, "For Your State Bulletin: Something Should Be Done about the Movies," Legislative Committee of 1930, papers of Elizabeth Tilton, box 8, folder 238, Radcliffe.

132. "The following national organizations have been enlisted in the movement for federal supervision during the past year. The North American Congress of Home Missions . . . representing 28 Communions and 23,000,000 constituents and adherents: The National Grange, Women's Foreign Missionary Society and Home Missionary Society of the Methodist Episcopal Church, Northern Baptists, United Presbyterians, Reformed Presbyterians, General Convention of the Protestant Episcopal church, Board of Bishops of the Methodist Episcopal Church" (Maude M. Aldrich, "Motion Pictures," *Minutes*, 1931, 116).

133. For books focusing on women in urban life, see Joanne Meyerowitz, *Women Adrift: Independent Wage Earners in Chicago, 1880–1930* (Chicago, 1988); Kathy Peiss, *Cheap Amusements: Working Women and Leisure in Turn-of-the-Century New York* (Philadelphia, 1986); Christine Stansell, *City of Women: Sex and Class in New York, 1789–1860* (1982; rpt., Urbana, Ill., 1987); Judith Walkowitz, *Prostitution and Victorian Society: Women, Class, and the State* (New York, 1980).

134. Peiss, *Cheap Amusements*, 68–69, 73.

135. Leslie Woodcock Tentler, *Wage-Earning Women: Industrial Work and Family Life in the United States, 1900–1930* (Oxford, 1979), 73, 111.

136. Paul Johnson, *A Shopkeeper's Millennium: Society and Revivals in Rochester, New York, 1815–1837* (New York, 1978), 122–23, 127.

137. Roy Rosenzweig, *Eight Hours for What We Will: Workers and Leisure in an Industrial City, 1870–1920* (New York, 1983), 205–6.

138. Ibid.

139. "I wish here to thank Mr. T. V. Powderly and his Council for sending out ninety-two thousand of those petitions [to raise the age of consent to 18] to local

assemblies of the Knights of Labor" (Frances E. Willard, "The Ideal Home and Purity," *The Philanthropist* 2.12 [Dec. 1887], reel 31, sec. 3, scrapbooks 9–12).

140. Deborah Leeds, "Department for the Suppression of Impure Literature," *Minutes*, 1888, 183.

141. Rosenzweig, *Eight Hours for What We Will*, 206.

142. Ibid., 207 (emphasis in original); Tentler, *Wage-Earning Women*, 100.

143. Dorothy Salem, *To Better Our World: Black Women in Organized Reform, 1890–1920* (Brooklyn, 1990), 21–22.

144. Ladd-Taylor, *Mother-Work*, 62.

145. Salem, *To Better Our World*, 36–37, 22.

146. Minnie Finch, *The NAACP: Its Fight for Justice* (Metuchen, N.J., 1981), 21.

147. Meyerowitz, "Beyond the Feminine Mystique," 1472–73.

148. Martin, "Purity," 1893, 395.

CHAPTER 2: THE SUPPRESSION OF IMPURE LITERATURE

1. Jean McArthur Hyde, "Immoral Tendency of Modern Fiction: A Paper Read before the National WCTU Convention, Philadelphia, PA, November 30, 1904," *Signal*, Jan. 12, 1905, 5.

2. For books on culture at the turn of the century, see Robert Allen, *Horrible Prettiness: Burlesque in American Culture* (Chapel Hill, N.C., 1991); Stephen Kern, *The Culture of Time and Space 1880–1918* (Cambridge, 1983); Rubin, *Middle/Brow Culture*; John Tebbel, *History of Book Publishing* (New York, 1972).

3. The *Signal* had a circulation of almost 100,000 by 1890. See Bordin, *Woman and Temperance*, 90.

4. Hyde, "Immoral Tendency of Modern Fiction," 6 (emphasis added).

5. Ibid., 5.

6. See Fiske, *Understanding Popular Culture*, 4–5; Janice Radway, *Reading the Romance: Women, Patriarchy, and Popular Literature* (Chapel Hill, N.C., 1984), chap. 5.

7. Hyde, "Immoral Tendency of Modern Fiction," 5.

8. Mary Allen West, *Childhood: Its Care and Culture* (Chicago, 1892), 584–85, located at Willard Memorial Library, Evanston, Illinois.

9. Significantly, poverty was never mentioned as a possible reason for crimes committed by youths. See, for example, Naomi Tomlinson, "Department for the Suppression of Impure Literature," *Signal*, Mar. 3, 1887, 12; Pritchard, "Purity," 1898, 190; Harriet Pritchard, "Purity in Literature and Art," *New York A.R.*, 1910, 170.

10. West, *Childhood*, 588.

11. Ann Douglas, *The Feminization of American Culture* (New York, 1977), pt. 2.

12. Dorothy Horning, "The Best Book I Have Read This Year and Why I Liked It," *Signal*, Nov. 8, 1900, 7.

13. Ann Scott MacLeod, *American Childhood: Essays on Children's Literature of the Nineteenth and Twentieth Centuries* (Athens, Ga., 1994), 82–83.

14. A.K.H., "Pernicious Literature," *Signal*, Apr. 22, 1886, 5.

15. Ibid. See also "The National Congress of Mothers," *Signal*, May 19, 1904, 3.

16. Higham, *Strangers in the Land*, chaps. 9–11.

17. Elizabeth A. Perkins, "Children and Books," *Signal*, Mar. 24, 1921, 5.

18. Philip Johnson, "What Can We Do for Our Children," *Signal,* May 10, 1900, 4–5.

19. Frances Willard, "Romance versus Reality," *The Chautauquan* 5.2 (Nov. 1884): 88.

20. Ibid. See also Frances E. Willard, "The Novel," *Alliance News,* Dec. 1893, reel 31.

21. Willard, "Romance versus Reality," 88.

22. These views remained constant for at least two decades. See Mrs. S. B. Hill, "Impure Literature," *Signal,* June 14, 1888, 6; "For Purer Fiction," *Signal,* July 4, 1907, 8–9.

23. A Friend of Girls, "Novel Reading," *Signal,* Feb. 13, 1890, 10.

24. Hill, "Impure Literature," 1888, 6; Harriet S. Pritchard, "Work for the Promotion of Purity in Literature and Art," *Signal,* Feb. 19, 1914, 10.

25. Hill, "Impure Literature," 1888, 6. See also "For Purer Fiction," *Signal,* July 4, 1907, 8–9.

26. Hyde, "Immoral Tendency of Modern Fiction," 6.

27. Addie Davis Fries, "Mothers' Meetings and Good Literature," *Signal,* Dec. 13, 1900, 5.

28. See Gene Smith and Jayne Smith, eds., *The Police Gazette* (New York, 1972), 14–18. For a discussion of the *Police Gazette* in its early years (1845–50), see Dan Schiller, *Objectivity and the News: The Public and the Rise of Commercial Journalism* (Philadelphia, 1981), chaps. 4–5. For a study of borderline forms of popular culture, see Allen, *Horrible Prettiness,* 199.

29. Smith and Smith, *Police Gazette,* 16.

30. For a discussion of WCTU movie censorship efforts, see chapter 5.

31. Smith and Smith, *Police Gazette,* Oct. 1878, 22. See also Bordin, *Woman and Temperance,* 84–85.

32. Smith and Smith, *Police Gazette,* Oct. 1878, 23; ibid., May 1891, 136.

33. Ibid., Feb. 1895, 210.

34. Ibid., Mar. 1895, 188; ibid., Apr. 1895, 190.

35. Ibid., Mar. 1882, 33.

36. Ibid., Feb. 1888, 87.

37. Chambers, "Pure Literature and Art," 1894, 31.

38. Lucy J. Holmes, "Report of the Department for the Suppression of Impure Literature," *Minutes,* 1884, c–ci.

39. Corresponding Secretary's Report, *Minutes,* 1885, 112.

40. Holmes, "Suppression," 1886, p. cxxi.

41. Ibid., p. cxxiv.

42. "Eleven states have passed laws against the sale of police papers and kindred publications" ("Signal Notes," *Signal,* Apr. 15, 1886, 14).

43. "Fourteenth Annual Report of the Board of Managers of the New York Society for the Suppression of Vice, 1887–1888," 7–8, in WCTU microfilm collection, Frances Willard's scrapbooks 57–58, sec. 3.

44. Superintendent Narcissa M. Smith, "Temperance Literature," *Iowa A.R.,* 1887, 57; Kepley, "Suppression," 1887, 111. For a discussion of local WCTU enforcement of Scientific Temperance Instruction in the public schools, see Zimmerman, " 'Queen of the Lobby.' "

45. Smith, "Temperance Literature," 56–57. Note that Iowa's pro-censorship work took place through its Temperance Literature Department.

46. See Holmes, "Report of the Department," 1884, c–ci; Kepley, "Suppression," 1887, 112.

47. D. Leeds, "Suppression," 1888, 178–83.

48. Mrs. Samuel Clements, "Department of Purity in Literature and Art," *Minutes,* 1889, ccvii–ccxi.

49. Martin, "Purity," 1892, 188–95; see also Emilie Martin, "Purity in Literature and Art," *Minutes,* 1906, 317; "Law against Impurity," *Pennsylvania A.R.,* 1905, 273–74.

50. Contrast Holmes, "Suppression," 1886, cxxi–cxxiv, and Martin, "Promotion of Purity," 1894, 454–63.

51. See Smith and Smith, *Police Gazette,* 14–18.

52. Adella Curtis Firman, "Newspaper Literature," *Signal,* Oct. 2, 1885, 7.

53. It also recommended that parents remove from the home any French novels that could be accidentally discovered by a son or daughter. See Emilie Martin, "Work for the Promotion of Purity in Literature and Art," *Signal,* July 6, 1899, 14.

54. "Promotion of Purity in Literature and Art," *Minutes,* 1894, 455.

55. "Editorial," *Signal,* May 2, 1895, 12.

56. Emilie D. Martin, "Purity in Literature and Art," *Signal,* Apr. 7, 1898, 12.

57. "Help the Children to Read," *Signal,* Oct. 26, 1905, 8.

58. Tomlinson, "Suppression of Impure Literature," Mar. 3, 1887, 12.

59. Mrs. E. M. Adams, "A Mothers' Meeting," *Signal,* May 1, 1902, 6.

60. Mrs. Kipp, "The Anti-Dime Society," *Signal,* Mar. 14, 1889, 6.

61. "How to Form a Book Club," *Signal,* Feb. 26, 1885, 6.

62. The article "Books as Moral Educators" stressed the importance of character development in early childhood and suggested that stories in first- or second-grade readers (textbooks) permanently affected children. See Jean Hyde, "Books as Moral Educators," *Signal,* Apr. 11, 1907, 5.

63. Jean Hyde, "A Book Conscience," *Signal,* July 19 and 26, 1906, 4–5.

64. Jean McArthur Hyde, "What Is Modern Fiction?" *Signal,* June 22, 1905, 5.

65. Josiah W. Leeds, "Against the Teaching of War in History Text-Books," *Signal,* Apr. 28, 1896, 3–4; "Is War a Tonic to Literature?" *Signal,* Oct. 19, 1899, 6.

66. Hyde, "A Book Conscience," 14 (emphasis added). Although Hyde's statement could imply that all creeds and ceremonies, even Catholic ones, were inherently good and worthy of respect, WCTU members generally associated Catholicism with the Irish and other "wet" immigrants who opposed Prohibition.

67. Josiah Leeds, "The Domination of the 'French Novel,' and the Struggle against It," *Signal,* Oct. 30, 1890, 3.

68. "A Literary Scourge," *Signal,* Sept. 22, 1904, 8.

69. Walkowitz, *Prostitution and Victorian Society,* chap. 5.

70. See "The Religious Element in Fiction," *Signal,* July 24, 1902, 8; "Influence of Reform Movements upon Literature," *Signal,* Mar. 4, 1897, 8.

71. Dr. John Madden, "Unconscious Pro-Alcohol Influences in Literature," *Signal,* Aug. 18, 1904, 5.

72. Duncan C. Milner, "Modern Fiction and Drink," *Signal,* Nov. 11, 1920, 6.

73. Emilie Martin, "Department of Purity in Literature and Art," *Minutes*, 1895, 302.

74. Rubin dates the creation of a middlebrow culture to the 1920s. See Rubin, *Middle/Brow Culture*, 29–33.

75. John L. Wright, "Tainted Literature," *Signal*, Jan. 18, 1894, 5–6.

76. "Our Library Table," *Signal*, Nov. 10, 1898, 14.

77. "Purity," *Minutes*, 1907, 130.

78. Elites also experienced alienation from American popular culture. See T. J. Jackson Lears, *No Place of Grace: Antimodernism and the Transformation of American Culture, 1880–1920* (New York, 1981).

79. Willard, "Romance versus Reality," 88; Willard, "The Novel," reel 31.

80. Some of these authors published in the popular secular children's magazine *St. Nicholas*. See Fries, "Mothers' Meetings and Good Literature," 5. For a discussion of fiction writing in *St. Nicholas*, see Erisman, "There Was a Child Went Forth," 96–126.

81. "Among the Books," *Signal*, Dec. 6, 1888, 5; "Our Library Table," *Signal*, Nov. 22, 1900, 14. The boyhood literary tastes of the Prohibition leader General Neal Dow of Maine were extensively reported in the *Union Signal* and served as another reading guide for youths. See Mrs. C. B. Hopkins, "General Neal Dow and His Books," *Signal*, Mar. 12, 1896, 3; Mrs. M. A. Rodger, "Keeping the Boys at Home in the Evening," *Signal*, July 22, 1886, 4–5; Emily A. Kellogg, "Books and Book-Lovers: A Talk to Girls," *Signal*, July 23, 1891, 10; Olive Clark, "With Louisa Alcott," *Signal*, Mar. 5, 1903, 13.

82. "Book Notices," *Signal*, Dec. 3, 1885, 3.

83. "'Bring a Book' Evening with the Y.P.B.," *Signal*, Oct. 31, 1925, 11. For discussions of the 1920s youth culture, see Paula Fass, *The Damned and the Beautiful: American Youth in the 1920s* (New York, 1977); Lewis Erenberg, *Steppin' Out: New York Nightlife and the Transformation of American Culture* (New York, 1981).

84. The *Union Signal* also published lists of books sold by the WCTU's own publishing house in Illinois. For examples, see "The Best Juvenile Books," *Signal*, Dec. 6, 1888, 17; "List of Books for Libraries," *Signal*, Dec. 21, 1911, 11.

85. "Our Young People: Books That Will Help You Grow," *Signal*, July 19, 1923, 12.

86. See Harriet Pritchard, "Work for the Promotion of Purity in Literature and Art," *Signal*, Dec. 11, 1913, 15; "Women's Campaign for Clean Literature Brings Prompt Action," *Signal*, Apr. 9, 1925, 3. See also Boyer, *Purity in Print*, 106–7.

87. Stone, "Purity," 1924, 86.

88. Martin, "Purity," May 19, 1910, 10.

89. "Workable Ideas for Local Unions: Book Censorship," *Signal*, Apr. 11, 1912, 14; Martin, "Purity," 1893, 394–99; Martin, "Department of Purity," 1895, 302–6; Tomlinson, "Suppression of Impure Literature," Mar. 3, 1887, 12.

90. "Purity," *Minutes*, 1891, 180.

91. Harriet Pritchard, "Purity in Literature and Art," *Minutes*, 1911, 350–52.

92. Tomlinson, "Suppression of Impure Literature," Mar. 3, 1887, 12; Harriet Pritchard, "Purity in Literature and Art," *Minutes*, 1914, 271.

93. Emilie Martin, "Purity in Literature and Art," *Minutes*, 1905, 340; Martin, "Promotion of Purity," 1896, 356; Emilie Martin, "Purity in Literature and Art,"

Minutes, 1900, 309–11. The WCTU records are often frustratingly silent on specifics about what exactly made books offensive. Usually, a blanket charge of "immorality" is all that we find.

94. D. Leeds, "Suppression," 1888, 181; Emilie Martin, "Purity in Literature and Art," *Minutes,* 1910, 347; Lucy Holmes, "Report on the Department for the Suppression of Impure Literature," *Minutes,* Oct. 1884, appendix, c–ci. See also Zimmerman, "'Queen of the Lobby,'" 195.

95. Pritchard, "Purity," 1910, 172.

96. The *Minutes of the National WCTU* from 1885, 1891, 1903, 1915, and 1919 give examples of local endeavors.

97. Frances J. Barnes, "Circulating Libraries," *Signal,* Nov. 22, 1900, 10.

98. Clara A. Packard, "The Kentucky W.C.T.U. Circulating Library," *Signal,* Mar. 28, 1901, 6; "A Call for Books," *Signal,* Dec. 29, 1887, 3.

99. "Chats with Our Workers," *Signal,* Mar. 23, 1899, 11.

100. Ruth A. Perham, "Wisconsin's Lending Library Plan," *Signal,* Feb. 15, 1900, 7; Susanna M. D. Fry, "To Save the Boys," *Signal,* Aug. 31, 1900, 4.

101. Jean Hyde, "What Is Modern Fiction?" June 22, 1905, 5; Hyde, "Immoral Tendency of Modern Fiction," 5. For a discussion of women's clubs' educational efforts, see Karen Blair, *The Clubwoman as Feminist: True Womanhood Redefined, 1868–1914* (New York, 1980).

102. Harriet Pritchard, "Purity in Literature and Art," *New York A.R.,* 1915, 127.

103. Pritchard, "Purity," 1916, 175.

104. Stone, "Purity," 1922, 79.

105. Ibid., 1924, 86.

106. See, for example, D. Leeds, "Suppression," 1888, 181; Martin, "Purity," 1910, 347; "Dangerous Literature," *Signal,* July 6, 1916, 9; "National's Library Project," *Signal,* Sept. 6, 1930, 8.

107. Rev. Harry Adams Hersey, "A Good Letter to Pass on to Your Librarian, General Sunday School Association of the Universalist Church," Department of Temperance, *Signal,* Apr. 27, 1916, 16.

CHAPTER 3: GUARDIANS OF PUBLIC MORALS

1. Lasch, *Haven in a Heartless World,* chaps. 2, 5–6; Donzelot, *Policing of Families,* chap. 3.

2. Mellen Chamberlain, "Report on Fiction in Public Libraries," *LJ* 8 (1883): 208; George Iles, "The Appraisal of Literature," *LJ* 21 (1896): 26. See Garrison, *Apostles of Culture,* chaps. 7–8.

3. Daniel Walkowitz, "The Making of a Feminine Professional Identity: Social Workers in the 1920s," *American Historical Review* 95 (Oct. 1990): 1051–75. For discussion of the process of professionalization, see Haskell, *The Emergence of Professional Social Science;* Bledstein, *The Culture of Professionalism.*

4. See Walter Learned, "The Line on Exclusion," *LJ* 21 (July 1896): 320–23; Peter Cowell, "On the Admission of Fiction in Free Public Libraries," *LJ* 2 (1877): 155.

5. Garrison, *Apostles of Culture,* chap. 5.

6. The 1893 survey quoted by Woodruff states that "the American Library Association, voiced by 60 of the 75 librarians to whom letters were sent, gives forth no

uncertain sound as to the necessity and duty of restricting the provision for fiction (novels, strictly so speaking) to the smallest possible quantity of the best quality" (Edwin H. Woodruff, "Fiction in Public Libraries," *LJ* 20 [Oct. 1895]: 342–45).

7. Garrison, *Apostles of Culture*, 219–21. For another discussion of the ALA and political censorship, see Wayne Wiegand, *"An Active Instrument for Propaganda": The American Public Library during World War I* (New York, 1989).

8. See, for example, Hubbart, "Report of the Department," 1905, 215.

9. L. E. C. Story, "Purity in Literature and Art," *New Hampshire A.R.*, 1918, 70; Harriet Pritchard, "Purity in Literature and Art," *New York A.R.*, 1917, 138.

10. Pritchard, "Purity," 1917, 140. Pritchard also noted: "Wrote to the Cosmopolitan objecting to a story in it that had been brought to my notice by the newsdealer, and the second month it was not published, and never finished" ("Purity," 1916, 175).

11. See A. W. Whepley, "Common Novels in Public Libraries," *LJ* 19 (1894): 21–22; F. B. Perkins, "Free Libraries and Unclean Books," *LJ* 10 (Dec. 1885): 396–99.

12. A. L. Peck, "Common Novels in Public Libraries," *LJ* 19 (1894): 137.

13. Theodore C. Burgess, "Means of Leading Boys from the Dime Novel to Better Literature," *LJ* 21 (Apr. 1896): 144–47.

14. William H. Brett, "Improper Books," *LJ* 20 (Aug. 1895): 36.

15. Louis N. Feipel, "Questionable Books in Public Libraries—II," *LJ* 47 (Nov. 1, 1922): 907–11. Feipel also wrote: "Librarians appear to be unanimous in believing that it is inadvisable to give general publicity in their communities to the fact that certain works are not approved by them for acquisition" ("Questionable Books in Public Libraries—II," 907).

16. Theresa H. West, "Improper Books: Methods Employed to Discover and Exclude Them," *LJ* 20 (Aug. 1895): 32; J. N. Larned, "Improper Books," *LJ* 20 (Aug. 1895): 35.

17. See Bernard C. Steiner, "Some Problems Concerning Prose Fiction," *LJ* 28 (1903): 33–35.

18. "Editorial," *LJ* 14.9 (Sept. 1889): 390.

19. See Michel Foucault, *History of Sexuality*, vol. 1: *An Introduction* (1976; rpt., New York, 1980), 61; "Editorial," *LJ* 20 (May 1895): 162; F. M. Crunden, "Concerning Library Censorship," *LJ* 20 (June 1895): 198.

20. Steiner, "Some Problems Concerning Prose Fiction," 33–35; J. C. Dana "Fiction in Public Libraries," *Springfield Republican*, rpt. in *LJ* 24 (Dec. 1899): 670–71.

21. See "The Question of Fiction Reading," *LJ* 27 (Jan. 1902): 18.

22. Charles Francis Adams, Jr., "Fiction in Public Libraries and Educational Catalogues," *LJ* 4 (1879): 330–38; Elizabeth P. Thurston, "Common Novels in Public Libraries," *LJ* 19 (1894): 16–18.

23. W. M. Stevenson, "Weeding Out Fiction in the Carnegie Free Library of Allegheny, PA," *LJ* 22 (Mar. 1897): 133.

24. Miss C. M. Hewins, ed., "Literature for the Young," *LJ* 8 (Feb. 1883): 36.

25. Ibid., 37.

26. Ibid.

27. Miss C. M. Hewins, ed., "Literature for the Young," *LJ* 8 (Dec. 1883): 342. See also Miss C. M. Hewins, ed., "Literature for the Young," *LJ* 8 (July 1883): 132. For a description of this book, see MacLeod, *American Childhood*, 152–54.

28. Mary U. Rothrock, "Censorship of Fiction in the Public Library," *LJ* 48 (1923): 454–56 (emphasis added).

29. "Novels may be roughly classified as follows: First, classics, among the older of which we may name Fielding, Smollett, and Richardson; and among the modern, George Eliot, Thackeray, and Dickens. Second, the common run, varying in the degrees of commonness from Hardy, Black, and Howells to Roe, Holmes, and Southworth. Third, the vicious and immoral, such, for example, as those of the so-called decadents" (Woodruff, "Fiction in Public Libraries," 342–45).

30. "Fiction at the Boston Public Library," *The Boston Herald*, rpt. in *LJ* 6 (Aug. 1881): 205–6.

31. Feipel, "Questionable Books—I," 857–59. See also Learned, "The Line on Exclusion," 320–23.

32. Feipel, "Questionable Books—I," 857–59.

33. Rothrock, "Censorship of Fiction," 454–56.

34. Chamberlain, "Report on Fiction in Public Libraries," 208; Caroline H. Garland, "Common Novels in Public Libraries," *LJ* 19 (1894): 15. See also George Watson Cole, "Fiction in Libraries: A Plea for the Masses," *LJ* 19 (1894): 18–21.

35. Isabel Ely Lord, "Open Shelves and Public Morals," *LJ* 26 (Feb. 1901): 66.

36. Thurston, "Common Novels in Public Libraries," 16–18.

37. Garrison, *Apostles of Culture*, introduction; Chamberlain, "Report on Fiction in Public Libraries," 208. For a detailed account of librarians' professional in-fighting, see Wiegand, *Politics of an Emerging Profession*.

38. Perkins, "Free Libraries and Unclean Books," 396–99.

39. Isabel Ely Lord, "The Use and Value of Fiction in Education," *LJ* 28 (1903): 28–31.

40. R. B. Poole, "Fiction in Libraries," *LJ* 16 (Jan. 1891): 8–10.

41. Frances Willard, "The Do Everything Policy," *Signal*, Oct. 16, 1893, 32–33.

42. Larned, "Selection of Books," 270–72.

43. Rubin, *Middle/Brow Culture*, introduction.

44. Larned, "Selection of Books," 270–72.

45. "Address of Professor WM. P. Atkinson," *LJ* 4 (1879): 359–62.

46. Mr. J. D. Mullins, "Library Conference," *LJ* 2 (1877): 256.

47. Adams, "Fiction in Public Libraries," 330–38.

48. Burgess, "Means of Leading Boys from the Dime Novel," 144–47.

49. The use of the word "stimulant" is ironic, considering that they were talking about depressants.

50. George McLean Harper, "The Encouragement of Serious Reading: 'Profit You in What You Read?'" *LJ* 28 (May 1903): 217–21.

51. Josephine Gerry, East Broadway Library, Oct. 1907, NYPL, 2.

52. Ethel Sullivan, St. Gabriel's Park Branch, June–Sept. 1910, NYPL, 3. Irish youths were singled out and criticized as bad or indifferent readers: "The children in the neighborhood of our library are Irish and Italian. The Irish care very little for reading, and the younger Italian boys are afraid to come to the library because they say their books are taken from them by the Irish boys" (Amy F. Sutton, Hudson Park Branch, Oct. 1907, NYPL, 1). See also Amy F. Sutton, Hudson Park Branch, Nov. 1908, NYPL, 6; Charlotte H. Meade, "Notes on Children's Reading," *LJ* 29 (Sept. 1904): 476.

53. Josephine Gerry, East Broadway Library, Apr. 1908, NYPL, 2.

54. C. A. Cutter, "Supervision of Children's Library Use," *LJ* 23 (Apr. 1898): 149; "Editorial," *LJ* 23 (Apr. 1898): 1.

55. Linda A. Eastman, "The Library and the Children: An Account of the Children's Work in the Cleveland Public Library," *LJ* 23 (Apr. 1898): 142–44; Mary Wright Plummer, "The Work for Children in Free Libraries," *LJ* 22 (Nov. 1897): 679–86.

56. Arthur E. Bostwick, "The Purchase of Current Fiction," *LJ* 28 (1903): 31. See also Lord, "Use and Value of Fiction," 28–31.

57. From Bostwick, "The Purchase of Current Fiction," 31.

58. Larned, "Selection of Books," 270–72.

59. Poole, "Fiction in Libraries," 8–10.

60. Miss C. M. Hewins, ed., "Literature for the Young," *LJ* 8 (May 1883): 85; C. M. Hewins, ed., "Literature for the Young," *LJ* 8 (Mar.–Apr. 1883): 57.

61. S. S. Green, "Sensational Fiction in Public Libraries," *LJ* 4 (1879): 345–55.

62. Cole, "Fiction in Libraries," 18–21.

63. J. Schwartz, "New York Apprentices' Library," *LJ* 15 (Sept. 1890): 261; "Peccator," "As to Novel-Reading—A Confession," *LJ* 5 (1880): 104.

64. B. W. Pennock, "The Other Side of Paternalism," *LJ* 25 (Feb. 1900): 61–63.

65. Gertrude Sackett, "Home Libraries and Reading Clubs," *LJ* 27 (1902): 72–73.

66. Adams, "Fiction in Public Libraries," 330–38.

67. William Kite, "Fiction in Public Libraries," *LJ* 1.8 (1876): 277–79; Mary A. Bean, "Report on the Reading of the Young," *LJ* 8 (1883): 217–27.

68. See chapter 7 for a discussion of ALA members' reasons for disliking Horatio Alger's books. Anne MacLeod asserts that "for Alger the essence of democracy was class mobility" (*American Childhood*, 81).

69. Caroline M. Hewins, "Yearly Report on Boys' and Girls' Reading," *LJ* 7 (1882): 182–90.

70. Garland, "Common Novels," 15.

71. Poole, "Fiction in Libraries," 8–10.

72. Woodruff, "Fiction in Public Libraries," 342–45.

73. Feipel, "Questionable Books—I," 857–59.

74. "City Children and the Library," *LJ* 25 (Apr. 1900): 170.

75. Mary E. Comstock, "The Library as an Educational Factor," *LJ* 21 (Apr. 1896): 147–49.

76. Ibid. See also "Good Literature Taking the Place of the Bad," *LJ* 10 (Nov. 1885): 377.

77. A Worcester, Massachusetts, librarian, quoted in "Editorial," *LJ* 1 (1876): 79. See also W. H. Brett, a Cleveland librarian, quoted in Hannah P. James, "Yearly Report on the Reading of the Young," *LJ* 10 (1885): 278–91.

78. Annie Carroll Moore, "Special Training for Children's Librarians" (pt. 1) *LJ* 23 (1898): 80–82. Hewins, "Yearly Report," 182–90. For a eulogistic biography of Moore, see Frances Clarke Sayers, *Anne Carroll Moore: A Biography* (New York, 1972).

79. Dorothy Ross, *G. Stanley Hall: The Psychologist as Prophet* (Chicago, 1972), 113–27.

80. Moore, "Special Training," 80–82.

81. F. M. Crunden, "Special Training for Children's Librarians" (pt. 2) *LJ* 23 (1898): 82.

82. "Fiction at the Boston Public Library," *The Boston Herald*, rpt. in *LJ* 6 (1881): 204.

83. "In 1910, 78.5 percent of library workers in the United States were feminine [*sic*]" (Garrison, *Apostles of Culture*, 173, 207, 210). Another historian estimates that "about 20% of all librarians had been women in 1870; over 90 percent were women in 1930" (Stanley Coben, *Rebellion against Victorianism: The Impetus for Cultural Change in 1920s America* [New York, 1991], 101).

84. Moore, "Special Training," 80–82. For a discussion of the professionalization of the social sciences, see Dorothy Ross, *The Origins of American Social Science* (Cambridge, 1991).

85. Moore, "Special Training," 80–82.

86. Plummer, "The Work for Children," 679–86.

87. Ibid.

88. Annie Carroll Moore, "The Work of the Children's Librarian," *LJ* 28 (Apr. 1903): 160. See also Walkowitz, "The Making of a Feminine Professional Identity," 1051–75.

89. Moore, "The Work of the Children's Librarian," 160.

90. Ibid.

91. Ibid.

92. Ibid.

93. Ibid.

94. Lasch, *Haven in a Heartless World*, 10, 15, 18.

95. Ibid., 9–10, 169.

96. For a discussion of professional authority and the power of metaphor, see JoAnne Brown, "Professional Language: Words That Succeed," *Radical History Review* 34 (1986): 33–51.

97. Donzelot, *Policing of Families*, 227.

98. Garrison, *Apostles of Culture*, chap. 11.

99. Feipel, "Questionable Books—II," 907–11. See also Garrison, *Apostles of Culture*, 89; Geller, *Forbidden Books*, 132–35; MacLeod, *American Childhood*, 178–81.

100. The 47th (1898) Report of the Library, "The Fiction Committee of the Boston Public Library," *LJ* 24 (Sept. 1899): 528–29.

101. Ibid.

102. Director's Report (1898), N.Y. State Library, "'Evaluation' of Fiction at New York State Library," *LJ* 24 (Sept. 1899): 529.

103. Green, "Sensational Fiction," 345–55; S. S. Green, "The Selection of Books for Sunday-School Libraries and their Introduction to Children," *LJ* 7 (Oct. 1882): 250.

104. Green, "Sensational Fiction," 345–55.

105. For a brief mention of Swift, see Geller, *Forbidden Books*, 61.

106. Lindsay Swift, "Paternalism in Public Libraries," *LJ* 24 (Nov. 1899): 609–18.

107. Ibid.

108. Ibid. (emphasis added).

109. J. A. Mangan and James Walvin, eds., *Manliness and Morality: Middle-Class Masculinity in Britain and America, 1800–1940* (New York, 1987), introduction.

110. "Children's Aid Society of Boston," *LJ* 17 (Oct. 1892): 426.

111. Sackett, "Home Libraries and Reading Clubs," 72–73.

112. C. G. Birkwell, "The Home Libraries of the Children's Aid Society," *LJ* 16 (Sept. 1891): 278; Mary C. Thurlow, "Encouragement of Serious Reading by Women's Clubs," *LJ* 28 (May 1903): 227–29.

113. "Children's Aid Society of Boston," *LJ* 17 (Oct. 1892): 426. The creation of the Children's Library Association demonstrates the multiple connections between reform groups on a casual, daily level—in this case between the YMCA, the South Reformed Church, the Woman's Christian Temperance Union, and Grammar School No. 28 in New York City. See Emily S. Hanaway, "The Children's Library in New York," *LJ* 12 (May 1887): 185–86; "The Children's Library in New York, and Its Constitution," *LJ* 12 (June 1887): 224–25.

114. "Bureau of Library Information at General Federation of Women's Clubs" (editorial), *LJ* 25 (July 1900): 336.

115. See Lasch, *Haven in a Heartless World*, 171–73; Donzelot, *Policing of Families*, 18–19.

116. James, "Yearly Report," 278–91; Mellen Chamberlain, quoted in Minerva A. Sanders, "Report on Reading for the Young," *LJ* 15 (1890): 58–64.

117. "Female Influence on Reading," *LJ* 3 (1878): 380–81 (emphasis added). This rhetoric is similar to that of "Republican motherhood" in the early national period. See Linda Kerber, *Women of the Republic: Intellect and Ideology in Revolutionary America* (Chapel Hill, N.C., 1980).

118. Charles Welsh, "The Evaluation of Children's Books from the Point of View of the History of Literature for Children," *LJ* 27 (1902): 76–79.

119. It was the unusual librarian who went so far as to deny that the regulation of fiction should be the domain of the American Library Association. One such librarian (a Miss Adams of the public library at Somerville, Massachusetts) said that "in my opinion parents are entirely responsible, and should know and examine every book read at home" (quoted in Bean, "Report on the Reading of the Young," 217–27). See also James, "Yearly Report," 278–91.

120. Burgess, "Means of Leading Boys from the Dime Novel," 144–47.

121. Miss Chandler, a librarian in Lancaster, Massachusetts, is quoted in Bean, "Report on the Reading of the Young," 217–27. See also Lutie E. Stearns, "Report on Reading for the Young," *LJ* 19 (1894): 81–87.

122. Burgess, "Means of Leading Boys from the Dime Novel," 144–47.

123. Caroline A. Blanchard, a librarian in Weymouth, Massachusetts, is quoted in "Reading by School-Children and College Students," *LJ* 13 (1888): 89–90.

124. Plummer, "The Work for Children," 679–86; Stearns, "Report on Reading for the Young," 81–87.

125. Bean, "Report on the Reading of the Young," 217–27; Cutter, "Supervision of Children's Library Use," 149. See also Miss M. A. Bean, "The Evil of Unlimited Freedom in the Use of Juvenile Fiction," *LJ* 4 (1879): 341–43.

126. Burgess, "Means of Leading Boys from the Dime Novel," 144–47 (emphasis added). See also Lasch, *Haven in a Heartless World*, 19.

127. J. C. Sickley, "Plan for Course of Reading for Pupils of the Poughkeepsie Public Schools," *LJ* 12 (1887): 372.

128. Learned, "The Line on Exclusion," 320–23. MacLeod notes that "genteel

and popular audiences alike before 1910 resisted strongly realistic literature, in particular, sexual frankness . . . [was] rejected by most of the reading public" (*American Childhood*, 125).

129. Higham, *Strangers in the Land*, 149–57.

130. Linda A. Eastman, "Books for Mothers' Clubs," *LJ* 22 (Sept. 1897): 436–37.

131. Mr. Kite of the Friend's Free Library in Germantown, Pennsylvania, quoted in Bean, "Report on the Reading of the Young," 217–27 (emphasis added); Dr. Elizabeth B. Thelberg, "The Home and the Library," *LJ* 24 (Apr. 1899): 145–47; Green, "Sensational Fiction," 345–55.

132. For a biography of Moore, see Sayers, *Anne Carroll Moore*.

133. Hester Conway, Hamilton Grange Branch, Nov. 1907, NYPL, 5.

134. St. Agnes Branch, Apr. 1910, NYPL, 6.

135. Hester Conway, Hamilton Grange Branch, Oct. 1909, NYPL, 6–7.

136. Tompkins Square Branch, Sept. 1910, NYPL, 11.

137. Agnes White, Hamilton Grange Branch, Nov. 1908, NYPL, 7.

138. Henrietta Sherwood, Jackson Square Branch, July 1908, NYPL, 4.

139. Port Richmond Branch, Nov. 1910, NYPL, 5.

140. S. E. Warn, Jackson Square Branch, Sept. 1908, NYPL, 6.

141. Predictably, Lindsay Swift offered a late objection to children's rooms: "Personally, I am exceedingly distrustful of 'Children's rooms'—they are very much like Sunday-schools—convenient places for parents who don't go to church to unload their offspring. They relieve parents also from a task peculiarly their own—an especial danger of civic and state paternalism, through an assumption of artificial prerogative. . . . I do not chance to agree with . . . the mental sequestration of children in libraries" (Swift, "Paternalism in Public Libraries," 609–18). Swift's argument favoring parental responsibility aligns him, ironically, with Kate Gannett Wells (see note 142).

142. Kate Gannett Wells, "The Responsibility of Parents in the Selection of Reading for the Young," *LJ* 4 (1879): 325–30. For a biography of Wells, see Mary Huth, "Kate Gannett Wells: A Biographical Study of an Anti-Suffragist" (M.A. thesis, University of Rochester, 1980).

143. Wells, "Responsibility of Parents," 325–30.

144. Ibid.

145. Boyer, *Purity in Print*, 3–5; Carl Kaestle, *Literacy in America: Readers and Reading since 1880* (New Haven, Conn., 1991), introduction.

146. Bean, "Report on the Reading of the Young," 217–27.

147. "City Children and the Library," *LJ* 25 (Apr. 1900): 170. For an account of the work of James M. Sawin, see W. E. Foster, "Some Successful Methods of Developing Children's Interest in Good Literature," *LJ* 20 (Nov. 1895): 377–79.

148. Linda A. Eastman, "The Child, the School, and the Library," *LJ* 21 (Apr. 1896): 134–39; Perkins, "Free Libraries and Unclean Books," 396–99.

149. "Editorial," *LJ* 23 (Apr. 1898): 1.

150. The metaphor of the library as "storehouse" would certainly not increase librarians' professional claims or prestige. See Eastman, "The Child, the School," 134–39; Bean, "Report on the Reading of the Young," 217–27.

151. Green, "Sensational Fiction," 345–55; Evelyn N. Lane and Ida F. Farrar,

"Methods of Evaluating Children's Books," *LJ* 26 (Apr. 1901): 194–97; Perkins, "Free Libraries and Unclean Books," 396–99.

152. James, "Yearly Report," 278–91.

153. Caroline M. Hewins, "Report on List of Children's Books with Children's Annotations," *LJ* 27 (1902): 79–82.

154. Bean, "Report on the Reading of the Young," 217–27.

155. Arthur E. Bostwick, "Efforts to Improve the Character of Reading in New York City," *LJ* 28 (May 1903): 229–33.

156. Swift, "Paternalism in Public Libraries," 609–18. Mr. Upton of the Peabody, Massachusetts, library is quoted in Hewins, "Yearly Report," 182–90. See also Bean, "The Evil of Unlimited Freedom," 341–43; Kite, "Fiction in Public Libraries," 277–79; Pennock, "The Other Side of Paternalism," 61–63.

157. S. E. Warn, Jackson Square Branch, Feb. 1909, NYPL, 5.

158. Mott Haven Branch, Mar. 1909, NYPL, 4.

159. James Sully, "Child-Study and Education," *International Monthly*, rpt. in *LJ* 27 (Apr. 1902): 195–96.

160. Plummer, "The Work for Children," 679–86.

161. Burgess, "Means of Leading Boys from the Dime Novel," 144–47. From Plummer, "The Work for Children," 679–86.

162. Sully, "Child-Study and Education," 195–96.

CHAPTER 4: AMATEUR CENSORS AND CRITICS

1. Levine, *Highbrow/Lowbrow*, chap. 2.

2. Ibid., 195, 239. For information on amusement parks and dancing styles as twentieth-century working-class leisure activities, see Peiss, *Cheap Amusements*, chaps. 4–5; John F. Kasson, *Amusing the Million: Coney Island at the Turn of the Century* (New York, 1978). In *The Sociology of Culture* (New York, 1982), Raymond Williams presents a typology of cultures as oppositional, alternative, and affirmative, suggesting that a "cultural free space" can be any of these three types.

3. Rubin, *Middle/Brow Culture*, xii–xiii.

4. Levine, *Highbrow/Lowbrow*, 164.

5. Rubin, *Middle/Brow Culture*, xi–xx.

6. Rubin's "genteel intellectuals" are the founders of journals and museums, who guided the reading of "many Americans" in search of "stability, insight, and pleasure" (ibid., 27). See also George Santayana, *The Genteel Tradition: Nine Essays*, ed. Douglas Wilson (Cambridge, 1967); Henry May, *End of American Innocence: A Study of the First Years of Our Own Time, 1912–1927* (New York, 1959); Robert Dawidoff, *The Genteel Tradition and the Sacred Rage: High Culture vs. Democracy in Adams, James, and Santayana* (Chapel Hill, N.C., 1992).

7. Levine, *Highbrow/Lowbrow*, 176, 228; Bordin, *Woman and Temperance*, appendix.

8. Barbara Novak, *American Painting of the Nineteenth Century: Realism, Idealism, and the American Experience* (1969; 2d ed., New York, 1979), 201.

9. Leonard Everett Fisher, *Masterpieces of American Painting* (New York, 1985), 25.

10. For a discussion of Americans' embarrassment with the human body, see

John F. Kasson, *Rudeness and Civility: Manners in Nineteenth-Century Urban America* (New York, 1990), 114, 217.

11. Kilpatrick, *Smut Peddlers*, 38.

12. *Minutes*, 1889, p. ccvii.

13. The marble sculptures and casts all over the exteriors of the buildings in the "White City" had drapery and fig leaves carefully covering private body parts and were not the source of the WCTU's concern. See Allen, *Horrible Prettiness*, 227.

14. For a sample of typical subjects for American painters, see Novak, *American Painting of the Nineteenth Century*. Peter Selz discusses the Armory Show in *Art in Our Times: A Pictorial History, 1890–1980* (New York, 1981), 123–24. For an excellent discussion of the nude in art, see Beisel, "Upper Class Formation."

15. Emilie Martin, "Purity in Literature and Art," *Signal*, Mar. 17, 1892, 12–13.

16. Mrs. Samuel Clements, "Department of Purity in Literature and Art," *Minutes*, 1892, 190.

17. Martin, "Purity," 1893, 394–95.

18. "Since Our Last Issue," *Signal*, May 11, 1893, 1.

19. Martin, "Purity," 1893, 394–95.

20. Willard, "The Do Everything Policy," 32–33.

21. Abby Felton, "The Nude in Art II," *Signal*, May 24, 1894, 5–6.

22. "The Key to the Problem of Purity in Art," *Signal*, May 19, 1898, 8.

23. Willard, "The Ideal Home and Purity," scrapbooks 9–12.

24. Ibid.

25. Martin, "Purity," 1893, 396; Emilie Martin, "The Power of Literature and Art," *Signal*, Sept. 6, 1900, 4.

26. Frances Willard, "The 'Do Everything' Policy: Address before the Second Biennial Convention of the World's Woman's Christian Temperance Union, and the Twentieth Annual Convention of the National WCTU," World's Columbian Exposition, Chicago, Illinois, Oct. 16–21, 1893, Willard Memorial Library, Evanston, Illinois.

27. Pritchard, "Purity," 1908, 207.

28. Roger Shattuck, *The Banquet Years: The Origins of the Avant Garde in France, 1885 to World War I* (New York, 1958), chap. 12. For a discussion of the Society of American Artists, see Keith L. Bryant, Jr., *William Merritt Chase: A Genteel Bohemian* (Columbia, Mo., 1991).

29. Pritchard, "Purity," 1908, 207.

30. Ibid., 1898, 191; Martin, "Purity," Jan. 9, 1908, 359.

31. Pritchard, "Purity," 1922, 99 (emphasis added).

32. Ibid.

33. Frances Willard, Presidential Address, *Minutes*, 1890–91, 134–35.

34. Martin, "Power of Literature and Art," 4.

35. Paul and Schwartz, *Federal Censorship*, 12.

36. Kern, *Culture of Time and Space*, 313–18.

37. For extended analyses of mass consumption in advertising, see Herbert Marcuse, *The Aesthetic Dimension: Toward a Critique of Marxist Aesthetics* (Boston, 1978); Marshall McLuhan, *Culture Is Our Business* (New York, 1970); Roland Marchand, *Advertising the American Dream* (Berkeley, Calif., 1985). Thanks to Paul Boyer for suggesting the parallels to Marcuse and McLuhan.

38. Bordin, *Woman and Temperance*, 136.

39. Pritchard, "Purity," 1898, 192.

40. Martin, "Purity," 1907, 329.

41. Pritchard, "Purity," 1910, 172.

42. "Purity in Literature and Art," *New York A.R.*, 1908, 209–10.

43. "Resolutions," *Minutes*, 1887, 45.

44. Frances J. Barnes and Associates, "A Time to Frown," *Signal*, May 6, 1897, 10.

45. "For Clean Plays and Clean Advertising," *Signal*, June 16, 1910, 9. One state superintendent asked: "are advertisements true to the result desired? If shoes are to be sold as a result of an advertisement, are shoes the center of interest?" (Goddard, "Purity," 1927, 83).

46. Emilie Martin, "Purity in Literature and Art," *Signal*, Aug. 7, 1902, 10. This rhetoric has a contemporary ring to it, as late twentieth-century feminists try to delegitimize the use of sexualized female bodies to market products ranging from cars and FAX machines to men's razors.

47. President Willard's Annual Address, *Minutes*, Nov. 14–18, 1890, 28.

48. Martin, "Purity," Aug. 7, 1902, 10 (emphasis added).

49. J. F. Cowan, "The Décolleté in the Magazines," *Signal*, Dec. 24, 1896, 3.

50. Whereas the upper and middle classes had previously mingled with the lower classes to see theatrical productions of Shakespeare, by the 1880s or 1890s Shakespeare was claimed exclusively by the "cultured" elite, who were also expected to patronize operas (performed in German) and the newly established symphony orchestras. See Levine, *Highbrow/Lowbrow*, 68.

51. Josiah W. Leeds, "The Theater Route to Crime," *Signal*, Aug. 23, 1906, 4.

52. Pritchard, "Purity," 1898, 190.

53. Ibid.

54. Ibid., 189.

55. Martin, "Purity," 1900, 308.

56. "27th Annual Convention NWCTU," *Signal*, Dec. 27, 1900, 1.

57. Martin, "Purity," 1893, 395.

58. Reformers asked that children not be allowed to go to the theater on Sunday. See Joseph F. Flint, "The Theater Ensnaring the Children," *Signal*, Jan. 3, 1907, 6. See also Palmiter, "Purity," 1899, 125.

59. "Notes," *Signal*, June 4, 1896, 1.

60. Martin, "Purity," 1909, 334.

61. For instance, a Massachusetts WCTU member protested to the mayor about a local production of a play by Elinor Glyn and succeeded in having the play closed. See Stone, "Purity," 1924, 85 (in the WCTU microfilm collection, University of Michigan, Ann Arbor).

62. From "Censors of Plays: Miss Willard Says Uncle Sam Should Provide One . . . ," *New York Morning Advertiser*, Dec. 3, 1894, reel 32, scrapbooks 13–16.

63. Pritchard, "Purity," 1921, 96.

64. Pritchard, "Purity," 1908, 208.

65. Martin, "Purity," 1908, 361.

66. Martin, "Purity," 1900, 308.

67. The text provides a summary of information from Charles C. Baldwin, *Stanford White* (1931; rpt., New York, 1971), 303–12.

68. Although early films still relied on the printed word in the form of subtitles to move the plot along, movies reflected a gradual shift in American culture toward the visual. See Martin, "Purity," 1907, 334.

69. Karen Halttunen, *Confidence Men and Painted Woman: A Study of Middle-Class Culture in America, 1830–1870* (New Haven, Conn., 1982), 174–76.

70. Robert Allen's work on burlesque adds the corrective that working-class audiences in store-front shows and concert saloons had been enjoying relatively "titillating" living pictures since the 1850s. See Allen, *Horrible Prettiness*, 93.

71. Edith Wharton, *The House of Mirth* (1905; rpt., New York, 1982), 138–39.

72. "The Living Pictures," *Our Message*, Sept. 1894, reel 32, scrapbooks 13–16 (emphasis added). President Frances Willard, who traveled frequently in Europe and was good friends with members of Britain's aristocracy, was inconsistent regarding the acceptability of representing nudity in art: "There is as wide a difference between the Venus de Milo and the acres of human epidermis in a French picture gallery as there is between the planet Venus in the heavens and her reflection in a mud puddle" (President's Address, *Minutes*, 1890–91, 134–35). The membership at large was less likely to make such fine distinctions when condemning nudity in art.

73. "Make War on Nudity . . . ," *Chicago Mail*, Sept. 24, 1894, reel 32, scrapbooks 13–16. See also "No Living Pictures . . . ," *New York Press*, Nov. 28, 1894, reel 32, scrapbooks 13–16.

74. "The Limits of the Shocking," *Weekly Examiner*, Dec. 1894, reel 32, scrapbooks 13–16.

75. "WCTU Convention Report," *Signal*, Dec. 6, 1894, 12.

76. "The Living Pictures: Miss Frances E. Willard's Address before the WCTU," *Albany Journal*, Sept. 1894, reel 32, scrapbooks 13–16.

77. Willard, "The Ideal Home and Purity," scrapbooks 9–12.

78. "Censors of Plays . . . ," *New York Morning Advertiser*, Dec. 3, 1894, reel 32, scrapbooks 13–16.

79. "The Living Pictures," *Our Message*, Sept. 1894, reel 32, scrapbooks 13–16.

80. Edward Said, *Orientalism* (New York, 1978), introduction.

81. Frances Willard, "Address at the World's WCTU Convention," *Minutes*, 1895, 29; President's Address, *Minutes*, 1893, 151.

82. From "Censors of Plays . . . ," *New York Morning Advertiser*, Dec. 3, 1894, reel 32, scrapbooks 13–16.

83. Frances Willard, President's Address, *Minutes*, 1893, 152. Willard's desire to regulate images of violence in the living pictures anticipates the position of anti-pornography groups such as Women against Violence in Pornography and the Media.

84. "The Living Pictures," *Albany Journal*, Sept. 1894, reel 32, scrapbooks 13–16 (emphasis added). See also Willard, "Address to the World's WCTU," June 19, 1895, 29.

85. Tomlinson, "Suppression of Impure Literature," Mar. 3, 1887, 12.

86. "Purity in Literature and Art," *Minutes*, Oct. 1895, 303; "Editorial," *Signal*, July 6, 1896, 11.

87. "Make War on Nudity . . . ," *Chicago Mail*, Sept. 24, 1894, reel 32, scrapbooks 13–16.

88. "Purification of the United States Mail Service," *Minutes*, 1896, 357.

89. See Martin, "Purity," 1893, 395. For a discussion of Rebecca Felton, see Joel Williamson, *A Rage for Order: Black-White Relations in the American South since Emancipation* (New York, 1986), 90–95, 183–84.

90. Smith and Smith, *Police Gazette*, Dec. 1895, 203.

91. Leeds's wife, Deborah Leeds, ran the Department of the Suppression of Impure Literature from 1888 to 1890. See Allen, *Horrible Prettiness*, 92; President's Address, *Minutes*, 1890–91, 135.

92. Pritchard, "Purity," 1921, 95. "Work to place one woman on the Board of Concessions that fairs and carnivals may be clean" (Ward, "Social Morality," 1923, 71). See also Hubbart, "Report of the Department," 1905, 216; Pritchard, "Purity," 1925, 162.

93. "Special Correspondence," "The Show 'For Men Only'," *Signal*, Feb. 24, 1921, 10.

94. Wilbur F. Crafts, "Corrupt 'Shows,'" *Signal*, Jan. 25, 1900, 5.

95. The decision was *Miller v. California* (1973). Leon Hurwitz, *Historical Dictionary of Censorship in the United States* (Westport, Conn., 1985), introduction and 73–74.

96. See Martin, "Purity," 1893, 395; "Kansas Gleanings," *Signal*, Nov. 9, 1893, 12; *Minutes*, 1902, 329.

97. "The Show 'For Men Only,'" 10.

98. Pritchard, "Purity," 1922, 101.

99. "The Show 'For Men Only,'" p. 10.

100. Similarly, in today's feminist anti-pornography rhetoric, the boundary between viewing pornography and raping is erased, as viewing pornography becomes a form of rape. To argue that the man in the audience or the man reading pornography is a whoremonger or a rapist implies that the person watching a show or looking at a magazine will automatically transgress the boundary from viewing into action. See Russell, *Making Violence Sexy*, 120–50, 194–216; Catharine A. MacKinnon, "Turning Rape into Pornography: Postmodern Genocide," *Ms. Magazine*, 4.1 (July–Aug. 1993): 24–33. Thanks to Nicki Beisel for her helpful comments on this point.

101. Pritchard, "Purity," 1922, 101; Carolyn P. Lindsay, "Your Influence Needed to Rout the Vulgar Carnival and Obscene Show," *Signal*, July 1, 1920, 11.

102. Foucault claims that "power over sex . . . operates according to the simple and endlessly reproduced mechanisms of law, taboo, and censorship" (*History of Sexuality*, 84). Similarly, the feminist theorist Judith Butler suggests that "the effort to produce and regulate it [sexuality] in politically sanctioned forms ends up effecting certain forms of exclusion that return . . . to undermine those very efforts" ("Force of Fantasy," 108).

CHAPTER 5: MOTHERING THE MOVIES

1. For discussions of youths, progressive reformers, and the movies, see Miriam Hansen, *Babel and Babylon: Spectatorship in American Silent Film* (Cambridge, 1991), 320; Richard de Cordova, "Ethnography and Exhibition: The Child Audience, the Hays Office, and Saturday Matinees," *Camera Obscura* 23 (1990): 103;

Garth Jowett, *Film: The Democratic Art* (Boston, 1976), 77; Robert Sklar, *Movie-Made America: A Social History of American Movies* (New York, 1976), 134–39.

2. The film historian Richard de Cordova controversially argues that the nineteenth-century ideal of the child as having a culture separate from adult culture was disrupted by the advent of cheap movies attended by all age groups. For further discussion of the local movements for child matinees, see de Cordova, "Ethnography and Exhibition," 91–106.

3. Alta B. Norton, "Motion Pictures," *Ohio A.R.*, 1930, 127; Mary Sayers, "Crusade," 1930, 108.

4. See Hansen, *Babel and Babylon*, 1–2, 119. For a discussion of prizefighting, see Elliott Gorn, *The Manly Art: Bare-Knuckle Prize Fighting in America* (Ithaca, N.Y., 1986).

5. Terry Ramsaye, *A Million and One Nights: A History of the Motion Picture* (New York, 1925), 286–89. For other work on early film, see John L. Fell, ed., *Film before Griffith* (Berkeley, Calif., 1983); Anthony Slide, *Early American Cinema* (New York, 1970); Tino Balio, ed., *The American Film Industry* (rev. ed., Madison, Wis., 1985).

6. "Prize Fight Moving Pictures," *Signal*, July 21, 1910, 8.

7. Pritchard, "Purity," 1910, 169. The WCTU's "Executive Committee of [Minnesota] State sent a petition to the Governor urging him to use his influence to prohibit the use of the kinetoscope exhibitions of the Corbet-Fitzsimmons fight in the state" (Martin, "Promotion of Purity," 1897, 449). See Emilie Martin, "Purity in Literature and Art," *Minutes*, 1899, 283; Hubbart, "Report of the Department," 1905, 214. See also Ramsaye, *Million and One Nights*, 287–88; Sklar, *Movie-Made America*, 18.

8. The continued popularity and accessibility of prizefighting shows that in the long run these laws were ineffectual. See Martin, "Purity," 1910, 346–53.

9. Pritchard, "Purity," 1910, 169–70; Margaret Dye Ellis, "Our Washington Letter," *Signal*, July 25, 1912, 2; Pritchard, "Purity," 1917, 138.

10. Movies in vaudeville shows represented a middle stage of motion picture presentation, familiarizing a middle-class audience with movies before the growth of nickelodeons. See Allen, *Horrible Prettiness*, 265–71.

11. Rosenzweig, *Eight Hours for What We Will*, 190–93.

12. The National Board of Censorship was financed by the movie industry. The board created a Committee on Children's Pictures and Programs, run mainly by women from the General Federation of Women's Clubs, to urge parents to control their children's movie-viewing experience, rather than fight for censorship. See Charles Matthew Feldman, *The National Board of Censorship (Review) of Motion Pictures, 1909–1922* (New York, 1977), 194.

13. The advent of motion pictures in the late 1890s did not alleviate concerns about the power of the printed word, as indicated by the large number of *Union Signal* articles on "immoral" literature in the first three decades of the twentieth century.

14. "Five Cent Schools of Crime," *Signal*, Oct. 18, 1906, 8.

15. For a discussion of America's emerging fascination with a popular youth culture, see Fass, *Damned and the Beautiful*.

16. In 1907, the "first movie censorship ordinance . . . in this country" was passed in Chicago (Carmen, *Movies*, 186).

17. "Five Cent Schools of Crime," 8.

18. "The Nickel Theater," *Signal,* Apr. 25, 1907, 8.

19. Douglas Gomery, *Shared Pleasures: A History of Movie Presentation in the United States* (Madison, Wis., 1992); Douglas Gomery, "The Movies Become Big Business: Publix Theaters and the Chain Store Strategy," *Cinema Journal* 18.2 (Spring 1979).

20. Martin, "Purity," 1909, 334 (emphasis added).

21. Helen W. Barton, "Motion Pictures," *New York A.R.,* 1939, 86–88.

22. See Martin, "Promotion of Purity," 1897, 449; Martin, "Purity," 1899, 283; Hubbart, "Report of the Department," 1905, 214; "Prize Fight Moving Pictures," *Signal,* July 21, 1910, 8.

23. Pritchard, "Purity," 1910, 170–71.

24. This estimate is probably higher than the average of children's movie attendance rates. See M. Evelyn Killen, "Motion Pictures," *Delaware A.R.,* 1931, 87; Miller, "Motion Pictures," 1926, 161.

25. Norton, "Motion Pictures," 127; Sayers, "Crusade," 1930, 108.

26. Norton, "Motion Pictures," 127.

27. Maude M. Aldrich, "Motion Pictures," *Minutes,* 1930, 174–75; Mary Sayers, "Department of Motion Pictures," *Pennsylvania A.R.,* 1929, 103.

28. Pritchard, "Purity," 1917, 139.

29. Ibid., 1916, 309.

30. Ibid., 1917, 139.

31. Larry L. May, *Screening Out the Past: The Birth of Mass Culture and the Motion Picture Industry* (New York, 1980), 49–60; Sklar, *Movie-Made America,* 124.

32. Cora B. McGregor, "Motion Pictures," *Kentucky A.R.,* 1931, 107.

33. See also "Resolutions Adopted by the Jubilee Convention," *Signal,* Nov. 27, 1924, 8.

34. Leonard, "Motion Pictures," 1928, 84.

35. Miller, "Motion Pictures," 1926, 162.

36. Mrs. Bristol French, "Motion Pictures," *Missouri A.R.,* 1933, 90.

37. Barton, "Motion Pictures," 86–88.

38. Maude Aldrich, "Moral Standards of Motion Pictures," *Signal,* Oct. 6, 1928, 13. See also Emilie D. Martin, "Higher Standards for Women in Literature and Art," *Signal,* June 22, 1911, 11; Harriet Pritchard, "Purity in Literature and Art," *Minutes,* 1916, 309; Martin, "Purity," 1908, 362.

39. Ida Mabel Apgar, "Motion Pictures," *New Jersey A.R.,* 1933, 105.

40. Maude M. Aldrich, "Motion Pictures," *Minutes,* 1929, 174; Lulu Freeman Larry, "Motion Pictures," *Illinois A.R.,* 1929, 82; Mary Sayers, "Motion Pictures," 1929, 103; Aldrich, "Motion Pictures," 1930, 174–75; Norton, "Motion Pictures," 127; Millie C. Munson, "Social Morality," *New Jersey A.R.,* 1921, 67.

41. For an exploration of women's role in the National Board of Censorship, see Andrea Friedman, " 'To Protect the Morals of Young People, and Likewise Womanhood': Women and the Regulation of Obscenity in Early Twentieth-Century New York" (paper presented at the Berkshire Conference on Women's History, Rutgers University, June 1990). See also Charles Matthew Feldman, "The National Board of Censorship (Review) of Motion Pictures, 1909–1922" (Ph.D. diss., University of Michigan, 1975).

42. Carrie A. Clark, "Motion Picture Department," *Northern California A.R.*, 1936, 83. See also Jessie L. Leonard, "Motion Pictures," *Massachusetts A.R.*, 1933, 79.

43. Florence Havens Ayres, "Motion Pictures," *New Jersey A.R.*, 1938, 97.

44. Laird, "Motion Picture Department," 1931, 51.

45. Pritchard, "Federal Motion Picture Commission," 10.

46. Margaret Ellis, "Motion Picture Censorship Bill Should Pass," *Signal*, June 25, 1914, 2.

47. "Hughes-Smith Censorship Bill Needs Help," *Signal*, Oct. 1, 1914, 9; Harriet Pritchard, "Work for the Promotion of Purity in Literature and Art," *Signal*, Mar. 2, 1916, 10.

48. Pritchard, "Purity," 1916, 175. See also Nancy F. Cott, *The Grounding of Modern Feminism* (New Haven, Conn., 1987), chap. 1.

49. For discussions of these issues, see Carmen, *Movies*, chap. 1; Murray Schumach, *The Face on the Cutting Room Floor: The Story of Movie and Television Censorship* (New York, 1964).

50. Miller, "Motion Pictures," 1926, 161. For a discussion of Jews in Hollywood, see Neal Gabler, *An Empire of Their Own: How the Jews Invented Hollywood* (New York, 1988).

51. For descriptions of the scandals, including Mary Pickford's divorce and quick remarriage and the death of an actress in Fatty Arbuckle's suite, see Slide, *Early American Cinema*, 146–47; Ramsaye, *Million and One Nights*, 803–21. Leonard J. Leff and Jerold L. Simmons document resistance from film directors to "cleaner" pictures in *The Dame in the Kimono: Hollywood, Censorship, and the Production Code from the 1920s to the 1960s* (New York, 1990).

52. "Cleaning Up the Movies," *Signal*, July 13, 1922, 9.

53. See Pritchard, "Purity," 1923, 121; Cora McGregor, "Motion Pictures," *Kentucky A.R.*, 1928, 93; Stone, "Purity," 1922, 80; Pritchard, "Purity," 1922, 98. See also Ramsaye, *Million and One Nights*, 308.

54. Francis Couvares, "Hollywood, Main Street, and the Church: Trying to Censor the Movies before the Production Code," *American Quarterly* 44.4 (Dec. 1992): 584–616. See, for example, Harriet Pritchard, "Purity in Literature and Art," *Minutes*, 1911, 352–53; Maude Aldrich, "Motion Pictures," *Signal*, Dec. 5, 1925, 12; Martin, "Purity," 1910, 348; Apgar, "Motion Pictures," 1933, 105; Mary Sayers, "Motion Pictures," *Pennsylvania A.R.*, 1927, 104–5. See also Jowett, *Film*, 243; Carmen, *Movies*, 184.

55. For information on New York State film censorship, see Jowett, *Film*, 159. See also Pritchard, "Purity," 1916, 175.

56. New York, Maryland, Virginia, and Kansas still had active censorship programs in the 1960s, although much of the legal support for movie censorship had been eroded by Supreme Court rulings dating from 1952. See Carmen, *Movies*, chap. 3.

57. Sayers, "Motion Pictures," 1927, 104–5; LuAnna Wilson, "Motion Pictures," *New York A.R.*, 1934, 121; Maude M. Aldrich, "Motion Pictures," *Minutes*, 1933, 175; ibid., 1926, 176.

58. Aldrich, "Motion Pictures," 1930, 174–75; ibid., 1928, 156–59.

59. Sayers, "Crusade," 1930, 108; Sayers, "Motion Pictures," 1929, 103.

60. Pritchard, "Purity," 1925, 160.

61. State unions had separate departments of purity in literature and art as late as 1927. See Goddard, "Purity," 1927, 83.

62. Pritchard, "Purity," 1925, 161.

63. Maude Aldrich, "Motion Pictures," *Minutes*, 1926, 175.

64. Maude Aldrich, "Moral Standards of Motion Pictures," *Signal*, Sept. 22, 1928, 12.

65. Pritchard, "Purity," 1916, 175.

66. In their first joint venture, the council and the WCTU cooperated to fight the movie industry's efforts to overturn a film tax and license law in Connecticut that gave the state control over the distribution of films. See Maude M. Aldrich, "Motion Pictures," *Minutes*, 1925, 192; Sayers, "Motion Pictures," 1927, 104–5.

67. Aldrich, "Motion Pictures," 1926, 176.

68. Ibid., 1932, 182.

69. Killen, "Motion Pictures," 88; Alice W. Mann, "Department of Motion Pictures," *Pennsylvania A.R.*, 1932, 109.

70. Block booking was not prohibited by the Supreme Court until 1946. For information regarding the legal history of block booking, see Michael Conant, *Antitrust in the Motion Picture Industry: Economic and Legal Analysis* (Berkeley, Calif., 1960). See also "Congressional Proposal Prohibits Blind and Block Booking of Films," *Signal*, May 10, 1930, 2–3.

71. Maude Aldrich, "The Motion Picture Problem," *Signal*, Jan. 25, 1930, 12.

72. Maude Aldrich, "What the Exhibitor Wants," *Signal*, May 28, 1925, 6.

73. Aldrich, "Moral Standards," Sept. 22, 1928, 12.

74. Miller, "Motion Pictures," 1926, 161; Sayers, "Crusade," 1930, 107.

75. Maude Aldrich, "What the People Want," *Signal*, Mar. 5, 1925, 6.

76. "Do the Liquor Dealers Control Censorship of Moving Pictures?" *Signal*, Apr. 20, 1916, 3; "Department of Motion Pictures," *Signal*, Jan. 1, 1927, 10; "Motion Picture Producers Adopt Policy of Support of Prohibition Law," *Signal*, July 24, 1926, 3.

77. Joy was a retired official of the American Red Cross and had worked in the War Department. See Ruth Inglis, *Freedom of the Movies: A Report on Self-Regulation from the Commission on Freedom of the Press* (1947; rpt., New York, 1974), 103.

78. The WCTU's Department of Social Morality had experimented with a version of this "boost the best" plan in 1920 but had quickly disavowed its utility. See Gertrude S. Martin, "What about the Movies?" *Signal*, Mar. 25, 1920, 5.

79. Jason S. Joy, "How Women Can Help for Better Films," *Signal*, June 2, 1928, 15.

80. Aldrich, "Motion Pictures," Dec. 5, 1925, 12.

81. Maude Aldrich, "Indorsing Motion Pictures," *Signal*, Oct. 27, 1928, 15.

82. Aldrich, "Moral Standards," Sept. 22, 1928, 12.

83. Ibid.

84. See Pritchard, "Purity," 1921, 94. Unfortunately, state records are incomplete or exist only from the late 1930s on. Surviving reports provide tantalizing hints regarding organizations such as the Syracuse Federation of Women's Clubs and the Commission of Public Safety that cooperated with the state WCTUs to regulate movies at a local level.

85. Elizabeth U. Ussher, "Motion Pictures," *Southern California A.R.*, 1930, 96 (emphasis added).

86. Ibid.

87. Jessie L. Leonard, "Moving Pictures," *Massachusetts A.R.*, 1925, 85.

88. Jessie L. Leonard, "Motion Picture Department," *Massachusetts A.R.*, 1927, 77 (emphasis added).

89. Lulu F. Larry, "Motion Pictures," *Illinois A.R.*, 1931, 78; Leonard, "Motion Pictures," 1928, 83.

90. For a detailed account of the World's WCTU, see Ian Tyrell, *Woman's World/Woman's Empire: The Woman's Christian Temperance Union in International Perspective, 1880–1930* (Chapel Hill, N.C., 1991).

91. Aldrich, "Motion Pictures," 1926, 176; Maude Aldrich, "Motion Pictures," *Signal*, Oct. 23, 1926, 14.

92. In 1922, President Obregon of Mexico imposed an embargo on all films from the United States. See Inglis, *Freedom of the Movies*, 99.

93. Miller, "Motion Pictures," 1926, 162; Pritchard, "Purity," 1922, 99; Pritchard, "Purity," 1925, 160; Aldrich, "Motion Pictures," *Minutes*, 1928, 156–59.

94. Lulu Heacock, "Motion Pictures," *Southern California A.R.*, 1938, 94. In New York, newsreels were not subject to state and local censorship regulation after 1927. See Carmen, *Movies*, 142–43.

95. Articles published during World War I added an international focus, asking children to donate to the Red Cross and to raise $3.50 each for the benefit of French war orphans. See "The Lad Who Gave Away His Coat," *YC*, June 1918, 5; Vera Whinery, "Help the Little Frenchies Find Happiness: Orphan Fund Program—Loyalty and Love," *YC*, June 1918, 5.

96. Miller, "Motion Pictures," 1926, 162.

97. Aldrich, "Motion Picture Problem," Jan. 25, 1930, 12 (emphasis added). See Ramsaye, *Million and One Nights*, 642–43; Harriet Pritchard, "Purity in Literature and Art," *Minutes*, 1917, 194.

98. Miller, "Motion Pictures," 1926, 162; Helen Andruss Miller, "Motion Pictures," *New York A.R.*, 1932, 136. For accounts of women's missionary work, see Patricia Hill, *The World Their Household: The American Woman's Foreign Mission Movement and Cultural Transformation, 1870–1920* (Ann Arbor, Mich., 1985); Pascoe, *Relations of Rescue*.

99. For a discussion of colonialism and censorship, see Ruth Vasey, "Foreign Parts: Hollywood's Global Distribution and the Representation of Ethnicity," *American Quarterly* 44.4 (Dec. 1992): 627.

100. "Recent Publicity Concerning Film Censorship," *Signal*, Mar. 30, 1929, 14.

101. Aldrich, "Motion Pictures," 1926, 176; ibid., 1925, 192.

102. For a recent biography of West, see June Sochen, *Mae West: She Who Laughs, Lasts* (Arlington Heights, Ill., 1992). For an "unauthorized" account, see Kenneth Anger, *Hollywood Babylon* (New York, 1975), 259–70.

103. Helen Andruss Miller, "Motion Pictures," *New York A.R.*, 1930, 164.

104. Aldrich, "Motion Pictures," 1930, 173.

105. Ibid.

106. Maude M. Aldrich, "Motion Pictures," *Signal*, Dec. 13, 1930, 12.

107. Aldrich, "Motion Pictures," 1931, 116.

108. Aldrich, "Motion Pictures," 1929, 173. In 1929, Aldrich, as national director, spoke to a wide variety of religious conventions, such as the National Convention of the Disciples of Christ, the New York Synod of the United Presbyterian Church, and the Methodist Episcopal Church, and successfully convinced them to pass "resolutions for federal supervision of motion pictures providing higher standards at the source of production" (ibid.). See also Sayers, "Motion Pictures," 1929, 103.

109. Gusfield, *Symbolic Crusade*, 162.

110. Aldrich, "Motion Pictures," 1933, 176.

111. Mann, "Department of Motion Pictures," 108.

112. Maude M. Aldrich, "Motion Pictures," *Minutes*, 1934, 171.

113. "Motion Pictures," *Pennsylvania A.R.*, 1938, 99.

114. Quoted in Jowett, *Film*, 248.

115. John Higham cites the election of 1928 as an important turning point in the history of anti-Catholicism in the United States because Al Smith waged a viable campaign and won the democratic presidential nomination. See Higham, *Strangers in the Land*, 329.

116. Aldrich, "Motion Pictures," 1934, 172 (emphasis added).

117. Ibid.; LuAnna Wilson, "Motion Pictures," 122.

118. Jacobs, *Wages of Sin*, chap. 5.

119. Jowett, *Film*, 254.

120. Ayres, "Motion Pictures," 97.

121. Harriet S. Pritchard, "Moving Pictures as Educators," Literature and Art Leaflet No. 5, 1911, 4–5, Willard Memorial Library, Evanston, Illinois.

122. For extensive discussions of maternalist discourse, see Seth Koven and Sonya Michel, eds., *The Origins of Welfare States* (New York, 1993).

CHAPTER 6: THE PRODUCTION OF "PURE" CHILDREN'S LITERATURE

1. Alternative "pure" culture was linked to "genteel" Victorian ideas regarding acceptable and morally elevating art. See Rubin, *Middle/Brow Culture*, 11–15.

2. From Caroline Hewins, ed., "Literature for the Young," *LJ* 8 (Aug. 1883): 152. See also Caroline M. Hewins, ed., "Literature for the Young," *LJ* 8 (Nov. 1883): 326.

3. None of the WCTU's children's magazines are included in the University of Michigan's microfilm collection but are available at the Willard Memorial Library, in Evanston, Illinois. The *Oak and Ivy Leaf* (*O&IL*) was first published in 1887, the same year as the *Young Crusader*, under the editorship of Margaret A. Sudduth. There are copies available at the Willard Memorial Library in Evanston, Illinois, for the years 1887–95. A 1904 *Young Crusader* article spoke to males "anywhere between the ages of fourteen and twenty-eight," whereas a 1931 article asserted that the paper was "especially intended" for "boys and girls between six and twelve" (Herbert C. Shattuck, "How to Interest Young Men in the Senior Legion," *YC*, May 1904, 15; "The Front Cover Contest," *YC*, July 1931, 15). In its first year the *Young Crusader* was published twice a month, and for a time it was called the *Monthly Crusader*. See also Ada Melville Shaw, "The Cocaine Enemy,"

YC, Apr. 1907, 13; Anna A. Gordon and Ella W. Brown, "Our 'Twenty-five Thousand' Celebration," *YC*, Jan. 1908, 12; "Editorial," *O&IL* 2.12 (June 1889): 2. By comparison, in 1890 the WCTU's official organ for its adult members, the *Signal*, had a circulation of about 100,000. See Jane L. McKeever, "The Woman's Temperance Publishing Association," *Library Quarterly* 55.4 (Oct. 1985): 374–75; Bordin, *Woman and Temperance*, p. 90.

4. I am modeling my examination of the WCTU's "pure" children's fiction on Dee Garrison's analysis of women's romance novels (*Apostles of Culture*, chap. 4) and on Judith Walkowitz's readings of artifacts of popular culture (*City of Dreadful Delight: Narratives of Sexual Danger in Late-Victorian London* [Chicago, 1992]). For other approaches to borderline children's literature, see Michael Denning, *Mechanic Accents: Dime Novels and Working-Class Culture in America* (New York, 1987); Kimberly Reynolds, *Girls Only? Gender and Popular Children's Fiction in Britain, 1880–1910* (Philadelphia, 1990).

5. By 1892, as mandatory Scientific Temperance Instruction was introduced into many public schools, the *Crusader* changed its strategy and published quarterly temperance lessons that included "Hints for Primary Teachers." See "A Word for the Teachers," *YC*, Mar. 4, 1887, 1–2. See also Lucia E. F. Kimball, "Crusader Supplement—Quarterly Temperance Lesson," *YC*, Jan. 17, 1892, 1–4; "Our Heroes," *YC*, Feb. 1897, 4; Mrs. O. W. Scott, "A False Knight," *O&IL* 5.9 (Mar. 1892): 6; Anna Gordon, "Miss K.'s Way," *YC*, Sept 23, 1887, 1; "What She Did," *YC*, Aug. 26, 1887, 2.

6. In contrast to the *Crusader*, the WCTU's *Oak and Ivy Leaf*, written for an older audience of females between the ages of about fifteen and twenty-five, had a few stories with explicitly romantic or even titillating plots. See Mary Wood Allen, "Poor Meldora," *O&IL* 7.11 (May 1894): 1; Anna M. Vail, "A Girl's Influence," *O&IL* 4.7 (Jan. 1891): 6–7.

7. "Editorial," *YC*, Jan. 21, 1887, 3–4. See Fiske, *Understanding Popular Culture*, 106–8.

8. For discussions of medievalism in the United States, see Gusfield, *Symbolic Crusade;* David Glassberg, *American Historical Pageantry: The Uses of Tradition in the Early Twentieth Century* (Chapel Hill, N.C., 1990); Mark Caldwell, *The Last Crusade: The War on Consumption, 1862–1954* (New York, 1988); John Fraser, *America and the Patterns of Chivalry* (Cambridge, 1982); JoAnne Brown, "Tuberculosis: A Romance" (paper presented at the Berkshire Conference on the History of Women, Vassar College, June 1993, copy in the author's possession).

9. M.A.C., "One Way to Do Good," *YC*, Dec. 2, 1887, 2.

10. Geo. C. Hall, "The Danger of Too Much Liberty," *YC*, Feb. 4, 1887, 1.

11. J. F. Cowan, "Doing as You Please," *YC*, Apr. 1895, 2.

12. For an extended analysis of the nexus of reform, professionals, and the child, see Lasch, *Haven in a Heartless World*.

13. George C. Hall, "Scene from Chicago Police Court," *YC*, Jan. 7, 1887, 4.

14. Smith-Rosenberg, *Disorderly Conduct*, 245, 256, 264.

15. Fanny R. Rastall, "Safe Business Openings for Girls," *YC*, Mar. 1892, 6.

16. See Rev. Kittredge Wheeler, "Self-Support and Marriage," *Young Women* 8.3 (Sept. 1894): 4. See also "What Our Girls Think," *YC*, Mar. 1892, 7–8; "A Labor Operetta," *YC*, Aug. 1893, 6; Mabel Gifford, "The Y's Thinking-Cap: Without Money and without Price," *O&IL* 5.4 (Oct. 1891): 6–7.

17. See Alice Kessler-Harris, *Out to Work: A History of Wage-Earning Women in the United States* (Oxford, 1982), 141–48, 171.

18. Dolores Hayden argues that although the WCTU employed a rhetoric idealizing domesticity to gain broad public support, WCTU leaders from Frances Willard to Mary Livermore supported socialized domestic work and the cooperative housekeeping experiments of the settlement houses. See Hayden, *The Grand Domestic Revolution: A History of Feminist Designs for American Homes, Neighborhoods, and Cities* (Cambridge, 1981), 127 and chap. 6.

19. To summarize the women's educational backgrounds and early careers: (1) Maude Rice of Pennsylvania, college-educated teacher and elocutionist; (2) Lucie E. L. Rising, New York, Loyal Temperance Legion (LTL) organizer and public speaker; young married woman who gave "51 addresses and 15 talks" in two months may have been a salaried LTL worker; (3) Alice Roberta Linvill, Pennsylvania, completed a B.A. at Swarthmore College and then a two-year degree in domestic science at Drexel Institute; taught "at the Hartley District [New York City] on the College Settlement plan, with basketry added to her teaching"; passed the teacher's exam enabling her to teach in New York public schools; (4) Bessie Lee Clink, Michigan, finished high school, had "kindergarten training at the Ferris Institute," and then at age nineteen decided to take a full-time paid job as an LTL worker in Bridgeport, Connecticut; (5) Mary J. Money, Wisconsin, salaried LTL secretary for fourteen LTL's in Milwaukee; (6) Edith Hillis, Indiana, finished high school, spent a short time at music school at De Pauw University, then worked as a stenographer; (7) Lillian Norton, Massachusetts, taught in a district school in Maine but "will soon commence special training for missionary work in India." The sources for this material are: "Some Pen Pictures of Our Seniors at Philadelphia, *YC*, Jan. 1905, 9; "The Senior Loyal Temperance Legion: Seniors Who Have Won Success" [same title for all], *YC*, Apr. 1904, 8; Mar. 1905, 8; Feb 1905, 8; July 1905, 8; Oct. 1905, 8; Apr. 1905, 8.

20. "Bits of History," *YC*, May, 1892, 5. For discussions of U.S. Indian policies, see Patricia Nelson Limerick, *The Legacy of Conquest: The Unbroken Past of the American West* (New York, 1987); Richard White, *"It's Your Misfortune and None of My Own": A New History of the American West* (Norman, Okla., 1991).

21. Susan B. Anthony, "A Patriotic Message to Girls," *YC*, July 1898, 8.

22. Margaret Dye Ellis, "What Our Young People Can Do for Temperance Legislation," *YC*, Jan. 1909, 3.

23. Margaret Dye Ellis, "The Post Office Department," *YC*, June 1909, 3; "Our Legislative Bodies," *YC*, Mar. 1909, 3; "The Supreme Court," *YC*, May 1909, 3; "Uncle Sam's Bank," *YC*, July 1909, 3; "The Congressional Library," *YC*, Aug. 1909, 7.

24. Erisman, "There Was a Child Went Forth," 72–94.

25. See Betty Longenecker Lyon, "A History of Children's Secular Magazines Published in the United States from 1789 to 1899" (Ph.D. diss., Johns Hopkins University, 1942), 316–24.

26. George P. Brown, "The King and His Wonderful Castle" (chap. 3), *YC*, Mar. 1911, 5.

27. Erisman, "There Was a Child Went Forth," 103.

28. Ibid., 104.

29. Ibid., 120.

30. Ibid., 73.

31. MacLeod, *American Childhood*, 152–53.

32. For a discussion of Willard's remarkably similar autobiography, see ibid., chap. 1. See also Frances Willard, *Glimpses of Fifty Years: The Autobiography of an American Woman* (Evanston, Ill., 1904).

33. As late as the 1880s, most children did not attend school past the seventh grade; those in rural areas had farm responsibilities, and working-class urban children worked in factories, attending school irregularly, if at all. See Carl F. Kaestle, *Literacy in the United States: Readers and Reading since 1880* (New Haven, Conn., 1991), 19–25.

34. Willard described in detail the "Board of Trade" set up by the children. See Willard, "Three Children and How They Amused Themselves," chap. 4, *YC*, Jan. 28, 1887, 14; ibid., chap. 3, Jan. 21, 1887, 10.

35. Ibid., chap. 13, Apr. 1, 1887, 51.

36. Kate eagerly congratulated Jamie on his sermon, commenting, " 'That was *gospel*. How happy you are to be a preacher. That's what I'd be, if I dared' " (ibid., chap. 27, Apr.29, 1887, 67). See also ibid., chap. 39, Oct. 7, 1887, 159; ibid., chap. 14, Apr. 8, 1887, 55; ibid., chap. 16, Apr. 22, 1887, 63; Nellie Blessing Evster, "Jessica; or, *Ich Diene*," *O&IL* 2.3 (Sept. 1888): 4.

37. Willard, "Three Children," chap. 7, Feb. 18, 1887, 3.

38. Ibid., chap. 39, Oct. 7, 1887, 159.

39. Bordin, *Woman and Temperance*, 123–25.

40. Willard, "Three Children," chap. 9, Mar. 18, 1887, 35. Producing the paper increased their writing skills and taught them discipline: "It taught them to be prompt, because the paper must be ready on a certain day each week. It taught them to spell, use capital letters, punctuate, etc. So, though there was no school for them to go to, they were getting a first-rate stay-at-home schooling" (ibid.).

41. A Little Girl, "Just before Election," *YC*, Mar. 25, 1887, 4.

42. "Women's Votes, Motion Song," *YC*, Sept. 1915, 13.

43. Willard, "Three Children," chap. 9, Mar. 18, 1887, 35.

44. Ibid., chap. 22, June 3, 1887, 87.

45. Here, the city promoted gender equality. See ibid., chap. 9, Mar. 18, 1887, 35.

46. Lucie E. L. Rising, "Talks on Parliamentary Law," *YC*, Apr. 1904, 9.

47. In another contrast to Alcott's novel, purity was of greater import to Willard; accordingly, her characters used no slang and apparently had no romantic thoughts or interests. See Sarah Elbert, *A Hunger for Home: Louisa May Alcott and 'Little Women'* (Philadelphia, 1984), chap. 10. For an article on young women and health, see "Courage of the Modern Young Woman," *O&IL* 5.11 (May 1892): 4. See also Smith-Rosenberg, *Disorderly Conduct*, 182–216.

48. Willard, "Three Children," chap. 10, Mar. 11, 1887, 39.

49. Reversing conventional sex roles, Kate served as an authority on nature for three neighborhood brothers, as she taught them how to "drown out a gopher." Gophers, she explained, ate the corn crops before they could be picked, so her father had sanctioned their destruction. The children would pour water into the gopher hole and slam the gopher on the head with a shovel when it

popped out. "Father told us that . . . when they spoil our work, we are obliged to spoil them, for the general good" (ibid., chap. 11, Mar. 18, 1887, 43).

50. Willard praised Mr. Hill and Atherton's facility in the kitchen: "Both father and son were famous cooks" who took turns preparing the elaborate Sunday dinner (ibid., chap. 13, Apr. 1, 1887, 51).

51. Ibid., chap. 21, May 27, 1887, 83.

52. Ibid. (emphasis added).

53. Ibid., chap. 3, Jan. 21, 1887, 10.

54. Ibid., chap. 12, Mar. 25, 1887, 47; ibid., chap. 47, Dec. 9, 1887, 195.

55. Ibid., chap. 4, Jan. 28, 1887, 14.

56. Mrs. Hill had been skilled at horseback riding in her youth; she finally succeeded in overruling her husband's prohibition when Kate was fifteen years old (ibid., chap. 10, Mar. 11, 1887, 39).

57. Ibid., chap. 12, Mar. 25, 1887, 47.

58. Ibid., chap. 22, June 3, 1887, 87.

59. Under these circumstances, "Fort City" was, indeed, a crucial means for home education. The children created the "Fort City Board of Education" and asked their parents to hire a young woman who had been educated in the urban area of Albany, New York, to tutor Kate and Nell in their own summer school (ibid., chap. 22, June 3, 1887, 87).

60. Ibid., chap. 25, June 24, 1887, 99.

61. Bob, "How the *Young Crusader* Is Made," pt. 1, *YC*, Sept. 1929, 4–5; Frances E. Willard, "Hints about Authorship," *O&IL* 2.2 (Aug. 1888): 3; Willard, "Three Children," chap. 8, Feb. 25, 1887, 31; ibid., chap. 9, Mar. 18, 1887, 35.

62. Willard, "Three Children," chap. 13, Apr. 1, 1887, 51.

63. Ibid., chap. 14, Apr. 8, 1887, 55. At times, however, as when a prairie fire threatened their property, nature dominated. Even then, as they labored with their father to fight the fire, the girls learned to appreciate nature's power; Kate and Nell emerged as heroines, "covered all over with dirt and glory, and both told at once about the 'hair-breadth escape' " (ibid., chap. 19, May 13, 1887, 75).

64. See ibid., chap. 39, Oct. 7, 1887, 159; ibid., chap. 20, May 20, 1887, 79; ibid., chap. 17, Apr. 29, 1887, 67.

65. Ibid., chap. 47, Dec 9, 1887, 195 (emphasis added). See also ibid., chap. 17, Apr. 29, 1887, 67.

66. Ibid., chap. 39, Oct 7, 1887, 159.

67. Ibid., chap. 43, Nov. 4, 1887, 176. In another moment of slippage, Mr. *Hill* said, "'I want the three children always to remember . . . that their great grandfather, Elijah *Willard*, was a Baptist minister'" (ibid., chap. 47, Dec. 9, 1887, 195).

68. Ibid., chap. 43, Nov. 4, 1887, 176.

69. Ibid.

70. Perhaps that was Willard's point; Kate gained her strength from country life and physical activity. See ibid., chap. 3, Jan. 21, 1887, 10.

71. See ibid., chap. 20, May 20, 1887, 79. Especially in its first year of publication, the *Crusader* published many stories, songs, and poems that urged children to obey all their mother's orders and requests for help, avowing that "Mamma knows best." See, for example, Alice M. Tucker, "A Brown Towel," *YC*, May 6,

1887, 4; Mrs. L. A. Hopkins, "Home" (poem), *YC,* May 27, 1887, 2; "Kindergarten Song—The Mother Hen," *YC,* June 3, 1887, 2.

72. Hewitt, *Women's Activism,* chap. 1; Ryan, *Cradle of the Middle Class,* chap. 5.

73. Willard, "Three Children," chap. 16, Apr. 22, 1887, 63 (emphasis added).

74. Ibid., chap. 14, Apr. 1887, 55.

75. Ibid., chap. 47, Dec. 9, 1887, 195.

76. Both the author and *Crusader* editors viewed this story as a mobilizer, inspiring readers to become Loyal Temperance Legion members, along with almost 250,000 other children.

77. Lynde Palmer, "The Little Captain," chap. 4, *YC,* Apr. 1911, 2.

78. Ibid., 2, 13.

79. For the basis of such beliefs, see Jean-Christophe Agnew, *Worlds Apart: The Market and the Theater in Anglo-American Thought, 1550–1750* (Cambridge, 1986).

80. Palmer, "Little Captain," chap. 4, June 1911, 3.

81. Women writers often published under a male pseudonym, so the identity of this author remains uncertain.

82. Palmer, "Little Captain," chap. 5, May 1911, 3.

83. Ibid., chap. 6, July 1911, 3.

84. Ibid., 13.

85. Ibid., 2; Lasch, *Haven in a Heartless World,* 8–9.

86. Palmer, "Little Captain," chap. 7, Aug.–Sept. 1911, 2.

87. The story included examples of how to organize cold-water armies, how to explain the cause to friends, and what types of speeches to give in front of saloon keepers and their inebriated patrons. A monthly column for Loyal Temperance Legion superintendents in the *Crusader* suggested that the young male members should participate directly in law enforcement, being "constantly on the watch for saloons which violate the judge's orders in minor details—closing time, lunches, screens, slot machines, selling to minors and on Sunday" ("Superintendent's Round Table: Suggestions from the Keystone State," *YC,* Aug. 1905, 15).

88. *The Compact Oxford English Dictionary* (New York, 1971), s.v. "melodrama," 1765. See also Judy Walkowitz, "Patrolling the Borders," *Radical History Review* 43 (Winter 1989): 25–31; Walkowitz, "Science and the Seance," *Representations* 22 (Spring 1988): 3–29.

89. See chapter 5 for a discussion of movie censorship.

90. Palmer, "Little Captain," chap. 8, Oct. 1911, 2.

91. Ibid., chap. 7, Aug. 1911, 14.

92. Ibid., chap. 8, Oct. 1911, 2.

93. Walkowitz, *City of Dreadful Delight,* 91.

94. Harriet Beecher Stowe, *Uncle Tom's Cabin* (1851; rpt., New York, 1981), chap. 25. Barbara Sicherman suggests that male heroes could be used by girls as well as boys as possible role models, so that girls were not necessarily dependent on finding or identifying with female heroines for self-esteem. See Sicherman, "Reading and Ambition: M. Carey Thomas and Female Heroism," *American Quarterly* 45.1 (Mar. 1993): 73–103. See also Douglas, *Feminization of American Culture,* 3–13.

95. Palmer, "Little Captain," chap. 9, Dec. 1911, 2.

96. Ibid., 13.

97. Ibid., chap. 10, Jan. 1912, 14.

98. Zimmerman, "'Queen of the Lobby,'" 520, 549.

99. See "Jac" Lowell, "Who Admires Her? Isn't She a Blot on Woman's Honor? A Bit about the Blot," YC, Aug. 1911, 6; Will H. Brown, "Are Smoking Women Entitled to Respect?" YC, Apr. 1929, 7; "Mr. Edison's Oft Repeated Views," YC, Dec. 1917, 5.

100. From Jennie N. Standifer, "Roger Hillman's Honor," chap. 1, YC, Jan. 1913, 2–3.

101. Ibid., chap. 2, Feb. 1913, 2.

102. See Anne Firor Scott, Natural Allies: Women's Associations in American History (Urbana, Ill., 1992), chap. 4.

103. The Crusader reprinted racist selections from other papers, too: "All the children loved Nig. He was just a black cur dog who did not belong to anyone" ("Helping Poor Nig," Sunday School Advocate, rpt. in YC, Oct. 1916, 13).

104. Standifer, "Honor," chap. 3, Mar. 1913, 2.

105. Ibid.

106. See ibid., chap. 2, Feb. 1913, 15.

107. Ibid., chap. 4, Apr. 1913, 2, 10.

108. Ibid., chap. 5, May 1913, 2.

109. Other Crusader stories had similar themes, arguing that "the highest type of manhood could not be traced to the smell of tobacco" ("A Novel Valentine," YC, Feb. 1917, 6).

110. Black women were appointed as WCTU organizers of other blacks in the North but were often organized by white women in the South. See Bordin, Woman and Temperance, 83–85.

111. John Bodnar, The Transplanted: A History of Immigrants in Urban America (Bloomington, Ind., 1985), 98–99.

112. A strict anti-immigration law was passed by Congress in 1924. See Higham, Strangers in the Land, 324; James R. Barrett, "Americanization from the Bottom Up: Immigration and the Remaking of the Working Class in the United States, 1880–1930," Journal of American History 79.3 (Dec. 1992): 996–1020.

113. Bordin, Woman and Temperance, 86–87, 122–23.

114. Ida Buxton Cole, "A Word about Equal Suffrage," O&IL 3.2 (Aug. 1889): 2.

115. Ladd-Taylor notes that "in 1918, the National Congress of Mothers and Parent-Teacher Associations established its own Department of Americanization. . . . Americanization literature characterized ethnic women as 'timid,' 'shy,' and 'diffident,' innocent victims of social upheaval and male lust, childlike in their need of guidance and assistance" (Mother-Work, 56).

116. Jessie E. Wright, "The House of Good Will," YC 29.1 (Jan. 1916): 2.

117. Ibid., chap. 2, Feb. 1916, 2.

118. Ibid., chap. 3, Mar. 1916, 2.

119. Ibid., chap. 4, June 1916, 2.

120. Ibid.

121. Lane and Farrar, "Methods of Evaluating," 194–97.

122. Wright, "Good Will," chap. 6, May 1916, 2.

123. Ibid., chap. 4, Apr. 1916, 2.

124. Ibid., chap. 5, May 1916, 2.

125. Ibid., chap. 7, July 1916, 2.

126. Ibid.

127. For an example of the WCTU's home-decorating campaign, see Jeanhette M. Dougherty, "The Household: Art Education in the Home," *Signal*, Oct. 31, 1901, 6.

128. See Stone, "Purity," 1924, 85.

129. Wright, "Good Will," chap. 8, Aug. 1916, 2 (emphasis added).

130. Ibid., chap. 9, Sept. 1916, 2.

131. Walkowitz, *City of Dreadful Delight*, 88.

132. Wright, "Good Will," chap. 9, Sept. 1916, 2. See Zimmerman, " 'Queen of the Lobby,' " 30, for an extended discussion of social scientists' debates about alcohol and temperance.

133. Wright, "Good Will," chap. 11, Nov. 1916, 2. Patriotic songs and holidays as a means to inspire immigrants to be loyal U.S. citizens were illustrated in other *Crusader* stories. See Elizabeth P. Gordon, "A Great Day for Karl and Petro," *YC*, June 1924, 8; Mary B. Wilson, "A New True Fairy Story," *YC*, Aug. 1907, 2.

134. Wright, "Good Will," chap. 11, Nov. 1916, 2. A 1918 story emphasized that Italians and eastern Europeans were following in the esteemed tradition of the Pilgrims, who came to America so "that they and their children might have religious liberty and better advantages" (Grace Boteler Sanders, "The Castaways," *YC*, Oct. 1918, 3).

135. Stories from the late 1920s and 1930s, the Great Depression era, highlighted benevolence and generosity as the most desirable character traits for youths. See Lois Snelling, "Robin's Thanksgiving Offering," *YC*, Nov. 1931, 3; Roy A. Keech, "Come in and Get Warm," *YC*, Nov. 1931, 5.

CHAPTER 7: HEARTS UPLIFTED AND MINDS REFRESHED

1. "Editorial," *LJ* 23 (Apr. 1898): 1.

2. Mary A. Jenkins of the Boston Public Library, Miss A. L. Hayward of the Dana Library in Cambridge, Massachusetts, and J. C. Houghton, a librarian in Lynn, Massachusetts, are quoted in James, "Yearly Report," 278–91.

3. Sanders, "Report on Reading for the Young," 58–64.

4. Wells, "Responsibility of Parents," 325–30.

5. Stearns, "Report on Reading for the Young," 81–87.

6. Caroline M. Hewins, "Report on Children's Reading," *LJ* 23 (1898): 35. "As late as 1893 children under the age of twelve were barred from almost half of the large public libraries in the nation," and the first children's room opened in 1890. See Garrison, *Apostles of Culture*, 173, 207, 210.

7. Ellen M. Coe, "Common Novels in Public Libraries," *LJ* 19 (1894): 23.

8. MacLeod, *American Childhood*, 121.

9. *New York Tribune* article reprinted in *LJ* 6 (1881): 183.

10. Bean, "The Evil of Unlimited Freedom," 341–43.

11. Myra F. Southworth, a Brockton, Massachusetts, librarian is quoted in Sanders, "Report on Reading for the Young," 58–64 (emphasis added); Clara W. Hunt, "Some Means by Which Children May Be Led to Read Better Books," *LJ* 24 (Apr. 1899): 147–49.

12. Hester Conway, Hamilton Grange Branch, Nov. 1907, NYPL, 3–4. For more information, see Poole, "Fiction in Libraries," 8–10; Abby L. Sargent, "Children's Books and Periodicals," *LJ* 25 (1900): 64–65; Comstock, "The Library as an Educational Factor," 147–49; Robert C. Metcalf, "Reading in the Public Schools," *LJ* 4 (1879): 343–45; "The Children's Room: Report of the Examining Committee of the Boston Public Library," *LJ* 22 (Sept. 1897): 439.

13. Superintendent of Boston Public Library, "Address of Mellen Chamberlain," *LJ* 4 (1879): 362–66. On masculinity, see Mark C. Carnes and Clyde Griffen, eds., *Meanings for Manhood: Constructions of Masculinity in Victorian America* (Chicago, 1990).

14. Hunt, "Read Better Books," 147–49.

15. MacLeod, *American Childhood*, 153–54.

16. Ellen M. Coe, "What Can Be Done to Help a Boy to Like Good Books after He Has Fallen into the 'Dime Novel Habit'?" *LJ* 20 (Apr. 1895): 118–19.

17. By implication, adults often viewed librarians' regulatory efforts on their behalf as unwarranted intrusions. See Hunt, "Read Better Books," 147–49.

18. Dee Garrison argues that librarians divorced themselves from all censorship by 1923; surveys conducted at that time by the American Library Association found its members less willing to censor adult fiction. See Garrison, *Apostles of Culture*, 87–89, 213. See also Rothrock, "Censorship of Fiction," 454–56.

19. MacLeod, *American Childhood*, 179.

20. Rothrock, "Censorship of Fiction," 454–56.

21. Superintendent, "Address of Mellen Chamberlain," 362–66. "When we consider the dime-novels, the class of literature known as Sunday-school books, the sensational newspapers, the vicious literature insinuated into schools, and the tons of printed matter . . . we cannot help seeing that *the librarian*, in his capacity as selector of books for the library, *has the initial responsibility*" (Plummer, "The Work for Children," 679–86 [emphasis added]).

22. Burgess, "Means of Leading Boys from the Dime Novel," 144–47.

23. "Address of James Freeman Clarke," *LJ* 4 (1879): 355.

24. Superintendent, "Address of Mellen Chamberlain," 362–66.

25. Bean, "Report on the Reading of the Young," 217–27.

26. Green, "Sensational Fiction," 345–55.

27. Poole, "Fiction in Libraries," 8–10. See also Superintendent, "Address of Mellen Chamberlain," 362–66.

28. In that respect, it is comparable to contemporary claims regarding the inherent truthfulness of documentary films and even the television news.

29. Bean, "Report on the Reading of the Young," 217–27.

30. Ibid., 218.

31. Hester Conway, Hamilton Grange Branch, Sept. 1908, NYPL, 8.

32. Schwartz, *Federal Censorship*, 16–17.

33. "Address of Professor WM. P. Atkinson," *LJ* 4 (1879): 359–62. Miss Stevens of the Toledo, Ohio, Public Library is quoted in Bean, "Report on the Reading of the Young," 217–27.

34. Wells, "Responsibility of Parents," 325–30.

35. Bean, "Report on the Reading of the Young," 217–27.

36. Stevenson, "Weeding Out Fiction," 133; Eastman, "The Child, the School," 134–39.

37. Hewins, "Report on List of Children's Books," 79–82. See a relevant article by Dee Garrison, "Cultural Custodians of the Gilded Age: The Public Librarian and Horatio Alger," *Journal of Library History* 6 (Oct. 1971): 327–36.

38. Miss Chandler, a librarian in Lancaster, Massachusetts, is quoted in Bean, "Report on the Reading of the Young," 217–27.

39. Sargent, "Children's Books and Periodicals," 64–65.

40. Henrietta Sherwood, Jackson Square Branch, Oct. 1907, NYPL, 4. Miss H. P. James of the Osterhout Library in Wilkes-Barre, Pennsylvania, is quoted in Mary Sargent, "Reading for the Young," *LJ* 14 (1889): 226–36. See Hewins, "Yearly Report," 182–90. See also the quote by Mr. Watson, a Portland librarian, in Bean, "Report on the Reading of the Young," 217–27.

41. Mr. Beardsley of a Cleveland, Ohio, public school library is quoted in Bean, "Report on the Reading of the Young," 217–27.

42. Stearns, "Report on Reading for the Young," 81–87. See also Bean, "Report on the Reading of the Young," 217–27; Solon F. Whitney of the Watertown, Massachusetts, Library, quoted in Sargent, "Reading for the Young," 226–36.

43. Miss M. A. Bean of the Brookline, Massachusetts, Library is quoted in Sargent, "Reading for the Young," 226–36.

44. Thurston, "Common Novels in Public Libraries," 16–18. See also S. S. Green, "Library Conference," *LJ* 2 (1877): 256; F. J. Soldan, a librarian in Peoria, Illinois, quoted in James, "Yearly Report," 278–91; Stearns, "Report on Reading for the Young," 81–87.

45. "Address of T. W. Higginson," *LJ* 4 (1879): 357–59.

46. Green, "Sensational Fiction," 345–55.

47. C. H. Garland of Dover, New Hampshire, is quoted in Sanders, "Report on Reading for the Young," 58–64.

48. "T. W. Higginson," *LJ* 4 (1879): 357–59; A. L. Peck, "What May a Librarian Do to Influence the Reading of a Community?" *LJ* 22 (Feb. 1897): 77–80. Note the use of the term "real" in Higginson's address.

49. "The main thing is that neither should know you have intentions to change his or her reading-matter. . . . Keep near to the delivery-desk a number of carefully-selected novels and hand these to any reader who is willing to select from books. In this manner, without giving offence, the character of the reading of this class of readers will gradually be improved" (Peck, "What May a Librarian Do?" 77–80).

50. Josephine Gerry, East Broadway Library, Oct. 1907, NYPL, 3–4 (emphasis added).

51. Hester Conway, Hamilton Grange Branch, Apr. 1908, NYPL, 5.

52. Grace Judd, Morrisania Branch, Dec. 1908, NYPL, 2.

53. Rivington Street Branch, Sept. 1908, NYPL, 15 (emphasis added).

54. Rivington Street Branch, Jan. 1909, NYPL, 3–4.

55. See Reynolds, *Girls Only?* 25–26.

56. "Books for Boys and Girls," *Boston*, rpt. in *LJ* 6 (1881): 182.

57. "Only 17 [authors] are mentioned by both, Louisa M. Alcott and Horatio Alger are apparently the only ones who enjoy at all anything like equal favor" (from a study by Clara Vostrovsky in *The Pedagogical Seminary*, Dec. 1899, rpt. in "A Study of Children's Reading," *LJ* 25 [Apr. 1900]: 171).

58. Frieda Jonas, 67th Street Branch, Feb. 1908, NYPL, 4–5.

59. Plummer, "The Work for Children," 679–86.

60. Elsie Otis, Kingsbridge Branch, Jan. 1909, NYPL, 3–4.

61. Hewins, "Yearly Report," 182–90.

62. Miss S. C. Hagar of the Fletcher Free Library in Burlington, Vermont, is quoted in Sargent, "Reading for the Young," 226–36.

63. Thurston, "Common Novels in Public Libraries," 16–18.

64. "A Study of Children's Reading," *LJ* 25 (Apr. 1900): 171.

65. Eastman, "The Child, the School," 134–39.

66. Lane and Farrar, "Methods of Evaluating," 194–97.

67. Ibid.

68. Sargent, "Children's Books and Periodicals," 64–65.

69. "Miss Phelps' Gypsy Breynton books, and Miss Woolsey's *What Katy Did,* and *What Katy Did at School,* are as near the ideal type as anything I know" (Hewins, "Literature," Aug. 1883, 152). See also ibid., Nov. 1883, 326.

70. Irma Horak, Muhlenberg Branch, Nov. 1907, NYPL, 3–4; Elsie Otis, Kingsbridge Branch, Jan. 1909, NYPL, 3–4.

71. Irma Horak, Muhlenberg Branch, Nov. 1907, NYPL, 3–4. See also Mable Norman, 135th Street Branch, Feb. 1909, NYPL, 2; Mary Griffin, Hamilton Grange Branch, Feb. 1909, NYPL, 2.

72. A Harlem Branch librarian, Alice Lawrence, reported that the "older boys and girls are asking to be transferred to the adult department, because they want historical novels, detective, boarding school, college, and rail-road stories" (Alice M. Lawrence, Harlem Branch, Jan. 1909, NYPL, 13). See also ibid., Jan. 1908, NYPL, 5; Josephine Gerry, E. Broadway Branch, Dec. 1908, NYPL, 4; Hester Conway, Hamilton Grange Branch, Nov. 1907, NYPL, 4.

73. Port Richmond Branch, Mar. 1908, NYPL, 5.

74. Hewins, "Literature," Aug. 1883, 152. See also ibid., Nov. 1883, 326.

75. Ibid., Aug. 1883, 152. See also ibid., Nov. 1883, 325.

76. Martin, "Purity," 1900, 309.

77. Martin, "Purity," 1899, 282

78. Saul E. Zalesch, "What the Four Million Bought: Cheap Oil Paintings of the 1880s," *American Quarterly* 48.1 (Mar. 1996): 77, 78, 80.

79. Martin, "Work for the Promotion," July 6, 1899, 14; Sue M. D. Fry, "Corresponding Secretary's Notes," *Signal,* Jan. 16, 1902, 10.

80. Dougherty, "Art Education in the Home," 6; Emilie Martin, "The Spirit of Purity in Literature and Art," *Signal,* Oct. 6, 1910, 4. See Walter Benjamin, "The Work of Art in the Age of Mechanical Reproduction," in *Illuminations,* ed. Hannah Arendt (New York, 1968), 219–54.

81. MacLeod, *American Childhood,* 118–19.

82. For discussion of America's fascination with medieval symbolism, see Fraser, *America and the Patterns of Chivalry;* Lears, *No Place of Grace;* Gusfield, *Symbolic Crusade;* JoAnne Brown, "Tuberculosis: A Romance."

83. Dougherty, "Art Education in the Home," 6.

84. Willard, "The Novel," reel 31.

85. Dougherty, "Art Education in the Home," 6. See also Levine, *Highbrow/Lowbrow,* 176–77, 200; Rubin, *Middle/Brow Culture,* chap. 1.

86. See especially Sklar, *Movie-Made America,* chap. 2.

87. "A Visit to Mr. Thomas A. Edison," *Signal,* June 6, 1912, 2. See also May, *Screening Out the Past,* 24–25.

88. For discussions of the implementation of scientific temperance instruction in public schools, see Zimmerman, "'Queen of the Lobby',", 2; Bordin, *Woman and Temperance,* 135–38.

89. See *Minutes,* 1912, 328; *Minutes,* 1913, 340; "Motion Pictures an Ally of Temperance Teaching," *Signal,* June 6, 1912, 8; Pritchard, "Moving Pictures as Educators," 7–8.

90. "A Visit to Mr. Thomas A. Edison," p. 2.

91. Pritchard, "Moving Pictures as Educators," 7–8; Mary M. Coman, "Y.P.B. 'Movies' for Midsummer Nights," *Signal,* Aug. 14, 1913, 11.

92. *Minutes,* 1910, 346.

93. Mann, "Department of Motion Pictures," 108.

94. Leonard, "Motion Pictures," 1928, 84.

95. Talking films from the early 1930s, such as those featuring Mae West, indicate that directors allowed their stars to speak quite freely.

96. *Minutes,* 1913, 340.

97. *Minutes,* 1912, 329.

98. Kathryn Fuller separates Protestant critics from the small-town audiences, but the case of the WCTU suggests that they were often the same people. For a recent discussion of attempts by local people to watch and support alternative types of movies, see Fuller, "Shadowland: American Audiences and the Movie-Going Experience in the Silent Film Era" (Ph.D. diss., Johns Hopkins University, 1992), 80, 97, 141, 164.

99. For a discussion of the British categorization of those films geared to the "inculcation of morals" as "propaganda" films to be excluded from public movie theaters, see Kuhn, *Cinema,* chap. 3; Aldrich, "Motion Pictures," 1928, 156–59.

100. De Cordova, "Ethnography and Exhibition," 101. First local theater managers and then the big studios became concerned about competition from "alternative film programs" between the mid-teens and the 1920s. See Fuller, "Shadowland," 185.

101. Harriet Pritchard, "Purity in Literature and Art," *Minutes,* 1919, 190.

102. Ibid., 189–90.

103. The WCTU films were entitled "The Beneficent Reprobate" and "Pay-Off." See "Motion Pictures," *Pennsylvania A.R.,* 1938, 99.

104. Sayers, "Motion Pictures," 1927, 104–5.

105. Harriet Pritchard, "Purity in Literature and Art," *Minutes,* 1915, 285. "In every line there has been progress. Especially has this been so in the adaptation of moving pictures to educational purposes. . . . We spent a great deal of thought, time and strength in the preparation of our revised leaflet on the subject 'Moving Pictures as Educators'" (Pritchard, "Purity," 1915, 127).

106. Fuller, "Shadowland," 175.

107. Harriet Pritchard, "Purity in Literature and Art," *New York A.R.,* 1914, 112.

108. There is no indication that librarians showed educational movies in public libraries before the 1930s. Motion pictures are not mentioned in Garrison's *Apostles of Culture* or in the *LJ* before 1933.

109. Maude M. Aldrich, "Visual Education in Kentucky and Iowa," *Signal*, May 7, 1927, 10.

110. Cora B. McGregor, "Motion Pictures," *Kentucky A.R.*, 1927, 78.

111. Jowett cites a government study from 1935 concluding that "only 10 per cent of the public schools made systematic use of motion pictures for instruction" (*Film*, 150). See also Leonard, "Motion Pictures," 1927, 77.

112. Mary Sayers, "Department of Motion Pictures," *Pennsylvania A.R.*, 1928, 128–29.

113. Sayers, "Motion Pictures," 1929, 103.

114. "Safeguarding the Nation," *Signal*, Mar. 23, 1922, 13.

115. Ruth M. Whitfield, "Educators Advocate Motion Pictures," *Signal*, Mar. 23, 1922, 13.

116. "Safeguarding the Nation," *Signal*, Mar. 23, 1922, 13. Educational films in today's public school health classes try to serve a similar function: for example, by graphically representing the black lungs of cigarette smokers.

117. Sayers, "Motion Pictures," 1928, 128–29. See also Sayers, "Motion Pictures," 1927, 104–5. The department's national director, Maude Aldrich, confessed her fear that some WCTU members had taken their objections to films in an unproductive direction and had stopped attending movies altogether. This presented a unique problem; Aldrich thought that WCTU members needed to attend movies relatively frequently in order to maintain the high level of indignation and anger necessary for concerted activism in favor of federal censorship. Boycotting films, Aldrich worried, "gives little idea of the real problem to these women" ("Motion Pictures," 1926, 175).

118. Aldrich, "Motion Pictures," 1931, 116; Lucy A. McClintic, "Motion Pictures," *Northern California A.R.*, 1932, 89. *Ten Nights in a Barroom* was a theatrical play years before it became a motion picture.

119. Laird, "Motion Picture Department," 1931, 53; Larry, "Motion Pictures," 1931, 78.

120. Aldrich, "Motion Pictures," 1933, 174.

121. Robert Sklar criticizes the Motion Picture Research Council for entering its studies with a pro-censorship bias. See Sklar, *Movie-Made America*, 135–39. See also Fuller, "Shadowland," 75, 255, 257, 291–96.

122. Jacobs, *Wages of Sin*, 107; Aldrich, "Motion Pictures," 1934, 172; McClintic, "Motion Pictures," 88.

123. Aldrich, "Motion Pictures," 1933, 174.

124. Larry, "Motion Pictures," 1929, 74.

125. Miller, "Motion Pictures," 1926, 162.

126. Sayers, "Motion Pictures," 1929, 103. See also Sayers, "Motion Pictures," 1927, 104–5.

127. Mann, "Department of Motion Pictures," 108.

128. Leonard, "Moving Pictures," 1925, 85.

129. "Motion Pictures," *Pennsylvania A.R.*, 1938, 99.

130. Quoted in Clara Lloyd Jones, "Department of Radio," *New York A.R.*, 1940, 118.

131. Virginia Reum, "Department of Radio," *Northern California A.R.*, 1942, 61–62.

132. Jones, "Radio," 1940, 118.

133. Reum, "Radio," *Northern Calif. A.R.*, 1938, 79.

134. Jones, "Radio," 1940, 118–19.

135. Ibid., 1943, 101–2.

136. Ibid., 1940, 118–19.

137. Mrs. John C. Urquhart, "Department of Radio," *Southern California A.R.,* 1938, 95.

138. Reum, "Radio," 1938, 78–79.

139. Elizabeth Gibson, "Radio Department," *Pennsylvania A.R.,* 1938, 104–5.

140. Jones, "Radio," 1943, 101–2.

141. Ibid., 1941, 123–24.

142. Ibid.

143. Ibid.

144. Ibid., 1943, 101–2.

145. Reum, "Radio," 1942, 61–62.

146. I would like to thank Kathryn Oberdeck for her helpful comments at the Organization of American Historians meeting in 1995. Oberdeck suggested that the WCTU's activities in the public sphere should not be understood through the Victorian meaning of public and private spheres but rather through Habermas's notion of a "bourgeois public sphere."

CONCLUSION

1. See Bordin, *Woman and Temperance.*

2. See Suzanne Lebsock, *The Free Women of Petersburg: Status and Culture in a Southern Town, 1784–1860* (New York, 1984); Nancy F. Cott, *The Bonds of Womanhood: "Woman's Sphere" in New England, 1780–1835* (New Haven, Conn., 1977); Hewitt, *Women's Activism.*

3. Celia Morris Eckhardt, *Fanny Wright: Rebel in America* (1984; rpt., Urbana, Ill., 1992).

4. See, for instance, Maurine Weiner Greenwald, *Women, War, and Work: The Impact of World War I on Women Workers in the United States* (Ithaca, N.Y., 1980); various essays in Ruth Milkman, ed., *Women, Work, and Protest: A Century of U.S. Women's Labor History* (New York, 1985).

5. Estelle B. Freedman, *Their Sisters' Keepers: Women's Prison Reform in America, 1830–1930* (Ann Arbor, Mich., 1981).

6. Ladd-Taylor, *Mother-Work.*

7. Baker, *Moral Frameworks of Public Life,* esp. chap. 3.

8. Significantly, the WCTU's pro-censorship movement included both small-town and urban women. On the one hand, it appealed to rural Protestant Americans who, perhaps, feared an emerging commercial culture they barely knew. On the other hand, from 1891 to 1925, the Department of Purity in Literature and Art had its headquarters in the heart of New York City's business district.

9. Levine, *Highbrow/Lowbrow.*

10. Rubin, *Middle/Brow Culture.*

11. Butler, "Force of Fantasy," 121.

Index

Abbot, Francis E., 4

abortion. *See* birth control and abortion

Adams, Charles Francis, Jr., 88

Adams, William T. ("Oliver Optic"), 108, 198–202

Addams, Jane, 55, 70

African-Americans, 21, 36; racism against, 56–57, 154, 183–87; and riots, 135–36; support for censorship, 46–48

ALA. *See* American Library Association

Alcott, Louisa May, 167; *Little Women,* 171; *The Old Fashioned Girl,* 69; as "pure" reading for girls, 205–6

Aldrich, Maude: movie censorship campaign of, 153–56; national director of the Department of Motion Pictures, 145–46; and temperance films, 213–14. *See also* Department of Motion Pictures

Alger, Horatio: appeal to working class, 87; librarians' critique of, 108, 198–202; and upward mobility, 53, 89, 98

Alien and Sedition Acts, 2

alternative cultural hierarchy, 158, 211, 214, 226–27. *See also* middlebrow culture; "pure" art

Americanization, 53, 90, 140, 189, 203; in fiction, 187, 191–94; resistance to, 46–47

American Library Association (ALA): admission of children into libraries, 90, 196–97; apostles of culture, 83; boys' reading, 198, 201, 204; censorship of children's literature, 15; challenged by the WCTU, 68, 71–74; children's literature, 195, 207–08; children's reading rooms, 197, 199; definition of "immoral" books, 78, 82–83, 109–10; evaluation of children's literature, 81, 87–90, 104–6, 189, 203–7; as expert, 14, 98–102; girls' reading, 204–7; as guardian of public morals, 76, 83, 109, 196; immigrants, 196, 201–2; and legal censorship, 14, 16, 78–79; misogyny and sexism, 98–99; non-fiction preferred by, 101, 103, 196–200, 203–5; parents, relation to, 75, 94–95, 100–106, 108; political censorship, 14, 77–78, 228; as professional organization, 6, 14, 71, 99; as public servant, 79–81, 87; reading clubs, 203; realism in literature, 200; teachers, relation to, 79, 90, 93–96, 106–8. *See also* censorship; children's librarians; *Library Journal;* organizational goals and methods; women librarians

—members of: authority over parents,

Alison M. Parker is an assistant professor of American history at the University of Texas at Arlington. She has contributed to *Movie Censorship and American Culture*, edited by Francis Couvares, and is editing a collection tentatively titled *Political Identities: American Women and the Emergence of a Secular State.*